Domestic and Foreign Finance in Modern Peru, 1850–1950

Financing Visions of Development

Alfonso W. Quiroz

Associate Professor of History
Baruch College, City University of New York

University of Pittsburgh Press

Published in the USA by the University of Pittsburgh Press,
Pittsburgh, Pa. 15260

Published in Great Britain by The Macmillan Press Ltd,
in association with St Antony's College, Oxford

Printed in Hong Kong

Library of Congress Cataloging-in-Publication Data

Quiroz, Alfonso W.
     Domestic and foreign finance in modern Peru. 1850–1950 / Alfonso
W. Quiroz.
        p.   cm. — (Pitt Latin American series)
     Includes bibliographical references.
     ISBN 0–8229–1174–4
     1. Finance—Peru—History.   2. Finance, Public—Peru—History.
3. Peru—Economic conditions.   I. Title.   II. Series.
HG185.P4Q56   1993
336.85—dc20   92–36947
                                                          CIP

To Daniela Irene de los Reyes

Contents

List of Figures and Tables

Figures

Tables

Preface

This book is an historical interpretation of the relationship between finance and development in a Latin American export economy. In particular, this study assesses the impact on Peru's economic growth and diversification of three key factors, private domestic finance, public finance, and foreign finance. The main challenge in writing this book has been to organise information on the complex interaction between these financial factors. Instead of presenting a chronological description I have opted for a thematic treatment. In this regard, cross references between chapters are inevitable. Thus what the study might lose in linear exposition it is hoped it gains in explanatory coherence.

The book's approach to the issue of financial obstacles to growth can be applied to other underdeveloped economies, and is especially relevant to the current discussion on Latin American financial and debt problems. Studies on Latin American financial issues seldom integrate into a single framework of analysis of private, public and foreign finance despite their obvious links. This neglect perhaps stems from the assumption of the preeminence of international financial factors over domestic ones. I assume, however, that in the evolution of the global economy international and native factors complement each other.

An integrated approach to the analysis of financial factors allows the revision of commonly accepted views on the presumed insignificance of domestic private finance and elite groups. It is widely accepted, for example, that *private domestic finance* played a negligible role in pre-1950 Peru. This book challenges that assumption. It argues that private financial resources, and the institutions through which they were channelled (banks, insurance companies, the stock exchange), entered into a combination of competition and collaboration with foreign finance, and took a pivotal role in the export economy's initial modernisation, diversification and integration. Moreover, institutional finance was complemented by local élite groups and oligopolies as early as the 1890s. However the continued trend towards financial concentration, especially in the 1930s and 1940s, undermined financial autonomy and hindered social and regional distribution of credit.

Furthermore this book claims that *public finance* had, on balance, a negative effect on Peru's economy. The need to finance government deficits and ambitious developmental projects led to dependence on foreign loans and a rise in inflation. Preference was given to meeting Peru's external commitments; default and repudiation of internal debts were chronic and domestic investors incurred crippling losses. Public debt problems were compounded by corruption and poor investment decisions. Despite important infrastructural advances in the 1920s and 1930s, regional and income inequalities did not decrease. This was due in part to inefficient financial policies which contributed to the enhanced oligopolisation of domestic financial markets.

International loans have historically funded the expansion of government spending, as well as providing profitable, though risky, business to a few foreign negotiators and investors. The flow of foreign capital followed, predictably, international lending cycles. These cycles exerted a significant influence on private domestic credit and public finance. Foreign capital tended to exclude domestic capital from the most profitable investments, as well as to hindering effective financial collaboration between the private and public sectors by provoking unbalanced state intervention.

Thus, despite the occasional dynamism shown by the private financial sector in response to economic incentives, financial activities in Peru suffered from distortions caused by an overemphasis on public and foreign finance which hindered long-term financial efficiency. Thus inappropriate financial strategies and decisions made a crucial difference to Peru's efforts to attain economic and social development.

The book is organised as follows. Chapter 1 introduces the problem, discusses the method of approach, and provides an international financial context and the Latin American and Peruvian economic and financial settings. Chapter 2 analyses the historical background of the pre-1884 financial transformations brought about by the early interaction of private, public and foreign finance. Chapter 3 focuses on the private institutional interests behind the post-1884 financial recovery, and evaluates their contributions to economic diversification and financial autonomy. Chapter 4 evaluates the financial performance and evolution of private élite groups, while Chapter 5 assesses the regional and income distribution effects of financial concentration between 1884 and 1950.

Chapter 6 discusses the role of public finance, regulation, and intervention in relation to the local financial structure and sectoral interests. Finally, Chapter 7 considers the financial effects and trans-formations brought about by foreign loans and other types of foreign finance. It should be noted that my main argument to explain the 1884–1950 financial evolution in Peru starts with an analysis of the private financial sector in Chapters 3 and 4. The decision to discuss private finance first, instead of commencing with the more straight-forward public or foreign finance arose from a desire to bring the often neglected importance of private finance to the attention of the reader. The importance of private finance in the analysis of Latin American financial problems will be stressed in my concluding remarks.

Acknowledgements

Without the help of several persons and institutions this book would not have been written. Columbia University and the Social Science Research Council supported early stages of the study. An advanced grant from the Social Science Research Council allowed research in Peru in 1987. A World Bank Robert S. McNamara fellowship and a CUNY Incentive Award generously funded research and writing whilst I was in residence at Oxford in 1989–90. The graceful hospitality of St Antony's College made my stay in Oxford most rewarding and pleasant. The Alexander von Humboldt Stiftung supported research in Berlin during 1990–1. The Rockefeller Archive Center provided a grant in 1991 for research on the Nelson Rockefeller collection. Additionally, the School of Liberal Arts and Sciences, Baruch College, and the Professional Staff Congress of the City University of New York granted release time for research, as well as providing multiple facilities for travel and manuscript preparation.

I want to express my thanks to the staff and directors of the following libraries and archives: in Lima, Archivo de la Superintendencia de Banca y Seguros, Archivo General de la Nación, Biblioteca Nacional, Biblioteca Félix Denegri Luna, and Archivo Histórico Riva Agüero; in New York, Columbia University Library, and New York Public Library; in Washington, National Archives; in Madrid, Biblioteca Nacional and Archivo Histórico Nacional; in Seville, Archivo General de Indias; in Paris, Archives du Ministère de l'Economie et des Finances, Société Générale, Archives Nationales, and Archives du Ministère des Affaires Etrangères; in London, the Public Record Office, British Museum Library and Guildhall Library; in Oxford, the Bodlein Library; in Berlin, Staats-Bibliotek, and Ibero-Amerikanisches Institut Bibliotek; in Potsdam, the Bundesarchiv.

I also acknowledge the permission granted by the Oral History Research Office, Columbia University, to quote from the typescript of William Cumberland's reminiscenses. Likewise, the *Journal of Latin American Studies*, *The Americas*, the McNamara Fellowship Program, and the editor of the Congress on Latin American Debt in Historical Perspective, Berlin 1989, gave permission to use and quote material from articles and contributions I have published.

I am deeply indebted to Herbert Klein, Shane Hunt, Rosemary Thorp, Rory Miller, Reinhard Liehr, Michael Edelstein, Paul

Gootenberg, Franklin Pease, Felipe Portocarrero Suárez, Richard and Linda Salvucci, John Coatsworth, David Brading, Bill Albert and Paul Drake, among others, who read and commented on earlier drafts and chapters. My work benefited enormously from their suggestions; they should not be held responsible for any of its flaws. I owe to my colleagues at Baruch College, including Thomas Frazier, thanks for their unremitting support, and to friends and relatives in New York and elsewhere their vital sustenance. Above all I wish my daughter to know, when she learns to read these words, how much I cherish the special meaning she has given to my work and life.

A. W. Q.

1 Introduction

The crucial influence of financial factors on Latin American development is being stressed today in view of mounting debt problems. An historical perspective can help elucidate this complex and evolving interaction between finance and modern economic growth. In order to explain Latin American financial and developmental issues one must look back in time and consider, in particular, the extraordinary impact of export-led growth.

By the end of the nineteenth century, radical changes related to export growth in Latin America had raised hopes of continued development. Domestic and foreign financial capital had dramatically promoted modernisation in the areas of export production, transportation, infrastructure, urban development and industrialisation.[1] The financial system that supported these changes was based to a large extent on income from exports and foreign loans. Foreign and domestic debts were secured by liberal policies and investments that promised enhanced diversification and eventual self-sustained growth.[2] Without financial backing, the liberal vision of development could not have left a significant mark on the evolving Latin American economies.

However by the 1930s financing development in Latin America had become problematic. Because of a decline in the income from exports, the states' increased indebtedness and their persistent economic intervention, new forms of financing had replaced liberal measures on stable currency, incentives to foreign capital, and conservative foreign exchange reserves.[3] This crucial transition of financial strategies was influenced by three key interacting factors, which were well established in most of Latin America by the 1920s: private domestic finance, public debt finance, and foreign financial flows.

In order to measure the shifting impact of these different financial factors, this study examines them both individually and in relation to each other, as well as investigating whether the private and public financial sectors and foreign capital acting in Peru were able to meet the challenges of development linked to export growth, and make efficient use of domestic and foreign financial resources to promote development.

According to still widely accepted theories, Peru was largely dependent on foreign finance prior to 1950, with private domestic credit

1

playing an insignificant or subservient role.[4] I argue that domestic financial resources were central to the export economy's original modernisation. I also argue that public finance suffered from a legacy of interventionist policies and poor management of domestic public debts, leading to damaging financial repression. Moreover, foreign capital displaced private domestic financial capital and ultimately encouraged economic intervention by the state.

A reassessment of the Peruvian financial model will contribute to the broader debate on the character of Latin American modernisation during the heyday of export-led growth. Financial episodes have had a powerful impact in the economic history of a region haunted by contrasting poverty and progress. Despite the growing literature about the bearing of debt on developmental policies, there has been scant treatment of the problem from a broader historical perspective.[5] Yet it is only when financial events are seen in their economic, social, political and international contexts that we can pose historically pertinent questions about the underlying interests and motives of individuals and groups.

The financial interests of agro-exporters provide the key to Peruvian financial history between 1884 and 1950. The cycles of Peru's modern financial development reflect the agro-exporters' search for financial autonomy and diversification, their influential relationship with the state and foreign capital, and their ultimate demise (complemented by the rise of state- and foreign-sponsored industrialists and importers of capital goods) towards the end of this period.

FINANCE AND ECONOMY: METHODS OF INQUIRY

Financial decisions and strategies can influence the pattern of economic growth and responses to economic incentives.[6] The literature relevant to this study can be divided into two groups. To examine the interaction between finance and the economy, the first group focuses on the role of financial institutions and investor groups in channelling funds from lenders to the most productive sectors and borrowers, a process defined as financial intermediation. Using this method, significant criteria for measuring financial efficiency include productive allocation of funds, adequate financial legislation to allow unhindered financial flow and unrepressed capital markets (leading to a positive 'financial deepening'), and the use of public indebtedness to aid development rather than to patch up public deficits.[7]

A second group of studies centres on foreign debt issues. Here the central debate is whether international financial crises were caused by debtor countries or were the result of the lending cycles of developed economies. According to the latter position, the supply side of international credit, rather than the demand side, seems to have determined Latin America's financial problems.[8]

I propose combining the relevant elements of these different studies on financial processes. I am interested in studying the domestic traits often neglected due to an overemphasis on foreign debt issues. Domestic financial institutions and groups are essential in any process of development financing; one cannot disregard *a priori* their participation, as is done by certain authors of the dependency school.[9] The literature on financial intermediation, financial deepening and investment groups provides a framework for an analysis of the domestic working of financial activities; it also helps explain the local élite's motivations. Foreign financial inflows and outflows, on the other hand, can either aid or disturb the pattern of domestic finance. In consequence, the literature on foreign debt problems provides a necessary and complementary international scope.

In economies like Peru's prior to 1950, economic surplus was generated in the export sector. Theoretically, in order for an export economy to diversify, cheap and efficient fund transfers from the export sector to other sectors (industrial, services, urban development, infrastructure) must take place. If, on the other hand, financial resources are concentrated in a few hands, retained in the export sector, diverted unproductively by the state to incompetent firms and investors, or transferred abroad, financial inefficiency can be expected.[10]

Domestic finance in Peru obviously has had its particular history, and through this we can assess the degree of efficiency domestic financial efforts were able to achieve. In studying these matters, I will first examine broadly those financial traditions and innovations which might have had important effects on Peru's early financial evolution.

FINANCIAL TRADITIONS AND INNOVATIONS

Certainly by the Renaissance period, if not earlier, debtors and creditors in some European societies were expected to observe certain rules, and these became sanctioned by custom and law. States, as well as individuals, engaged in systematic credit transactions, domestic as well as international, which fill the pages of the best-known financial histories. Most of these accounts are the success stories of bankers, institutions and states that skillfully used innovative credit instruments to their advantage.[11]

Important studies on financial themes have established general patterns which reflect the workings of efficient and successful capital markets.[12] However, some individuals and states have not followed the path of success and have not complied precisely with the rules of bourgeois credit. Before participating fully in international capitalist financial markets they followed their own financial traditions. For example, in the Spain of the Reconquista Rodrigo Díaz de Vivar, El Cid, considered it fair game to provide his Jewish creditors, Raquel and Vidas, with fake collateral in order to obtain badly needed funds.[13] In another instance, in 1757 Indian communities in Peru were owed more than two million silver pesos by Spanish and creole officials and landowners, most of which remained unpaid in 1821.[14]

In the 1870s, the Ottoman and Peruvian states, newly incorporated into the 'civilised' markets, were considered unreliable and deceitful by the conservative press agents of European creditors, who expected debtors to behave in certain customary ways. They concluded that these two states should be made to suffer dearly for the consequences of their foreign debt defaults.[15] However, since default by debtor states could trigger serious international financial problems, common sense eventually prevailed over resentment and led to a questioning of the reasons behind the debtors' inability to repay loans. It became apparent that the cause of insolvency lay not only in the ebbs and flows of international finance, but also in the individual countries' credit and developmental history.[16]

In the now more developed countries, financial revolutions seem to have prepared the way for radical industrial and economic transformation. Financial innovations contributed to the formation of modern capital markets. Local and international financial transactions were facilitated by institutional cost-reduction. In these innovative markets, private, public and foreign financial factors worked together to support economic growth because it was to their mutual advantage.[17]

Economic historians trace the first signs of modern financial breakthrough to the Dutch practices of public and private finance which made Amsterdam the trading and financial centre of Europe in the seventeenth century.[18] The Dutch practices served as models for subsequent innovations in eighteenth-century England. The traditional absolutist role of the state in taxation and the collection of funds was changed in order to promote private confidence in long-term public finance, official exchange, and monetary regulation. Instead of increasing taxes, or undermining the value of local currency, the state created a reliable and often gainful public debt structure. This stimulated national capital markets, and as a result, private financial interests were readier to support state financial endeavours.[19]

By contrast, well into the eighteenth century Spanish imperial finance continued to exemplify the traditional absolutist handling of state finance. The Spanish Crown imposed stultifying taxation on dynamic private activities and often contracted costly emergency loans to cover its bureaucratic and military expenses. Spain's main creditors were Genoese, German and Portuguese moneylenders in the sixteenth and seventeenth centuries, and the French, Dutch and English in the eighteenth century.[20] In addition, Spanish aristocrats, merchant guilds and private lenders provided an internal source of credit through donations and enforced loans. Local and foreign loans were generally guaranteed by privileges such as slave trade licences, colonial trade monopoly, official posts, and noble titles. However, the 'institutionalisation of default' and 'emergency borrowing' made loans highly risky and expensive, and prevented Spain from developing a stable, reliable source of credit.[21]

Ironically the Dutch were able to afford their largely successful struggle against Spanish imperial designs by taking full advantage of innovative state finance between 1572 and 1648. As in many other instances, war actually served to increase the efficiency of the Dutch Provinces' private and public financial and monetary transactions.[22] Relatively democratic institutions in the Dutch Provinces made it possible for private investors to support public securities and bonds connected with war financing. Private lenders were enticed with the promise of interest and repayment instead of increased taxation or other arbitrary means levied to keep state finance afloat. Moreover the state's ability to meet its debts punctually fostered private confidence in public credit mechanisms. Following the same basic principles, the Bank of England was created in 1694 and soon became a powerful element in the eventual transformation of the London capital market into the financial centre of the world.[23]

While these momentous changes were taking place in Protestant Europe, the Spanish colonies in America continued to be bound to a stifling state financial structure. This meant that war efforts (increasingly against British attacks and smuggling) placed a heavy burden on the colonial private sector. It was not until the late 1770s that the excessive reliance by colonial governments on emergency finance – expropriations, donations, loans without interest which were rarely repaid, and the exchange of privileges for cash advances – underwent modification. These changes were accompanied by mainland Spain's efforts to improve its credit-worthiness via interest-bearing notes (*vales reales*) handled by the Banco de San Carlos created in 1782.[24] However by the early nineteenth century Spain's continued fiscal difficulties had undermined these financial reforms.

The struggle for independence in Spanish America exhausted and eventually destroyed the system of colonial public finance. As long as the colonial tax structure and mining production had been maintained, the Spanish colonies had been able to finance their local government expenses themselves, and had even managed to send sizeable funds to Spain. Financial problems became acute, however, when colonial bureaucratic management ceased. War and increasing operational costs halted mining production, and the resources of local lenders were drained by patriotic and royalist exactions.

Borrowing from abroad was adopted as an alternative emergency recourse.[25] This use of foreign finance was the first instance in which the financial innovations of Protestant Europe clashed ominously with the tradition of default and emergency finance in Spanish America. Foreign loans raised in London, as well as the interest on these loans, were expected by creditors to be punctually and regularly repaid. However the newly independent exchequers were by no means prepared to comply with this. As we have seen, the tradition of repayment was weak at best, and it was definitely secondary to the new political objectives of independence and early national formation. Thus the first foreign loans were soon defaulted. From then on, this tendency of poorly serviced public debts acquired structural dimensions in several Latin American countries.

IMPACT IN LATIN AMERICA

The nineteenth-century 'Great Transformation' of Europe's economy and society – stemming from long-term peace backed by *haute finance* – which brought about increased demand for raw materials and tropical food products, as well as shipping improvements, all had crucial implications for Latin America.[26] As early as 1840–60 new commercial and financial institutions had made their way to Latin America to facilitate export-related activities.

However, due to recurrent budget crises, state finance continued to rely periodically on emergency measures. Domestic creditors still had little confidence in state finance, and as a consequence only speculators (*usureros* or *agiotistas*) were willing to lend to governments, and then only at very high interest due to the risk involved.[27] When non-emergency internal debts were occasionally serviced, frenzied speculation took place, benefiting mainly the few merchants and negotiators who had timed well their participation and were prepared to use their influence on the frequently changing and unstable governments.

Foreign borrowing became the preferred way of financing deficits, state expenditure, and developmental projects which served as proxy for collateral. These projects were not always sound or genuine. Corruption existed, and poor financial investment choices were also made, although the latter improved with time, and the former naturally varied in accordance with the moral scruples of the politicians in office.

The incompetent handling of state finance was one of the most important obstacles facing private finance prior to 1880. As a result, the private financial market became selfish, highly informal as opposed to institutional, and bitterly opposed to taxation or to any form of income distribution that might interfere with its own strategies for accumulation and diversification. Latin American private financial markets, with obvious differences among the different countries, thus functioned on a fragmented base, in constant peril of state intervention, foreign penetration and a lack of collaboration with state finances.[28]

Those foreign merchant houses handling international trade received European financial resources. So too did negotiators of foreign loans to governments. Foreign loans were highly speculative and vulnerable to a wide array of political and economic variables, while foreign trade provided good and fairly constant profits (at least after 1850) without disturbing conservative merchant practices.[29]

The bill of exchange became a preferred financial instrument in the financing of Latin American foreign trade. Providing thirty, sixty or ninety days credit, bills of exchange allowed foreign merchants to pay for Latin American exports and encouraged domestic merchants and buyers to purchase imported goods. Bills were bought and sold in Latin American markets and their price was the prevailing exchange rate of the local currencies. By the 1860s branches of foreign commercial banks had been established in Latin America to engage in commercial and exchange activities.[30] Additionally, domestic banks of issue also emerged to promote internal credit business.

In the heyday of Latin American modernisation, between 1880 and 1914, the gold standard became the preferred monetary unit. Unlike other Latin American countries, Mexico delayed the adoption of the gold standard due to a strong attachment by exporters to silver currency. As a consequence Mexico suffered temporary losses in foreign trade as it had to pay for imports in a depreciating silver currency.[31] The adoption of the gold standard seems to have had the effect of imposing a temporary 'automatic' discipline on Latin American monetary systems and budgets, despite alleged disadvantages forced upon producers and exporters.[32] This modernisation in financial and monetary matters appears to have reinforced the profound changes brought about in the years 1880–1930, a crucial period for capitalism in Latin America.

The period of accelerated modernisation at the turn of the century has been typified as one of 'extreme dependency' or 'neo colonialism' by those who criticise the export-led model of growth.[33] Standard textbooks on Latin American history refer dismissively to the 'illusory prosperity' of Argentina at that time, or to the period having provided the Porfirian background (1876–1911) to the Mexican revolution, both cases representing a late continuation of nineteenth-century transformations. Even in those texts which point out the important changes which took place after 1880, the process is depicted as having been externally driven and thus 'dependent'.[34]

Ardent exponents of the dependency school consider the post-1930 period as the most relevant for autonomous growth and modern (import-substitution) transition. They do recognise that the 1880–1930 period brought about transformation not only of the export sector, but also of services, infrastructure, industry, urban development and finance. Nevertheless they prefer to typify the period as one of 'prosperity' rather than one of radical transformation.[35] Moreover, in the specific case of Peru, whose economy did not perform as well as that of Argentina or Brazil during the classical period of modernisation, it is widely accepted that there were few or no developmental consequences resulting from foreign economic 'enclaves' and 'oligarchical' dominance.[36] This despite new research which bring to light important national and regional signs of modernisation at least since the 1890s.[37]

Questioning the current interpretations, I consider that the 1880–1930 period is perhaps the most important one in terms of the capitalist transformation of Latin America (Peru included), where radical changes transformed economies to a degree unseen before. In general, modernisation in Latin America consisted of a dramatic increase in export products, marked urban development, economic diversification, budding industrialisation, and political stability, which resulted from the consolidation of the national ruling élite and the reformist effects of the emerging middle and working classes.

During this time, backward and forward linkages contributed to an extensive evolution. The *haciendas* and *saladeros* developed into plantations, agro-industrial and meat-packing plants. Local transportation and infrastructural networks multiplied, especially railways, tramways, motorways and seaport facilities. Urban centres such as Buenos Aires and São Paulo expanded. There was a proliferation of flour mills, tanning factories, wineries, breweries, cotton and wool textile factories, repair shops, foundries and construction firms. Most important for the present study, the service and financial sectors, which acted as crucial agents of economic growth, experienced unprecedented expansion.

By contrast, evidence has been provided by recent studies of the Argentinian and Mexican economies that during the 1930–50 period (even earlier in the case of Mexico) the developmental progress achieved earlier had reduced or even reversed (despite the frail economic recovery of the 1930s). This reversal may have had its origin in enhanced and over-extended state financial and economic intervention.[38]

In the 1930s and 1940s unorthodox financial and economic policies were based on monetary expansion, exchange controls and import substitution. Populist as well as authoritarian leaderships in Latin America distorted the benefits of export-led growth to engage instead on a supposedly more 'autonomous' course through a new partnership with foreign capital. These historical limitations of the import substitution model of growth are just beginning to be explored in the quest to explain the persistent problems of foreign indebtedness and the recent economic downturn of most Latin American countries.[39]

THE EXPORT ECONOMY IN PERU

In the long term the evolution of the Peruvian economy has been largely determined by export cycles of 'boom and bust'. Statistical analysis of the Peruvian export trade reveals three such cycles.

The first covered the years 1830–83, achieving its zenith in the 1860s thanks to the export of guano (a fertiliser); silver exports were also important in the early years of the period, and nitrates towards the end. The period's nadir was reached during the War of the Pacific (1879–83) between Peru and Chile. Pre-war levels in export trade were not achieved again until thirty years later, during the First World War, when the second export cycle attained its highest point. This second export cycle, the key to understanding the modern evolution of local financial institutions, lasted from 1884 to 1934, with the international depression of the 1930s contributing to its end.

The third export cycle spanned the years 1935–79 and had its peak in the 1950s. It was dominated by cotton, fishmeal and copper exports.[40] During this last cycle, however, industrial production played an increasingly greater role in the domestic economy and industrialists became a leading force in Peruvian economic and financial policies.

The highest annual average rate of export growth in the three cycles described above, 5.9 per cent, occurred in 1884–1934. This was a period of remarkable transformation, in which sugar and cotton shared, at times, a third to three-fifths of total Peruvian exports. Sugar dominated from 1895 until 1921. Cotton's share had started increasing by 1905, but obtained first place only around 1922–5. The balance of trade, though not the balance of payments, showed a nearly constant surplus throughout the whole period.

Despite overall export growth, a decline in the international price of exports occurred most notably in 1892–4, 1902–4, 1907–8, 1913–15, 1921–2, 1924–6 and 1929–31, with disturbing effects on Peruvian business and finance. Diversification of Peruvian export production diminished the effects of these sudden reductions in income from exports.[41]

Contrary to the opinion of those who argue that Peru had an economy dominated by foreign-controlled export 'enclaves', it has been recently established that the production of sugar and cotton, as well as that of wool and rubber, was controlled by the local élite, although foreign participation in the commercialisation of these products was substantial before the First World War. As indicated earlier, between 1884 and 1950 sugar and cotton provided a major share of Peru's total export value, together accounting for 37 per cent in 1890, 72 per cent in 1920 (an export boom year) and 29 per cent in 1930. These exports provided a high returned value and constituted the base of the native capitalists' economic and financial activities.[42]

Britain was the principal recipient of Peruvian exports until 1913, at which time the US market began to absorb up to 60 per cent of exports. Germany was the distant third competitor throughout the period 1900–39, minus the years of Allied blacklisting of German trade with Latin America during the First World War. The war also had a crippling effect on British trade and thus US trade became unrivalled. However between 1920 and 1928 British participation in Peruvian exports recuperated, taking an almost equal share of 30–35 per cent with the US. After 1928, however, the British share diminished steadily because of a decline in British importation of Peruvian petroleum and minerals which were gaining in importance among Peruvian exports.

British exports to Peru did less well than US products in capturing the bulk of the Peruvian market because Britain depended on the export of its textiles, which faced strong competition with domestic Peruvian manufacturing. Far more saleable US imports included foodstuffs, wheat, mining equipment and hardware supplies. As a result the US garnered almost 60 per cent of the Peruvian import market in the years 1916–20 and 42 per cent in the years 1921–30. British imports amounted to only 15 per cent and 17 per cent, respectively, for the same periods. Moreover British direct investment in Peru slowed down considerably while US investment increased sharply. Consequently profit remittances from British investments in Peru also lost ground. US direct investment grew from 38 million dollars in 1914 to 162 million in 1929, compared with an increase from 58 to 66 million dollars for Britain. However British merchant firms still continued to play a major role in the import–export trade with the US after 1930.[43]

During the period of modernisation the Peruvian population rose significantly. According to available statistics, the total population increased from 2.7 million in 1876 (census figure) to 6.2 million in the census year of 1940, with an intermediate estimate of four million by 1918. In other words, there was an approximately twofold expansion between 1876 and 1940. A recent study measures the increase of the urban population (towns and cities with more than 2000 inhabitants) from 1.1 million (or 25 per cent of the total population) in 1876, to 2.2

million in 1940 (28 per cent).[44] The figures for the growth of Lima's urban population are even more impressive: an increase of 40 per cent between 1876 and 1908, 23 per cent between 1908 and 1920, and 57 per cent between 1920 and 1931 – a total increase of 173 per cent between 1876 and 1931.[45] This urban population explosion brought with it a boom in Lima's real estate. Much of the increase in Lima's population was due to migration from the provinces.

The basic rigidities characteristic of the modern Peruvian economy are related to its dual character: on the one hand, Peru has a modern sector producing for the international market or for the small internal capitalist market, and on the other, it has a subsistence or non-capitalist sector which can not easily be integrated into the market economy. Technological backwardness has also constrained productive efficiency. Even when expensive modern industrial technology was adopted, the extremely unequal distribution of income caused imperfections of the market and the demand structure. As a result, resources were underutilised, markets were glutted, and there was an overabundance of low quality manufactured products.

Another serious structural constraint was the economy's dependence on international prices that produced negative terms of trade in times of decline, disturbing the balance between imports and exports. Deterioration in the terms of trade led to the need for foreign credit. The excessive acquisition of funds from abroad at certain times upset the domestic financial sphere and its connections with the local economy. This was the case with British and French capital imports to Peru in 1910–14 and US bank loans in 1925–9, which were determined substantially by the economic conditions of the lending countries themselves.[46]

Despite the structural constraints listed above, export gains did fuel a degree of economic diversification in Peru from 1890 to 1950. Like other modernising Latin American economies, there were improvements in the urban, industrial, infrastructural and service sectors. Numerous questions arise in this regard. To what extent did financial institutions, the élite related to them, and the state, contribute to the observed diversification? How did the financial structure relieve bottlenecks to allow and encourage an efficient transfer of funds from the export sector to the rest of the economy? Did income distribution improve as a result of domestic financial intermediation? Apart from oiling the export trade credit structure, what other functions did local financial institutions perform? Did financial institutions contribute to the peculiar diversification of the Peruvian economy, which was skewed towards the concentration of capital resources on the coast and particularly in Lima? (The industrial sector, for example, was – and still is – predominantly situated in the Lima–Callao area, despite some industrial advance in Arequipa, Trujillo and Cuzco). To answer these questions, different periods of financial development in Peru must be scrutinised.

PERIODS OF PERUVIAN FINANCIAL HISTORY

There are four important periods in Peruvian financial evolution which are relevant to the perspective adopted in this book. In the first period, between approximately 1780 and 1850, state emergency finance predominated. During the second period, between 1850 and 1883, the guano trade opened up new financial opportunities, and private and public interests clashed over key financial matters, leading to ill-timed foreign indebtedness and financial disaster. The third period, 1884–1930, was marked by institutional recovery and the search by agro-exporters for financial autonomy and diversification, which was reversed by 1930. In the fourth period, 1931–50, the state increased its financial intervention and sheltered increased oligopolisation of capital markets.

The years of modernisation coinciding with the third financial period formed the core of Peruvian financial development. The costliness and destructiveness of Peru's war with Chile (1879–83), however, had resulted in default of the Peruvian public foreign debt and left commercial finance in profound disarray. Aware of the situation, alert businessmen active in Peru at the time obtained sound financial backing before embarking on any enterprise that seemed at all risky. If the risk was high, though, so too was the return. But financiers had to be convinced not only of the feasibility of the projects, but of the wealth and moral standing of the prospective borrowers.[47] Despite the risks involved, commercial activities backed by financial resources were the ones most likely to encourage the private sector.

The Peruvian state lost many of its old Hispanic rights and characteristics following the war with Chile. State monopoly over resources and key economic activities was weakened. Instead of political determinants for economic privileges, the 'free' forces of the international markets gradually introduced new forms of monopoly or oligopoly based on financial backing and technological advantage. The new forces of 'High Imperialism' based on financial concentration thus made their successful appearance: 'It is no longer cannons that attain triumph', wrote a Peruvian contemporary, 'but trusts, cartels and comptoirs'.[48]

The years 1884–1930, which encompass the third financial period, can be categorised as the most important in the evolution of Peruvian capitalism. Recent studies have demonstrated the profound effects of capitalist penetration into Peru at the time, most particularly in the coastal region but also in the hinterland.[49] According to interpretations emphasising the role of foreign investment, the economic and financial role of native resources and the participation of the élite were negligible during this period. In this study it will be argued that the process of capitalist change in Peru involved a complex (and to date relatively unexplored) financial restructuring which evolved from the activities of domestic as well as of foreign agents.

Financial institutions and groups supported the initial process of oligopolisation of the production and service sectors from 1884–1930. The resulting reallocation of resources had mixed effects in terms of whether control was in native or foreign hands. It contributed to land property and technological innovation being concentrated in coastal plantations, as well as paving the way for the command of the domestic financial structure by locally-based banks linked to native investment groups. But it also led to foreign companies controlling the bulk of mining and petroleum concerns.

In the fourth financial period, 1931–50, oligopolisation of the financial structure was critically influenced by the Banco Italiano, renamed Banco de Crédito in 1941. This bank, unlike the failed Banco del Perú y Londres which had been active in the previous period, adapted its activities to the changing reality of declining agro-exports, consolidation of multinationals in the petroleum and mining industries, and a rise in state-sponsored industrial and service businesses. In the long run, however, relevant financial and statistical indicators discussed in Appendix A attest to a chiefly positive though variable financial evolution of modern Peru, lagging considerably behind developed countries but ranking favourably (behind Mexico and ahead of Colombia) in the Latin American context. The following chapters will analyse in detail this financial evolution starting with its pre-1884 foundations.

2 The Colonial and Post-Independence Heritage

The private and public use of credit in Peru went through significant changes between 1780 and 1883. The customary way of financing agriculture, mining and trade (old pillars of the colonial economy) was transformed. In terms of economic principles, the concepts of profit and rate of interest gradually replaced those of morally condemned usury and traditional rent.[1] By the 1860s new credit instruments had been instituted. Rural mortgages, for example, formerly secured by meagre colonial land rent, relied increasingly on agricultural commercial ventures. Likewise public finance (based on internal credit which heavily taxed the private sector) became increasingly dependent on newly acquired foreign loans.

This chapter traces the colonial and early republican roots of the credit practices which were central to private and public finance from about 1780, and the effect of foreign borrowing from its introduction around 1822–5 up to the damaging debt default of 1876–9. I aim to evaluate whether the terms and use of public indebtedness facilitated or impeded the capacity of native financial institutions and the élite to efficiently allocate financial resources. In more general terms I ask whether or not the relationship between public and private finance contributed to early economic growth.

The interaction between the public and private sectors in the early capitalist evolution of Peru has been approached from different perspectives. On the one hand authors like Cotler, Yepes and Bonilla argue that an inept economic and financial (liberal) élite, in collaboration with foreign capital, controlled and mismanaged the state's finances in order to advance their own interests.[2] On the other hand Hunt considers the economic stagnation in nineteenth century Peru was due to poor public investment decisions which did little to solve overwhelming structural constraints. Likewise, Gootenberg and Mathew explain that traditionally protectionist forces under urgent fiscal pressure acted against the implementation of adequate liberal trade policies and modern private and public financial management.[3] I consider that the views of Hunt, Gootenberg and Mathew offer the most adequate interpretation of the evidence produced by research on the issue.

15

This chapter will show that factors of patrimonial state finance constrained pre-modern finance in Peru by hindering the development of private commercial and mortgage credit and related institutions. I argue that the disproportionate public indebtedness of the late 'Guano Age' was in part a result of the factors which disturbed the overall pre-1884 financial development of Peru. The subsequent financial history of Peru has been affected by these impediments to a lasting compromise and collaboration between private and public finance.

I start with an analysis of the impact of the Bourbon financial reforms of the late colonial period, when the colonial state and the official merchant guild replaced ecclesiastical control over key colonial credit mechanisms. Subsequently the chapter will centre on the consequences of early-republican and Guano Age private and public internal and external borrowing.

THE BOURBON FINANCIAL REFORMS

Credit had multiple uses in the currency-scarce early Peruvian economy. A tradition of ecclesiastical, mortgage, commercial and public credit existed before independence from Spain, and Peru, with its distinct financial history rooted firmly in its colonial past, remained virtually detached from international capital markets until 1822.

In order to overcome a shortage of currency, private credit contracts had been fairly common since the beginning of Spanish colonial rule.[4] Credit was essential to the economy since silver bars and coins were exported to pay for imports and make sizeable remittances to Spain. The effect of the endemic currency shortage was reduced by several credit mechanisms – mainly colonial mortgages (*censos*),[5] and notarial loans (*escrituras*) – but the periodic extraction of bullion, and monetary contractions such as the 1772–83 re-minting of 10.5 million pesos of debased coins (*moneda macuquina*), into only 2.7 million pesos '*fuertes*', served to increase the problem.[6]

Mortgage loans on real estate was the main form of traditional credit supply used to partially ease the shortage of currency among the colonial élite. One of the most important mortgage mechanisms was the *censo al quitar*. This resembled the present-day mortgage loan: a redeemable long-term loan subject to a certain annual rate of interest (*rédito*) with real estate as collateral. This type of *censo* could be repaid by debtors at will and thus differed from the *censo enfitéutico*, which could not be cancelled while the lender was alive, or the *censo perpetuo* which was not redeemable at all.[7]

The *censos* adapted well to an agrarian economy based on the rent of the land. However, the *censos* were not necessarily used for productive prupuses or to improve property, but more generally for consumption or prestige purposes by landlords. Although the *censos* were repayable in the medium or short term, debtors repaid only on rare occasions, preferring to delay their *rédito* payment or to default on their loan repayments in order to avoid parting with precious currency. This became a customary practice among *censo* debtors, except for the most productive properties or when *censos* at lower *réditos* were available.

The most important creditors, the ecclesiastical institutions, accepted this practice because they were more interested in the secure allocation of their loans than in profitable credit business.[8] Thus in colonial times *censos* were in essence rent-extraction mechanisms rather than profit-seeking activities.

As shown in Table 2.1, *censos* to *haciendas* (rural estates) accounted for more than three-fourths of all credit belonging to the expropriated Jesuit assets (*Temporalidades*) in 1769; and 51 per cent of a total of one million pesos in *censos* pertaining to Indian funds (Caja de Censos de Indios de Lima) between 1757 and 1781. *Censos* granted to the state with the guarantee of fiscal rents did not amount to more than one-fifth of the total *censos* of these two lenders at that time. Another traditional mortgage creditor, the Inquisition, derived the bulk of its rents from 1.5 million pesos attached to *censos* (mostly on urban property), of which more than 60 per cent carried devotional and charitable obligations and should, more appropriately, be defined as liens (Table 2.2).

Monasteries also lent heavily to landed estates, as evidenced by the Lima Archbishophric's archive and the work by Hamnett.[9] Among the most important monastic lenders were the convents of Santa Rosa, Encarnación, Concepción and Nazarenas. In general, ecclesiastical and traditional credit provided a long-term, low-interest (3–5 per cent) mortgage type of credit which adapted to the low productivity and rentier character of colonial agriculture and landowners. According to contemporary observers, ecclesiastical lenders controlled approximately 50 per cent of the total mortgage credit available in the colony.[10] By custom, merchants were granted only limited *censo* loans due to canonical limitations on ecclesiastical lending for profit.

The origins of Peruvian public debt can be found in the late

Table 2.1   Distribution of *censos* pertaining to Jesuits (1769) and Lima's Caja de Censos (1757–81) by type of mortgaged property (in pesos)

	Haciendas	Fiscal Rents	Urban Property	Merchant Property	Official Posts	Total
Jesuits	446 534	119 445	21 700			587 679
(%)	(76)	(20)	(4)			(100)
Caja	527 560	220 428	143 260	78 000	67 516	1 036 764
(%)	(51)	(21)	(14)	(7.5)	(6.5)	(100)

Source: 'Libro mayor y general . . . de la negociación de Temporalidades', 1769, Sección Jesuitas, Lima, libro 443, AHN (Madrid); Audiencia de Lima, Juzgado General de Censos, legs. 31–93, AGN; Protocolos Notariales, testamentos y tasaciones, AGN.

Table 2.2   *Censo* funds (*fondos de censos*), value of properties (*fincas*), and income of Lima's Holy Office of the Inquisition, 1813 (in pesos)

	Value	Percentage	Annual Rent	Unpaid Debts
Censo funds	484 637	32	17 094	99 512
Suppressed chaplaincies	–	–	19 100	–
Liens of entails (*patronatos*)	532 897	35	21 323	33 893
Properties of entails	122 000	8	–	–
Liens of charities (*obras pías*)	368 984	25	12 694	21 298
Total	1 508 518	100	70 211	154 703

Sources: Francisco Echevarría, 'Estado demostrativo', in 'Expediente sobre la ocupación del Tribunal de la Inquisición', Lima, 7 Dec. 1813, Sección Inquisición, leg. 4800[2], AHN; also Gobierno, Lima, leg. 1605, AGI and Colección Moreyra, leg. 44, AGN.

colonial period. This was the time when the colonial state and the official merchant guild were able to take control of the main sources of colonial credit. In the background lay the creation in 1782, by the Spanish imperial state, of the first central bank of Spain, the Banco de San Carlos, with the intention of financing war efforts through the issue of royal interest-bearing notes (*vales reales*).[11] International conflicts fostered increasingly the role of the state in both the metropolitan and colonial credit systems. Neo-mercantilist and physiocratic ideas also lay behind imperial reformist and interventionist projects which were rationalised by 'enlightened' royal advisors (Campillo-Ward, Jovellanos, Olavide).[12]

Ecclesiastical credit was the first casualty of the Bourbon financial reforms in late-colonial Peru: the expropriation of Jesuit properties in 1767, the *consolidación de vales reales* (1806–9), and the abolition of the Inquisition (1813–1815) resulted in the partial disentailment of ecclesiastical liens and land property towards a stronger fiscal and commercial presence in credit matters. The Bourbon determination to reform the economy set an important precedent in the relationship between public and private financial interests.

The *consolidación de vales reales* was particularly objected to by large sections of the creole élite, especially by the Lima town council (*cabildo*) and important landowners. The measure was an attempt by the Crown to back its depreciating royal notes with liquid funds obtained from private debtors of ecclesiastical *censos* in Spain and its colonies. By decree the royal government became the single debtor of ecclesiastical *censos*, compelling former debtors to repay their old credits to newly appointed *consolidación* officers instead of to creditor ecclesiastical institutions. In Peru the *consolidación* obtained from debtors approximately 1.5 million pesos between its introduction in 1806 and its interruption in 1808 following continued native protest. The cessation of the measure did not impede the shipping of approximately 1.3 million pesos in *consolidación* proceeds to Spain in 1809, and in consequence colonial mortgage loan interests increased from 3–4 per cent to 5–6 per cent.[13]

Thus the traditional forms of mortgage credit granted by ecclesiastical institutions, and by the official Indian Caja de Censos, to traditional colonial landowners were seriously disrupted. However new fiscal debt mechanisms under the administration of the merchants' guild (*Consulado*) were introduced.

In the seventeenth and early eighteenth centuries the relationship between the state and the merchant guild was based on monopoly rights and privileges granted to the guild in exchange for 'services' to the crown, which included donations, enforced loans and loans without interest. Gradually however the proceeds of new trade taxes controlled by the *Consulado* were used as guarantees for loans granted to the state by merchants and other private lenders. From 1777 these public loans were entitled to 3–6 per cent annual interest.[14]

After 1750 there was an increase in colonial trade and mining in

Peru, probably linked to reformed trade practices.[15] By 1800 the Lima merchants had managed to channel funds from traditional lenders into the increased commercial activities of the late colonial period. The *escritura de riesgo*, a sort of merchant credit and insurance instrument, made possible inter-oceanic commercial transactions by establishing a contract between the lender (who assumed the responsibility for any loss or risk) and the merchant (who used the borrowed amount to buy merchandise) at high levels of interest. Important merchants were thus able to raise working capital without having to engage directly in mining finance (*avío*), which they avoided because of the risks involved, or provide advances to miners when purchasing silver (*rescate*).[16] (Credit for mining was scarce; capital was acquired by the continued exploitation of the Indian labour force, the miners' own savings or access to the funds of family networks. From 1780 limited credit was provided by the short-lived Bancos de Rescate, which were sponsored by the state and the official miners' guild.)[17]

Between 1751 and 1774 the interest (*premio*) on *escritura* loans decreased from 65 per cent to 16 per cent because of increased trade and competition in trade financing.[18] Lima merchants protested against the erosion of their monopoly interests and the bankruptcies which had occurred as a result of the relative over-supply of the colonial market. *Repartos de mercancías* (the forced distribution of imported and local produce among the Indian population), was just a temporary solution – backed by local credit chains – to the rise in the supply of imports. More satisfying arrangements to enable the Lima merchants to maintain some of their monopoly control included the formation of a regional closed market comprising Lima, Guayaquil and Chile, and the creation of new trade taxes to guarantee public loans.[19]

Peru was one of the last Hispanic American colonies to become independent. A relatively solid system of indebtedness, which had its roots in the late eighteenth century and was strengthened by viceroy Abascal in the early nineteenth century, constituted the financial basis for Spanish resistance to allowing independence.[20] The local private sector – especially merchants – was the main creditor of the state, which offered fiscal revenues as collateral for cash advances. According to a sample of the colonial fiscal debt (Table 2.3), merchants held 26 per cent, aristocrats and rentiers 21 per cent, and ecclesiastical institutions 17 per cent of a total of 3.6 million pesos between 1777 and 1819.

Table 2.3 Sample of main creditors of the colonial state in Peru by social sectors, 1777–1819

	Pesos	*Percentage*
Merchants	930 444	26
Aristocrats and rentiers	766 499	21
Ecclesiastical institutions and clergy	624 172	17
Fraternities (*legas*)	248 049	7
Charities	152 977	4
Charitable institutions	114 963	3
Military	95 600	3
Lenders (*prestamistas*)	88 000	3
Other (bureaucrats and professionals)	164 305	5
Not classified	400 276	11
Total	3 584 885	100

Sources: Tribunal del Consulado, 'Toda Imposición, 1819', leg. 349, libro 1237A, serie H-3, AGN; Protocolos Notariales, AGN.

A degree of trust or loyalty existed among the creditors of the king. Perhaps the introduction of interest-bearing loans guaranteed by *imposiciones* (pledges) of new fiscal rents (new trade taxes such as *ordenanza, corsarios, derecho patriótico, subvención, arbitrios*[21]), administered by the *Consulado* from 1777, also contributed to public confidence. Abascal was certainly aware of the need to provide adequate security and interest to local creditors, as well as to exploit their fidelity to the crown.[22] One independence fighter observed in 1823 that 'the blood and treasures of the land of the sun were used to extinguish the sacred fire set alight by the love of independence'.[23]

With independence the relative trust in the state as a debtor completely disappeared, together with the organising principle of the tax structure. The new republican government refused to honour the considerable amount owed by the colonial state to the private sector. In the official surrender by the Spanish army to the independent army on 9 December 1824 the fate of the colonial debt was discussed: Spanish officials considered the new government should honour the debt, while the victors dictated that a future Peruvian Congress would decide on the issue.[24] In August 1831 the Peruvian Congress recognised in principle the rights of the colonial creditors, and in 1851 there was a serious attempt by corrupt officials to integrate this 'old debt of the Spanish government' with the national debt.[25] The

Table 2.4   Total colonial public debt by type of creditors and debts, 1821 (in pesos) (official classification)

Creditors	Consulado	Consolidación	Tobacco, Mintage	Total	Percentage
Private individuals	4 989 484		394 756	5 384 240	44
Chaplaincies/cults	1 237 297	684 012	725 331	2 646 640	22
Monasteries	585 934	450 028	1 434 234	2 470 196	20
Former ecclesiastical funds	203 907	105 453	829 639	1 138 999	9
Charitable funds	232 252	21 252	69 112	322 616	3
Hospitals	226 528	20 840	36 753	284 121	2
Total	7 475 402	1 281 585	3 489 825	12 246 812	100

Source: 'Informe que presenta la comisión de la deuda española y secuestros', 20 Feb. 1865, Manuscritos 1865–D2845, BNL.

unsettled debt also became a major issue in the Spanish–Peruvian conflict of 1864–66.[26] However the debt was never actually repaid.

It was calculated that the outstanding debt owed by the colonial state to the private sector amounted to 12.2 million pesos,[27] that is, approximately £2.5 million in 1865 (compared to a total public external debt of £9 million in the same year). As shown in Table 2.4, 44 per cent of the debt in 1821 was owed to private individuals and 51 per cent to religious institutions (mostly monasteries), pious funds (chaplaincies and religious cults), and former ecclesiastical funds (*censos*). The amount of the debt was considerable if we take into account that, as a proxy for the amount of capital available in Lima in 1815, the funds invested in rents by major institutions amounted to approximately 12.7 million pesos.[28]

A policy of expropriation (*secuestros*) of private Spanish assets, considered necessary to stop private aid to the loyalist army, was practised between 1821 and 1823. According to the zealously anti-Spanish Bernardo Monteagudo, the number of Spaniards in Lima was reduced from 10 000 to only 600 between 1820 and 1823.[29] The total amount expropriated from the Spanish and their supporters is difficult to assess. Expropriations consisted mainly of rural and urban property and private and public credit documents, rather than cash. Approximately 43 *haciendas*, some of which were valued at 4–500 000 pesos, were taken over by the state from Spanish or pro-Spanish owners in the central coastal region alone. The expropriated property was given as a reward to military officers who had led the independence army, including Antonio José de Sucre, Bernardo O'Higgins, Blas Cerdeña, José María Plaza and others.[30]

The newly independent state weakened to the extreme the private sector of the old colonial order. The tax structure was in shambles and was dependent on inadequate import and silver mintage taxes and, until its final abolition in 1854, the Indian head tax. War costs, the costly presence of Colombian troops, and fiscal disorder forced the republican state to appeal for the first time for foreign loans.

EARLY REPUBLICAN DEBTS

The first foreign loans, amounting to £1 816 000, were raised in London in 1822 and 1825 and defaulted as early as October 1825,[31] remaining unpaid until 1849 when the new revenues from guano, a fertiliser in growing demand for European agriculture, allowed sufficient funds for the conversion (refinancing) of the 1820s debt, which by then had accrued to £3.7 million. The early recourse to foreign borrowing resulted in failure due to over-optimism on the part of the new state about its capacity to repay, and the political and military pressures of the struggle for independence. After the 1825–6 default the state had no alternative but to rely on traditional forms of domestic finance.

Between 1826 and 1849 the Peruvian state depended on a series of emergency financial mechanisms (merchant loans and *abonos*, or advance payment of customs duties)[32] and domestic privileged high interest loans guaranteed by *arbitrios* taxes on domestic trade. As was the colonial practice, the independent state relied on credit from monopoly-minded lenders who in return demanded the revenue from trade taxes to secure their loans. Republican governments rarely repaid these loans in cash; instead they granted their creditors several privileges over commercial tax revenues, which served to slow foreign trade expansion. Unlike the colonial state, the republican state lacked an organised tax structure. The result was an endemic practice of deficit finance.

After independence the private sector was weakened, but it retained some influence in overall political–economic matters due to the emergency finance mechanisms, budgetary problems and political instability. State finance had become a crucial instrument in forming support groups for military leaders competing for control of the state. By 1837 it was still possible to find some of the former colonial creditors among those who contributed to emergency loans. One loan that year came from 328 lenders contributing between 50 and 1000 pesos each, totalling only 66 075 pesos.[33]

However, in the list of the 1841–3 loans on *arbitrios*, the names of former creditors were less plentiful. In those years the loans on *arbitrios* totalled approximately 790 000 pesos, and included higher individual sums (up to 37 000 pesos) and more lenders (553) than previous emergency loans. By 1852–5 the names of the former creditors had practically disappeared.[34] This change represented a process by which the state gradually moved in borrowing away from traditional groups favouring protectionism, concessions and privileges, towards new groups of private lenders of merchant origin with a more liberal outlook and foreign connections.[35]

The guano *consignaciones* (temporary lease or contract of guano sales abroad) served as a model for a subtle transformation in public finance, and cash advances from the first guano contractors became another source of state finance. Conspicuous among these contractors was the British merchant house Antony Gibbs & Sons, which remained the only supplier of guano to Great Britain between 1842 and 1861.[36] Continuing political instability made the practice of financing government expenditure through guano cash advances a customary practice.

The Peruvian state from 1825–49 thus combined the eighteenth century practice of offering future fiscal revenue as collateral to domestic creditors (due to the absence of foreign credit resulting from the 1825 default) and the introduction of guano trade contracts against cash advances by primarily foreign merchant creditors. The state, endowed with rights inherited from the colonial past, was the sole owner of the guano deposits in the islands off the Peruvian coast. This placed the state in a position of relative strength, despite its fiscal problems. However, the state monopoly on guano complicated rather than simplified fiscal debt problems by enhancing the capacity for military and bureaucratic expenditure through foreign credit. The overall linkage and redistributive effects of the guano income were thus limited.[37]

Mining also faced serious problems during and after independence due to the weakness of private entrepreneurs, outmoded mining property legislation, and heavy taxation by the state. Foreign and native merchants supplied expensive credit in order to buy silver, the most important of the Peruvian export products until the 1840s. Miners in Cerro de Pasco had to confront credit shortage, political instability and price controls on silver by the state and Lima merchant creditors. The miners organised to complete in 1839 the Quiulacocha drainage channel, which had been started in 1806. However in the 1850s and 1860s additional drainage works and pumping machinery were needed, but venture capital had by then been concentrated on the coastal region. Only the scarcity of coins in the 1870s revived efforts to exploit Peruvian mining, but despite the limited efforts of private finance, silver mining continued to stagnate for the rest of the century.[38]

In 1850 the first effective repayment and servicing of the outstanding internal debt (*consolidación*) worked mainly in favour of merchant creditors and speculators. After three decades of neglect in the midst of economic stagnation, the state distributed 6 per cent interest-bearing bonds among those private individuals who had made reparation and credit claims against the different independent governments since 1821. The 1850 *consolidación* did not include the colonial debt. Only those domestic creditors who had lost property (through expropriation, damage or levies) and salaries, or had held internal debt IOUs since independence, were entitled to claim *consolidación* bonds.

Corruption was a prominent factor in the whole process of debt acknowledgement and bond issue.[39] Corrupt officials and their merchant partners obtained large sums through forgery, false recognition of claims and other illegal means, and rapidly sold their tainted bonds to avoid prosecution. These persons were indicted following an official inquiry in 1855, although few were in fact punished.[40] Beneath the surface, the corruption of the *consolidación* was an expression of the political struggle between the opposing supporters of the military leaders José Rufino Echenique and Ramón Castilla. As a result of the shady *consolidación* politics, public opinion was outraged and popular protest broke out.

In the business realm, particular domestic and foreign merchants acquired old and new bonds at initially low quotations in order to speculate and press for a rise in their value. Merchants were also allowed to pay part of their customs dues with internal debt bonds. These privileged negotiators of bonds displaced the original creditors by buying out their claims, thus making the *consolidación* measure ineffectual as a means towards a more equal distribution of wealth. On the contrary, an exclusive mercantile élite achieved influence through the *consolidación* to press for improved conditions of debt repayment and liberal economic reforms.

Table 2.5 Social background of major *consolidación* bondholders, 1850–1857

	1850–1852			1857		
	No.	Amount[1]	%	No.	Amount[1]	%
Merchants	45	6.05	38	25	2.36	51
Landowners	21	2.75	17	4	0.28	6
Government officials	21	2.05	13	–	–	–
Urban owners	12	1.93	12	4	0.35	8
Charitable institutions	2	0.36	2	2	0.27	6
Ecclesiastical institutions	1	0.21	1	2	0.24	5
Professionals	1	0.04	–	1	0.07	1
Other[2]	5	1.57	10	–	–	–
No information	18	0.97	6	16	1.04	23
Total	126	15.93	100	54	4.60	100
(% of total debt)		(66)			(42)	

1. Millions of nominal pesos in *vales de consolidación*
2. Includes debts to Chile and the heirs of Simón Bolívar.

Sources: Alfonso Quiroz, *Deuda defraudada*, Tables 8 and 19; 'Libro de la deuda interna consolidada . . .' and 'Liquidación de intereses . . .', Libros Manuscritos Republicanos, AGN.

In 1852 a group consisting mostly of merchants controlled 38 per cent of a representative sample of internal debt bonds. By 1857 their control had risen to 51 per cent (see Table 2.5). The concentration of bonds among merchants, apart from speculation and political lobbying, was due to credit repayments and loan guarantees offered by debtors, especially indebted landowners, in the form of internal debt bonds. In addition, the freeing of slaves was financed in 1855 by manumission bonds, which were used by landowners in a similar way as the internal debt bonds. The partial financial recovery of the agricultural sector can thus be traced to the release of funds by the *consolidación* and manumission transactions.[41] However, more productive use of these funds was limited by the absence of an institutional financial framework, which started to appear only with the first banks in the 1860s.

Several merchants and speculators of the *consolidación* participated in yet another controversial transaction: the partial conversion of the internal debt into 4.5 per cent interest-bearing foreign debt bonds issued in London. Approximately 38 per cent (9 million pesos) of the 24 million pesos (£4.8 million) total internal consolidated debt was converted in 1853.[42] Only a handful of well-connected merchants and speculators participated in the conversion. In 1854 some members of the London stock exchange objected to the admission of the Peruvian converted domestic bonds because 'two thirds of this debt . . . was made in an irregular manner through fraudulent means, by the favourites of the present government'.[43] However native and foreign creditors in Lima petitioned jointly in favour of the servicing without exception of the converted and non-converted internal debt. President Castilla complied in 1857, urged on by his rich supporters and by internal political difficulties.[44] Despite the proven legal irregularity of the transaction, the Peruvian government continued honouring the interest payment and amortisation (4 per cent sinking fund) of the converted debt through its financial agents in London, Antony Gibbs & Sons.

The conversion of the internal debt to an external one reinforced the move of the new financial strategy away from domestic borrowing towards renewed foreign borrowing. In 1849 the deferred 3 per cent Anglo–Peruvian debt had been settled; this was substituted in 1853 for new 4.5 per cent bonds brokered by the London firms Cristobal de Murrieta & Company and C. J. Hambro & Son.[45] In short, because of corruption and conversion measures the internal debt mechanism had been thoroughly ruined as a potential local and democratic vehicle of public finance for future purposes. As a consequence the Peruvian state renewed its reliance on foreign debt mechanisms and only used domestic borrowing in critical situations, with mostly ruinous effects on the national economy and the private sector.

Based on detailed information on the internal debt and its repayment between 1850 and 1865, I have challenged elsewhere the point of view of Bonilla, Cotler, and Tantaleán, who consider that the *consolidación* and conversion were measures that aided to fund and create a new domestic élite for future guano rentier ventures.[46] On the contrary, evidence shows that the funds released by the *consolidación* were rapidly concentrated among creditor merchants despite official designs to benefit political supporters. These merchants had previous accumulation patterns and foreign connections backed by trade and speculation in a capital- and currency-scarce economy.

Two important local merchant creditors were the Chilean Pedro Gonzales Candamo and the Spaniard Julián Zaracondegui.[47] They participated extensively in the *consolidación* and conversion deals, engaged in import and credit activities and kept very good friends among the military leaders. Zaracondegui was also very active in politics and merchant guild leadership. These men contributed very little to the formation of the national élite because their main motivation under the circumstances of a weakened private sector was individualistic rather than group or class oriented. A comment by a fellow merchant and partner in 1858 is quite revealing:

> Don Pedro Gonzales Candamo had a well known tactic in Lima's commerce of obtaining all possible gains and guarantees without labour or responsibility in capital concerns. . . . Don Julián Zaracondegui . . . wanted absolute control and had no scruples in business management . . . señor Candamo usually took a revolver with him on his rare visits to Zaracondegui's office, and señor Zaracondegui had his always ready: this was the measure of understanding and harmony in which my two partners lived – two of the highest persons in Lima's trade.[48]

These two merchants had interests in the first guano contracts as well as in many other kinds of import businesses, railways, and even some failed manufacturing ventures. Taking advantage of the shortage of capital and currency prior to 1850 they had granted loans at 18–24 per cent annual interest, and negotiated their own drafts with success.[49] They were good friends of President Castilla who, with the help of guano contracts and revenue, centred government control in Lima against regional secession.[50]

A second generation of assertive private capitalists appeared in the 1860s and 1870s.[51] Their main economic activities were guano contracts, trade, commercial agriculture, mining and eventually banking. These men played an important role in channelling funds into the sugar, cotton and nitrate export sectors through note-issuing, commercial and mortgage banks which appeared in Peru in the early 1860s.[52]

THE 'GUANO AGE' PRIVATE BANKS

> If there had not been banks, if 'credit' had not been used, if transactions had been limited to what was permitted by metallic currency, would agriculture and trade had achieved the level they have today?[53]

The Guano Age (1840–79) has been defined as a case of developmental 'failed opportunity'.[54] However the guano trade had some economic repercussions which have not been sufficiently analysed. Probably the most important effects of the private use of income from guano by the 1860s was a noticeable agrarian recovery, and the institutionalisation of credit in banks, which provided much needed financial instruments and contributed to the transfer of funds between the commercial and export sectors.

The first banks appeared in Lima in response to the increased financial requirements for commercial activities during the peak (1860–79) of the Guano Age. The use of commercial bills (*vales a la vista*) had increased considerably among Lima merchants to supplement the shortage of currency. The excessive export of silver currency resulting from trade imbalances and the rise in the international price of silver since 1848 had stimulated the circulation of debased national and Bolivian coins (*moneda feble*).[55] Currency instability thus contributed to the circulation of commercial bills, which were used by merchants as a more reliable means of payment.[56] However in the 1860s the circulation of bank notes which could be freely converted into silver provided a better institutional guarantee for monetary payments than the commercial bills. In addition the national currency was reformed in 1855, 1857 and 1862–3 in order to discourage its exportation and to allow the withdrawal of the *moneda feble* from circulation.[57]

The first note-issuing bank, the Banco de la Providencia, started its activities in Lima in 1862. Soon other issuing banks appeared, the most important being the Banco del Perú and Banco Nacional. These banks issued private notes which circulated as money without regulation or control by the state.

Local banks granted commercial loans and discounted bills guaranteed by either two well-established commercial cosigners, or with one cosigner and collateral in the form of public debt bonds, guano consignment companies' shares, IOUs from third persons and other stock and financial assets (which were kept in custody by the bank until the loan was fully repaid). As a consequence of these financial activities approximately 42 million *soles* (S/) in stocks and bonds existed in the Lima capital market in 1874. These securities included the stock of 12 banks and various companies: three insurance, four railway, four gas, three guano consignment, two immigration, three nitrate and nine various other companies.[58]

Under this initially liberal banking system, however, private bank administrators had ample opportunity to abuse the confidence of depositors and stockholders. Domingo Porras, manager of the Banco de la Providencia, led his institution into severe liquidity difficulty in February 1866 and it had to suspend operations until 1867. Porras had appropriated cash, disguised withdrawals with valueless or false credit documents, and faked the withdrawal from circulation of excess notes, for a total amount of S/747 934 (40 per cent of the bank's capital). Protests by the bank's clients followed, and demands were made for appropriate backing of bank notes, increased official supervision and legislation to limit indiscriminate issues by banks.[59] 'Frankly', wrote a merchant in 1868, 'except for the Banco del Perú, the other banks do not inspire great confidence because their managers are young men with neither capital nor experience'.[60]

Other critics accused local banks, especially the Banco del Perú, of forming a monopoly or 'financial dictatorship' led by the joint interests of guano contractors and bankers who took advantage of the lack of appropriate banking legislation.[61] The Banco del Perú, went through difficult times due to the sizeable indebtedness of one of its important clients, the Eten-Ferreñafe Railway Company. This company had raised S/720 000 in public stock, and S/600 000 in additional 8 per cent interest bonds with the mortgage of its tangible assets as a guarantee. Among the creditors of the railway firm were important directors of the Banco del Perú who, in 1872, granted an exceptional one-year term loan and additional current account credit for a total of S/643 000 (16 per cent of the bank's capital). These loans had low profit expectations due to competition from a rival railway and the poor financial situation of the Eten-Ferreñafe Company. In 1876 the Banco del Perú was still debating whether it should become the owner of the Eten-Ferreñafe Company.[62]

However, despite such cases of dishonesty and favouritism among managers and directors, the Guano Age issuing banks filled an important vacuum and assisted the mobilisation of capital within the Peruvian export economy. Furthermore, mortgage banking credit aided the revitalisation of post-1840 coastal agriculture. In late colonial times traditional ecclesiastical credit in the form of *censos* provided support to an aristocratic landowning class only marginally interested in commercial agriculture. The Bourbon reform of a portion of ecclesiastical *censos* and liens offered increased opportunity for some landowners to commercially exploit landed estates (as was the case with the landowning families Orué y Mirones and Carrillo de Albornoz). Peruvian sugar became an important merchandise, consolidating the Pacific trade in Chilean wheat. This trade pattern continued in the early post-independence period, although with serious limitations.[63]

With independence the landowning class lost most of the prestige and social position it had held during the colonial period. This was due to expropriation, a shortage in the slave labour force, limited foreign markets, and credit and capital shortage in a depressed economic situation. *Hacendados* (landowners) were forced to depend on very high credit rates when *censo* and family credit were not available. The surviving ecclesiastical institutions continued to lend at low interest rates (6 per cent per annum) during the post-independence period, but the loans went only marginally to agriculture and more to urban properties. A few *hacendados* were able to provide mortgage loans to others at 12 per cent annual interest, but many landowners could not raise funds for their own use because of legal uncertainties over their property titles caused by lien burdens and earlier expropriations.[64]

On the other hand merchants provided expensive credit through 'consignment' contracts, by which the merchant obtained the right to the *hacendado*'s crop in exchange for short-term credit at 18–24 per cent annual interest, or through direct loans at 24–30 per cent annually. By the 1850s consignment credit had become the norm with regard to sugar and cotton crops, as exemplified in the close business relationship between lender Pedro Gonzales Candamo and *hacendado* Fernando Carrillo de Albornoz, and Zaracondegui's cotton consignment deals with Ramón Aspíllaga.[65]

The 1850 consolidation of the internal debt nominally provided the landowners with up to three million pesos in bonds as compensation for the expropriation and destruction which had occurred during the first decades of independence. However, most of these funds – as we have seen – passed into the hands of their merchant creditors to repay previous debts or as collateral for new loans (as in the credit granted by Lachambre & Company and Green Nicholson to Domingo Elías).[66] Landowners thus reduced their participation as major internal debt bondholders from 17 per cent in 1850–2 to 6 per cent in 1857 (see Table 2.5). The freeing of slaves in 1855 provided landowners with up to eight million pesos in manumission bonds, which were used to repay merchant creditors and to replace slave labour with an indentured labour force.[67]

However the decisive contribution to the availability of credit to commercial agriculture was the appearance of the first mortgage banks. These institutions allowed diversification from the guano business by private entrepreneurs at a time when the international price of cotton increased as a consequence of the US Civil War.[68] Engelsen's research in notarial archives establishes that the first mortgage bank, the Banco de Crédito Hipotecario (1866), lent approximately S/12 million in the 1867–81 period, mostly to medium and large estates in the northern and central coastal valleys specialising in cotton and sugar production. A second mortgage bank, the Banco Territorial Hipotecario, was established in 1870. These mortgage banks granted loans to rural commercial ventures in preference to urban ventures by a ratio of 3.5:1. Note-issuing banks also lent to the agrarian commercial sector, especially in the boom years of 1865–73. Thus the interest on credit to agriculturists was lowered from the customary merchant rate of up to 18 per cent to the banking mortgage of 12 per cent by the late 1860s.[69]

The legal basis for the establishment of the mortgage banks was laid down at the completion of the republican disentailment legislation which freed landed properties from *censo* and lien obligations. As early as 1838 the state had decreed the substitution of *censo* credits for internal debt bonds, but little was done in practice. In 1825 the interest (*rédito*) on *censos* was reduced from 5 per cent to 2 per cent; thereafter it oscillated between 3 per cent and 5 per cent. Between 1851 and 1855 the state accepted internal debt bonds to redeem *censos*, these amounting to 404 677 pesos.[70] In December 1864 a new law was promulgated to allow property owners (*censatarios*) to convert up to 75 per cent of their *censo* and lien debts to 12 per cent interest-bearing state bonds (*cédulas de reconocimiento*). The state thus assumed the *censo* and lien debts and became the exclusive *rédito* debtor to *censo* creditors (*censualistas*) for a total of S/800 000. This measure encouraged the subsequent sale and speculation of the 12 per cent interest-bearing bonds.

In January 1865 the Lima ecclesiastical chapter (*cabildo eclesiástico*) protested against the 1864 law, arguing that it was neither constitutional nor economically sound (because it placed a heavy burden on state finances), and unjustly damaging to ecclesiastical property.[71] Similar protests had occurred in 1808 against the Bourbon *censo* amortisation process.

Soon after the application of the law redeeming *censos* and liens, in August 1866, the most important lenders and commercial landowners subscribed S/1.5 million in capital stock for the formation of the Banco de Crédito Hipotecario – despite opposition by a sector of the press. The detractors of this bank argued that it would lend at high interest rates. The bank granted 20-year loans on urban and rural property at 10.5 and 12 per cent annual interest, and issued mortgage bonds (*cédulas hipotecarias*) bearing 6 per cent and 8 per cent annual interest. The mortgage debtors thus received loans in the form of *cédulas*, and they were able to obtain cash by selling the bonds at the current discount to the public (approximately 88 per cent of their nominal value). The bank's gross profits derived from the difference between the loan interest and the interest on the *cédulas*, and between the nominal and current value of the bonds.[72]

In 1868 a project to form a state-sponsored mortgage bank was announced. This was a clear attempt to encroach on the agricultural consignment credit business of merchants by offering lower interest rates. The project did not succeed due to loopholes in the legislation concerning property rights and judicial procedures for executive action on the assets of defaulted debtors.[73]

The Banco de Crédito Hipotecario also granted loans to pay existing mortgages or for the purchase of property, and to finance improvements in production methods. Between 1870 and 1877 one debtor, María de Arauzo, an urban proprietor, renewed her loan with the bank three times.[74] Mortgages were also granted in some provinces (La Libertad, Ancash, Arequipa, Ica, Moquegua). As a result, the bank contributed to the doubling of the price of agricultural land for sugar production. Despite the political instability which almost caused the liquidation of the Banco de Crédito Hipotecario in 1867, the Guano Age mortgage banks succeeded in establishing significant links between the agrarian and commercial sectors at least until the beginning of the financial crisis of 1873–81. As a contemporary analyst argued, the competitive environment of Guano Age liberal banking seemed not to have been responsible for the financial crisis. (On the contrary, the crisis could have worked as a safety mechanism to expel inefficient institutions from the market.) It was rather the state's intervention and its foreign indebtedness which precipitated the crisis and bailed out the inefficient and unsound firms.[75]

FOREIGN PUBLIC DEBT PROBLEMS, 1850–79

The liberal conditions of the early Peruvian private banking system evolved alongside the state monopoly over guano deposits and deficit-led fiscal finance. This contradiction at the core of the transitional export economy continued to place serious limits on the development of a stronger private sector despite the opportunities offered by the guano income.

Until 1869 the external public debt was kept under relative control by strict guarantees on guano revenues administered by private financial agents in monopolistic conditions. Between 1849 and 1861 Antony Gibbs and Company had adhered strictly to interest and amortisation payments to foreign creditors.[76] Such punctuality was in the interest of political stability and international support for governments which strived to maintain good national credit abroad.

The native guano contractors who replaced Gibbs in 1861 also hired the services of a foreign firm, Thomson Bonar & Company, to handle the Peruvian external debt in London. The external debt conversions and loans of 1862 and 1865 provided fresh amounts for governmental expenditure. However the loans also brought with them a wave of controversial allegations. One negotiator of the 1865 loan of £10 million, the liberal future president Manuel Pardo, had family ties with partners of Thomson Bonar. Moreover the London firm was sued by the Peruvian government in 1872 for charging unfair commissions of up to £46 700 in the brokerage of the 1862 and 1865 loans.[77]

Guano contractors charged up to 35 per cent for interest, commissions and other charges on short-term loans advanced to the government between 1864 and 1869. The state remained in constant financial need and some officials thought that private native and foreign lenders were taking advantage of the state.[78] By 1869 the fiscal guano revenues had achieved very little in terms of improvement to domestic infrastructure and development, while public deficit reached S/17 million. Most of the proceeds of the short- and long-term loans were consumed by bureaucratic and military expenditure and the cost of commissions and interest.[79]

Part of the reason behind the public sector's dependence on the guano contractors' advances and external bonded credit was the underdeveloped tax structure. Customs and silver taxes were insufficient to provide internal autonomy of revenues. Guano was therefore increasingly essential as a fiscal guarantee to attract external credit. As early as 1855 tax reformists had warned against the excessive reliance on guano revenues.[80] Moreover, the Indian head tax had been abolished in 1854. Also, since the abandonment of old internal debt strategies by 1850–4, auxiliary trade taxes had been curtailed. However any small attempt at introducing tax reforms and taxes based on income was vehemently opposed by different social sectors. In 1866 minister of finance Manuel Pardo's plan to institute new taxes on capital and labour suffered relentless attack. Pardo's original tax reform achieved only the establishment of new export and indirect taxes, which remained in use until the 1890s.[81]

The liberal revival of 1866–8 declined and was replaced by a traditionalist faction led by colonel José Balta, who became president in 1868. This was, however, a conservative government with a difference. Balta adopted an apparent 'developmental' attitude. His strategy and that of his ministers of finance was to increase the external debt to a disproportionate level with respect to the increasingly unreliable but still mortgageable guano revenues. Justification of their policy was based on condemnation of the guano contract system and the need to develop a national railway system. The burden of increased foreign indebtedness was to be transferred to subsequent governments. In only one year, between 1871 and 1872 the Peruvian external debt increased dramatically from S/90 million (£18 million) to S/185 million (£37 million); the debt had been only £9 million in 1865 (Table 2.6). The annual servicing of the external debt thus increased to S/13.5 million in 1872, clearly rendering inadequate the S/15 million guano revenue of that year.[82]

The 1870s debt spiral began with the signing of the Dreyfus contract in 1869. Traditionally-minded minister of finance Nicolás de Piérola set the tone by displacing the domestic guano contractors and bankers from the administration of guano revenue funds, replacing them with a single French firm, Dreyfus Frères et Cie, which was contracted to sell two million tons of guano against advances to the government. The Peruvian Congress moved that the Dreyfus contract exceeded the congressional authorisation for deficit arrangements. The displaced contractors, the '*hijos del país*' (native sons), took the issue to court but remained powerless against the executive decision.[83] The head of the French house, Auguste Dreyfus,[84] had financial backing from a group of bankers in Paris (Société Générale, Leiden Premsel) and London (J. Henry Schröder & Company). Huge advances were supplied by the speculative Dreyfus, who strived to monopolise the guano business at all costs. Dreyfus also became the financial agent of the Peruvian debt in Europe.[85] Unlike Gibbs, Dreyfus was not careful in calculating safe guano guarantees for the expanded credit to the Peruvian government.

Piérola has been seen by sympathetic historians[86] as a popular leader who was able to displace an élite which took advantage of

Table 2.6   Estimated Peruvian (internal and external) public debt, 1821–80* (millions of pesos of 1850)

Years	Mer-chant[a]	Arbi-trios	Consol-idation	Manu-mission	Banks	Total Internal	Guano	Loans	Total External
1821	0.5	–	–	–	–	14.5[b]	–	–	–
1825	–	–	–	–	–	14.5	–	9.1	9.1
1830	1.2	–	–	–	–	1.2	–	9.1	9.1
1835	0.2	0.4	–	–	–	0.6	–	9.1	9.1
1840	0.7	0.7	–	–	–	1.4	0.3	9.1	9.4
1845	1.1	1.0	4.8	–	–	6.9	0.2	9.1	9.3
1850	–	1.3	6.6	–	–	7.9	1.8	19.0	20.8
(1852)	–	–	24.0	–	–	24.0	–	11.1[c]	–
1855	–	–	12.4	7.9	–	20.3	2.0	25.0	27.0
1860	–	–	7.8	1.8	–	9.6	5.9	27.5	33.4
1865	–	–	–	–	12.5[d]	12.5	–	45.0	45.0
1870	–	–	–	–	–	–	–	60.0	60.0
1875	–	–	–	–	11.0	11.0	–	165.0	165.0
1880	–	–	–	–	48.0	48.0	–	250.0	250.0

* Approximations to nearest year, according to source used
a. Includes loans and *abonos*
b. Includes colonial debt and *secuestros*
c. Conversion of internal to external debt 1853–4
d. Guano advances

Sources: Paul Gootenberg, *Between Silver and Guano*, pp. 168–73; Alfonso Quiroz, *Deuda defraudada*, pp. 44–7, 89–91; W. M. Mathew, 'The First Anglo-Peruvian Debt'; Carlos Palacios Moreyra, *La deuda anglo-peruana*, pp. 89–93; Emilio Dancuart, *Anales de la Hacienda Pública*, vol. 5, pp. 46–8; Carlos Marichal, *A Century of Debt*, p. 244; Ernesto Yepes del Castillo, *Perú 1820–1920*, p. 83; Carlos Cambrubí, *Historia de bancos*, p. 245.

fiscal business to advance their own interests. However he can be seen in a different light if we consider his conservative background. Piérola was the son of a Spanish-educated scholar turned politician and state bureaucrat who served as a controversial minister of finance under President Echenique in 1853. Before occupying the same post as his father did sixteen years earlier, the young Piérola had been a seminarist of traditional education and convictions closely linked to conservative leaders Echenique and Balta.[87] Piérola became the civilian heir to the *caudillo* tradition, which was bitterly opposed to the liberal civilianist party and its leader, Manuel Pardo. Unlike Pardo's reformist attempts, Piérola was in favour of continuing to borrow from abroad in order to maintain the independence of fiscal finances and the manoeuvring of his political clients.[88]

According to Piérola's wishes an external loan contract was signed with Dreyfus in 1870 for almost £12 million. This loan at 6 per cent interest was used mainly to finance the railway projects of contractor Henry Meiggs, a yankee Pizarro, for the lines Lima–Oroya and Mollendo–Arequipa–Puno. According to a British financial review of 1874, the Peruvian railway system was 'unsurpassed in "grandeur", costliness, and total hopelessness of profit returns'.[89] Despite the increase in the foreign debt with the 1870 loan, in 1871 Piérola took out another loan contract with Dreyfus, the funds to be used mainly for conversion purposes.

In the minutes of a meeting of the Council of Ministers in July 1871, handwritten by Piérola himself, one can read the persuasive and authoritative arguments which he used to convince the other ministers to approve the new loan. He argued that the conversion of previous foreign public debts (the 1865 loan, the 1866 Chile–Peru debt, and the 6 per cent interest bonds of 1870 floated at a price of 82.5 per cent) was possible and urgently needed. The reasons given were (a) to meet debt servicing and current expenditure on public works and the police; (b) to allow time for the expected proceeds from railways to materialise; and (c) because there was no legal impediment for including a conversion loan as part of the £15 million loan limit authorised by Congress in February 1871. This congressional authorisation was, however, granted only for a loan for railway and irrigation works. According to Piérola, since the interest of the conversion loan would be 1 per cent lower than that of 1870, his proposed loan conversion contract also complied with the conditions set by Congress to contract only advantageous public loans.[90] In accordance once again with Piérola's designs, a new loan contract was signed with Dreyfus on July 1871. However the sudden interruption of the negotiations days later by order of President Balta brought about Piérola's immediate resignation. It is not clear whether the disagreement between the president and his minister was due to personal interests involved in the loan negotiations.

Only in December 1871 was a new deal arranged with Dreyfus, without Piérola's participation, which raised the loan amount to £36.8 million.[91] This mammoth 'consolidated' loan bore 5 per cent interest and was floated at the low issue price of 77.5 per cent.[92] Everything was set to raise the funds in the London, Paris and Amsterdam markets early in 1872 when a letter, by the Peruvian citizen Carlos Elías, was made public in European newspapers. Elías disputed the legality of the loan transaction and pointed out the impossibility of a poor country such as Peru being able to repay the loan. Distrust spread quickly among bankers and investors and, consequently, the loan negotiation faltered before coming to a halt.[93] Only £15 million was initially allowed to be floated by the London stock exchange committee. The remaining portion was carefully meted out during the next months.

Observers have commented that the 1872 loan 'cannot be termed a satisfactory success. Bonds have been sold, it is true, thanks to the vigorous and untiring efforts of the syndicate [backing the loan] . . . but the figure at which the loan had been floated in the greater part is not flattering to the credit of the republic'.[94] It was in 1873 that London bondholders begin to protest against the 'unjustifiable depreciation' of the Peruvian external bonds. The quotation of Peruvian foreign loan bonds in London had already been declining by 1872, as had other Latin American bonds.[95]

Contemporaries had no trouble pointing out the flaws in the use of the Peruvian foreign debt to cover current expenditure, refinance existing loans, and carry out colossal railway projects with uncertain returns. The increased foreign debt also allowed wider opportunities for corruption – a constant though 'invisible' factor in Latin American public indebtedness. The politicisation of the public debt became a serious problem due to frequent deadlocks in Congress between opposing sides and impulsive actions on the part of the executive power. It was only a matter of time until private banking capital was 'pulled into the unfortunate destiny of public finance'.[96] As one observer commented in 1876:

> It has been several years now that Peru has been slipping towards the abyss. . . . What has pushed Peru in that direction? The careless loans, the banking mania, the railway mania and, above all, the witchcraft remedies used against such follies and others; in a word, the contempt towards mercantile principles.[97]

The sudden inflow of foreign capital triggered a temporary banking boom between 1869 and 1872. In 1869 there were only three banks of issue (one of them, the Banco del Perú, co-owned by Pardo) and one mortgage bank. However in 1873 there were sixteen main offices of banks (13 issuing, two mortgage, one savings), six branches and five agencies. Discount rates declined from 15 per cent in 1869 to 6–8 per cent depending on the maturity date, which could be up to six months. Camprubí considered this to be a banking 'hypertrophy' out of proportion with the Peruvian economy.[98]

Serious domestic financial and currency problems coincided with the world recession of 1873. According to Pardo, currency difficulties had been experienced in Peru since 1872 because of inflationary pressure linked to foreign indebtedness.[99] The resulting tendency was an outflow of silver currency to cover trade deficits, and therefore the issuing banks could not easily pay note holders with silver currency or provide bills of exchange on London. In August 1875 domestic banks had to suspend the specie payment of their note obligations. The suspension was observed to be caused by 'the extreme scarcity of exchange on Europe which rendered it absolutely necessary for merchants to make their remittances in silver coin, bar-silver or foreign gold'.[100] Foreign companies confronted, apart from depressed commercial conditions, difficulty in remitting their considerable profits abroad (in some cases profits of up to an annual average of 60 per cent for the 1868–1873 period).[101] A foreign merchant wrote in March 1876:

> The state of business matters in general shows no signs of improvement and sales are extremely dull. Were it not for the large exportation of sugar it would be impossible to obtain remittances as with the exception of a small quantity of bar silver there is nothing else in the open market to draw for.[102]

President Manuel Pardo had to deal with the imminent banking and fiscal failure in 1875–1876. Public debt servicing and amortisation were suspended in January 1876 when new refinancing loans failed to materialise. The quotation of Peruvian bonds plunged from 77.5 per cent in 1875 to 17.15 per cent in 1876.[103] Under fiscal pressure, the state began to use the pledged guano revenue for current expenditure following the debt default. Public works were paralysed. The reduction in credit from abroad led to a dramatic reversal of liberal financial conditions and of stable monetary policies. Banking regulation had been introduced in 1873, but rigid intervention by the state in banking matters was targeted as a means to confront the financial crisis.

The private banking sector was forced to assist the state in the critical 1875–9 period, beginning with an agreement between the government and the banks in September 1875.[104] The state guaranteed the banks' monetary issues with internal debt instruments, and the banks lent S/18 million to the state with the rapidly depreciating paper currency. Bank notes were declared legal tender of mandatory inconvertible circulation, backed by valueless consolidated internal debt instruments. The establishment of a central bank was criticised and feared.[105] Ultimately in August 1877 the state converted the private bank notes into a national currency, the *billetes fiscales*, which continued to depreciate even further.[106] The banks continued lending to the state until 1880. These manoeuvres between public and private interests enabled each to cover up in inefficiency.

Inflated internal credit thus replaced the inflow of foreign capital. Absolute fiscal and banking collapse was avoided but inflation loomed, as did currency depreciation, and long- and short-term credit conditions foundered. According to a press report in 1878 'Peru suffered from the necessary consequences of importing larger quantities of merchandise than she had produced to pay for, and of having nothing but a depreciated currency with which to make good the balance of trade against her'.[107]

Another interventionist policy on the part of Pardo was the expropriation in March 1875 of nitrate concerns in southern Peru. Both foreign and native private owners were affected by the measure. A stock company had been formed in 1873 by the native banks Perú, Nacional and Providencia to administer the sale of nitrate at officially fixed prices.[108] Private interests collided with this attempt to establish another public monopoly. Nitrate certificates were then issued by the state in payment for the expropriation of nitrate fields in 1875. The associated banks also administered and financed the expropriation process by making loans to the government and subcontracting the sale of monopoly nitrate to Antony Gibbs & Sons.[109] At the end of Pardo's term of office in 1876 his administration and interventionist policies were bitterly criticised in Peru and abroad.[110]

Between 1874 and 1876 there had been frustrated attempts to refinance the external debt. During the administrations of Presidents Manuel Pardo and Mariano Prado (1876–9) the foreign debt renegotiations failed to halt the approaching financial collapse. After a series of unfruitful deals with Dreyfus and the Société Générale, Prado signed in 1876 the Raphael contract under pressure from the Council of Foreign Bondholders and its chairman Charles Russell.[111] The contract established that a foreign creditor company, the Peruvian Guano Company, would administer the guano income to service the defaulted Peruvian debt, but legal conflicts with Dreyfus, who also had rights over the guano revenue, resulted in difficulty in implementing the contract.[112]

Even so there were still hopes that a transformation of the export economy could lead to recovery and renewed possibilities for development. Meiggs had found ingenious ways of financing his railway, mining and nitrate projects with the scrip of his Public Work Company (totalling S/5.3 million) which quoted higher than the *billetes fiscales*. The circulation of national currency was later limited to only S/20 million.[113] Income from the export of sugar had eased the exchange crisis by December 1876, and the rate of exchange had increased from 18–20d. (pence) per sol to 22–24d. by June 1877.[114]

However the War of the Pacific removed all remaining hope of recovery. The Peruvian Guano Company and the Committee of Peruvian Bondholders made separate financial arrangements with Chile, thus depriving Peru of its guano income in the middle of the war. In a stern and conservative British newspaper the epitaph of the Peruvian financial and military disaster was written in 1879: 'After the shameless way in which Peru has played fast and loose with her creditors, she can not expect to be treated as if she had been all along an honourable state. She will not attract the sympathies of the civilised world however loudly she may protest; and Chili, the victorious state, is certainly entitled to exact compensation for her expenditures and losses'.[115]

To make things even worse, after his coup against Prado in the middle of the War of the Pacific, Piérola ultimately contributed to the destruction of local banking activity by issuing in 1879 the worthless incas to replace the *billete fiscal*. The Banco Garantizador was an early casualty when it converted all of its cash into incas under the influence of some of its directors who were involved in business and politics with the Piérola regime.[116] This and other financial blunders weakened further Peru's war efforts.

In conclusion, in Peru's financial evolution prior to 1884 the private economic and financial leadership was neither able nor allowed to take firmer command of the national economy, and thus remained vulnerable to chronic public intervention with damaging effects on domestic monetary and institutional bases. Public and private inefficiency continued because of monopoly and privilege arrangements. Traditional debt and fiscal strategies contributed to the decline in the effectiveness of domestic financial intermediation. With these harmful legacies, which hindered collaboration between public and private interests, financial evolution was arrested until institutional reconstruction followed the end of the Chilean military occupation in 1883. It is no accident that of the only three institutions to avoid bankruptcy, two were strictly commercial banks – one native, the Banco del Callao (established in 1877), and the other a branch of a foreign bank, the London Bank of Mexico & South America (1863) – which avoided the issue of notes and concentrated rather on short-term commercial credit, the basis for the next period of banking and financial activity in Peru.

3 The Domestic Financial Structure, 1884–1950

In line with adverse appraisals of the financial legacy of the Guano Age, it is commonly believed that private domestic finance continued to play a damaging role in the Peruvian economy after 1883. Major causes of Peru's underdevelopment and dependence have been found in the financial bases of the *República Aristocrática* (1895–1919) and President Leguía's *Oncenio* (1919–30), periods during which private finance was prominent.[1] Thereafter the private financial system has been seen as the key link between national economic resources and the foreign interests which supposedly controlled its direction.[2] It has also been suggested that true modern financial evolution only started as late as 1931 thanks to increased state intervention and regulation in banking and financial matters.[3] In this chapter, and in Chapter 4, new evidence on private finance contributes to a revision of these accepted views.

The relevant issue is whether Peru's national financial structure was able to meet the challenges of development linked to export growth and thus establish a clear break with the guano past. I approach the issue by evaluating whether the private sector helped channel funds for productive and autonomous diversification within and beyond the agricultural export sector. I argue that private financial interests and institutions after 1883 were at the centre of initial economic recovery and modernisation, contributed to the relative diversification of the Peruvian export economy, and combined competition and collaboration in their deals with foreign interests. The complementary role of the public sector in Peru's financial development, especially between 1931 and 1950, and the financial system's shortcomings at the regional and wealth distribution levels will be focused on in more detail in later chapters.

Within the two broad divisions of the fluctuating but mainly positive modern financial evolution in Peru – the mostly liberal years 1884–1930 and the more interventionist period of 1931–50 – described briefly in the Introduction and evaluated in Appendix A, I will analyse here the development of key financial institutions and organisations in five relevant sub-periods: 1884–1901, a period of institutional recovery and the diversification of financial services led by commercial credit; 1902–15, characterised by increased financial support to oligopolisation and foreign participation in native institutions under the gold standard; 1916–30, a key sub-period for agro-exporters in search of financial autonomy in a context of growing financial ties with the internal market; 1931–9, a time of internal financial adaptation to the depression under the influence of one dominating institution, the Banco Italiano; and finally 1940–50, a decade of inflationary expansion and subsequent fall in financial activities strongly linked to sheltered industrial interests.

1884–1901: REGENERATION AND COMMERCIAL CREDITORS

The reemergence of financial institutions in the 1880s and 1890s did not enjoy the advantageous conditions of the export bonanza of the 1860s. Immediately after the War of the Pacific, an acute shortage of venture capital and credit arose from the low international credit-worthiness of Peru and the extreme drop in value of the national paper money. In general, an aversion to credit was widespread due to profound distrust by the public of financial institutions.[4]

Not surprisingly, businessmen and savers regarded state intervention in financial and monetary matters as a serious impediment, already experienced in the late Guano Age with disastrous results. Hence public institutions offered only a weak challenge or no challenge at all, to the increasingly dominant commercial banks – the native Banco del Callao and the foreign London Bank of Mexico and South America – which had survived financial collapse by avoiding note issues. In order to capture scarce funds, these banks had to display an ultra-liberal financial policy opposed to state arbitration, high liquid reserves of hard currency, and perform on a strictly short-term basis when granting credit. Those individuals and firms who had some confidence in the few surviving financial institutions expected the immediate restitution of their funds in hard currency upon demand, and looked to banks as a source of effective short-term credit whenever needed. Thus financial institutions reinitiated their local activities in the face of swift action by the saving public in depositing and withdrawing their funds. These conditions compelled Peruvian financial activities to be conservatively based on strict commercial and merchant credit terms during the initial phase of financial recovery.[5]

Moreover, the legacy of the extensively defaulted, long-term agricultural debt left by the Guano Age ensured that commercial banks avoided agricultural credit; they preferred to provide credit to merchants rather than to planters.[6] Thus, during the first few years after the War of the Pacific there was an apparent absence of direct links between the local banking sphere and export activities.

In these circumstances, one might ask how it was possible for the thoroughly weakened export sector to recover and finance the investment needed in sugar and cotton plantations. Lacking adequate banking and mortgage credit, sugar and cotton planters depended largely on few *casas fuertes*[7] – powerful merchant companies, most of them foreign – to provide competitive commercial credit.[8] That most plantations were Peruvian-owned was due in part to the fact that foreign companies did not want to assume the risks of direct control over export production.[9] In the main, coastal landowners with good commercial connections, plus some merchants and informal mortgage lenders who held credits on certain properties, acquired the land of traditional landowners unable to repay their debts.[10]

By 1900, when the international price of sugar and cotton had improved temporarily (attracting renewed investment in commercial agriculture), native planters were heavily indebted to and financially dependent on these foreign merchant creditors.[11] Dissatisfied agro-exporters voiced their complaints about the lack of adequate agrarian credit institutions, proposing in 1902 an agrarian bank and other forms of agricultural credit.[12] But the fact that this bank only became a working reality in 1931 indicates that their needs were not shared by other financial interests.

'It should be the steady and consistent object of a commercial firm like ours', wrote a top manager of the London-based Antony Gibbs & Sons with reference to their Peruvian interests, 'to do the maximum amount of commercial business (so long as profitable) with the minimum outlay of capital'.[13] Other influential merchant houses acting in Peru between 1884 and 1930 followed strictly the same financial leitmotiv. The strongest were the North American W. R. Grace & Company, the French T. Harth et Cie, and the British Graham Rowe, Duncan Fox and H. M. Beausire.[14] The golden years of the Guano Age, which allowed an average net profit of above 50 per cent for traders, were long gone.[15] After the war of 1879 foreign trade on the west coast of South America concentrated mainly in Chilean ports. Those companies which remained in Peru were still attached to the impoverished market through previous unfruitful investments, such as immobilised assets in credits to sugar estates and the government. Although greatly discouraged, foreign trade did not lose its hold on the heavily indebted country. One dominant merchant house even obtained a net profit of 40 per cent in 1883, a year of deep economic depression in Peru.[16] It appears that the business objective of these firms was to attain a controlling position and enhance monopoly gains after Peru's expected economic recovery.[17]

It had been common practice among large foreign commercial houses to engage not only in lending to local retailers and consumers of imported goods, but also in export trade, government and railway financing, among many other activities. In a backward economy foreign merchant houses were the heralds of modern business.[18] Business innovations earned a premium both when they were first introduced with a competitive advantage and then monopolised to avoid competition. Capital outlays were unavoidable in controlling certain areas of business. However less orthodox methods, such as bribes, pay-offs and monopoly agreements, were concurrently applied to keep the overall investment as low as possible. Bribery was used widely, both locally and abroad, to 'remove difficulties', starting at low levels with gifts of golden watches accompanied by '*cartitas de atención*' (reprimand memos) offered to capricious collaborators.[19]

Large merchant houses were themselves debtors to merchant bankers abroad, as well as creditors to local agriculturists and smaller commission merchants all over the country. These houses' success in the reduced Peruvian market depended on the full and most profitable use of their lenders' capital, and a strict credit policy towards their debtors. Initially the only area where they had a competitive relationship with local banks was over commercial paper discounts and exchange commissions. More commonly however, merchant houses collaborated in joint ventures with local financial institutions when the opportunity arose. The prominent position of these major merchant houses in financial initiatives was recognised in the Peruvian business scene. This was especially so with regard to the prolonged negotiations on the foreign debt, which was finally settled in 1890 with the signing of the Grace Contract, and the corresponding formation of the British-based Peruvian Corporation to administer the assets surrendered by the Peruvian government to its foreign creditors.[20]

Merchant credit for the marketing of agro-exports was based on the *habilitación* system that left a considerable part of price fluctuation risks in the hands of local producers. *Habilitación* consisted of monetary advances, which were never more than 75 per cent of the previously agreed value of the export crops consigned by planters as collateral. This was done in order to protect the merchant from a possible fall in price between the harvest and the final sale of the product. After the crops had been sold abroad, the merchant deducted from the proceeds the loan's principal and the interest charged to the planter, as well as trading, shipping and insurance commissions and any additional or unexpected costs. Merchant creditors also acted as agents of the agro-exporters for the purchase of agricultural equipment. Export credit was granted by merchant houses to fill the loading capacity of steamers departing from Peruvian ports, thus obtaining maximum advantage in the import–export trade.

In periods when the price of export products declined, merchant creditors swiftly withdrew their services, leaving local producers in a critical financial situation. A senior manager of a merchant firm in New York wrote to his Lima subsidiary in 1898, during a temporary collapse of the agro-export business:

> we have decided that the benefit derived from commissions earned on the sales of produce does not and will not at any time warrant our giving credits. . . . Take, for example, credits lately given to Céspedes and to José Figallo [of Piura]. We will have sold in a few days the balance of this latter friend's cotton, and will send on the account, showing a considerable debit balance, the collection of which we will no doubt confide to your care. . . . No guarantee which you would be likely to get in Peru would be of much value; we know that mortgages there are of very questionable value, and can be disputed in court for years . . .[21]

Less important local merchant houses conducted the *habilitación* business on more risky terms than the large merchant houses and local banks. A good number of these were agents of foreign firms and engaged in import representation in addition to granting agricultural credit. They also worked with short-term credit granted to them by local banks. Quite often these merchants offered securities as collateral to obtain from local banks the working capital necessary to advance the customary 75 per cent on account to producers for the sale of products abroad.[22]

Strong foreign firms abroad hesitated however to commit themselves to employing local representatives due to their assumed unreliability: 'although . . . you say that the "soundest" way of doing business [in Peru] is to own cotton estates, I have no doubt you only mean that it is the way to avoid the risks inherent in dealing with weaker or fraudulent consignors or "habilitados" . . .'[23]

Thus some *casas fuertes* invested directly in sugar and cotton estates. There were two main reasons for following this course of action, despite the risk involved: either they had to take direct ownership of landed estates due to the inability of native landowners to pay back outstanding debts (for example Grace's credit on Alzamora's Cartavio estate in 1882, Graham Rowe's and Terry's on Salas del Real's San José estate in 1883, and W. & J. Lockett's on Swayne's Cañete estates in 1900); or to modernise and make profitable certain estates – some perhaps acquired through foreclosure – and thus secure a reliable supply of products for export–import business and industrial concerns.[24]

Political and diplomatic support was also sought to protect large foreign merchant investments in commercial agriculture. Agro-exporter, and future president, Augusto B. Leguía did not hesitate to use diplomatic pressure to his and his creditors' advantage. In 1895 Leguía protested at the attempt by the Peruvian government to force the purchase of S/10 000 in government bonds, 'a worthless paper', on the Casa Blanca estate in Cañete, and demanded from the British minister the protection 'due to English interests' because the estate belonged to Mrs Swayne, the widow of a British subject and Leguía's mother-in-law, and was 'hypothecated to a Liverpool firm for a large amount'.[25]

To facilitate their export and import trade, merchant houses widely used the bill of exchange as the main instrument of credit. The inflow and outflow of these foreign currency drafts had a strong bearing on the exchange rate of the Peruvian currency. The major importers employed local travelling representatives and provincial agents to provide the credit information needed to extend the customary 60- and 90-day paper credit in the pre-First World War period.[26] A US commercial attaché stated that 'credit is the basis of all local trade, much more so than in the case with regard to foreign trade. This applies especially to the provincial business'.[27] Bills extended by prestigious houses to local retailers and consumers of imported goods were endorsed, discounted and rediscounted in local banks, which regarded them as representing top quality financial value. Conversely, merchant houses discounted and rediscounted the commercial bills endorsed by local banks. Thus a solid commercial credit network developed among foreign traders and local merchants and banks.[28] Their credit activities gave impetus to the expansion of the import–export trade. Native and foreign merchant creditors thus constituted one of the primary factors in the post-1883 reconstitution of the Peruvian financial structure.

The other participating financial institutions of the period were commercial banks. These institutions had to face a sceptical and conservative savings sector with limited capital accumulated through traditional, prudent thrift. Between 1883 and 1895, for example, several 'runs' occurred against the most important banking institution of the time, the Banco del Callao. This bank was fortunately able to pay out the S/40 000 in silver which was demanded by its depositors when an important commercial firm closely related to the bank, Prevost & Company, went bankrupt in 1885.[29] Likewise deposits were demanded when news arrived that the bank's London bankers, Murietta & Company, were deeply involved in the Baring crisis.[30] Unease spread in 1893 due to the heavy loss inflicted on the bank by the failure of Toso y Sánchez, the wheat and flour concern of Sr Angel Sánchez, a member of the Banco del Callao's board of directors.[31] As a consequence local bankers began to realise that considerable foreign credit was needed as protection against these unpredictable runs.[32]

The volatile behaviour of the depositors was a result of there being few reliable options for the investment of their cash due to the extremely weakened state of the economy. Bankers needed to contribute to the formation of secure financial investment opportunities in order to stabilise depositors' trust in local financial conditions and institutions. The only alternative was to expand the financial structure.

The first task for bankers in that direction was the liquidation of the Guano Age banks, a process which involved long and cumbersome legal procedures. The repayment of these banks' credits involved, between 1883 and 1887, decisions about the use of the depreciated paper currency. The monetary situation was disadvantageous to creditors, who fought for a stable currency based on silver. On the other hand indebted agro-exporters argued in court that their defaulted debts to the old banks should be repaid in the official paper currency, not in silver.[33]

In practice, during the Chilean occupation of Lima (1881–3), the use of silver currency in tax collection and trade transactions had already been securely established, and fiscal notes were limited to retail transactions. Foreign importers supported the use of silver currency and it was not long before the exhausted public treasury recognised the problems of financing deficits with devalued notes.[34]

Paper currency, worn out by the general lack of an alternative means of payment, remained in the hands of consumers in Lima and the northern provinces. Fiscal notes amounted to a nominal total of approximately S/86–97 million. In 1881–7 Chilean and Bolivian fragmented silver coins and illegal notes coexisted with the old fiscal notes. In the south, Bolivian currency served as a basic exchange medium. Much of the Peruvian silver coinage had been taken abroad as a crude way of correcting extreme trade and foreign payment imbalances.[35]

In November 1887 the merchants of Lima and Callao organised themselves to 'repudiate' the fiscal notes, refusing to accept them for retail sales. Soon violent protests by note holders erupted. In Laredo, a sugar plantation town in the northern province of La Libertad, a mob targeted as scapegoats the Chinese retail traders who had repudiated the notes.[36] When, in response to merchant pressure, the government declared that there would be no mandatory acceptance of the *billetes*, there were protests by consumers in Lima, but these were easily repressed. In 1889 the fiscal notes were declared part of the internal public debt, the consolidation of which in later years meant heavy losses to the public.[37]

The effective eradication of the paper money in 1887, a triumph for merchants and bankers over consumers and debtors, established a firmer base for financial activities in Lima. The brief increase in the international price of silver in 1890, buttressed by the US Sherman Silver Purchase Act, favoured the temporary consolidation of silver monometallism. Banks strongly agreed with the adoption of a silver currency regimen and this partly reestablished depositors' confidence in banking institutions. The Banco del Callao had established its capital in silver *soles* as early as April 1883. This bank also took an active role in the minting of five million *soles* in 1890, a measure which established a minimum supply of silver currency.[38] The banks' policy of dealing in silver currency was coupled with the conservative practice of keeping large reserve funds and ready cash on hand (around 30 per cent of total liabilities).[39]

Trade and speculation in Guano Age securities – nitrate certificates, railway shares, and government foreign bonds – of doubtful appraisal value (since their value was linked directly to political decisions) seemed to have provided an initial impulse to the diversification of commercial banks' and savers' financial assets. In 1887 the Chilean government decided to redeem pre-war nitrate certificates. This measure mainly benefited speculators in the certificates, such as J. T. North and M. P. Grace, who used them to consolidate land and railway ownership in Chilean-occupied nitrate fields,[40] but it also brought positive benefits to certificate holders in Lima. The death of a Peruvian nitrate capitalist living abroad, José Sevilla, permitted his nitrate certificates and railway and the water company shares, amounting to S/402 674, to enter the Lima market through donations, lawsuits and inheritance. Contemporaries recognised that this individual fortune had an important impact on the reduced local capital market.[41]

Certificates and donations amounting to an influx of S/5 million (approximately £735 000 in 1888) actually had a miraculous effect on Peruvian financial transactions. Contemporary periodicals reported a low demand for Lima securities between 1883 and 1887, but an abrupt increase in their popularity occurred at the end of 1887 because 'this brisk appearance of capital avidly seeks placement in what is preferably at ready reach: securities'.[42] Such was the upsurge of demand in Lima's reduced financial market that before it reached its height between August and September 1890, native financiers had cited the decline in interest rates for discounts (from 12 per cent to 8 per cent between 1887 and 1889) as proof of a relative 'abundance of capital'.[43]

Contrary to this opinion, a foreign observer, James Dorion, argued in 1889 that the decrease in the interest rate was really due to the limited opportunities for capital investment resulting from low Peruvian productivity. Financial transactions, he continued, benefited only a privileged minority and a handful of speculators in Lima who received preference from managers of the few existing banks; discount terms did not exceed thirty days; other financial assets were demanded as collateral by banks from their clients; and at least one of the cosigners was required to have a current account at the bank in charge of discounting.[44] Dorion concluded that commercial bills of exchange discounted in such conditions did not facilitate the open or long-term credit transactions so necessary to stimulate agriculture and industry. The function of Peruvian banking was not to satisfy the needs of the country but simply those of a reduced number of bank clients. As a consequence, if the observations of this interested witness were correct, the modern origins of the local banking structure were oligopolistic in nature and adapted to economic backwardness.[45]

Part of Dorion's argument was verified in the early stages of modern banking in Peru. A clique of financiers and merchants benefited from cheap commercial banking credit. José Payán, the most influential financier in Peru, stated in 1888 that 'in our transactions [banking] credit is a privilege enjoyed only by those who exercise the profession of trade; this is true to such an extent that while the [Callao] bank discounts bills at 9 per cent annually, other [lenders] grant mortgage and pawn contracts at 18 per cent and 24 per cent'.[46] Another institution, the Banco Italiano, was established in 1889 to supply the credit needs of resident Italian merchants.

In 1887 the internal and external liabilities of banks increased faster than their credits due to the increase in capital supply from abroad. The limited amount of trade in Lima could not absorb these new funds. The Banco del Callao had to pay more in interest on deposits, while the revenue it received from loans decreased. Consequently, and paradoxically the bank's profits diminished.[47]

However facilitating trade was not the only intermediary function fulfilled by commercial banks. In fact the share of trade credit in total bank assets began to diminish in the 1890s. Payán himself noted on several occasions the gradual decline of commerce's share in local banking transactions, especially at times of import reduction linked to exchange rate fluctuations. Bankruptcies of important merchant houses in those years corroborate his assertions.[48] With time the financing of securities, urban mortgages, group associations and insurance companies became important and complementary activities of domestic banks. Thus, contrary to Dorion's observations, banks aimed at diversifying their activities away from trade credit specialisation by means of expanding the financial structure.

The financing of securities was strongly encouraged by local banks. The Banco del Callao's Board of Directors meetings (which were held two or three times a week) gave evidence of numerous occasions when the bank purchased certificates, bonds or securities, and accepted them readily as collateral for discounts and short-term promissory notes (*pagarés*) between 1886 and 1890. In attempting to expand their limited activities, the banks contributed to the increase in value of securities. Investor–speculators supported the initiative of the banks.

By 1897 new stock issues had appeared in the volatile Lima capital market. The Lima Exchange (Bolsa Comercial de Lima) was established in 1896 through the initiative of financiers like Payán, its director in 1898. Among its managing members were the most important bankers in the city. Although the Lima stock market was to experience extreme fluctuations in the future, the banks had managed to secure a helpful appendix to their intermediary role.[49]

Ambitious securities schemes between domestic banks and powerful merchant houses active in the Lima Exchange developed from the base of the already consolidated commercial credit system. The large commercial concerns displayed a unique ability to coordinate various factors in order to guarantee the success of particular fundings through securities. Persuasive deals with powerful investors and merchant bankers in London, Paris and New York secured the capital necessary to control strategic monopolistic and oligopolistic concerns, which attracted native participation. For example, W. R. Grace & Company formed several syndicates with important foreign and local financiers, as well as receiving credit support in different periods from foreign bankers such as J. P. Morgan & Company National City Bank, Kuhn Loeb & Company, Baring Brothers, Deutsche Bank and Henry Schroeder & Company.[50]

This cooperation between native bankers and capitalists, local officials of the Lima Exchange, and prestigious commercial houses, not only allowed foreign and domestic capital to be invested locally in 'sound' securities, it also discouraged competition. The participation of José Payán, 'manager and soul of the Bolsa', in important security issues was eagerly sought by foreign firms because

with Mr. Payán interested in this business [Vitarte Cotton Mill] . . . it would very materially tend to do away with the floating of any new companies to compete in this business, besides being advantageous in other ways. His influence with the Government is at present very considerable and is likely to be with the coming Administration. I think he would also become a considerable shareholder if he were on this Committee.[51]

Payán and other local financial interests did participate in the abovementioned concern, and in a host of similar monopolistic and oligopolistic ventures. These included, apart from Vitarte Cotton Mill (later named Peruvian Cotton Company), Fósforos 'El Sol', Fábrica Nacional de Sombreros de Lana, and Cía. Arturo Field, all of which had initially high quotations on the Lima Exchange but later performed in an average or poor fashion. Bonds, also quoted on the Lima Exchange, were an alternative source of finance for these industrial concerns. Additional credit support of up to 7–10 per cent of the capital of Fósforos 'El Sol' and Sombreros de Lana – according to their annual balance sheets – was provided by local commercial banks.[52] While favourable internal conditions remained, until 1901–2, banking credit was granted to factories, mainly to finance the importation of foreign equipment. The form of commercial banking credit made available to manufacturers was the standard 30- to 90-day IOUs, which were sometimes extended beyond their maturity period with added interest. Current accounts and mortgage loans were also used on occasion. The debtor's factory shares were commonly accepted as collateral.[53] Credit to factories declined at approximately the time of the sugar crisis of 1901–2 as a result of financial contraction, inefficiency on the part of the factories, and defaulted debts to banks and merchants.

As well as dealing in securities, local banks also strove to find other more secure sources of investment. In 1889 one commercial bank, the Banco del Callao, took over the responsibility for liquidating the old Guano Age mortgage banks and redeveloping the mortgage loan market. Payán, whose bank – together with the London Bank of Mexico – in 1888 owned 41 per cent of the defunct Banco de Crédito Hipotecario's shares, and who was also in charge of the old Banco Territorial's liquidation, proposed a new mortgage law based on contemporary French and Argentinian 'positive' legislation. Payán's proposal pointed out the need for efficient property registration and the granting of loans in silver currency, and recommended that the responsibility for acting on defaulted mortgage debts should be transferred from the judicial power to the executive realm. The influential banker's proposal was enacted as law in 1889.[54] The law was praised by the financial élite but criticised by legal experts, who pointed out its shortcomings with regard to long-term credit to small owners and farmers who had to 'fall in the hands of the usurer or export merchant' in their search for credit.[55]

The reward for the initiative of the Banco del Callao (which merged in 1897 with the London Bank of Mexico to form the Banco del Perú y Londres) was its monopoly over the mortgage credit business between 1889 and 1900. The bank's mortgage section was considered 'undoubtedly one of the most important' of the institution.[56] Only in 1900 did other banks enter the mortgage business. The mortgage bonds issued and marketed by the banks (and not by the debtors themselves as in the Guano Age) had immediate success in the small financial scene of Lima because they constituted the most solid alternative for prudent investors. At first these bonds bore 10 per cent interest and were widely quoted on the Lima Exchange. The bonds were cancelled periodically and randomly by the issuing institutions with amounts received from loan amortisations. Bank profits on mortgage credit were obtained from commission surcharges paid by loan recipients over and above the bonds' interest rates. Mortgage bonds constituted a first-class security used widely as collateral in other banking transactions.[57]

In 1895 a shift was identified in local investment away from securities and towards real estate.[58] Lima investors were reinforcing the belief, stated in 1890, that 'more than the rate of interest [in local investments], taken into consideration should be the security and soundness of the return, and the only investment that offers these advantages in the present economic situation of the country is the acquisition of urban properties'.[59] The Banco del Callao profited from this shift. Mortgage loans were a blessing in periods of foreign exchange decline: 'the discount section . . . has not fared well this semester, so much so that if it were not for our mortgage section, we would have had considerable funds without profitable allocation'.[60] Bank mortgages were more of a windfall source of credit for urban landowners than for rural ones. According to relevant samples, urban proprietors received the second largest amount of bank credit (22.5 per cent of a total £1 243 680) in the period 1884–98, especially in long-term mortgage loans (see appendix D). Likewise industrial and mining firms rarely received these long-term credits from banks.

Mortgage transactions between lending institutions and private borrowers constituted a very important base for institutional reconstruction and financial diversification because credit institutions and traditional thrift practices were engaged in a new compromise. Traditionally-minded proprietors had previously been reluctant to mortgage their properties – during times of economic uncertainty, currency hoarding and real estate acquisition were the favourite methods of averting risk. According to a leading financier, an important reason for the limited development of the mortgage business in Peru was that 'Peruvians are very much attached to their urban properties. In consequence, they avoid every occasion conducive to mortgaging those properties. It is pertinent to add that they are not enterprising so they do not actively commercialise their properties'.[61] However, under the new legal basis and with the increased supply of

10- to 21-year term mortgages, substantial capital was placed in the hands of property-owners (a large proportion of whom were widows) who, in their turn, opened new deposit accounts in banking institutions, enhancing the confidence of traditional bank depositors. At the same time, mortgage credit helped to move property away from its customary pattern of stationary ownership by increasing the availability of mortgage and short-term credit to buyers and sellers of real estate.

However the basic feature that made real estate in or near Lima a sound long-term investment was its periodic appreciation during different business cycles. Investment in real estate also provided extremely high speculative profits during short inflationary periods (as discussed in Chapter 5). Only religious properties remained outside the increasingly active real estate market in Lima, to which financial intermediaries were making decisive contributions. A further effect of the increased value of Lima's real estate was that it provided a solid base for the establishment of new insurance companies, which were introduced by native bankers and financiers who eventually controlled their local operation.[62] Local banks invested gainfully in these domestic insurance companies. While fire and maritime insurance had been introduced early on by foreign companies acting through local merchant-agents, foreign life insurance companies did not operate consistently until 1899.[63]

A number of foreign companies, especially British, initially shared the small market in Lima for freight insurance and urban property insurance. In 1888 nine local agents, four of whom were also managers of foreign trading houses, acted as representatives for twenty foreign insurance companies. Foreign companies were unwilling to increase their investment in Peru and operational costs were kept to a minimum, consisting almost entirely of commissions paid to agents. Any official attempt to introduce regulation or increase licence (*patente*) charges on the part of the needy state was vigorously opposed by the insurance agents. Insurance premiums were maintained at a high level by agreement among agents of foreign companies.[64]

The establishment of the first three local fire and maritime insurance companies, Cía. Internacional in 1895 and Cía. Rímac and Cía. Italia in 1896, coincided more or less with the first regulatory laws, which were enacted on 21 December 1895 and 9 November 1897. The laws required from all companies a minimum capital investment of S/100 000 in silver, mandatory guarantees in the form of deposits in local banks, and investment of 30 per cent of the insurance company's capital in Peruvian real estate, bonds and national currency.[65]

Locally-funded companies partially complied with the regulatory demands, especially those concerning investment in urban property of rising value. Native investors seized the opportunity to capture the insurance business by cutting the premium rate by 50 per cent.[66] However all the foreign companies resisted compliance with the new regulatory measures, and several of them preferred to liquidate their interests in Peru rather than engage in local real estate investment. In 1898 eleven foreign companies had not fulfilled the legal requirements and had already lost an important section of the Lima insurance market to native companies. The shifting preference of the local insurance policy purchaser was expressed in an article signed by 'an insured' protesting against the authorities' soft hand in dealing with foreign companies: 'Is it that in Peru laws are enacted only for nationals while foreigners enjoy special privileges which allow them not to comply with the law?'[67]

Although they did invest in urban property and lodged guarantee deposits in banks, the native insurance companies did not comply fully with the legal minimum requirement for capital stock, averaging only 30 per cent of the supposed minimum capital requirement. This was possible through the accounting device of adding to the assets column of their balance sheets the unpaid portion of capital (*capital adeudado por accionistas*), thus permitting the continuation of business with a limited cash investment.

Financing group associations, in which each member pledged all his possessions as guaranteed for the loan, proved to be another diversification taken by banks. These associations became the favourite of the Banco del Perú y Londres' loan policy. The Sociedad Industrial Santa Catalina; a group of Ica grape growers organising canalisation work; Piura cotton estate owners; Chinese merchants; Chincha's Unión Vinícola; Empresa Socavonera del Cerro de Pasco; and organised cocaine producers; all received significant loans from local banks.[68]

Despite the institutional regeneration described so far, the recovery, expansion and diversification of Peru's financial structure depended ultimately on the financial institutions' ability to respond to export and exchange rate variations. Available data on the fluctuations of aggregate bank loans and deposits – one of the few statistical indicators of financial development at the time – indicate close links to an overall pattern of export boom and bust cycles and related fluctuations in the exchange rate.

The fluctuations in the Peruvian exchange rate, whether caused by foreign trade or monetary effects, was an indicator widely used at the time to explain banking and financial cycles. The exchange rate served as an extremely sensitive financial and investment pointer. The higher and firmer the exchange rate, the safer depositors felt. Conversely, exchange rate depreciation had the effect of reducing deposits and limiting the growth of banking business. Contemporaries expressed the issue as follows: 'When the exchange rate remains stable or shows a tendency to improve, traders deposit their currency. When it decreases (especially if the decline is fast), traders hasten to withdraw their currency to protect it from danger'.[69]

The troublesome fall in the Peruvian exchange rate between 1890 and 1897 was caused predominantly by a decline in the international price of silver, whose intrinsic value was tied to the monetary value of the official silver currency.[70] The adoption of the gold standard by an increasing number of countries around the world contributed to the decline in the price of silver. However local banks could not avoid having large quantities of silver coins to meet sudden fund withdrawals by depositors. Thus the strict silver currency policy initially favoured by banks brought its own inconveniences and imposed rigid limitations on banking activities.[71]

During periods in which silver quotations recovered somewhat, banks experienced additional complications because silver coins were in danger of being exported when other export products could not provide sufficient income to balance foreign trade. In 1890 there was the fear that a reduction in the stock of currency would be experienced as a result of increases in imports and the consequent rise in demand for bills of exchange on London. The same happened in 1894 when banks raised their silver discount rates from 12 per cent to 18 per cent to offset the dangers of a reduction in currency arising from the scarcity of bills of exchange and the exportation of coins.[72] As early as October 1886 the leading banks sought to protect themselves from variations in the value and supply of silver currency by converting their capital to British gold pounds. Nonetheless by January 1893 the inconvenience of keeping profit accounts in gold and borrowing from abroad in pounds while lending locally in silver became obvious. Bankers realised that their capital had to be restricted to silver in order to avoid the risk of drastic profit and dividend reductions resulting from their attempts to keep up with the equivalent in gold.

The preference for silver currency by government officials and private individuals became well entrenched after the eradication of paper money. For this reason banks could not shirk in keeping up their silver reserves to provide for emergencies, as in the case of the contraction produced by the Baring Crisis.[73] Another reason for the continued local use of silver currency was that the exchange rate of the silver sol was overvalued – despite a decline in the international price of silver – due to the scant money supply and the heavy exportation of silver currency. The Peruvian silver sol did not exactly follow the tendency of the silver price oscillations. In May 1894 the price of the sol was 26d. while according to the price of the international silver ounce it should have been worth 22.5d., that is to say, 17 per cent less.

Declines in the exchange rate had negative effects on import merchants, but provided at the same time a 'natural' protection for local manufacturers (as Thorp and Bertram have argued) and gave exporters certain advantages. Exchange depreciation allowed exporters to obtain a relative appreciation of their income in gold from the sale of their products abroad. Agro-exporters were thus favoured as recipients of foreign gold currency and debtors in silver currency. Not surprisingly, leading agro-exporters and miners thus favoured the continuation of silver monometallism.[74] Trade in foreign goods declined drastically, due partly to the adverse import and exchange situation. From 1892 onward, top financiers in support of importers endeavoured to switch the country's monetary regime to the gold standard. They argued against 'protectionists' and, from their perspective, the unjust privilege exercised by exporters who earned in gold abroad and paid native costs and salaries in depreciated silver currency.[75]

However, a period of stabilisation of the exchange rate at around 24–25d. per sol (linked to a temporary recovery of both the international price of silver and Peruvian exports) resulted in an improvement in local financial conditions by February 1895. It was stated at the time that 'the rise in [the quotation of] securities corresponds to the decline in the interest rate'.[76] There existed a relationship between the greater availability of money due to exchange stabilisation (less money was exported) and its investment in established securities, among which bank securities and mortgage bonds were preferred. Bank interest rates on discounts and deposits in silver were reduced by up to two percentage points. Paradoxically, total term and cash deposits in banks began to increase as the supply of currency and public confidence in the monetary unit rose. Loans and discounts did not increase at the same rate, indicating a search for increased liquidity by bankers.

A factor which also contributed to the growing confidence of depositors in banks and the financial structure was the renewed political success of the popular leader, Nicolás de Piérola, in March 1895. The seven previous months of tense civil warfare in the interior provinces against the military dictatorship of Andrés Avelino Cáceres had caused uncertainty in Lima's financial circles. Piérola, 'the Regenerator', had good friends among foreign merchants and native financiers who were ready to take advantage of the new political situation.[77] Payán, himself a Cuban ex-revolutionist, had a longstanding friendship with Piérola who, in turn, was also friendly with Michael P. Grace (despite Grace's previous deals with Cáceres). Thus expectation of political and economic stability was beneficial for financial transactions.

Financial optimism continued into 1896. New securities were quoted, including those of financial institutions (the insurance companies International, Rímac and Italia, and the short-lived savings house La Acumulativa), and industrial and agricultural enterprises. In May 1896 the discount rate reached a very low 6 per cent and interest on current accounts was suppressed. The reorganisation by private managers of the deficient public tax collection added to the banks' confidence in the government. The newly chartered collection company, Cía. Recaudadora de Impuestos, was quoted on the Lima Exchange.[78]

By the end of 1896 optimism in the Lima Exchange receded when the price of silver and the exchange rate resumed their fall. Scepticism about investing in securities temporarily raised deposits in banks, but a panic which had gradually built up in the preceding months occurred among bank depositors in March 1897. Discount rates now rose two percentage points. Total loans outstanding, including discounts and current account advances, remained stationary. Loans were not repaid at the same speed as deposits were withdrawn. Prudent anticipation by banks in the run-up to these events had limited the granting of loans and current account advances with securities as collateral. A contraction in the amount on deposit diminished the collateral value of securities. Thereafter liquidity reduction at times when heavy loans were outstanding became a constant worry to bankers.

These brisk alterations in the exchange rate under silver monometallism proved to be negative to the prestige of the banks. Something had to be done to eliminate the effects of unpredictable events. In June 1897 the two most important banks in Lima, the Banco del

Callao and the foreign London Bank of Mexico & South America, merged (in a 3:2 ratio favouring native capital) under the trust-inspiring name, Banco del Perú y Londres, in order to reduce competition during periods of financial crisis. Monetary legislation became the next targeted means of effecting banking stability.

In April 1897 the pro-gold standard group of financiers and import merchants obtained its first significant victory over the influential pro-silver group of export agriculturists, miners and related business-men. President Piérola, a believer in the gold standard, influenced the outcome. The minting of silver coins was halted, causing a 27 per cent revaluation of the Peruvian currency over its intrinsic silver value. To introduce the replacement of silver, payment of customs charges in gold became mandatory. The business sphere awaited the results, which in the short term proved highly beneficial to financial transactions. By October 1897 discount rates had declined after their initial rise, the stock exchange recommenced activity, and the ex-change rate stabilised, creating renewed confidence among deposi-tors. A parallel effect detected in April 1898 was an increase in local prices.[79] Opponents of the attempts to introduce the gold standard soon complained that measures taken to improve the exchange rate were inadequate. Gold, they argued, had not entered the country as expected and could not attract the desired foreign capital; on the contrary, the national currency was in alarmingly short supply in the interior provinces, which adopted instead the use of Bolivian coins to fill the gap. Monetary limitations hindered industrial development and added to the problems of agro-exporters. The banks, which could grant only limited credit, raised their interest rates. They were ac-cused of causing 'crisis and ruin' for agricultural and mining activities. Some anti-gold standard individuals not only defended the silver currency but also praised the old fiscal notes.[80]

Detractors of the movement toward the gold standard had to admit by June 1898 that, under the favourable international conditions for Peruvian exports arising from the Spanish–American War, the domestic coinage of gold currency was increasing as a result of an inflow of gold to the country. There was an overall upsurge in financial transactions, mortgage loans in particular. Securities were exchanged with ease. Under the favourable conditions two new na-tive banks were established, the Banco Internacional in 1897 and the Banco Popular in 1899.

However interest rates increased in September 1898 despite the apparent sufficiency of currency. According to some, the increased economic activities exerted pressure for an increase in interest rates. Nevertheless monetary disturbances continued to appear periodically in the interior provinces because gold had concentrated and accumulated in Lima. In the country's capital, gold currency was highly treasured because of its overvaluation and the fear of future monetary shortage.[81] In October 1900 the equivalence between the new gold Peruvian libra (Lp) and the silver sol was set at a ratio of 1:10.

In October 1901 a large amount of gold seemed to have been 'hidden or lost'. Residents of Lima wondered about the whereabouts of the £800 000 estimated to have entered Peru during the temporary export recovery of 1895–1900. Banks were no longer cashing cheques in gold as they had formerly, but in silver. This in practice meant the suspension of payment in gold. Some put the blame for gold hoarding on financial 'trusts'. Others explained the problem of gold scarcity during the brief financial crisis in 1901–2 as having been caused by the drop in the price of sugar, cotton and silver. At times of adverse export prices, the gold coins in circulation became too few to replace silver currency. Beginning in March 1901, economic, financial and commercial activities entered a period of temporary stagnation, but local prices were still rising as a result of adjustments to international price levels.[82] To attract gold from abroad an incentive had to be offered. This was accomplished by the 1901 law which officially established the gold standard in Peru.

1902–15: BANKS AND OLIGOPOLIES

The law formally establishing the gold standard in Perù was enacted on 14 December 1901. Although banks received deposits in gold, they agreed among themselves not to carry their accounts in gold currency (to avoid paying liabilities in gold) until May 1903, by which date the official monetary regime would have had sufficient time to encourage depositors to increase the banks' gold funds. Consequently total deposits and cash accounts steadily increased from the end of 1901 until the slump of 1908–9. Imports also increased significantly as a result of the adoption of the gold standard, the high exchange rate, and the reduction of tariffs. As a consequence the Peruvian trade balance, which had been positive until then, reached the negative figure of Lp290 698 in 1904.[83]

Banks did not suffer much from the decline in the trade balance since they closely assisted import traders. For example, between 1898 and 1906 the Banco del Perú y Londres allocated approximately 29 per cent of its total loans to the commercial sector, as opposed to 20 per cent to urban mortgages, 13.5 per cent to government short-term credit, 11 per cent to industry, and only 8 per cent to commercial agriculture.[84]

Thus the formal introduction of the gold standard mainly benefited importers, financiers and owners of real estate while the high and stable exchange rate raised internal costs for the export-related sectors. It is not surprising that representatives of the agro-exporters in the Peruvian Congress were still against the gold standard in the early 1900s. Critics pointed out that the high legal equivalence of gold currency over silver currency implied, in practice, a premium intended to attract the flow of gold from abroad.[85]

Foreign capital certainly was attracted to Peru under the favourable conditions of the gold standard. The North American Cerro de Pasco Corporation deposited foreign funds in Lima banks to pay for the approximately 19 million soles invested in the mining centre of Cerro. In addition profitable native banks enjoyed heavy foreign participation in their stock. The obstacles to foreign investment posed by the Peruvian Corporation and French creditors with claims dating from the Guano Age were by-passed by competitive US and German direct, trade and banking investment which made a fresh appearance in the country. A branch of the Deutsche Bank was established in Lima in 1905, increasing local banking assets and introducing new and competitive techniques to the banking system. As a result of an arrangement between the German bank and the Peruvian government, the first foreign public loan since 1879 was agreed upon in 1905–6 for purposes of 'national defence'. Until then native banks had been practically the only providers of credit to the government, as in the case of the Banco del Perú y Londres' loan of £360 000 for the acquisition of military equipment during President López de Romaña's administration (1899–1903). Thus a new source of business for foreign and native banks functioning as intermediaries in public credit matters was inaugurated with the effective reestablishment of the Peruvian government's credit abroad.[86]

The investment in sheltered securities by banks constituted the most important development of the 1902–15 financial period. From 1903 there was an increase in the aggregate portfolio investments of banks. This declined considerably in 1908–9, but then resumed its upward movement until the First World War. These two well defined banking cycles had steep peaks in 1908 and 1912 respectively, as

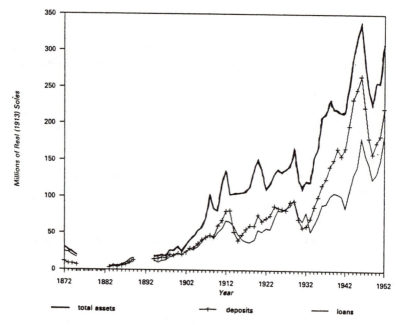

Figure 3.1   Commercial and savings banks: Total assets, deposits and
loans, 1872–1952

Sources: Appendix B

shown in the curve of banks' total assets in Figure 3.1. The distinctive
banking practice of securities financing was an attempt to overcome
the extreme liquidity limitations imposed on banking assets by the
gold standard. Under the strict conditions requiring the maintenance
of highly liquid assets in order to satisfy in gold the brisk demand on
bank deposits, banking transactions had fewer opportunities for diversification. Mortgage loans and bonds were very secure but only
provided a fixed rate of profit. New possibilities for enhanced profits
centred on the Lima Exchange at a time when deposits in banks were
relatively high.

However several oligopolised stock issues supported by banks and
foreign interests were unable to fulfill the excessive profit expectations of foreign and domestic security investors. In a 1907 interview
on the issue of the Banco del Perú y Londres' excessive credit support
to 'trusts' like the electricity merger, Empresas Eléctricas Asociadas
(EE.EE.AA) – which had received credit against its shares for up to

20 per cent of the bank's capital – the by now famous banker, Payán, revealed that 'inventories of real assets were appraised with exaggeration and, on this accounting base and high expectations, new shares were issued for up to seven times the primitive capital stock'.[87] In 1908 the firm's stock had a particularly poor performance; fears soon arose of its 'imminent crash'.[88] Clearly this was a case of stock speculation of a financially overcapitalised concern. Contemporaries commented that 'trusts in general present serious inconveniences by facilitating the abuse of [securities] issues'.[89]

The justification used by banks and their defenders in funding such oligopolistic companies generating low stock dividends was the need to finance industrialisation in Peru. However very little diversified and competitive industrialisation was possible under the prevalent method of financing monopolies and oligopolies. The result was a growing amount in securities in the banks' investment portfolios, which reduced the high liquidity standards expected from banks when loans with securities as collateral could not be paid back with the necessary speed.[90]

Together with the deteriorating internal financial conditions caused by speculation in securities, a shortage of cash stemming from the New York Panic of October 1907 affected the Peruvian banking system for approximately two years. Some commentators on the 1907 crisis found that 'the misuse of credit, and the unexpected inflation of certain securities which today weighs heavily on our small market . . . coincided with a general decline in the prices of our [export] products'.[91] To further aggravate the business depression, the renewed expansionary budget policy of the government, which was burdened by deficits, came to an abrupt halt in 1908. This unstable situation continued throughout 1909. Grave political and diplomatic issues, such as the 29 May 1909 attempted coup to overthrow President Leguía, and troubled relations with Bolivia, Ecuador and Chile, increased the feeling of insecurity in the financial sphere. As a result, banking activities slowed considerably in the years 1908–9 in terms of loans granted, deposits and cash on hand. The exchange rate suffered slight variations, causing alarm among a financial community accustomed by now to the gold standard exchange stability. The gold coin supply diminished markedly and there was evidence of currency exportation.[92]

The slowdown of financial development in 1908–9 can be explained by the structural oligopolistic characteristics of private finance in this period. After the initial reconstruction, local commercial banks and insurance companies had become an end in themselves for investors. Their high profits and dividends made them attractive to both foreign and native capitalists.[93] The French minister in Lima noted in 1904 that '. . . in Peru it is customary to make money produce high interest and preferably in those businesses which can provide rapidly such results. This explains for the most part the good results obtained by the Lima banks'.[94] Banking institutions also strove to capture and secure financial markets with modern merger, cartel and cooperation techniques. Due to heavy foreign participation in the leading banks' stock and managing boards, the principal banking institutions contributed to capital importation, the formation of oligopolies of expected high returns, and exportation of banking profits abroad during the full operation of the gold standard. As a consequence the native character of the financial structure during the operation of the gold standard is subject to doubt.

Distinguishing analytically between native and foreign banks acting in an open economy poses complicated methodological problems.[95] However from the national origin of directors and stockholders one can distinguish three types of bank operating in this period: foreign, foreign-resident, and native.

The foreign banks had limited leverage in domestic affairs because of the strong native representation in the financial sector and the initial hesitancy of foreigners to invest in domestic financing. Except for a brief attempt by a German and a US bank to control the export financing business by 1913–6, branches of foreign banks concentrated instead on exchange and international transfers. Foreign banks served primarily foreign commercial interests insofar as profit repatriation and preference toward their compatriot businessmen were concerned. The most important in this period were the Deutsche Ueberseeische Bank (Banco Alemán Transatlántico, established in 1905), the Mercantile Bank of the Americas (1916), and the Commercial Bank of Iquitos (1912), a branch of the London-based Anglo South American Bank. In spite of their efforts they were unable to capture the domestic banking market and, according to their scantly publicised balance sheets, they were not very profitable, except perhaps for the German bank. British and French financial interests preferred to participate in, and attempt to control, the most important native banks.

The foreign-resident category applied to a single institution, the Banco Italiano established in 1889. Beginning as a bank mainly providing commercial credit to the Italian community in Peru, it later evolved to claim an increasing share of the domestic banking market. It cannot be considered entirely foreign because an important number of its shareholders and clients reinvested their profits in Peru. According to the Italiano's statutes in 1899 'the objective of this society is to favor commercial development through the means of credit and facilitate relationships with Italy . . .'[96] However after 1913 Italian and Swiss financial interests started to augment their participation in this local bank.

The supremacy in Peruvian banking was held however by the most important native bank, the Banco del Perú y Londres, although it endangered its national character by absorbing substantial British and French capital during the years 1897–1914 in an attempt to gain oligopolistic dominance.[97] Foreign participation in the bank's board of directors and shareholders had been limited by the 1897 merger statutes agreed with the London Bank of Mexico to around 30 per cent of the bank's shares. However, after a decisive shareholders' meeting in March 1907 and subsequent capital expansions, foreign directors and stockholders raised their control to approximately two-thirds of the bank's decision-making bodies.[98] By 1915 Peruvians held only 15 000 of the bank's shares while 35 000 were owned abroad.[99] One example of the negative effects of foreign financial interests in this bank's administration was the formation of the Crédit Foncier Peruvien, a French concern (discussed more fully in Chapter 7) to which the Banco del Perú y Londres' profitable mortgage business was surrendered in 1912 in order to attract more foreign capital. The progress of foreign control over native institutions was recorded in 1915: '. . . as it has happened with a majority of capital ventures in the country, banks' decisions have passed over to foreigners, many of them absent. Instead of being targeted by widespread contempt and even hatred, banks could be sustained by the wealthy classes and would then merit the respect and consideration of everyone'.[100]

The other native banks, the Banco Internacional and the Banco Popular, performed as suppliers of credit for the emerging native élite groups (networks of diversified entrepreneurship discussed in the next chapter). Among the members of both institutions' boards of directors it is possible to identify prominent and politically influential native interests connected to a seemingly diversifying economy, especially agro-exports, mining, real estate and industry. Initially a savings cooperative, the Banco Popular was constrained by its by-laws to allocate its resources among its own members.[101] However by 1901 the Prado family network, an élite group linked to the budding

Table 3.1   Share of Peruvian commercial and savings banking market by national interests, 1885–1955

Year	Number of Offices				Percentage of Total Assets				Net Profits/Capital and Reserves			
	Natv[1]	*Res.*[2]	*For.*[3]	*Total*	*Natv*	*Res.*	*For.*	*Total*	*Natv*	*Res.*	*For.*	*All*
1885	2	0	1	3	55	0	45	100	–	–	–	–
1895	6	2	1	9	62	24	26	100	0.06	–	–	–
1900	11	3	0	14	82	18	0	100	0.09	–	–	–
1905	15	3	1	19	65	24	11	100	0.11	0.11	0.05	0.10
1915	19	5	3	27	58	17	25	100	0.04	0.01	–	–
1925	21	6	12	39	38	32	30	100	0.15	0.17	0.05	0.13
1935	5	27	5	37	26	45	29	100	–	–	–	0.08
1945	147	0	3	150	92[4]	0	8	100	–	–	–	0.15
1955	269	0	3	272	95[5]	0	5	100	–	–	–	0.12

1. Native banks
2. Foreign resident bank
3. Foreign banks
4. In 1941 the Banco Italiano changed its name to Banco de Crédito and was considered a national institution but Italian and Swiss capital participation continued.
5. The Banco Continental and other native banks allowed US and French capital participation.

Sources: Inspección Fiscal de Bancos, *Informe* (1921–30); institutions' balance sheets; Alfonso Quiroz, 'Financial Institutions', pp. 432–9; Carlos Cisneros, *Sinópsis estadística del Perú*; Superintendencia de Bancos, *Memoria* (1931–66); *Situación de las empresas bancarias* (1931–66).

industrial sector, began to influence the direction of the institution. Between 1902 and 1912 the bank was in charge of managing the tax collection company Sociedad Nacional de Recaudación. Although it occupied only a small portion of the banking market, the Banco Popular seem nevertheless to have channelled funds from the export sectors to sectors of the internal market.[102]

The distribution of the banking market and number of banking offices among these three types of banks, between 1900 and 1915, indicates native supremacy, as shown in Table 3.1. In 1900 native institutions controlled 82 per cent of total banking assets, largely due to the 1897 merger of the Banco del Callao and the London Bank of Mexico, which gave favour to native shareholders. However control of the market by native institutions declined to 65 per cent in 1905 and 58 per cent in 1915 due to an increase in foreign participation from 11 per cent to 25 per cent in the same years. The share of native capital in total banking capital did not decrease as sharply, according to capital and reserve figures. Also, native banks were definitely more profitable than foreign banks, competing in profitability with the foreign-resident institution, according to the profit figures of Table 3.1. This, together with their clear lead in the number of banking offices in Lima and the provinces, shows a greater hold on the local banking market by native institutions, especially the Banco del Perú y Londres. However, in terms of management native banks followed the advice of foreign specialists throughout the period. It is also important to note that foreign participation in native institutions increased substantially during the years 1907–14 and decreased after the First World War.

By 1902 the other profitable financial institutions, insurance companies, had expanded their business by providing insurance for highly priced urban properties supported by mortgage loans. This type of loan required fire insurance. Scarce native capital therefore successfully linked several of its strategic interests by virtue of this expansion. An analysis of the composition of the boards of directors of insurance companies proves that each competing insurance company was linked to a major local bank. Cía. Internacional was related to the Banco del Perú y Londres, Cía. Rímac to the Banco Internacional, Cía. Italia to the Banco Italiano, and Cía. La Popular to the Banco Popular. In 1902 fire insurance amounted to approximately Lp4.6 million or 86 per cent of total fire and maritime insured amounts.[103] Among the three leading local companies the average annual dividend increased from 11 per cent in 1900 to 36 per cent in 1905.[104]

Furthermore, stricter regulation in 1901 and 1902 persuaded foreign companies to abandon the insurance business in Peru. Nevertheless reinsurance abroad by native companies provided some foreign companies with an indirect share of the market.[105] Also, activity in life insurance continued under the control of the branches of the foreign companies Sud América (1899), La Equitativa (1899), La Previsora (1905), and El Sol de Canadá (1908), with the sole participation of the native El Porvenir as late as 1913. However local financiers were present among the directors of most life insurance firms.[106] Therefore native presence in the Peruvian insurance business must be understood more in terms of a trade-off and sharing with foreign interests than as a national market 'capture'.

Fire insurance premiums guaranteed handsome profits as there were few incidences of fire. Because of these favourable material conditions and the elimination of foreign competition, different local financial interests and their foreign coparticipants continued the struggle for dominance over the market. By 1905 the higher dividends went to those companies which had been established first. Newcomers posed a challenge in the competition for the profitable market. Premium rates decreased until just before the First World War, when an agreement was made among the competing fire and maritime insurance institutions to limit competition over premium rates and curb capital investment.[107]

From 1902–15 the Lima stock market attracted in particular capital for bank and insurance company securities, as well as those of a host of agricultural, livestock, service, public and semi-public firms.[108] Assuming the availability of only a limited amount of risk capital for investment in securities, the Lima market was geared toward oligopolistic capture of this secondary source of capital with its high speculative gains.

The three basic types of securities quoted were stocks, bonds, and public debt consols. In the long run, less risky bonds bearing a constant 8–10 per cent interest were preferred by Lima's medium and small investors over unstable stock with radical and unpredictable fluctuations. Bonds were certainly preferred to the poorly-serviced public debt consols. Because of their prestige in the highest financial sectors, which consisted of the principal members of the Lima Exchange, local commercial banks led and heavily influenced the securities' investing community. Under these circumstances the Lima Exchange had serious limitations as an open capital market for viable and competitive projects.[109]

The formation of merged companies and the underwriting of sheltered securities issues was encouraged and substantially enhanced by local banks between 1909 and 1914. In their attempts to guarantee oligopolistic gains for their clients and expand their financial activities, bankers and financiers risked rapid depreciation of stock during crucial periods. The most lamentable case was the huge internal and external stock issues of the EE.EE.AA. This overgrown concern ineffectively absorbed scarce financial resources in Lima and compromised the prestige of important banking institutions and personalities. It was a major cause of the prolonged stock exchange stagnation between 1913 and 1918.[110]

The EE.EE.AA. was by no means an isolated case. Other public utility companies were targeted by financiers for similar speculations. Scandals concerning insolvency and falsification of securities resulted – for example the Godoy family affair in 1913.[111] Important financial figures served on the boards of directors of disastrous concerns such as the Cía. Peruana de Vapores, Empresa del Agua, Empresa del Gas de Lima and the semi-public tax collection companies. Several of these companies initially performed acceptably but in the medium term they provided either a miniscule yield or no yield at all, their quotations falling several percentage points below par. Of course remuneration for the directors of these companies was deducted from the profit account before dividend distribution. Public discontent was aimed in particular at these large and monopolising public utility companies or 'monopoly enterprises'.[112]

The stock of agricultural concerns performed well only during export boom periods. Agricultural companies (*sociedades agrícolas*) relied on bond issues, which were more acceptable to the public. The stock issues of the dairy and livestock estates (*sociedades ganaderas*) Junín, del Centro and Corpacancha maintained successful quotations and high dividends between 1910 and 1925, years of favourable prices for their products. Also quite successful from 1905 was the real estate company Cocharcas.[113] It can be concluded that the few successful security issues, apart from insurance companies and banks, were those of demand-oriented enterprises (mortgage, real estate, housing, construction materials, food supply) tied to the urban expansion of Lima.

At the outbreak of the First World War the Banco del Perú y Londres was in deep trouble due to the depression of securities at the local and international levels. The investments in local speculative stock (especially EE.EE.AA, Cía. Peruana de Vapores, Cía. Recaudadora, Crédit Foncier), in which the bank had placed a disproportionate part of its assets, became huge financial disasters. The bank's management had been unable to forsee that in a time of war (as one specialist argued at the time) individuals and institutions prefer to convert any type of asset to gold ('wealth in the most liquid form'), thereby causing a fall in stock prices and the contraction of credit.[114] Moreover the bank's strong connections with London and Paris became a liability when the international credit system centred in London collapsed and the depressed French situation (which had started two years prior to the war) became aggravated in 1914.

The Banco del Perú y Londres suffered from a sudden paralysis in the availability of foreign credit for its general transactions. By 31 July 1914 the bank's directors had received telegrams from all its major European correspondents (Anglo South American Bank and Grace Brothers in London; Société Générale, Banque Française and

E. Ayulo in Paris; Swiss Bankverein; and M. M. Warburg in Hamburg) cancelling previous lines of credit.[115] In addition the decline in imports to Peru as a result of the war negatively affected importers and general traders, who represented a considerable proportion of the bank's clients. However the fiscal crisis caused by a severe decline in the state's revenues posed the most serious danger to the bank's stability, since loans to the government and the tax collection company had been areas of intense activity by the bank, especially since the formation of the Cía. Recaudadora de Impuestos in 1912.

In response to the withdrawal of foreign finance and to the poor financial situation of its major clients, banks restricted drastically the granting of credit, particularly on their current overdraft accounts which, in the case of the Banco del Perú y Londres, were all converted to IOUs. Interest rates were raised and a special 'Comité de Directorio' was created to monitor the credit situation more efficiently. In this manner this bank attempted to secure its gold reserves.[116]

Peruvian exporters were particularly affected by the first economic consequences of the war. Suddenly the European market for their products was closed. Shipping goods to Europe was almost impossible due to the risks of sea transportation. The different legal prohibitions to trading internationally with gold and the interruption in the flow of bills of exchange made the foreign proceeds from exporters extremely difficult to transfer to Peru. Furthermore European countries had built up stocks of raw materials in anticipation of the war. In October 1914 imports of sugar to Great Britain were forbidden. International export prices declined, and local credit for exporters was thoroughly restricted. Local banks and importers, led by the Banco del Perú y Londres, strongly opposed the trend toward a fall in the Peruvian exchange rate resulting from a fall in the number of bills of exchange in circulation. Thus exporters could not benefit from a depreciation of the Peruvian currency as had debtors and holders of scarce bills of exchange in the early 1890s. In terms of financial and monetary policies, the Banco del Perú y Londres clearly worked against the interests of the native exporters and agriculturists.[117] The amount of credit granted to agriculturists by the bank had not been particularly impressive before the war (only 3 per cent of the total credit granted between 1906 and 1914). In 1914 the bank was involved with just a few agricultural concerns.

Two main initiatives by the Banco del Perú y Londres further affected agro-exporters. Both their campaign for a stable paper-currency (*cheques circulares*), which replaced the gold currency, and their efforts to control negative fluctuations in the exchange rate in order to protect the bank's gold reserves, were resented by planters. In spite of the shortage of gold, the bank argued that 'the Peruvian currency has not depreciated, it is the foreign exchange which has declined . . .'[118] The objective of the Banco del Perú y Londres was to obtain for banks complete control of note issue while simultaneously maintaining the gold standard exchange rate. The bank brought to bear all its influence as the state's major local creditor to press for favourable legislation on paper currency and to oppose any increase in taxation on the banks.

In accordance with these policies, the bank also opposed the minting of silver currency which, the bank argued, would have negative effects on the exchange rate. This was in complete opposition to its previous strategy, that is, encouraging a shift towards the use of gold currency and away from paper money, against which Peruvians had a strong prejudice. The Banco del Perú y Londres was criticised in Congress and the newspapers for what was considered to be its opportunistic new monetary policy. Only the Banco Italiano remained a stern defender of the restricted issue of paper currency, a strategy that paid handsome rewards later on.

Agro-exporters shared the public distrust of the Banco del Perú y Londres. Although in desperate need for means of payment, which the issue of *cheques circulares* would partially alleviate, the exporters opposed attempts by the bank to artificially control the exchange rate of these notes to the advantage of private banks. In a frustrated attempt to bring about a compromise among merchants, bankers and agriculturists over the exchange rate, a meeting of the leaders of these three sectors was called for 20 November 1914. The position of the Banco del Perú y Londres on the problem reads as follows:

> it is convenient for everyone and for the country to avert the last strong fluctuations in the exchange rate which, initially, benefit agriculturists, but later affect them due to the increased cost of salaries.[119]

No further meetings with agriculturists to implement the Banco del Perú y Londres' compromise proposal was possible because several participants rejected the bank's appeal. Therefore only the banks and the most important foreign enterprises (W. R. Grace, Graham Rowe, Harth, Milne, Cerro de Pasco), who were all interested in keeping export prices and internal costs as low as possible, agreed to limit the discount rate on bills of exchange sold in Lima to 7.5 per cent. This agreement was ineffectual because bills of exchange continued to be sold at higher discounts (that is, lower exchange rates). In despair, manager Payán proposed the establishment of an official committee to monopolise the sale of bills of exchange and exert control over exchange brokers, even though his attempt to avoid exchange depreciation was at variance with his liberal principles. By August 1915 the Peruvian libra had depreciated by 16 per cent.[120] However monetary and financial disturbances would later ease considerably thanks to the boom in the price of Peruvian exports which was underway by 1916.

1916–30: PLANTERS BECOME BANKERS

A significant advance toward relative financial autonomy from foreign influence was achieved in 1916–30. Prominent agro-exporters managed to transform the proceeds of booming export cycles (1915–20 and 1923–25) into temporary independence from foreign creditors. During and after the First World War foreign investors, especially British and French, withdrew much of their investment in Peru due to war conditions and post-war international recession. Native capitalists readily filled the gap by taking over agro-industrial complexes and banking institutions.[121]

Leguía's successful second bid for power in 1919 cannot be fully explained without considering the support given by prominent agro-exporters, which was reciprocated by him in the 1920s through monetary and financial measures which served to assist them. Leguía could afford such favours because the financial structure in the 1920s was strongly influenced by the first effective state intervention since the War of the Pacific. Under President Leguía a series of financial reforms, together with increased reliance on public foreign loans, curtailed the formerly largely unchallenged authority of private banks on financial matters. The formation of the Reserve Bank in 1922, and firmer government control over the issue of money, taxation, tariffs, and mortgage and small savings institutions allowed Leguía the internal financial base to engage in an ambitious modernising strategy. This strategy had an unprecedented effect on Peruvian infrastructure, urbanisation and production.

Prior to 1916 most native producers of sugar and cotton had remained dependent on commercial credit and mortgages granted by foreign merchant firms and foreign merchant bankers abroad. Only during the 1915–20 export boom years were agro-exporters able to accumulate surplus earnings to repay debts and mortgages, and reassert or increase their holdings. A contemporary congressman, Aníbal Maúrtua, stated that sugar and cotton planters had noticeably improved their financial situation since the First World War.[122]

International demand for agricultural products expanded dramatically from 1915. The price of sugar and cotton soared, increasing the income of Peruvian agro-exporters to hitherto unheard of levels. The Hacienda San Nicolás had a net profit of 46 per cent in 1915 and an average profit of 38 per cent for the years 1916–18 – prior to 1915 its standard profit had been around 6 per cent.[123] By 1919 an unprecedented profit of Lp40 000 was declared by the sugar-producing concern Viuda de Piedra e Hijos. Banks did not participate fully in the early part of this economic boom because of their previous distance from exporters in financial matters.

In 1917 local commercial banks realised that native agriculturists were accumulating abundant funds abroad. Agro-exporters preferred to keep funds in foreign currency outside the country rather than to negotiate their bills of exchange at the inconvenient (overvalued) current local rate set by banks. At the same time, the exportation of gold from Great Britain and the US was prohibited during the war. A portion of these enforced foreign savings were spent on US imports (which displaced British imports during the war) for modernisation projects in agro-exporting estates. The foreign savings also allowed most of the agro-exporters' considerable foreign debts to be cancelled.

It was at this point that a change occurred in the traditional credit policies of the local banks towards agro-exporters. In 1917–20 the Banco del Perú y Londres started to expand its credit to agro-exporters with the hope of attracting their foreign funds and securing a large supply of the much disputed bills of exchange by other banks (especially the Mercantile Bank of the Americas). In view of increased production and rising local costs, exporters gladly seized the opportunity to finance their activities through previously restricted local credit. Sugar and cotton became readily acceptable as collateral for loans. Víctor Larco Herrera overcame the monetary shortage by using his own IOUs and US dollar bills as instruments of payment for his local transactions. The Banco del Perú y Londres' agency in Trujillo readily accepted Larco's monetary innovations. The percentage of credit allocated by the bank to the commercial agricultural sector rose to the unprecedented level of 27 per cent of the bank's total credit between 1914 and 1919. Mortgage credit also became more easily available to exporters. Such a credit policy towards commercial agriculture had not been practised since the 1870s.[124]

The Banco del Perú y Londres used its local networks to provide the most important native agriculturists with exceptional advantages and privileges in order to secure them as exclusive clients of the bank. To obtain an edge on the purchase of bills of exchange, the bank granted special interest rates on the current overdraft accounts of – and demanded exclusivity from – J. I. Chopitea (Hacienda Laredo), Víctor Larco Herrera (Hacienda Roma) – both of whom were prominent agro-exporters and senators – and Muñoz Nájar & Hnos of Arequipa (landowners and wool exporters).[125] Overdraft on current accounts, mortgage loans and medium-term loans, guaranteed by the stock of mushrooming *sociedades agrícolas*, were freely granted to Aspíllaga Hnos, Solar Hnos, Miguel Echenique and many other exporters of sugar and cotton. Special credit concessions were also granted to important native miners (Carlos Rizo Patrón, Gallo Hnos), rice growers (Nicanor M. Carmona) and provincial export merchants (Antonio Calvo & Company of Cuzco). As a result the term deposits of the bank increased to Lp469 211 by January 1918. The privileged and selective granting of credit was a device which the Banco del Perú y Londres exploited very efficiently, to the extent of displacing the Mercantile Bank from its competitive position in the Peruvian export finance market. However with this strategy the Banco del Perú y Londres also began its perilous specialisation in agro-export finance.

In 1919 the Anglo South American Bank, an old partner of the Banco del Perú y Londres, decided to open its own branch in Lima and to withdraw its participation from the Banco del Perú y Londres.[126] In March 1920 the Anglo started selling its holdings of the bank's stock (approximately 20 per cent of the Banco del Perú y Londres' total capital), with the apparent intention of making a good financial deal following a decline in the British exchange rate from 1919.[127] Massive withdrawals by other European investors followed, caused in part by the expectancy of an improvement in the pound sterling and the franc.

Similarly several British firms withdrew their investments. At the time of the stockholders' meeting of March 1920 European investors had represented 61 per cent of the Banco del Perú y Londres' stock, while in March 1921 they represented only 34 per cent.[128] Formerly close contact with British financial institutions started to deteriorate after the Anglo's withdrawal – although occasional business transactions with the London Joint & Midland Bank, and with the Anglo itself, did take place at later dates.

Simultaneously with the British withdrawal, important changes occurred in the composition of the Banco del Perú y Londres' board of directors. The trend was toward a stronger presence of native directors and stockholders. Between 1918 and 1921 several new directors included notable men tied to native agro-export interests, such as Francisco Mendoza y Barreda (Soc. Agrícola Paramonga), Manuel Vicente Villarán (brother of owner of Soc. Agrícola Cachipampa), and lawyer Pedro Gallagher.

The most crucial change in the direction of the Banco del Perú y Londres occurred in 1921 when, after the Anglo's withdrawal, Ramón and Antero Aspíllaga, powerful agro-exporters and politicians (*civilista* foes of Leguía), became the largest stockholders of the institution. The Aspíllagas held 3190 of the bank's total 22 328 shares in 1922 and were represented by John W. Stokes. Local participation increased even more in 1921 with the appearance of José I. Chopitea, Mansueto Canaval, Antonio Calvo, Demetrio Olavegoya, P. Mimbela, Pedro de Osma, Pedro Larrañaga, Alfredo Ferreyros and others as principal stockholders. The bank's most important investors were now mostly agro-exporters who, having paid their previous debts to British merchant houses and banks, were able to buy the stock of the most important lending institution in Peru.

The strong native presence in the Banco del Perú y Londres eventually led to complete control of the institution by Peruvians and confirmed the bank's agro-export orientation. A policy to eliminate foreign control over Peruvian agricultural concerns was implemented. In 1923 conflicts between local directors and representatives of foreign houses caused the resignation of the foreign directors Hammond (Graham Rowe & Company), Reid (Duncan Fox) and Grellaud (Harth et Cie). These individuals were replaced by Santiago Acuña, Pedro Larrañaga and Estuardo Marrou, all locals. Finally the bank's committee in Paris (previously helpful in attracting foreign capital), which was composed entirely of French representatives, was declared inoperative and was eliminated from the bank's statutes in 1924. As a result French financial connections were severed irreparably and the bank became almost exclusively locally directed and financed.

The strengthening of native agro-exporters' financial and property interests conditioned financial policy decisions during the 1920s. For the first time since the Guano Age, the Peruvian agrarian élite controlled and coordinated the core of the agrarian export sector's financing. This should not be overlooked, in spite of the continuing presence of American and British mining, petroleum and railways corporations (Cerro de Pasco, Vanadium, Northern Peru Mining; International Petroleum, Lobitos Oilfields; Peruvian Corporation).[129]

The withdrawal of foreign capital from native banks was due in part to the establishment of foreign institutions' own banking branches in Peru. The Anglo South American Bank and First National City Bank were established in Lima in 1919, and the Royal Bank of Canada (which acquired the assets of the Mercantile Bank) in 1924.[130] Also the Banca Commerciale Italiana of Milan substantially increased its participation in and control of the Banco Italiano in Peru in 1919–20.[131] The native banks' share of total banking assets was reduced from 39 per cent in 1920 to 32 per cent in 1929, due largely to the increase of the Banco Italiano's share from 28 per cent to 36 per cent in the same years. The strategy of opening branches of foreign banks was not successful since their profits amounted to only a third of those of native banks in 1925 (see Table 3.1). (Foreign concerns showed renewed interest in investing in native banks in 1928, when W. R. Grace & Company obtained a controlling share in the Banco Internacional.)

The withdrawal of foreign capital in 1920–1 seems also to have been part of a strategy to reduce the risks of an expected recession. Important foreign firms with foresight sold their land interests just prior to a contraction in the international market in 1921. This calculated disengagement from agricultural concerns in Peru is exemplified by W. R. Grace & Company's purchase of the Infantas estate from the Banco Alemán at a low price and reselling it profitably to Peruvian investors in 1920. The British Sugar Company's estates in Cañete, and other foreign-owned estates, were also sold to native landowners in 1920.[132]

A considerable decline in banking activities resulted from the 1921–2 market contraction. The slump was already noticeable in November 1920, when a French diplomat observed that producers of cotton and sugar were ceasing to export in reaction to the considerable decline in prices. Important foreign import–export houses had an excess of unsold stocks of sugar and cotton in Europe and the United States. Consequently the exchange rate declined in 1921. A frantic demand for bills of exchange depleted bank deposits and a substantial amount of capital was leaving the country.[133]

The situation continued into 1921. Some banks which had been extremely profitable in previous years were unable to distribute dividends in 1921. The banking slump reached its lowest ebb in 1922. A bank report in that year stated:

> Last year [1921] was not favorable for the regular course of business activities. Emigration of capital, which had begun by the end of the previous year [1920], was intensified last year, coincidentally with a decline of prices of our export products. Also, [official] domestic measures forced banks to restrict their transactions heavily. All of this caused an extraordinary decline in the foreign exchange rate, a considerable drop in the exchange of securities and a general stagnation in commercial transactions.[134]

A significant factor in the sudden withdrawal of capital from Peru was the attempt by Leguía's second government to increase regulation of the financial sphere. A ceiling on interest rates charged by commercial banks was established in May 1921, and other controls followed soon after: restrictions on capital exports, creation of the controlling institution Inspección Fiscal de Bancos, controversial projects for the first national bank, and finally the establishment of the Banco de Reserva in April 1922. These measures had an alarming impact on bankers. Huge public expenditure was also seen as a contributing factor to the financial crisis. Capping this were intensifying strikes and internal social and political strife which made financial activities more risky after 1918. However by 1922 Leguía and native agro-exporters and bankers had worked out a conciliatory solution with the creation of the Banco de Reserva, an institution with a substantial private representation.[135]

Banking assets had recovered from the slump by the end of 1922. Dividends on banks' stock had regained their customary high level although, according to specialists, the flight of capital from the country continued. The years 1923 and 1924 were considered particularly good in commercial terms because of a recuperation in exports. Nevertheless savers favoured having their bank deposits in foreign currency. The growth of both deposit and loan accounts in local banks in 1923 was due to increases in the foreign currency kept by the public, regardless of the relatively good standing of Peruvian exchange. Undoubtedly holders of currency did not trust the new monetary measures and financial regulation by the increasingly authoritarian regime, which relied heavily on foreign loans and financial advisors. However the fact remains that deposits in banks resumed their expansion coupled to an even steeper increase in loans and discounts between 1922–5 (see Figure 3.1). Banks' portfolio investment reached pre-war levels.[136]

Two events mark the end of the 1923–5 recuperation of banking activities, and both are related to cotton: disastrous floods in the northern coastal agricultural region in March 1925, and a sudden decline in the price of cotton during 1926. Banks were not able to sufficiently curtail their credit to the needy agricultural sector, as had happened in 1921–2, despite a considerable decrease in the liabilities of banks between 1925 and 1926. The Banco de Reserva's report on banking activities for 1925 expressed the hope that 'local banks would have applied their characteristic common prudence in their transactions because . . . credit distribution will be strictly controlled, particularly during periods of crisis'.[137]

However aggregate banking accounts indicate that banks were taking greater risks than in previous periods, and that the Banco de Reserva itself was increasing its rediscounting of local banks' credits. The curve representing total loans in Figure 3.1 runs almost parallel to that of total deposits from 1927 to 1929–30, at which point an excess of loans over deposits occurs. The same 1925 report indicates that the public had increased its demand for foreign currency from banks. Consequently the banking expansion of that time was explained by a 50 per cent increase in foreign currency transactions in a period during which the exchange rate declined by 14 per cent. The 1926 report insisted on the need to reassess the overrated portfolio assets of banks. Portfolio investment by banks had already diminished in July 1926 by 30 per cent of its December 1923 value.[138]

At this point there was a curious reversal in financial policy. Between 1928 and 1930 the government tried to stabilise the declining exchange rate, restrict credit and raise interest rates, while banking institutions strongly tied to export producers considered it better to allow the exchange rate to drop, to loosen credit and to maintain low interest rates. In previous similar situations private banks had espoused the opposite view. Shortly before this time the Banco de Reserva had been relatively free in extending credit to banking institutions by rediscounting. However in 1928, following the advice of US experts, it adopted a policy of exchange stabilisation by raising interest rates and restricting credit.[139]

Thus deprived of making the ultimate decision on financial policy, private banks engaged in a struggle to capture fluctuating and shaky local savings deposits and valuable mortgage business. There were two main competitors in this arena: the Banco del Perú y Londres and the Banco Italiano. In their respective bids to capture the greatest share of Peruvian commercial banking activities, the former failed and the latter succeeded.

The Banco del Perú y Londres lost its supremacy in the market around 1923. A great portion of this institution's foreign capital backing was forfeited between 1920 and 1923, but agro-exporters, merchants and provincial businessmen replaced it with their own. Conversely the Banco Italiano enhanced its foreign capital participation, which enabled it to invest heavily in securities (portfolio investment by banks resumed their increase between 1927 and 1929), and to provide credit to reliable Italian merchants and local clients oriented toward the growing urban demand. In the 1920s the Banco Italiano moved away from granting excessive agricultural credit and instead diverted its attention toward the more promising urban expansion and internal markets without losing the liquidity and mobility of its funds and assets. This proved to be a successful strategy.

The Banco Italiano also captured the confidence of depositors during the years when the exchange rate declined (1925–7 and 1929–30) and the demand for foreign currency increased. The bank's mortgage section also made important inroads toward dominating mortgage business – which boomed in the 1920s due to increased urbanisation – until mortgage issues were monopolised in 1928 by a state-sponsored institution, the Banco Central Hipotecario.

The sharp increase in internal consumer and real estate prices during the First World War had stimulated oligopolistic domestic industries (textiles, foodstuffs), and allowed those individuals oriented toward the domestic market (particularly the clients of the Banco Italiano) and urban property to share the export sector's gain. Insurance business linked to the internal market also grew considerably in the 1920s. Life insurance business doubled between 1921 and 1929, and the total assets of life insurance companies surpassed the assets of fire and maritime insurance companies in 1925. Total life insurance premiums reached approximately the same value, Lp350 500, in 1929 as that achieved by fire and maritime insurance premiums in 1916. Undoubtly the tremendous increase in Lima's population was the principal determinant in the observed expansion of the life insurance business.[140]

Thus it is fair to conclude that private and public finance in the 1920s contributed to and was benefited by the expansion of the internal market and increased urban development. However the government's practice of providing special licences for the establishment of factories increased oligopolisation of the industrial sector, as shown in the case of the company Cemento Portland which was the only cement producer in Peru.

Industrial monopolies and oligopolies limited the opportunities in industrial finance for those institutions already specialising in agricultural credit, such as the Banco del Perú y Londres. Unfortunately these institutions confronted serious problems in the late 1920s. The international price of cotton and sugar declined acutely (by around 60 per cent) between 1929 and 1932, presenting added financial problems to the banks' major debtors. The banks' financial weakening became too extreme to hide from depositors – in October 1930 the Banco del Perú y Londres was closed to the public following a run on it by depositors. The collapse of Leguía's public works programme, the deterioration of the state's credit abroad, and the withdrawal of political support, all contributed to the erosion of the bank. A military coup had taken Leguía out of office in August 1930, so lacking adequate political support the bank was forced to declare bankruptcy. Liquidation of the bank's assets started in 1931.

Private banking credit had been severely restricted since November 1929, and direct commercial credit to agrarian interests collapsed even further with the failure of the Banco del Perú y Londres. Thus in the late 1920s planters once again became reliant on credit from foreign merchant houses, despite the heavy involvement of leading native banks in agricultural credit at this time. Renewed concentration on land and sugar mills by creditor foreign firms was noticeable in the late 1920s and early 1930s.[141]

The most symbolic indebtedness during this decline of native agro-exporters was that of the Cía. Agrícola e Industrial Cañete, a 1926 reorganisation of the previous £250 000 debtor Anglo Pacific Estates. It was owned for the most part by President Augusto Leguía, by 1930 a heavy borrower from the London merchant bankers Frederick Huth & Company and Kearsley & Cunningham in the sum of £361 502, as well as from the local Banco del Perú y Londres for other sizeable personal loans.[142] The following remark by an American diplomat in 1927, in connection with the sale of Hacienda Roma to the Gildemeister group, is pertinent: 'A study of the history of the large Peruvian landholdings which have been devoted to sugar production, indicates a trend to foreign ownership and management'.[143] The world depression undermined very quickly a substantial part of native financial autonomy.

1931–39: COTTON, LIQUIDITY AND RECOVERY

With the fall of Leguía the state's financial links with the private sector entered a new phase. Despite Leguía's policy of ambitious infrastructural projects and increased state spending, levels of monetary and credit expansion had been kept within the limits acceptable to foreign creditors during his administration. However by March 1931 foreign debt default and abandonment of the gold standard – measures taken by most Latin American countries to avoid deeper internal recession – initiated a new working relationship between the state, agro-exporters, local industry, foreign capital and private finance.

The state now had only domestic credit to rely on for its expenditure. At the same time many agro-exporters were on the verge of bankruptcy and at the mercy of foreign private creditors. The Kemmerer Commission of US financial advisors hired in 1931 had recommended credit and monetary stringency, high reserves in the Central Bank, and the liquidation of the Banco del Perú y Londres, a bank with heavy liabilities abroad and substantial loans tied up with the ailing agro-export sector. State officials did not comply with most of Kemmerer's recommendations in order to save the agro-export sector from total collapse.

Instead of limiting currency issue and credit, the state devalued the currency and expanded its issue under the control of the totally public Banco Central de Reserva del Perú, established in 1931 to replace the previous Banco de Reserva which had operated with participants from the private sector. In the same year the first state-sponsored 'development' bank, Banco Agrícola del Perú, was created. Part of the Banco Central's reserve funds were allocated to provide the capital for the new institution, which mainly extended limited credit to cotton growers. Also the new Superintendencia de Banca, created to regulate private financial matters, delayed substantially the liquidation of the Banco del Perú y Londres, thus allowing many agro-exporters to escape bankruptcy.

In return the cotton growers, who had replaced sugar planters as the leading agro-exporters in the 1920s, provided necessary foreign exchange in the form of bills of exchange when cotton prices started to improve around 1932.[144] Thus the earnings of cotton growers did not stay abroad as had been feared. Amazingly the result was a temporary stabilisation of the Peruvian currency. However the strong reliance of the private agro-export sector on state financial manipulations for survival had costly consequences in the long run.

The foreign debt default did not imply a break with foreign capital. Foreign interests found new ways to adapt to the changing situation after 1929. Through official channels the largest foreign companies consolidated their position in Peru in the 1930s in exchange for financial support to the state. W. R. Grace & Company controlled important firms in the sugar, textile and commercial sectors. The Cerro de Pasco Corporation was able to withstand an acute export and labour crisis in 1931–3. The petroleum-producing sector was firmly in the hands of the International Petroleum Company (Standard Oil) and the Lobitos Oilfields. Foreigners were unwilling to divest themselves of their Peruvian interests on the scale of the 1914–21 period. The Peruvian economic recovery after 1933 drew foreign interests to those areas that promised high and secure monopolistic and oligopolistic returns, such as urban services (electricity, telephone, telegraph, radio), and the provision of credit – through the intermediation of the Banco Italiano and importing houses – to suppliers of the internal market.

According to contemporary accounts the progress of manufacturing in Peru was 'especially rapid' in the early 1930s.[145] (Industrial production consisted mainly of cotton and woollen textiles, processed food and beverages, matches, and construction materials.) However even though the industrial sector was expanding its share of the national income, obstacles such as the size of domestic market and its concentration in Lima limited its growth. The link between private finance and the industrial sector had also increased since the 1920s with a continued tendency to support industrial oligopolies.

The private financial institutions in this period followed a conservative and highly liquid credit policy, led by the Banco Italiano. This bank controlled 45 per cent of total banking assets in 1935, while native banks had 26 per cent, and branches of foreign banks accounted for 29 per cent (Table 3.1). The Banco Italiano had purchased the failed Banco del Perú y Londres' unsurpassed network and market share of provincial agencies. In the depths of the economic crisis the Banco Italiano declared handsome 10 per cent and 8 per cent dividends for the years 1931 and 1932 respectively.[146]

Moreover the Banco Italiano had Italian and Swiss financial backing, which enabled it to arrange the massive financing of the electrical monopoly (Empresas Eléctricas Asociadas), the telephone monopoly (Cía. Peruana de Teléfonos), the Callao dock works, the flour milling oligopoly and several oligopolistic industries in the hands of first or second generation Italians. In addition the Banco Italiano had strong interests in insurance, urban real estate (Cía. Inmobiliaria Ltda), and provided credit support to state institutions in return for political favours from the dictator Benavides.[147] As official recognition of its new importance in the local financial structure, the Italian bank was declared 'national' by the banking law of 1931, and its national status was officially reaffirmed in 1935.[148]

The Banco Italiano reinforced the tendency toward a higher level of deposits over loans and discounts that had prevailed since 1932 (Figure 3.1). Its reserves were five times in excess of those required by law. As a result of export recovery and the monetary expansion carried out by the Banco Central, commercial banks enjoyed an increase in deposits but they did not proportionately increase their loans. So how did they continue to be profitable?

The answer lies in an increasing liquidity (*fondos disponibles*) that was used to purchase public internal loan bonds. The first of such loans was the Patriotic Loan of 1932; road construction bonds followed. These bonds were then rediscounted by the Central Reserve Bank. High liquidity also allowed very profitable foreign exchange operations and services to exporters and importers (*otras cuentas del pasivo*).[149] The Lima stock market also benefited from this high relative liquidity. As a consequence, financial development in this period of export recovery experienced an important advance based on inflationary tendencies being kept to a certain limit by the understanding between private and public financial interests. This arrangement was substantially modified by 1939 with the political rise of an ex-president of the Banco Central, Manuel Prado.

1940–50: DEMISE OF AGRO-EXPORT INFLUENCE

Inflationary official financial and monetary policies advanced significantly in the 1940s. The counterpart to monetary and credit expansion was the introduction of exchange and price controls by the state to artificially curb the effects of inflation on the internal market. Between 1940 and 1948 the dollar exchange rate was officially fixed and controlled at S/6.50 per dollar. The price of agricultural food products was controlled to provide protection to the expanding urban population. Special import licences offered protection to local industrialists, and provided importers of capital goods with undervalued foreign currency.

During the Second World War the Peruvian version of import-substitution, although not as successful as in other Latin American countries, produced nevertheless the expansion of the industrial sector. New industrial oligopolies appeared: PERULAC, Leche Gloria, Eternit, INRESA, Cía. Goodyear, Vidrios Planos, Rayón Peruana, and Lanificios del Perú, among others.[150] The policies of the administrations of Manuel Prado (1939–45) and José Luis Bustamante y Rivero (1945–8) were favourable to the industrial sector's profits. However import substitution came together with financial repression, which had negative effects on financial activities.

The previous public internal debt policy was modified to include the formation of public corporations, which absorbed internal credit and added to inflationary pressures. Also, internal loan bonds depreciated significantly due to inflation, thus causing damage to holders of them, including commercial banks.

Banking deposits showed a small decline between 1940 and 1941, and then a sharp increase in 1941–6, as shown in Figure 3.1, corrected for inflation. Two new local banks (Banco Wiese and Banco Comercial) and one insurance company were established. However inflationary growth of bank deposits reached its limit in 1946 and a radical decline in deposits occurred between 1946 and 1949. On the other hand total loans dropped more than deposits in 1939–42 as a result of diminished opportunities of loan allocation due to official controls. Total loans increased between 1942 and 1946, but declined in real terms in 1946–9.

Native banks nominally controlled 92–95 per cent of total commercial banking assets in 1945, but foreign participation in some institutions was considerable. However the Banco Italiano, having changed its name to Banco de Crédito del Perú in 1941 to avoid being blacklisted because of its Italian connections during the war, had diminished its foreign capital participation from 50 per cent to 30 per cent of its total capital by 1942. The bank's Italian president, a renowned fascist sympathiser, resigned in 1939, perhaps under pressure from the Prado group with its increasing banking and political interests.[151]

At the same time cotton and sugar continued their long-term decline as export commodities, reflecting an overall loss of ground by agrarian export interests. Agro-exporters had merged their interests with other sectors (discussed in Chapter 4). Elite groups and new capitalists were now in control of industrial production, and credit allocation to the new sectors was the most significant policy of commercial banking institutions adapting rapidly to the changing economic conditions of the 1940s and 1950s.

LONG-TERM EFFECTS OF DIVERSIFICATION

To conclude this evaluation of the role of private finance in Peruvian financial and economic development, it is necessary to analyse the long-term effects of credit allocation in different sectors by private financial institutions. Detailed treatment by sub-periods needs to be complemented with an overall view of the years 1884–1950. Despite the gaps in historical statistical information due to institutional secrecy and the lack of official aggregate data prior to 1947, Figure 3.2 nevertheless provides some tentative approximations.

Commercial agriculture received an increasing share of commercial credit from the most important native bank between 1884 and 1930. The Banco del Perú y Londres increased its allocation to the agro-export sector from 3.5 per cent to 8 per cent during the last fifteen years of the nineteenth century. This fell to 3 per cent in the 1910s, but rose to 27–35 per cent of total loans in 1915–30. Thereafter loans to commercial agriculture declined, according to the official aggregate data of commercial and 'development' banks, to 12.8 per cent in 1947 and 11.2 per cent in 1951. Thus banking credit followed closely the growth of Peruvian agro-exports to their highest point in the 1920s and their subsequent gradual decline from the 1930s.

The share in credit to commercial agriculture was almost inverse to the industrial sector's credit share. The latter diminished from 13.4 per cent in the 1880s to 11 per cent in the 1890s, remaining more or less stationary at 4–6 per cent between 1907 and 1925 before increasing substantially to 22.7 per cent in 1947 and 27.7 per cent in 1951.

Except in the 1900s, when credit to trading activities reached a low share of 8.7 per cent, banking credit to commerce remained high and fairly constant from 1884–1950, accounting for approximately 30 per cent in the late nineteenth century (due to the central role played by

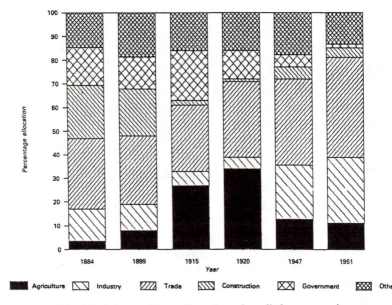

Figure 3.2　Banks' percentage allocation of credit by economic sector,
1884–1951

Sources: Appendix C.

merchant creditors in those years), 28–32 per cent in the 1920s, and increasing to 36.6 per cent and 42.2 per cent respectively in 1947 and 1951 (perhaps due to the increasing role played by import merchants in the process of import-substitution industrialisation).

Credit to urban properties and the construction sector diminished markedly from a high 20–22.5 per cent in the 1880s and 1890s to a low 1–2.1 per cent in 1915–30. The decline appears to be connected to foreign and then government monopoly over the mortgage credit business, despite the success of the Banco Italiano's mortgage business in the early 1920s. In the late 1940s commercial credit to the urban-construction sector had only risen to 4–5 per cent. The urban boom of the 1920s and the late 1930s seems therefore to have mostly benefited other financial institutions, notably 'urbanizadoras' and insurance companies.

The other major sector, the government and its institutions, made use of short-term commercial banking credit in the 1920s and 1930s. One important banking institution provided 13–16 per cent of its total loans and discounts to government and municipal institutions in the 1880s and 1890s, 37 per cent in the 1900s, 21 per cent in the 1910s, and between 12 and 31 per cent in the 1920s. If semi-private tax collecting institutions are also included, the share taken by the government would be higher in the 1900s and 1920s. However commercial credit to the government reduced significantly in the late 1940s to only 4–5 per cent, and 1.6 per cent in 1951.

Despite the unequal sources of information used so far, it is possible to identify some general patterns. The allocation of credit to commercial agriculture followed the evolution of this sector's economic importance. On the other hand, the share taken by industry clearly followed a pattern of substitution with respect to agro-exporting's share. Trading activities seemed to have been best and more constantly served by commercial banking credit. This could be interpreted as a change from commercial credit specialisation in agriculture to one in industry, which is typical of import-substitution industrialisation. Urban expansion was also facilitated by local banks in its early phase. The consistent growth of the share of credit going to industry and commerce is therefore related to limited modernisation and relative diversification.

In conclusion, this chapter has presented evidence to modify the view that private finance was either an irrelevant or an outright negative influence in Peruvian economic development and diversification. On the contrary, and despite tendencies towards oligopolisation and financial concentration (which will be analysed at the regional and social levels in Chapter 5), private financial institutions contributed to the initial recovery and modernisation of the economy after 1883, responded to the relative economic diversification within and beyond the export sector throughout 1884–1950 and, perhaps with more success prior to 1930, combined competition and collaboration with foreign financial interests. The causes of Peru's financial problems lay elsewhere.

4 Elite Groups and Private Financial Management

In studying private finance in underdeveloped economies it is not sufficient to consider financial institutions alone. Recent studies have demonstrated that informal (non-institutional) finance plays an important role in supplementing formal capital markets.[1] Elite investor groups constitute just such a type of informal private finance.

Attempts to explain Peruvian economic and financial problems have focused on the role of private élite networks and their financial decisions during the years 1884–1950. Some of these studies consider the leading élite groups as having been an obstacle to economic growth. According to these interpretations the economic behaviour of the élite was, first and foremost, traditionally 'aristocratic' or irrational.[2] In addition the native élite's collaboration with international capital permitted foreign penetration, which was considered adverse to national interests'[3] and their over-specialisation in agro-export concerns limited economic diversification, industrial capacity and financial decision-making.[4]

In order to evaluate these views, this chapter examines the financial decisions, diversification and autonomy of élite groups in their interaction with the financial system. Initially some debatable opinions on the élite's rationality are discussed. Subsequently an alternative argument is elaborated using documentary evidence of the activity of élite groups with financial capacities and strategies in the 1884–1930 and 1931–50 periods. Peruvian élite groups are found to have initiated their participation in modern and diversified economic evolution earlier than hitherto recognised. Finally, the shortcomings and limitations of the efforts by élite groups to achieve irreversible capitalist development are assessed.

PRIVATE GROUPS: OBSTACLE TO DEVELOPMENT?

For the business activity of the Peruvian economic élite to be described as 'retrogressive' is not new. Supporters of President Leguía, a reputed moderniser, used terms such as 'economic feudalism' and 'oligarchic trusts' during and after the 1920s to criticise opposing élite interests.[5] According to a contemporary economic analyst, Peru's lack of industrial development had its roots in the 'defective economic psychology' of Peruvians: 'The Peruvian race has little entrepreneurial spirit, an excessive liking for liberal professions and the bureaucracy, and a weak and fickle character'.[6] Likewise a US commercial attaché observed in 1925 that the Peruvian upper class exhibited the Hispanic aristocratic trait of a loathing for manual work.[7] The obvious ideological bias of these opinions should warn the historian not to take them at face value or as proof of a supposedly inherent entrepreneurial incapacity among the Peruvian élite. However, recent analyses continue to cite similar arguments as evidence of an inherent lack of modern economic methods among the private economic leadership, and so the debate continues.

A recent conclusion that the Peruvian élite was historically incapable of promoting development, originates from an intense discussion in the 1960s and early 1970s.[8] In the crucial years 1884–1950 'seigniorial' family groups, the argument goes, formed a closed and traditional 'oligarchy' with a pronounced disdain for industrial methods of production. Intermarriage between the members of its distinguished families, and its impenetrability by members of other social classes' provided the élite with exclusive property rights shared only with foreign allies. The scant diversification effected by the oligarchy was therefore intended merely to enhance its control over the economy through trade, finance and politics. Financial institutions performed as simple depositories for and suppliers of funds to oligarchic business in good times and facilitated the flight of capital in bad times. Critics of the private élite thus conclude that economic progress was limited to a few modernised sectors under the control of the oligarchy or foreign companies, with no positive effect on the rest of the economy.

Notwithstanding this now classic interpretation, the use of ambiguous concepts such as 'aristocratic', 'seigniorial', 'paternalistic', 'Old Régime', and even 'oligarchical', sets rigid limits when explaining the problem. New evidence, dug out by historians from primary sources and economists working from statistical reconstructions, does not fit into such rigid concepts. Data on the active and entrepreneurial participation of the élite in the modernisation of the economy of the time needs to be integrated into broader interpretations. Hence new alternatives in understanding the economic role of Peruvian élite groups are being put forward.[9]

Lately important revisions of the role of other Latin American élite groups have questioned the idea that irrational financial and investment decisions were the main cause of underdevelopment. For example, in Brazil during the early twentieth century, responsiveness to export prices coupled with an attentive financial policy by the state with regard to trade oscillations, show rational adaptations by the economic élite to the constraining conditions of economic backwardness. Furthermore the formation of investor groups in Brazil and other underdeveloped countries to pool capital resources for joint ventures has worked quite effectively in overcoming certain economic bottlenecks and political instability.[10]

In the case of Peru there is considerable evidence to support the view that, since the agro-export recovery of the 1890s, élite groups managed quite rationally to finance and promote business considering the economic constraints they faced, such as the effect of war, foreign competition in the export sector, decline in export prices, and shortage of venture capital. There is qualitative evidence to refute the idea of irrationality in connection with élite groups. To begin with, leading sectors of the élite had a strong desire to modernise and make more efficient the Peruvian economic base. The concept of 'development' at the time, although basically devoid of notions such as income distribution and social welfare, nevertheless followed contemporary capitalist prescriptions: the rationale of generous liberal incentives for capital investment, and the accumulation of profits to permit the exploitation of natural resources and the expansion of the domestic market.[11]

Development was closely associated with fomenting market-oriented production, particularly commercial agriculture and mining which were seen as the basis for an 'initial period of evolution' typical of 'incipient' countries: 'After studying Peru closely what can there be but agriculture and mining?'[12] The principal means considered by the élite for maximising economic activities were the liberalisation of state prerogatives, the attraction of foreign capital, increased mechanisation of agrarian and mining activities, the improvement of infrastructure (railways, ports, roads, urban development), huge irrigation projects, and the immigration of Europeans, preferably Anglo-Saxons. Clearly some members of the élite did not lack developmental know-how.

As a second priority, economic policymakers favoured the mobilisation of traditional properties belonging to the Church, Indian communities and old fashioned rentiers.[13] Monetary expansion in the provinces was sought. Likewise, as immigration objectives apparently failed to materialise (instead of the desired German and

British immigrants, arrivals consisted of Italians and Asians), the integration of the secluded, indigenous population into the national labour force was practiced.[14] Communal land ownership, which was widespread in the highlands, was considered 'incompatible with a civilised and progressive life'.[15] The bearer of this opinion, Manuel Vicente Villarán, was a progressive university professor of Law, who later became minister of justice, and director and chairman of the Banco del Perú y Londres. He had family ties with the coastal cotton export interests of the Sociedad Agrícola Cachipampa. Villarán nevertheless recognised that 'positive' efforts to legislate for the supression of communal property could do little to mobilise rural property in the Peruvian highlands. Independent farmers would not be able to compete over land ownership with 'feudalistic' *hacendados*. Therefore more economic development was needed before legally dealing with Indian communal lands.

Furthermore the costly experience of the War of the Pacific and the signing of the Grace contract (1890) taught the value of modern rationality to the élite. A consistent liberal policy had to be established, similar to that used by the mid-nineteenth century Chilean victors, since 'no better [policy] was known'.[16] The state's revenue and expenditure had to be balanced and its customary prerogatives kept to the basics. Strict control over legislative power and the election machinery was modified.[17] Twenty-one years after the implementation of the Grace contract, economic analysts considered it represented an advantageous transaction between the Peruvian state and foreign capital.[18]

Those élite members who survived economically and were able to rebuild their position after the war developed a new self-awareness. They realised that wealth was not to be obtained as easily as during the Guano Age; conscious efforts had to be made to develop new sources of income. Their preoccupation was to avoid a new reduction of national resources by an invading foreign power, be it Chile or another bellicose neighbour, and the erosion of their internal authority. This drove the Peruvian élite to search for modern and effective economic devices to ensure their survival. Augusto B. Leguía, minister of finance between 1903 and 1908, summarised the élite's change of attitude after the war: '. . . that prosperous and comfortable [pre-war] situation just had the appearance of being so; we were deceived, remained deceived and thus we succumbed. Today we do not live with largesse but we have honesty. Our budgets are balanced'.[19] To this Villarán added: 'for us today wealth is a matter of dignity, honour, perhaps independence, more than a matter of comfort and culture'.[20]

However, the long-term negative consequences of the War of the Pacific limited the élite's economic achievements. Dependence on foreign credit for private activities remained pervasive between 1884 and 1914. By 1920, however, important élite groups had achieved considerable financial autonomy and repaid much of their private foreign debts. Native firms also displaced foreign companies in the control of crucial areas (sugar and cotton production, insurance, trade finance, banking) using local financial institutions.[21] Unfortunately there was a reduction in these positive tendencies from the late 1920s to the 1940s. Although not representing a complete success story, Peruvian élite groups demonstrated distinguishable managerial and financial abilities in their capitalist quests. The study of the struggle for financial autonomy and diversification by élite groups constitutes a much needed complementary approach to the study of private finance, to avoid possibly unfruitful ideological discussions over the rationality of the Peruvian economic leadership.

INFORMAL AND INSTITUTIONAL FINANCE

A helpful concept in analysing how some of the élite maximised the use of financial institutions to execute the transfer of funds to and from the export and other economic sectors, is that of modern élite investment groups, which constitute a response by members of the entrepreneurial élite toward overcoming the deficiencies of unequally developed (formal) markets. This they achieve by coordinating intra-firm activities through the association of interests and kinship. Investor groups not only mobilise inactive family and group assets, but also tap capital from outsiders and maximise profits in common investments.[22] The antecedents of these modern élite groups were the 'notable family networks' of the late eighteenth and nineteenth centuries.[23]

Investor groups can be small or large, according to the scope and diversity of their investments. They function through interlocking directorships held by their members in different companies and economic sectors. Generally they have a common financial policy directed by a leading member, either the initiator of the group's accumulation or his/her successors. Bonds among the members go beyond the casual, business-like connections characteristic of anonymous stockholders in joint-stock ventures. Personal allegiance, family ties and moral codes solidify group cohesion and help establish the coordination necessary for the success of medium- and long-term projects.

The most successful groups are structurally integrated with formal capital markets through participation in or control of the policy of financial institutions. Unlike specialised firms and partnerships, the range of interconnections established by the groups provide them with a wealth of information and greater flexibility to adapt and respond to sudden changes in the economic situation.[24] These groups do not exclude partnership with foreign capital in areas where competition and risk are too high, although it is in their ultimate interest to secure autonomy and an unchallenged control over crucial sectors of the economy.[25]

In the case of Peru, historians have stressed evident fragmentation of the Peruvian élite from 1884–1930 along regional, sectorial, national and political lines. They portray a lack of the social class cohesion needed to unify the country.[26] In contrast, the findings of Maushammer for the 1950–65 period depict a well-established network of investor groups, some directed by the heads of important families in the 1890–1930 period, which were well represented in export activities but were also complementally attached to the industrial and financial sectors.[27] Clearly there is a gap in our understanding of the evolutionary process linking these chronologically separated activities of the Peruvian élite groups.

In an attempt to explain this apparent disconnection, I shall now analyse the patterns of grouping among the economic élite for two periods, 1884–1930 and 1931–50, and their integration into local financial institutions. I argue that during these periods a transition from group formation to group consolidation occurred. It appears that in the earlier period response to and imitation of foreign oligopolistic practices encouraged group formation, diversification and a search for privileged access to local institutional credit. Banks and other financial institutions at an early stage became the meeting and negotiating places for old and new group interests. Some traditional families adjusted to the trend, while others succumbed to the process equivocally termed 'the disappearance of colonial Peru'.[28] The evolution of investor groups into full operational activity by 1950 shows a move towards areas of specialisation other than agro-export, increased concentration, and an overall weakening in their negotiations with the state and foreign financial interests.

FORMATION AND TRANSITION OF ELITE GROUPS

The earliest trials for native Peruvians in their pursuit of cohesive entrepreneurial control over uncoordinated resources can be traced to the bustling Guano Age's commercial activities (1850 to 1879). Prominent family groups and guild-like interests had to face the advances of well-organised foreign merchant houses and new ambitious merchants attracted by the economic opportunities offered by guano.

However, the financial and foreign debt crises of the 1870s, erratic state intervention in banking, fiscal and money matters, limited overseas trading networks, and the War of the Pacific, truncated the economic transformation of the Peruvian élite.[29] The devastating effects of the war delayed the coordination of various activities and the diversification of long-term credit institutions. For most of the 1880s and 1890s, internal resources flowed to foreign creditors and commercial houses. As seen earlier, institutions offering short-term credit dominated the weak financial market. Concurrently there were signs of a reversion to former rentier attitudes by some élite families. The suffering élite had no alternative, in the midst of deep internal dissension, but to financially maim the thoroughly weakened state in order to pay foreign debts. Ultra-liberal representatives confronted the protectionists in Congress over several economic policy issues, which only after a long and painful struggle were turned into working compromises between the opposing factions.[30] This meant a significant break in the pre-War of the Pacific relationship between the private and public sectors.

At this juncture modest steps toward group formation were stimulated by the 'demonstration effect' of foreign companies and banking policies which selected groups and associations to be recipients of credit so as to minimise the financial risks. This tendency picked up momentum in the late 1890s and early 1900s. Initially only the merchant and financial sectors were capable of achieving the scale necessary to instigate multi-firm actions.

Important merchant houses of the first and second tax classification categories constituted the main organising economic agents after the war. As shown in the previous chapter, these houses undertook a wide range of activities: debt collection, participation in over-priced foreign and internal trade credit and commissions, intervention in the liquidation of bankrupted institutions, political lobbying, official contracting, retail business, and the attraction of comparatively cheap capital from abroad. They became most influential in pressing for liberal economic policies or privately run official monopolies, and arranging Peru's foreign debt.[31]

The degree of control over the economy by merchants and banks was such that there was little possibility for the first signs of economic recuperation to bypass them and directly benefit agro-exporters, the traditional core of the native élite. Monopolies, oligopolies and cartels were established in almost every promising activity to a degree and scale unknown before. They included railways (Peruvian Corporation), the Callao dock facilities (Société Générale), ocean transportation (Grace Line, Pacific Steam), copper mining (Cerro de Pasco Corporation), the cotton trade (Duncan Fox, Graham Rowe), wheat importation and flour milling (Milne & Company, Toso y Sánchez, Revoredo), and mortgage credit (Banco del Callao). Cooperation was established between foreign firms, Italian resident merchants and industrialists, who were considered 'élite strangers',[32] local banks and, most importantly, the first-formed domestic groups. These participants in oligopolies profited from exchange and protectionist measures in the 1890s. The calculated diversification strategies of the commercial–financial sector now began to permeate the affairs of the native élite and be absorbed into the previous pattern of family-based groups.

At the time, anti-trust sentiments in Peru and elsewhere criticised monopolies as unjust, anti-democratic and wasteful.[33] However the advantages to the economies of scale obtained by vertically and horizontally integrated mergers have been recently emphasised by economists.[34] This was a crucial lesson, learnt in part from foreigners by a domestic élite unaccustomed to the scale and complexity of late nineteenth-century mergers.

The most obvious way in which foreign managerial techniques initially influenced members of the Peruvian élite was through the extremely good results achieved by foreign business in Peru despite the depression, and their successful competition against traditional native houses. Correspondence between foreign executives of internationally spreading firms and influential Peruvians reveals an awareness on the part of natives of the need to improve their business methods.[35] The leading and competitive congressman and businessman Manuel Candamo, for example, critically praised Michael P. Grace and his manipulations during the Grace Contract discussion: 'Intelligent and active, practical and bold, with a clear understanding of our political scene, of our virtues and defects, from having grown among us and because his mercantile activities had given him extense and valuable relations which he sagaciously and carefully kept . . .'[36]

Another important way in which foreign 'demonstration effects' acted upon Peruvian businessmen was through their direct participation in joint ventures or competition with foreign firms. Key local financial figures (Payán, Pardo, Aspíllaga, Prado) collaborated with foreign capital to form oligopolies such as Grace & Company's Cartavio Sugar Company and Peruvian Cotton Manufacturing Company, and the EE.EE.AA trust. Thus, between 1900 and 1914, foreign interests were able to predominate in financial speculations which resulted in native displacement from secure investments and periodic stock market crises under the gold standard. Such was the case of the Banco del Perú y Londres in 1907, Crédit Foncier Peruvien in 1912 and EE.EE.AA. in 1913.[37]

Prominent Peruvians studied British, French and US methods abroad or worked as employees for foreign merchant and financial firms operating in Peru. This was the case with the future presidents, José Pardo, Augusto Leguía, Guillermo Billinghurst, and the élite members Miguel Pardo, Enrique C. Basadre and Alejandro Garland, among others.[38] Finally the effective collaboration between members of the Italian community, and the competitive advantage they gained from this, opened the eyes of the members of the native élite to the advantages to be gained by forming coordinated groups.

At first the native élite responded in an eclectic and fragmented manner to the advances of foreign influence. Combining traditional and new approaches in dealing with foreign capital, notable and influential Peruvians bargained quite tenaciously over the sale of mining, petroleum and other state rights. Taking advantage of exclusive state grants for mining sites in the central highlands, prospective petroleum lands on the northern coast and their monopoly over the drainage works of the native Empresa Socavonera del Cerro de Pasco, leading Peruvian families obtained rentier income from foreign corporations after years of judicial conflict. Other local mining interests, however, such as the Gallo Diez and Fernandini groups, were able to diversify their interests.

A host of lawyers and politicians, expert in the hybrid Peruvian patrimonial–liberal legislation, served the family interests and were also recruited by foreign firms.[39] Conciliation and agreement between the two groups of contenders, foreign corporations and native rentiers, was the most sensible outcome of long judicial trials, which in the meantime provided considerable income for local lawyers.

Prominent local attorneys were thus an integral part of the élite's transformation and occupied an important place in the management of financial institutions.

Merchants and financiers also participated in this process as creditors of almost ruined rentiers and as a decisive third force in charge of the floating of securities of rentier enterprises. By 1906–7 a group of merchants and financiers had obtained the crucial participation of at least one-third of the stockholders of the Empresa Socavonera. This enabled them in 1908 to conclude a highly lucrative agreement with the Cerro de Pasco Corporation for compensation for the rentier enterprise's right, established in 1900, over 20 per cent of all the ore produced in the Cerro mining area. Paradoxically active mining families were barely represented in the Empresa Socavonera.[40]

Miners were dealing separately with foreign firms and selling some of their properties with the intention of continuing their self-financed activities.[41] Consequently only after 1914 did native miners, such as Manuel Mujica y Carassa, Eulogio Fernandini and Gallo Porras, appear in prominent positions in several financial institutions (Banco Popular, Compañía de Seguros La Popular, Banco del Perú y Londres).

Among the groups of rentiers, landowners, lawyers and politicians who participated in the state grant scheme for petroleum and mining, the best represented were the Heeren, Riva Agüero, Aspíllaga and Alzamora families, as well as the diversifying Olavegoya and Alvarez Calderón families. Among the merchant and financier groups we find the ubiquitous Jose Payán, together with Raúl Godoy, J. W. Stokes, J. Normand and the Italians Isola, Orezzoli, Rezza, Nosiglia, Denegri, Piaggio.[42]

The Riva Agüero family is the best example of a traditional rentier family that did not develop into an investor group but was able to avoid ruin thanks to the appreciation of its properties and opportune use of local credit. José de la Riva Agüero y Osma grew up in a proud Catholic family with aristocratic ties in Europe. He became an influential intellectual and conservative politician, and has been portrayed as a typical 'oligarch' of seigniorial extraction. In reality the Riva Agüeros represent only the declining portion of the Peruvian élite unable or unwilling to adapt to the new circumstances of modernisation. In this sense they are an atypical case in relation to the evolving investor groups of the time. Reliance on past traditions, rather than vigourous action in the present or planning for the future, distinguished the Riva Agüeros.[43]

The family's main sources of income were landed estates near

Lima, used for cattle grazing and maize production (Haciendas Pando, San José, Palomino, Cayetano), and urban property in old Lima and Cocharcas (houses, stores and two tenements, *callejones*, with 153 rooms). The family's patrimony was consolidated through the disputes with relatives conducted by Ignacio de Osma. Married to a daughter of the Sancho Dávila family of late colonial nobility, Ignacio won several judicial suits which helped to consolidate his estates before his death in 1893.[44] His son-in-law, José Carlos de la Riva Agüero, who was married to Dolores de Osma y Sancho Dávila, continued the administration of the Osma's estates until 1906. An analysis of José Carlos' financial situation at the time of his death in 1906 reveals his dependence on merchants, exchange brokers and private lenders for credit. Attempts on his part to form a cartel of estate owners of the Magdalena, Maranga and La Legua valleys (1900) to raise the price charged to cattle herders for grazing land, and to form an agricultural society (1906), were unsuccessful.

The family's urban rent income, administered by Dolores' elder sister Rosa Julia, amounted to approximately S/1100 a month. At the same time, family consumption costs, which included banquets, donations to Catholic institutions, book purchases, newspaper subscriptions, general costs of administration and lawyers' and notaries' fees, added up to S/1050. In 1906 the rural estates' production of maize sold for only S/5907, which was insufficient to repay the advance payment of S/9628 for the harvest which had been received from the merchant firm Solari Hermanos nine months previously. The deficit was covered by signing a Banco del Perú y Londres promissory note bearing 2 per cent monthly interest. At the death of José Carlos his less entrepreneurial son, José de la Riva Agüero y Osma, simply rented out the family's landed concerns.

Fortunately for José, by 1918 the urban rental income of the family had increased to S/5246, which in nominal terms was 510 per cent higher than it had been in 1901. In 1919 he ran into political problems with Leguía and decided to travel with his mother and aunt to Europe, where he remained in self-imposed exile for approximately twelve years. The expenses for the stay in Europe were initially financed by an 8 per cent annual interest loan of £10 000 granted by the Banco del Perú y Londres, using the Fundo Pando as collateral at a time of booming prices for agricultural land and urban property.[45] Upon his return in 1931 he was appointed mayor of the city of Lima. In the meantime his traditional views had remained untouched. According to Mr. Forbes, the British Ambassador in Lima and a good friend of Riva Agüero in the 1930s, he possessed 'a viceregal mentality and [was] incapable of understanding modern ideas',[46] and if he had his way 'we should revert to the complete subjugation of the lower classes and the absolute domination of the Church. Don José should have lived two centuries ago and been a Viceroy'.[47]

The economically more influential families followed a path different from that of the traditional Riva Agüeros. Elsewhere I have identified some of the most prominent local élite groups and divided them into four categories according to the degree of diversification of their investment concerns: traditional coastal, transitional new coastal, provincial and foreign in origin.[48] One first observation is that even in the more traditional category of coastal families, we find that there is a distinct tendency toward expanding into sectors other than commercial agriculture and toward coordinating different enterprises.

The leading example in this respect is the Aspíllaga group. It concentrated on sugar production, which received large amounts of foreign and native mercantile credit. The group chose to diversify into mining, real estate, investment in financial institutions and securities, but demonstrated a certain reluctance to become involved in industrial investments. Gilbert identifies the Aspíllaga group's investment preferences as 'typically oligarchic' despite its relative diversification.[49] Another traditional group, the Miró Quesada, extended its interests from trade into the newspaper printing industry but remained less involved in other sectors. Neither family was even slightly aristocratic in origin in spite of their proud pretenses. Interestingly enough, Antero Aspíllaga and Antonio Miró Quesada were considered part of the liberal faction of the *civilistas* who opposed the old guard in the early 1900s.

The Carrillo de Albornoz family, like the Riva Agüero, can be considered as 'aristocratic'. Both were among the few families with dusty colonial titles of nobility dating from the late eighteenth century. At the centre of their interests were landed estates, which allowed them to maintain the status of privileged clients of banks even though their organic link with financial institutions was fragile. The Carrillos however were much more dynamic in modernising their sugar plantations in the Cañete and Bocanegra valleys. This was financed by sizeable mortgage loans obtained from the Banco del Perú y Londres.[50] In general, the groups in the category 'traditional coastal' benefited from mortgage or medium-term credit which allowed them to make full use of their properties.

The second category of élite groups, the new coastal, provides the clue to understanding the transitional character of the élite groups during their evolution into consolidated investor groups. The new coastal groups comprised old and new families with strong political and financial connections based on agro-exporting or mining, and oriented toward a diversification which included industrial concerns. The Leguía, Ayulo, Olavegoya, Larco, Echenique, Pardo and Prado groups were among the most prominent and modern-thinking of the native groups. The *civilista* representatives of these groups constituted the progressive-liberal sector opposing the conservative politicians Alzamora and Arenas and, in the case of Leguía, Larco and Echenique, a splinter faction that later controlled the reformist regime of the 1920s.

Before dashing into high-level politics around 1900–3, Augusto B. Leguía, who came from a modest though well-connected Lambayeque family, rose to become one of the most successful Peruvian entrepreneurs. From his education in a commercial English school in Valparaiso, Chile, his employment by the US–Peruvian merchant firm Prevost & Company in Lima, and his appointment as agent and manager of the New York Life Insurance Company for the Peruvian, Ecuadorian, Bolivian and Colombian markets, Leguía acquired modern business acumen and a first hand awareness of the foreign demonstration effect, which attributes he brought to his political career.

Leguía married the daughter of an English landowner, Henry Swayne. After the latter's death Leguía acted as the administrator of the Swayne sugar estates. Through credit obtained from Liverpool and London merchant-bankers, Leguía expanded and modernised the estates under the name of the British Sugar Company. Later he diversified into other sectors, principally insurance and finance. When New York Life abandoned its business in Peru following protectionist legislation, Leguía helped establish the Lima branch of the Sudamérica insurance company. Other financial investments in Leguía's portfolio included participation in Seguros Rímac and Banco Internacional.[51] He was thus able to link agro-export interests with financial management.

The marriage of Leguía's daughters allowed him to join with other prominent families to form an economically powerful group which guaranteed the obtainment of credit from British, American and local sources. His most important sons-in-law were Antonio Chopitea Hernández (Hacienda Laredo), Alberto Ayulo Laos and Alberto Larrañaga.[52] The latter became one of the most prominent road contractors in the 1920s and, together with Miguel Echenique, a major stockholder of the cement-producing Portland Peruana, a large industrial concern which was promoted by Leguía's government in the 1920s.

During his political career Leguía, the modernising representative of agro-exporters *par excellence*, obtained substantial credit support for his private activities from native banks, especially the Banco del Perú y Londres, and from foreign lenders. Some of Leguía's deals with foreign creditors exemplify his business procedure while president and are revealing of his strong interests as an agro-exporter.

Leguía was highly regarded by British creditors, but in August 1928 Messrs Kearsley and Cunningham of Liverpool filed a claim at the Foreign Office in London against him. Kearsley and Cunningham had supplied considerable credit between 1914 and 1921 to allow the financing of Leguía's cotton and sugar production in his Anglo Pacific Estates Ltd. As Leguía had mortgaged these estates in 1918 to the London merchant bankers Frederick Huth & Company in order to protect his property against political uncertainties, he was only able to repay the previous and current loans from Kearsley and Cunningham by allowing the purchase of cotton and sugar futures by the Liverpool firm. Leguía failed, however, to consign the promised amount of cotton to repay his obligations. Apparently he was unwilling to consign or sell his cotton because he was expecting higher prices after 1920: 'For a time Mr. Leguía's view of the market proved to be right, but unfortunately he held on until 1923 by which time the market had fallen very considerably'.[53] As a result in 1927 he owed Kearsley and Cunningham £469 741. After long deliberation the Foreign Office decided to carry only unofficial representations in favour of the British claimant despite a final comment that stated: 'This is a very bad case: President Leguía gambled in cotton futures with this firm's money and then refused to deliver the cotton or to repay the money'.[54]

When Leguía was ousted from power in 1930 he also owed Lp10 000 to the Banco del Perú y Londres, according to the accounts rendered to an official investigating committee. No clear proof of graft, corruption or hidden funds was found by this investigation. However, according to a British diplomat in 1929, it was difficult to find an honest man among Leguía's family and Cabinet. Leguía's three sons had influence, but also had bad reputations. His favourite son, Juan, was involved in a bribe scandal with US bankers.[55]

Leguía's assets abroad were not impressive at the end of his political life and he continued to be heavily indebted to British financial houses.[56] This proves that the main investment target of the Leguía group was coastal Peru and not abroad.

The Ayulo family firm was among the few native merchant houses that survived the War of the Pacific and maintained active import–export activity in the 1890s. Its success can be accounted for by two strategic transformations of the Ayulo family from its situation as state-protected consignee during the Guano Age. In the first place, it established secure trade and financial contacts in Paris which allowed the firm to obtain credit support in difficult times and a competitive edge to dispute portions of the Peruvian sugar (and later cotton) trade. Paris was an important focus of wealthy Peruvian émigrés whose funds were funnelled to and from Europe through the Ayulos' intermediation. In the second place, the Ayulos had family members in important managerial positions in several financial institutions in Lima, particularly in those under the influence of the leading local bank, the Banco del Perú y Londres.[57] In this way the Ayulo group was able to obtain sound financial information, as well as to coordinate its actions with the representatives of foreign commercial interests who dealt with the bank. The Ayulos also acted as import agents for textile industrialists, were stockholders of the Peruvian Steam Company, and participated actively in the funding of irrigation projects to develop cotton plantations. During the Leguía regime in the 1920s, the Ayulos, who were directors of banks at the time, were granted extensive local credit for their agro-export concerns. The Ayulo group was one of the outstanding debtors at the time of the Banco del Perú y Londres' bankruptcy.

The Olavegoya group's most remarkable achievement was the early channelling of funds from the Lima financial market to investment in livestock companies in the central highlands region. The Sociedad Ganadera Junín (1904), del Centro (1910) and Corpacancha, in which the Olavegoyas participated as major partners, were instrumental in the consolidation of landed properties, the rationalisation of large-scale production and an improvement in the quality of sheep and cattle. These transformations were sought in order to tap the growing demand by Lima and the mining centres.[58] Related to the Alvarez Calderón family, the Olavegoyas were successful in having their leading members appointed as directors of the local banks Italiano, Internacional and Perú y Londres. They invested in and obtained credit from these banks to develop their diversified concerns. From 1910–30 the *sociedades ganaderas* were among the most successful joint-stock companies quoted on the Lima Exchange.

Furthermore, through Italian partners the Olavegoyas secured the diversification of their interests beyond livestock, finance, urban and trade businesses and into the textile industry.

The native groups that became especially linked to industry were the Pardo and Prado groups. Like the Olavegoyas, these groups ventured into industry through partnerships with Italians who provided the industrial skills in such factories as La Victoria, Nacional de Lana, San Jacinto and Santa Catalina. What should be emphasised here is their wide range of interests, which were financed by local banks (especially the Banco Popular), and insurance companies where they participated as stockholders and directors. Participation in textile manufacturing, electric power companies, tramways and urban developments, as well as agro-export interests and financial investments, evidences the degree of their diversification. Furthermore their interests were not limited to the Lima region. By 1940 four large textile factories had been established in the provincial city of Huancayo, of which three were controlled by the Prado group and one by the Pardo group.[59]

The common characteristics of the modernising groups were: (1) their organisation of trusts that helped group formation in new areas where foreign capital and firms had not established their dominance (for example electrical supply trusts between 1896 and 1905, manufacturing, and mortgage credit); (2) their ability to control new financial institutions (Banco Popular, Banco Internacional, and insurance companies) with the objective of capturing local savings and competing with older institutions heavily influenced by foreign capital (Banco del Perú y Londres), and their gradual take-over of these same institutions; (3) their resourcefulness in obtaining capital internally and from abroad, and transforming short-term credit into long-term investments; (4) their investment in protected and exclusive industries, using oligopolistic price controls and production agreements, in cooperation with foreign industrial specialists who provided the know-how lacked by the members of the native élite; (5) their sensitive response to urban-led growth and booming real estate, which were more gainful areas of investment than were industrial concerns during certain periods.

Certainly traditional tendencies initially helped the new coastal élite groups to attain leverage over competing foreign and newly rising groups. This was the case with the native manipulation of state concessions, subventions and grants such as the Cía. Recaudadora, Cía. Peruana de Vapores, and the monopoly on the sale of tobacco, salt, and alcohol. However their ability to interest or coerce financial institutions to extend credit to and invest in domestic group concerns, using the attractive lure of low risk combined with potentially large profits, brought about the groups' consolidation and their rise toward managerial posts in those same financial institutions.

Between 1890 and 1914 banks encouraged the formation of élite associations and cooperative organisations among those native businessmen and producers able to establish monopolies and oligopolies to adequately secure the repayment of loans. For instance the Banco del Perú y Londres and the Banco Italiano supported financially the traditionally oligopolised sector of wheat milling and storage that had expanded to include the industrial production of noodles (Molineros y Depósitos de Bellavista). Since the eighteenth century this sector had been an arena for scandalous speculations and extremely high profits due to the huge demand for and the controlled supply of wheat flour products which depended almost exclusively on wheat imports. In 1888 Juan Revoredo, Juan V. Peral, Bucelli & Company, Milne & Company and Toso y Sánchez organised themselves into a cartel to control the price of their products. This practice was maintained from 1890 to 1930. As a result these companies were among the most profitable of the time. First the Banco del Callao (Angel Sánchez and José Bucelli were directors of the Callao between 1884 and 1895), and later the Banco Italiano (which counted among its directors Luis Nicolini and Federico Milne, owners of the largest mills in the 1920s) gave extensive credit to these oligopolistic associations.[60] The Banco Italiano itself began in 1889 as an association of Italian merchants (Prefumo, Nosiglia, Fracchia, Orezzoli, Debernardi, Carbone, Botto, Mombello and Lertora), and in September 1895 obtained from the Banco del Callao a huge loan of S/62 500 to expand its own activities.

Associations represented a diminished risk to banks when allocating loans. This is the reason for the generous financing of the following by Lima banks: the protected textile, hat and match industries, the electrical trusts (Lima 1900, Callao 1902, Trujillo 1911, Cuzco 1917), water enterprises, associations of agriculturalists in Ica (1900), Piura (1912), Chincha (1904), cocaine producers' collectives (1906), Chinese merchants (from 1903), livestock companies and in general, prominent élite groups.

Analysis of the evolving composition of the boards of directors of local banks and insurance companies also reveals a tendency toward diversification of financial interests among the élite. Table 4.1 surveys

Table 4.1   Sectorial interests among directors of important financial institutions, 1890–1930

Year	Agriculture	Trade	Industry	Real Estate	Mining	Finance	Law/ Politics	Total
Banco del Callao/Perú y Londres:								
1889	–	10	1	–	–	1	2	14
1905	–	6	1	–	–	2	1	10
1925	2	3	–	–	1	2	1	9
1930	2	4	–	–	2	1	1	10
Banco Italiano:								
1889	1	8	–	–	–	–	–	9
1905	–	9	–	–	–	–	–	9
1922	1	5	3	–	–	4	–	13
1930	2	2	2	2	–	4	–	12
Banco Internacional:								
1897	4	2	–	1	–	–	–	7
1905	4	2	–	–	–	–	2	8
1921	2	2	–	1	2	–	4	11
1929	2	4	–	1	2	1	2	12
Banco Popular:								
1901	4	6	–	–	–	1	5	16
1921	3	2	–	–	2	–	1	8
Cía. Internacional (insurance):								
1895	2	8	1	–	–	2	–	13
1921	2	5	–	–	1	2	1	11
Cía. Rimac (insurance):								
1901	2	5	–	–	–	–	2	9
1920	2	6	–	–	–	1	2	11

Sources: Board of Directors' lists in *El Comercio*, *El Financista*, *El Economista* and the institutions' annual reports.

the main activities of the directors of some financial institutions between 1890 and 1930. Each institution's change in the composition of its directorship reflects interesting tendencies. The two largest banks, the Banco del Perú y Londres and the Banco Italiano, showed in the 1890s an overwhelming presence of merchants among their directors. Around 1922–5 the principal activities of the directors of these banks had already undergone significant changes. In this process of diversification away from the dominant trading interests, the

Banco del Perú y Londres was more consistently represented by agro-exporters and miners in the 1920s, whereas the Italiano's directors tended to concentrate their interests on industry and foreign (Italian) financial connections. This depicts the diverging pattern followed by both institutions: the first specialised in native export sectors and the second, heavily supported by foreign capital, in servicing the financial needs of the domestic market.

In contrast the Banco Internacional and the Banco Popular started with a majority representation from the agricultural, trade, legal and political sectors, and by 1920–30 had gained representation from mining and real estate interests. In 1901 the Banco Popular counted among its directors Manuel Sotomayor (president), an estate owner in Lima and the third largest tax payer, and the landowners Bartolomé Araoz, Carlos Gildemeister and Pablo Sarria; in 1897 the Banco Internacional had the miner and landowner Elías Mujica (as president), Alfredo Benavides (influential agro-exporter and owner in Puente de Piedra), and 'proprietors' Demetrio Olavegoya and Pedro Oliveira. The two selected insurance companies do not reveal great changes between 1900 and 1920. Both maintain an almost constant representation in agriculture and trade, and professional and political activities.

Some individuals who held leadership positions in local financial institutions started to specialise exclusively in financial activities. There was a noticeable increase in better-trained financiers among managers of financial institutions in the 1920s. José Payán and Pablo La Rosa dedicated their full time to the administration of the Banco del Perú y Londres and to training employees. Other financiers with strong professional backgrounds were Santiago Acuña (Seguros Rímac, Banco del Perú y Londres), F. Pérez de Velasco, Francisco Echenique (educated in Argentina, employee of the Mercantile Bank and later manager of the Banco Internacional), and Oscar Arrús (a government official trained in statistics in Argentina). Several foreign managers (Martin B. Wells, Paul Richarz, Paul Widmer) constituted another example of the foreign demonstration effect. They trained Peruvian banking employees working in local institutions. Other managers remained heavily attached to their concerns and group interests. Foreign and native financiers followed the recommended precepts for the good banker, according to a contemporary foreign specialist on the matter: 'Firmness, decisiveness, a cold and calm grasp . . . little imagination, a good memory and much dedication. He who has irritable nerves, an active imagination, or too sensitive a heart . . . ought to choose another profession'.[61]

Although groups based in the provinces did not achieve the degree of diversification of the coastal and Lima-based groups, the tendency towards diversification was emulated in major provincial cities. The Gibson (Arequipa) and Lomellini (Cuzco) groups seemed to have been the more diversified by the 1920s. Their concentration on trade, local credit-granting and faint-hearted efforts to form regional financial institutions show a trend towards the achievements of the coastal groups. Trade and trade-financing constituted the main avenue of capitalist penetration into the provinces just as it had on the coast.[62] The next step was the rationalisation of wool and cattle production.[63] Urban and industrial investments followed between 1910 and 1930.

The invasion of Lima by provincial groups seeking to expand their interests illustrates a completely new phenomenom in Peruvian society. The most relevant case in point was the group led by Antonio Calvo, a merchant from Cuzco who had accumulated considerable capital by the 1920s and decided to transfer part of it to Lima. Calvo became the most important stockholder of the Banco del Perú y Londres between 1926–30, but unfortunately this was bad timing as the bank shortly afterwards collapsed, in spite of having distributed high dividends until 1929. The Calvo group held 9525 shares, that is 23.2 per cent of the total shares represented in the bank's meeting of stockholders in 1929.[64]

Cooperation among the members of the Italian community to form new investor groups led to impressive achievements. Italian groups were especially successful in trade, banking, construction, industry, and agricultural produce for the internal market. They developed a very effective network of finance for small- and medium-sized producers. The Italian community in Lima was composed overwhelmingly of merchants (67 per cent in 1887 and 79 per cent in 1910) competing for a place in the reduced internal market. The rationalisation and diversification of these merchants' efforts were critical to their survival. The difficulties which arose were overcome by the development of cooperative associations[65] which encouraged a feeling of entrepreneurial partnership among the directing members. In the long term, the best results obtained by the Italian businessmen were related to the supply of goods to the domestic market. Without doubt Italian capitalists in Peru demonstrated the effectiveness of group formation, cooperation, oligopoly, thriftiness and diversification of mercantile capital. Prominent Italian groups included the following (listed according to their specialisation): trade – Isola, Orezzoli, Rezza; construction – Matellini, Mannarelli, Fabiani; industry – Raffo, Piaggio, Boggio; and agricultural produce for the internal market – Nosiglia, Nagaro, Valle, Unión Vinícola Chincha.[66]

Both provincial and immigrant groups exerted pressure on the powerful transitional coastal groups. Through effective competition, the newly constituted groups of provincial and foreign origin undeniably controlled important sections of the internal markets of Lima and the provinces.

ACHIEVEMENTS AND SHORTCOMINGS IN THE 1920s

By about 1920 the native élite had been able to develop, through its groups and financial institutions after a long period of competition with foreign interests, private financial autonomy for its core economic activities – the production and commercialisation of sugar and cotton, finance, urban real estate and certain manufacturing sectors. Native banks, insurance companies, and agricultural and livestock concerns financed by the Lima stock market had displaced foreign companies and institutions. However, autonomy had its costs. First, the élite groups had been unable to compete successfully against the huge foreign corporations in areas where the élite's financial capacity was inadequate. Such was the case with mining in the central sierra and petroleum on the north coast. Thus the loss of control over mineral resources and the loss of profits derived from them can be understood as *quid pro quo* for obtaining key economic activities elsewhere.

Secondly, in the 1920s the élite had to endure adverse international market conditions for its basic products: sugar and cotton. The 1921 post-war market contraction, natural disasters and declining prices had a depressive effect on the most important native agro-export concerns. This situation limited the possibilities for increased diversification of the élite's financial system. Thirdly, manufacturing continued to encounter great problems which hindered its adaptation and expansion: oligopolistic protection, the high purchase and installation cost of technology, and the lack of technical staff resulted in productive inefficiency which deterred native investors and allowed foreign penetration. Finally, attempts by the state to increase financial regulation and intervention had negative long-term effects.

With their reforms Leguía and his developmentalist bureaucrats and supporters (Fuchs, Salomón, Rodríguez Dulanto) tried to aid primarily Peruvian up-and-coming export, industrial and urban-based groups. These endeavours declined considerably after the 1921–2 export collapse.[67] Ultimately the state came to rely excessively on foreign loans because of foreign banks' eagerness to supply funds and because of agro-exporting difficulties, but not without first expanding the urban internal market and benefiting the élite groups oriented toward it. Leguía's financial edifice eventually started crumbling from the pressure exerted on the one side by his native agro-exporter protégés and, on the other, by American financiers.

Bertram plays down the positive achievements of the Peruvian economy and the élite in the 1920s. Instead he cites the negative effects of US corporations' control over the export sector, the failure of the élite in sugar specialisation, and Leguía's foreign indebtedness. These factors contributed to limit the number of industrial concerns in comparison with the 1890–1900 period, and caused the rewards to be gained from urban expansion to be channelled to American contractors (Foundation Company and Ley & Company). He does however portray a better case for the more entrepreneurial cotton growers.[68]

Other indices temper Bertram's pessimistic view of the 1920s. Migration contributed to increased urban demand in Lima and the provinces. Small savings accounts flourished in local banks before inflation set in in the late 1920s. Road construction led to the displacement of railways and tramways in urban and rural transportation. A transition from small cotton farms to large agro-industrial complexes was observable. The élite was able to maintain its relative financial autonomy until the late 1920s. Also, the appearance of heavily capitalised industrial concerns, in which domestic groups participated with foreign capital, helped to offset the decline in the quantity of industrial firms from the 1890–1900 period with a rise in the quality of such firms.

Large enterprises with mixed native and foreign participation obtained from Leguía exclusivity in the construction of roads, sanitation works, public buildings, refrigeration facilities, slaughter houses, and other works. The integration of productive and financial activities by the Foundation Company, Walton & Schmidt, Warren Bros and others, counted on the participation and emulation of several native groups. The most active and privileged was the Leguía group and its satellite groups. Luis F. Larco obtained a contract for constructing the road between Miraflores and Callao in April 1928;[69] the Banco del Perú y Londres organised and financed the firms Autovías y Pavimentos Miraflores, Antonio Castro, Castro e hijo, and Sociedad Benavides-Alvarez Calderón.[70] Alfredo Larrañaga, Leguía's son-in-law, was awarded the contract for the Lima–Ancón road in April 1929.[71] Likewise the native stockholders of the highly successful monopoly Cía. de Cemento Portland Peruana learnt of the advantages to be gained from large-scale enterprise and were planning others such as Leguía's strategic plan for a steel industrial complex, which was to be 'founded on a great scale'.[72] In spite of the heavy criticism of Leguía's administration,[73] his infrastructural work facilitated, before it was abruptly interrupted, an increase in urban business and a considerable expansion of the internal market.

Some agriculturists, especially those with cotton growing interests, took advantage of the declining exchange rate to diversify from what could be seen as dangerous over-specialisation; first from sugar to cotton and finance, and later to industrial concerns such as cotton by-products and the production of construction materials. The most successful examples were Miguel Echenique, Demetrio Olavegoya, Pedro Larrañaga, Luis Albizuri, Santiago Poppe, Carlos Cillóniz, Calixto Romero, the Colomas and Solars. These men, protected by Leguía, constituted the new generation of economic and financial managers of the domestic élite groups. Successful miners (Fernandini, Gallo Porras, Mujica) shared the gains and participated in the diversification during the 1920s. The clients of the Banco Italiano also prospered during Leguía's term of office. Other less successful agro-exporters had to sell out to foreign interests despite their strong connections with Leguía, as in the cases of Víctor Larco Herrera and the owners of Sociedad Agrícola Paramonga. Also, the immobilisation of a large part of the Banco del Perú y Londres' credit resulting from its agricultural specialisation contributed decisively to the bank's bankruptcy in 1930–1. In the 1930s the agro-exporter representatives skillfully delayed repayment of their debts throughout the slow liquidation of the Banco del Perú y Londres. This was concurrent with a *de facto* moratorium on repayment of the public foreign debt.

ELITE GROUPS AFTER 1930

After the end of the world depression, Peruvian élite groups continued the trend toward diversification and establishing strategic links with local banks. Perhaps the most important change was the rising financial importance of those groups which in the previous period had specialised in industry and servicing the internal market, and which had gradually replaced in importance those groups with exceedingly heavy agro-export commitments.

However the rise of inward-oriented groups also meant enhanced oligopolisation. Instead of an expanding and diversifying élite, fewer groups controlled the links between the industrial and the financial sectors. Other groups became subordinate to the new arrangements between industrialists, bankers and the state. As a result, after 1930 the leverage of the private sector had reduced in comparison with the earlier period. The new industrial and importing groups increasingly relied on state protection for the defence of their interests.

Groups based on agro-export activities continued to have a degree of influence, although this was much diminished. Agro-exporters made demands to the state and orchestrated political campaigns. They managed to secure from the state, through the Banco Agrícola, limited credit for their economic activities. Some of the provincial groups linked to cotton production improved substantially their situation by integrating and diversifying their firms, as well as using 'habilitación' business to concentrate land under their control. The most successful provincial groups followed the already established pattern of diverting their funds to Lima banks, such as in the well-studied case of the Romero group, which became involved with the Banco de Crédito from 1950–1.[74]

From 1930 there was an overall relative decline in the importance of over-specialised groups of agro-exporters, who became allied to or merged with groups oriented towards the internal market. The best examples of this were those groups with a strong involvement in commercial agriculture who were closely linked to the Banco Popular in the 1940s. This bank ranked behind the Banco Italiano but had been able to survive bankruptcy in the 1930s. Among its directors were important heads of landowning families, who acted in coordination with groups such as the Prado which were enjoying rising industrial and political power. According to Portocarrero, the Banco Popular facilitated the financing of the Prado's industrial concern by channelling funds from the agro-export sector.[75] This was probably the reason why it escaped the fate of the Banco del Perú y Londres in the 1930s.

Out of 203 investor groups in Peru identified in Maushammer's study for the period 1950–65, 44 specialised in agriculture, 28 in real estate, 22 in commerce, 18 in industry (textiles, food and drinks), and 12 in fishmeal production.[76] The relative decline of agro-export groups, and the rise of élite groups oriented toward the internal market, however, is evidenced by information on the élite's wealth composition. According to a recent study based on quantitative information on inheritances, among more than two hundred of the wealthiest Peruvians there was a decline from 28 per cent to 14 per cent in the élite's share of financial assets between 1916–32 and 1950–9. There was also a decline in their agricultural assets, from 23 per cent to 20 per cent. On the other hand there was an increase in their industrial assets, from 4 per cent to 14 per cent, and their commercial assets, from 8 per cent to 13 per cent. All the remaining percentages of their rural, urban, mining and luxury assets remained almost unchanged.[77]

This evidence on the inverse relationship between the rise in industrial and industrially-related commercial assets and the decline in financial and agro-export resources after 1930, is consistent with the information on credit allocation by commercial bank by economic sector provided in Chapter 3. Thus investment in financial assets was apparently not a sound alternative for the élite by 1950. Most probably this was due to the adverse consequences of inflation on domestic finance. Elite groups seemed to benefit more as borrowers and allies of unsound and state-sponsored macroeconomic policies than as savers and independent forces in policy making. This adaptive tendency seems to have been reinforced in the 1960s and 1970s.[78]

In conclusion, the Peruvian élite undertook changes in several times of crisis using modern and rational methods of managerial and financial manipulation in response to serious external threats that endangered its existence (war, foreign competition, declines in export prices, shortages of resources, state intervention). Grouping and the association of élite interests had brought about a shift in emphasis from trade and agriculture to finance, manufacturing and urban expansion by 1930. Different stages in the formation of investor groups, from the most traditional to the clearly modern, facilitated the transfer of funds from the export sector to urban investments and resulted in the expansion of the domestic market. Elite groups utilised native financial institutions to their advantage in the application of inter-twining and conciliatory financial policy resolutions. Those families and incipient groups that were unable to successfully emulate foreign entrepreneurial examples and thus form investment group concerns were replaced by more resourceful representatives of the élite.

Thus it is misleading to portray the Peruvian élite as a retardant social class which hindered development. Nor is it apt to consider Peruvian financial institutions as simple recipients of rentier funds unable to promote modernisation. Their contribution before 1914 to group formation by providing credit support to domestic associations, cartels and oligopolies prepared the conditions for the consolidation and diversification of the élite's economic power. However, the exist-ence of a dynamic élite was not in itself sufficient for capitalist development.[79]

The moves toward autonomy by agro-exporters led to dangerous overspecialisation in agricultural concerns during periods of adverse export conditions (1921, 1925–7). This was the price they paid in their search for financial and credit independence. There were other nega-tive aspects arising from an excessive reliance on foreign financial capital and loss of control in the mining and petroleum sectors. Between 1930 and 1950 élite groups benefiting from import-substi-tution industrialisation and unsound financial policies contributed to the increased oligopolisation of the domestic market. The parallel growth of state intervention and the élite's adaptation to it nurtured the authori-tarian and economic dangers experienced by Peru in later decades. Regional and income inequalities were major set-backs in the general process of financial concentration – this will be analysed in Chapter 5. Thus, in spite of the capitalist efforts of the Peruvian élite, the limited opportunities for greater development opened in the 1884–1950 period were not taken complete advantage of.

5 Financial Aspects of Regional and Income Inequalities

In analysing the developmental consequences of financial activities, recent studies rarely consider the effect they have on regional areas and on income distribution. Emphasis has been placed rather on the role of financial systems in mobilising and allocating financial assets, or on discussing the proper regulation of and legal environment for financial efficiency.[1] However a study which aims to assess the historical contribution by the financial sector in an underdeveloped economy must also assess the locational and distributional consequences. Development is not only measured in terms of economic growth, but also in terms of a long-term improvement in the living conditions of the majority of the population[2] and the overcoming of regional disparities.[3] Consequently this chapter will assess the contributions or distortions introduced by financial development in Peru's various regions, as well as in income and wealth distribution between 1900 and 1950.

Two recurrent arguments have been employed to deny that positive developmental contributions have been made by the Peruvian financial structure. In the first place, the concentration and centralisation of financial and banking activities in Lima, and the rather weak financial presence in the rest of the provinces, are cited as evidence of a negative, or at best, negligible impact on the national economy.[4] Secondly, the abysmal inequality of wealth distribution in Peru is said to have been reinforced by an oligarchical financial tradition uninterested in the financial and social needs of the popular sectors.[5] These two views will be tested in this chapter by considering relevant evidence on the regional and distributional impact of private financial institutions, élite groups and public finance.

I contend, first, that efforts to overcome regional isolation were significantly aided by complementary informal and formal commercial credit, and partly by public infrastructural works carried out in the 1920s and 1930s. However in the 1940s and 1950s, with a disproportionate allocation of credit in and migration to Lima, a pattern of regional concentration was intensified. Secondly, with respect to the contribution of domestic finance towards better income distribution, I find that both private and public finance undoubtly fared poorly in the few attempts to redress the historical pattern of income and wealth concentration.

This chapter first discusses some of the general aspects underlying unequal regional development in Peru between 1884 and 1950. It then proceeds to treat in detail the main spatial characteristics of groups and financial institutions, together with their centralist and regionalist connections, with special reference to each of the major regions. A look at the political decisions and conflicts on the issue of regional finance complements the examination of the declining isolation of regions during the period. Subsequently a brief discussion of the weak attempts at regional banking leads to the treatment of perhaps the most successful financial business at the core of regional concentration of credit, the mortgage and real estate activities in Lima. Finally, an evaluation of the financial activities of small savers and investors provides the basic criteria for assessing the financial effects on income distribution.

THE DECLINE IN REGIONAL ISOLATION

There is considerable debate on whether Peruvian regional integration advanced during the period 1884–50. Doubt is cast on the ability of contemporary developmental efforts to establish links between the isolated hinterlands and the core areas of the export economy.

Those who observe a lack of national cohesion in Peru have a good case for the early part of the period, but fail to recognise a trend toward capitalist integration that had advanced decisively by 1940. Important elements which served to diminish the isolation of the regions have only recently been detected. These took place at a time (1914–29) when modern national integration, already delayed by capitalist standards, was not incompatible with new versions of imperialism.[6]

Following Mariátegui's hasty conclusion that domestic banks 'have a limited scope, and are closely tied to the interests of foreign capital and large agrarian properties',[7] it has been argued that the Peruvian financial system contributed to the marked concentration of financial resources in the Lima region. Financial activities in Lima, the argument continues, neglected the needs of and links with other regions. The regional élite ('oligarchies') in important provinces established close financial and trade links with foreign merchants and companies rather than with Lima's businessmen; enclaves or regional economies with primarily foreign connections resulted, and regional fragmentation prevailed over national integration.[8] The validity of these assertions needs to be examined through a detailed consideration of the concepts and historical evidence on regional development.

An underdeveloped region can be defined by features of its population, productive specialisation, transportation networks, domestic market, pre-capitalist components, social classes, local politics, and its national and international links.[9] A region is therefore not only an economic unit but also a societal and political entity. The political and cultural loyalty of social groups to their region is determined to a large extent by the specific economic conditions of the region. Conversely, nationalism, the ideological answer of those sectors pressing for national economic expansion (among other things), strives to integrate scattered regions into the sphere of attraction of growth poles.[10]

The first phase of modern development and social change within a region are those related to efforts to reorganise the production and social structures according to the demands of external markets.[11] Theoretically, productive specialisation results from the exploitation of underutilised local resources and the attraction of extra-regional capital. A region that enters this critical process before other regions becomes a growth pole and quickly diverges from the national average of productive specialisation, urban population and division of labour. Eventually a financial system develops in the growth pole through internal accumulation. This may or may not foster change in other regions. As a consequence of this irreversible capitalist rationale, inequality in initial regional development is unavoidable.[12]

The second phase of regional economic development is the gradual decline in the relative productive specialisation of leading regions towards a more diversified and geographically balanced national economic base. Transportation networks play an important role both in economic integration and in overcoming regional disparities.[13] I argue that this second phase of regional development was never completed in Peru. Lima and its region kept its supremacy and concentration while the regions of the northern coast and sierra, central sierra, southern sierra and eastern jungle lagged behind in varying degrees despite an improvement in transport. Peruvian national integration did not overcome regional inequalities the way the modernising European states did in the nineteenth century.

However it should be also stressed that the truncated regional development in Peru overcame regional isolation, separatism and dismemberment due to factors which have not been sufficiently studied.[14]

The Lima region already had the advantage over the rest of the country by the end of the Guano Age. Coastal regions benefited the most from Lima's growth. Also, regional responses to Lima's growth have been detected as early as the guano boom period in both the northern coast and sierra, and the central highlands through the expansion of market demand and internal credit.[15] The War of the Pacific delayed further capitalist penetration into the interior provinces. Just after the war, native economic retrogression led to a relatively strong presence of foreign capital and credit and increased separation of the regions. However Klarén and Mallon have demonstrated that by the 1920s native and foreign capital had stimulated capitalist penetration, which transformed the regional economies of the northern coast, central coast and central highlands.[16] In the southern highlands during the same period, according to specialists, this process was less successful.[17] Let us observe the magnitude and trend of such differentiated transformations according to available indicators.

According to national statistics for the census years 1876, 1940, 1961 and 1972 – as processed and analysed in recent quantitative studies[18] – the evolution in the percentage of 'urban' population (in towns of more than 2000 inhabitants) was, respectively, 16.8, 26.9, 40.1 and 53.2 per cent. For the population of cities of more than 20 000 persons the corresponding transition was 6, 14.8, 27, and 40.8 per cent. Thus between 1876 and 1940 Peruvian cities grew 2.5 times while the national population grew 2.6 times. This must be considered a key modernising factor despite the fact that even in the 1920s and 1930s endemic diseases in the coastal regions and urban centres affected migration from the highlands, while in the 1940s and 1950s health conditions on the coast improved much more rapidly than in earlier decades.[19]

Moreover the population of Lima grew from approximately 100 000 inhabitants in 1876 to 407 662 in 1940, an increase of 400 per cent. Between 1908 and 1940 Lima's population had grown by 285 per cent, far exceeding the national average of city urban growth. Lima's and Callao's urban growth was the most outstanding feature in the process of modernisation during the period. An important part of this growth was the result of internal migration, which started with the most prominent élite families from the provinces. In comparison, the city of Cuzco's population doubled between 1912 (pop. 19 825) and 1940 (40 657).[20] The growth in urban population was due primarily to the attraction of rural inhabitants to the specialised growth poles, and the improvement in national infrastructure and transportation.

Productive specialisation became the most salient characteristic of the coastal region. The northern coast specialised in sugar production, but gradually developed its regional hinterland through modern mining and cattle farming. The central coast, which had better communications with Lima, specialised in cotton and sugar production. Lima was the trade, financial and service centre. The central sierra specialised increasingly and very rapidly in technologically advanced mining, as well as coffee production on its eastern slopes, which had linkage effects on the surrounding valleys.

The southern region, however, dedicated extensive rather than intensive efforts to sheep wool and alpaca fibre production for the fluctuating export trade without significant improvements in efficiency until the 1930s. The traditional wool-producing area of Puno was linked primarily to the commercial centre of Arequipa, and to the rather limited highland textile manufacturing pole of Cuzco. The eastern provinces of Cuzco eventually specialised in rubber (until the bust of 1913) and coffee, providing a profitable export trade serviced by the city of Cuzco.

The eastern jungle or Amazonian region at first specialised in unorganised rubber exploitation, but regressed after 1913 into secular isolation. This was the least integrated of all the regions, and its territory was disputed by neighbouring nations. The short-lived rubber boom did not allow an adequate accumulation of surplus to finance diversification. Labour costs were very high, and this discouraged investment in other activities. The lack of lasting integration inhibited the participation of groups with centralist financial backing. By way of illustration, in 1913 the Banco del Perú y Londres had closed its branch in Iquitos (formerly the second trading port in the country) leaving a foreign bank, the Commercial Bank of Spanish America, as the only institution to provide financial services in the area until the 1920s.[21]

By 1920 the nation's network of interior transportation and communications was still limited. Steam navigation was the main means of transportation between coastal ports and cities, being cheaper than the undeveloped interior land transportation.[22] Even so the smaller ports had conspicuously backward facilities. It was again Callao which set the pace in port improvements, followed by Salaverry, Cerro Azul and Mollendo (the main outlets for sugar, cotton and wool exports, respectively), to meet the increase in ocean transportation. Lima, as the principal market, was the main beneficiary of the ocean transportation system because smaller ports relied on Callao for the transhipment of and demand for their products as a consequence of the lack of railroads and highways. However medium sized ports were able to export directly abroad. The port of Salaverry exported considerable quantities of high grade silver to New York, and Mollendo handled wool exports to Europe in the 1920s.

Railroads were few; the majority were controlled by foreign interests and ran from the coast to the highlands, rather than down the coast or following Andean valleys. Railways have been seen as part of the failure to bring about regional integration by causing disruption in traditional internal markets and contributing to Lima's centralism.[23] Railroad expansion did not progress much in later years due to delays in its construction, poor economic results and, eventually, competition from motorways. Poor results in backward (except for wages) and forward (except for copper production) linkages have been identified by Miller.[24] Probably the best results were obtained by urban railways and tramway before 1913, when the first Ford motorcar arrived in Peru and competition by bus transportation developed soon after. However it is difficult to argue that railways did not contribute at all to the initial though limited integration of isolated coastal regions with their highland hinterlands.

By the 1920s car and truck transportation and highway construction were booming. Although minimally studied, the few works on the subject consider truck transportation especially as having had a 'progressive' effect on the Peruvian highland regions.[25] The commercial firms acting as sales agents for Ford, Hudson and Dodge cars (A. C. Shumway & Company, Graham Rowe, Tirado), contributed to the expansion in the use of cars and motorways. Advertising slogans such as 'modern roads mean prosperity, wealth and national progress' appeared increasingly on Lima's billboards and in its publications in the 1920s.[26] Highways radically reduced the cost of transportation and connected regions previously isolated from each other. At first highways sprouted in all directions from the most important cities. Lima and Trujillo expanded their communications to all cardinal points. Highways penetrating the highlands, such as the Trujillo–Tayabamba, Lima–Chosica, Lima–Canta and Ica–Puquio highways, and sections of the jungle Pichis trail (Cerro–Huánuco), successfully complemented the limited railroad incursion into the interior.[27]

A road building policy was formulated as early as 1916 by the Cuerpo de Ingenieros de Caminos. There was no better example of the new economic opportunities (lower transportation costs, time saving, real estate valorisation) opened by this new system of transportation than the network which, in the course of not more than five or six years (1919–25), connected old Lima with Callao, Miraflores, Magdalena and Chosica via the avenues Progreso, Leguía, Magdalena, Miramar and Ejército.[28] Probably the local developer who benefited the most from the road development in Lima was Tomás Marsano, an Italian resident who – apart from his financial interests in Cía. de Seguros La Nacional and mines in Castrovirreyna – profited greatly from his urban speculation, the Urbanizadora Surquillo in Miraflores. The value of real estate near the Avenida Leguía rose from 30 Peruvian cents per square meter of land in 1918 to S/10 in 1923, a rise of 3333 per cent in only five years. The average increase in Lima's real estate values was approximately 90 per cent between 1913 and 1923.[29]

Rudimentary highways were cheap to open and their construction was spontaneously undertaken by enthusiastic highlanders. Under Leguía's regime road construction was centralised and boosted as a result of the 1920 *Ley de Conscripción Vial*. Critics of this legal measure point out that local authorities committed excesses in the recruitment and use of Indian labour for private purposes. The abusive execution of the conscription law may have contributed to protests by the Indians. Wilson finds that peasant communities near Tarma had lost their enthusiasm for road construction by 1927. They were unwilling to work on road projects outside their own territories, causing the authorities to use force in the labour recruitment process.[30]

In the meantime driving had become a national sport and a source of adventure for drivers of sturdily-built cars who braved dangerous and precarious terrain. A road between Ica and Puquio was said to have been made accessible to a single car in just 45 days, enabling its driver to establish yet another contemporary record in distance covered. Highway development swiftly erradicated other transportation alternatives, such as the curious project to use camels to cross coastal deserts.[31]

With time the transition from spontaneous road construction gave way to technical improvement in highway construction that was relatively easy to finance and execute. Under President Leguía around 10 000 miles of roads were constructed, while Benavides' *Plan Vial* effectively completed or upgraded 3700 miles. Benavides also claimed 4000 additional miles of road renovation.[32] The Peruvian section of the Pan American Highway and the Central Highway (1935) were completed under Benavides. Trucking – an activity undertaken by a growing provincial petit bourgeoisie who owned US trucks – can be considered as an important forward linkage of motorways.[33]

Commercial aviation also performed what might have seemed amazing services at the time. American and French missions helped to diffuse military and commercial aviation and aerial photography. The American pilot Elmer Faucett was a pioneer in inaugurating air routes (for example Lima–Iquitos), as well as being one of the first aviation entrepreneurs in Peru. Money transfers by plane to productively dynamic isolated areas became a common practice. One pilot flying his aircraft was shot at by bandits who apparently were aware of the contents of his cargo – the weekly payroll of the Pampas Imperial irrigation project.[34] Radio also became a modern technological innovation to improve internal communications.

Even before the widespread use of cars and planes the Lima-based banking system had developed a network of provincial branches which facilitated fund transfers to and from Lima, and between traditional and modern sectors within particular regions. A sample of clients of the provincial branches of the Banco del Perú y Londres in the late 1920s shows that creditors were in the main traditional savers (ecclesiastical, rentier institutions, widows) while debtors who received loans were principally merchants and exporters.[35] Branches of the Banco del Perú y Londres dominated the provincial banking business. Other banks tried to follow suit, but only the Banco del Perú y Londres was able to expand its network beyond the major provincial cities of Trujillo, Ica, Arequipa and Mollendo until its bankruptcy in 1930. The bulk of the flow of capital to and from the provinces passed, however, through informal élite group mechanisms that employed increasingly the services of branches of commercial banks. This complementation of formal and informal finance contributed greatly to the initial integration of capital markets, commerce and export production. This allowed an important degree of capital transfer in spite of the limitations of the Peruvian means of communications. The financial contribution of élite provincial groups to regional specialisation and interregional complementation will be analysed next.

GROUPS, REGIONS AND FINANCIAL CONCENTRATION

There have been many attempts to explain the considerable contrasts in Peruvian regional development. The explanations traditionally used include the obstacles posed by geographical barriers, the lack of means of communication, imperialist enclaves and Lima's economic and political centralism. I propose instead to explore the financial mechanisms developed by the local élite to overcome constraints, consolidate regional areas and hinterlands, and diversify their private resources. How did the élite use commercial credit, group association and domestic financial institutions, and to what degree did they oppose or collaborate with foreign capital? I argue that discussing these financial mechanisms can help to explain the unequal regional development as being not just a purely negative factor, but rather a reality akin to capitalist penetration.

By 1919 a capitalist core, which had strong ties with some interior provinces, had developed in Lima. The main strength of this core was the initiative of an active minority who developed group networks of activity in export-oriented production, urban markets, real estate and finance, as described in Chapter 4.[36] The principal means by which these groups were able to start penetrating and consolidating in provincial areas was through the import–export trade, agro-industrial stock companies (*sociedades* and *negociaciones*), and the granting of credit to small provincial producers (*habilitación*). Initially the strongest links existed between the Lima-based groups and the central coast, the central sierra, and the north coast. The *sociedades agrícolas* and *ganaderas* were able to tap capital from the Lima stock exchange, commercial companies and banks with relative ease between 1915 and 1929. The most important *sociedades* to raise capital in Lima (by the amount of their capital in 1921) were the Santa Bárbara complex, which included the Cerro Azul port in Cañete and which was controlled by the Osma–Beltrán groups (capital: Lp300 000); Puente Piedra in the Carabayllo valley near Lima, controlled by the Vargas Sariego and Mujica y Carassa groups (Lp150 000); Paramonga, controlled by the Alvarez Calderón group (Lp100 000); Ingenio Central Azucarero Huaura, controlled by the Ayulo group and Banco del Perú y Londres; and San Nicolás in Supe and Barranca, controlled by the Ayulo and Miró Quesada groups and the Banco del Perú y Londres.

Probably the best results of the transfer of funds to dynamic provinces through the financial intermediation of groups and institutions were obtained in the Pisco–Ica area south of Lima. Financial backing allowed Pisco and Ica to become both commercial centres and active areas of cotton production forwardly linked with cotton oil and soap manufacturing. Vineyards, traditional in Pisco and Ica since colonial times, were uprooted to give way to cotton plantations. 'The principal business houses are branches of well known Lima firms, engaged in export and import trade; buying cotton and other products of the country and selling machinery and supplies to the estates which produce them'.[37] Ica's prosperity was measured at the time by the existence of four daily newspapers, the diversified production of cotton, corn, wine and beef, and the presence of cotton gins, oil mills and soap factories.[38] The Banco del Perú y Londres and the Banco Italiano had branches there and these reported good results to their headquarters in the 1920s. Cotton production was also successful in Cañete, more so after the completion of the irrigation project, Pampas Imperial, and the Lima–Cañete road, which was initiated and funded by the Leguía government.[39]

Two revealing examples illustrate the important role of the Lima-based élite groups in integrating central coastal production, trade and financing with the financial centre of Lima by 1921. The society Coloma, Rehder y Cía., which had its commercial headquarters in Lima, was a good client of banks and had no trouble in obtaining commercial credit for its business. This business consisted mainly of organising the production of cotton in the company's estates in Chincha (Sociedad Agrícola Hoja Redonda among others), and the industrial processing of cotton by-products (oil, soap) in a new factory (Fábrica El Triunfo). The firm complemented its productive activities by transporting its products via its own steamship company, the Cía. de Cabotaje La Veloz, from the port facilities of Tambo de Mora which were also under the company's control. In addition it was involved in the wholesale and retail trading of national and imported products in Lima and the provinces, offered a sales service for consignments from small cotton producers; and – most important with respect to our argument – *habilitación* (agricultural financing) business on a systematic basis in the valleys of Pisco, Ica, Cañete and Lurín.[40]

Similar activities were carried out by Barber, Vargas y Cía. – a firm controlled by the Vargas Sariego group – which had its headquarters in Lima, interests in Cía. de Seguros Victoria, and agencies in Callao, Pisco and Chimbote. The group also had controlling interests in the sugar-producing *sociedades agrícolas* Puente de Piedra and Tambo Real in Chimbote, as well as a strong *habilitación* business.[41]

The evolution of the *habilitación* business in the agro-export estates of the coast is illustrated by the case of the cotton-producing Hacienda Palto. In 1903 the lending and advancing of cash to the estate's tenants by third parties was permitted by the owners, the Aspíllaga family. The administrator was the main *habilitador*, who was supplied with capital by Venn, Vargas & Company. The land-owners preferred the financing system of *compañeros*, by which the landlord contributed land, water, tools, seeds and half the cost of the cotton harvest and the compañero provided the labour and sold his share of the cotton to the landlord. However by 1918 the Aspíllagas had enough funds to provide profitable *habilitación* at 10 per cent interest to their own tenants, who had to sell to the landlords the cotton produced and deliver it to cotton factories in Pisco.[42] The *habilitación* business not only allowed relatively efficient fund transfers to the export-producing provinces but was also instrumental in a responsive 'restructuring' (from sugar to cotton production) of the commercial agricultural sector as a result of the effects of the 1929–32 crisis.[43]

The northern coastal region, which was further away from the capital, developed a relative autonomy without losing its connections with Lima. In the valleys of Chicama, Moche, Virú, Saña and Lambayeque the sugar plantations were not only highly capitalised, specialised and technologically advanced, but had also diversified in the interests of self-sufficiency. The *haciendas* and estates in the province of La Libertad were described by an observer in 1923 as '[each] a little principality unto itself, with its own shops, schools, towns, government, and, in the case of the big sugar estates, with their own railways'.[44] These technified landed estates (*latifundia*), together with the increasing trade in exports, were pointed out by a contemporary as being the source of agrarian dislocation and responsible for the displacement of small owners and merchants since 1914.[45]

The most important sugar complexes, such as Negociación Agríco-la Chicama Limitada (known before 1919 as the Sociedad Agrícola Casa Grande) which was controlled by the Gildemeister group, the Negociación Azucarera Laredo (Chopitea group), Chiclín (Larco group), Negociación Tumán (Pardo group), and Pomalca (Piedra group), were able to diversify part of their assets into cattle raising, alfalfa and grain production. This seems to have resulted in a degree of protection against the worst effects of the depression of the 1930s.

Chicama, the most advanced concern in the selective breeding of cattle, controlled a 425 000 acre property in Cajamarca (Andina concern). This provided diversification against possible falls in the price of sugar, complementation of resources to reduce labour costs by providing cheap food for workers, commercial use of Andean lands, and integration of highland areas into the coastal commercial and productive sphere. The sugar complexes were well served by railways, roads and port facilities and the financial centre of Lima provided abundant financing for development.

Another outstanding example of a diversified native sugar concern well connected with the financial centre of Lima was the firm Viuda de Piedra e Hijos, founded in 1905. From the beginning it received credit from the Banco del Perú y Londres. It had commercial import–export headquarters in Lima where Enrique de la Piedra, one of the owners, was a director of the Banco Popular as well as a Leguiísta politician and Senator for Lambayeque between 1911 and 1928.[46] The company had agencies in Chiclayo, Callao, Pimentel and Huacho. In the Chiclayo area its estates Pomalca and Collud produced sugar, Naranjal produced rice, and its factory produced chocolate using cocoa from Cajamarca. Its Udima property in the province of Hualgayoc, Cajamarca, raised cattle. It also owned the majority of the stock of Pimentel's port facilities and railway, administered the local customs agency, and managed its own steamship company. In addition it developed with 'abundant capital' an *habilitación* network in the provinces by providing credit to small producers of rice and cereals.[47]

Sugar production enabled Trujillo to develop into an important commercial centre. Urban development and road construction promised to make Trujillo 'a future motorist's paradise'.[48] Merchant intermediaries supplied the necessary imported equipment and also represented financial institutions from the capital. Ludowieg y Cía., established in 1872, was one of the most powerful commercial firms. Julio C. Ludowieg, born in Peru, formed a partnership with a Trujillo notable, Juan Julio Ganoza, in 1914. The firm's extensive trading activities took place not only in Trujillo but throughout the northern provinces: La Libertad, Cajamarca and Ancash. It kept branches in Chimbote, Quiruvilca, Chusgón and Pataz, and also owned mining and agricultural interests (Sociedad Agrícola y Ganadera Chusgón and Empresa Aurífera Pataz Ltda). Ludowieg also represented a number of special agencies of Lima's insurance companies, the Banco Alemán Transatlántico and the Banco Popular.[49]

The mining activity was very important in linking the northern highland area with the north coast. Although not as developed as in the central highlands, the mining of vanadium, silver and gold attracted foreign capital and native initiative. The Northern Peru Mining & Smelting Corporation (NPM&S Corporation, a subsidiary of the American Smelting & Refining Corporation), controlled the mining centres of Salpo and Hualgayoc through long-term leases on the properties of native miners Boza, Orbegoso, Piaggio and Boggio.[50] The corporation was able to develop infrastructure and back-linkage effects between the highlands and the coast. The Hacienda Motil, between Millauchaqui and Quiruvilca, was integrated into the Northern Peru complex through a lease from the Orbegoso family – owners of the *hacienda* Chiquitoy – thus providing necessary timber, meat and other foodstuffs for the corporation's mining sites: 'Abundant labour for the hacienda is procured from the Indian owner occupants of the neighbouring "chacaras", who prefer working during their spare time on the hacienda than in the mines, their preference for the hacienda being so great that wages in the mines are about three times higher than in the hacienda'.[51] The NPM&S Corporation had interests in other regions of Peru and counted with the services of the Alvarez Calderón group, very active in the transfer of funds to and from the financial and service sectors of Lima. Alfredo Alvarez Calderón was an executive of the NPM&S Corporation in 1926, as well as an organiser of the joint venture of the Frigorífico Nacional and participant in a project for an industrial bank which had substantial capital support from the Foundation Company.[52]

The native group Boza Aizcorbe Hermanos was competitive in the mining of silver in the northern region. Héctor Boza, a mining engineer who graduated from the Rolla School of Mines in Missouri, was able to develop the highly productive La Guardia mine in the Salpo river district, fifty miles from Trujillo. The Boza firm introduced its own innovative transportation system using cable cars, railway and road from the mining site to the technologically advanced Challuococha mill, a total distance of 25 miles. The mill was highly efficient and obtained 94 per cent silver extraction from minerals. In five years this mining complex was able to produce silver worth four million dollars, part of which was exported directly to New York from Trujillo. All of Boza's installation works were built without foreign investment and, according to a reporter, 'without resorting to borrowing or by hypothecation to finance the various operations'.[53] This is a clear case of local accumulation made possible by profitable and efficient production within the framework of an integrated private concern and a relatively modernised regional economy.

However in March 1924 the Boza firm struck a deal with the NPM&S Corporation – a twenty-year lease of the La Guardia silver and gold mine for one million dollars and 30 per cent of the Challuococha mill's return for the same period.[54] Although the Boza firm had been financially self-sufficient an offer like that was too good to resist. It seems therefore that mining (as well as the oil exploitation of Tumbes) provided native proprietors with a considerable income from rent. For the northern regional economy this seems to have had modernising effects similar to those observed in the central highlands. By the 1930s it appears that Boza had dissipated his fortune, although at the time he was active in politics and a member of the Fernandini syndicate.[55]

The development of mining in La Libertad's highlands served as a stimulus for construction of the Trujillo–Quiruvilca (later Otuzco) highway. Thus the northern region became connected with the sierra regions of Cajamarca and La Libertad through integrated estates, trade, native and foreign mining companies and recently developed highways. A recent study of Cajamarca's economic evolution challenges the idea of a pre-capitalist agricultural sector and emphasises the impact of the capitalist development of the northern coast on Cajamarca's highlands from 1900–35. Coastal markets were supplied with cereal and sundry agricultural production from Cajamarca. Commercial expansion and agricultural innovation in the area was financed with credit from Lima and Trujillo.[56] Increased specialisation in cattle around the city of Cajamarca was well advanced by 1944.[57]

In the sierra central region the Cerro de Pasco Corporation and the Peruvian Corporation, which controlled mining centres and railways respectively, were able to establish their integrated communication with Lima and Callao as early as the 1900s. With few exceptions, local mine owners were displaced by multinational capital.[58] However the foreign mining corporation still relied on local labour recruitment (*enganche*), in which local agents advanced cash to prospective workers in exchange for a binding commitment to work in the mines. Following a similar practice as in the modernising northern region, the use of credit in *enganche* combined coercion and monetary incentives to diminish peasant resistance to proletarianisation.[59] Complementary services provided by the local élite reinforced the transformation within peasant communities, villages and towns of the region.

The creation of new opportunities for the regional élite smoothed the process of foreign and capitalist penetration. Native mining owners who had sold out (Gallo Diez, Bentín, Proaño, Rizo Patrón, Tealdo) made an easy transition to investment in sectors other than mining.[60] The *enganchadores* and indigeneous merchants were able to combine contracts with the US corporation and tie their trading activities to the increasing urban demand in Lima and Huancayo. Cattle, wheat, aguardiente, and coffee production and trade allowed local accumulation of capital and land, and diversification of private interests. Native credit systems developed, as in the case of the Camacho and Arellano groups. According to Wilson, indigenous and immigrant 'credit hierarchies' should be seen as part of the same process of expansion in regional finance.[61] Peasant communities, of whose members a growing number worked in the mines, increased their participation in the regional market.

The regional élite thus reinforced its capacity for capitalist penetration in the area by taking advantage of the modernisation of the regional economy to enhance the efficiency of the livestock industry of the Olavegoya, Alvarez Calderón and Valladares groups, such as the *sociedades ganaderas* Junín and del Centro, funded by capital from the Lima Exchange.[62] In addition the regional élite diversified and modernised those native mining concerns which survived foreign competition, and profited from their activities (Fernandini, Proaño, Bentín groups).[63] Probably the most successful among the miners was Eulogio Fernandini who was able to resist the Cerro de Pasco Corporation by diversifying and complementing his mining assets (silver, copper, bismuth, mercury and coal mines) with foundries (Fundición Huaraucaca, 1900), electricity generators, and livestock and agricultural concerns in the central highlands and in valleys near Lima,[64] using 'a complex combination of collaboration and competition' with foreign capital.[65]

The élite in the central highlands also expanded local trade and money lending in the growing regional market, as in the cases of the Travezón, Alonso, and Calmell del Solar groups which gradually acquired agricultural properties that had been foreclosed due to debt.[66] As early as 1908 some members of the élite formed industrial concerns, in particular textile mills but also electrical, telephone and cereal milling oligopolies. An important industrial concern, the Sociedad Industrial Huancayo Limitada, by 1919 owned electrical, telephone, urban development, and wheat and barley milling concerns, the required capital of Lp40 000 having been raised by Salvador Nesanovich, José Hanza, Augusto Zapatero, Mateo Galjuf and Juan Bákula who had financial connections with Lima.[67] In the 1940s the Prado and Pardo groups based in Lima took control of the textile production previously held by textile factories established after 1927. In 1947 there were thirteen factories in Huancayo.[68]

One important aspect of the central highland's dominant élite was its strong contacts with the Lima financial market, through the local branches of the Banco del Perú y Londres (from 1919) and Banco Italiano, and with agents of important Lima trading houses (Grace, Wessel Duval, Milne, Duncan Fox). Manrique prefers to evaluate the process as one of displacement of the regional mining–commercial–landholding élite by a Limean bourgeoisie tied to foreign capital.[69] The credit of those groups with contacts in Lima was considered better than that of groups without them: 'indeed one of the greatest economic assets of Huancayo's élite was their access to credit'.[70] The city of Huancayo became an important organising centre for financial and judicial services, which came in very handy to *enganchadores* in advancing money and enforcing contracts. Thus the local élite's progress, accumulation of assets, regional modernisation and overcoming of peasant resistance could not have occurred without the existence of local systems of credit and finance.

In contrast to the capitalist dynamism of the central and northern regions, the following was written in 1924 about the southern region: 'There are few places in the world where it is literally true that one half the world does not know how the other half lives, than in Peru; particularly so, in Southern Peru, where each provincial community has its own distinct resources, industries and mode of life'.[71] This apparent lack of capitalist integration needs to be explained and explored to avoid false generalisations for the rest of Peru.

It seems that commercial capital, foreign investment and financial intermediation worked more slowly in the transformation of the productive activities of the southern countryside. Merchant networks based in Arequipa – funded by Lima or from abroad – have been blamed for appropriating local surplus from Puno without effecting radical economic transformation of its traditional productive structure, at least until the 1930s.[72] Local reinvestment in sectors other than trade, urban improvement and local manufacture was limited in the south in spite of several attempts in the 1920s to modernise livestock-producing estates.

In the cities of Cuzco, Arequipa and Puno 'merchant princes' – the Italian merchants in Cuzco, Cesare Lomellini and Antonio Calvo, are the best examples in this regard[73] – were able to accumulate substantial capital. At the beginning their method of accumulation was to trade imports against native exports. Afterwards they reinvested their capital either in Lima or in urban developments in the most important provincial capital cities. Through commercial liaisons Puno became the hinterland of Arequipa. Cuzco found in its eastern tropical slopes a favourable area to develop its own regional commercial circuit, neglecting the Altiplano.[74]

Merchant houses such as Ricketts and Gibson, established in Arequipa, Puno and Cuzco, have been described as simple middle men rather than active and modernising economic agents.[75] Credit from Lima backed these *compradore* activities.[76] However some southern merchant creditors eventually became landowners when traditional *hacendados* were not able to repay their debts.[77] In the 1920s capital transfers to Lima and other economically expanding regions or abroad – with just a portion remaining for the urban expansion of Cuzco and Arequipa – occurred more often than in other regions, to the detriment of regional financial institutions. Antonio Calvo, a widely despised Cuzco money lender during a currency shortage in 1918, invested his accumulated capital in Banco del Perú y Londres' stock. When the bank went bankrupt in 1930 Calvo was the largest single shareholder and he lost a considerable portion of his capital.[78] The Banco Gibson, an attempt at regional banking, also collapsed in 1930 after only a short existence.

Leaving aside the scant communication between the south and other regional growth poles prior to the construction of motorways (the Southern Railway seems to have had a limited economic impact), the main cause of the weak integration seems to relate to the particular relations between property and production at the base of the region's main exports, sheep wool and alpaca fibre. In spite of attempts to improve the production of local wool, such as took place at the Granja Modelo run by the Scottish Colonel Robert Stordy in Chuquibambilla, Puno, between 1919 and 1925, the Indian peasants continued to own the animal stock – especially alpacas – within the framework of rentier *haciendas*. The owners of these *haciendas* preferred to expand and absorb communal lands (allowing Indians to keep their traditional means of production) rather than introducing technological improvements.[79] Until the 1930s commercial and financial concerns were not able to control production as successfully as they did in the central and northern highlands. *Sociedades* and *negociaciones ganaderas*, the agents of rural productive modernisation, became firmly established in Puno only when Arequipean merchants had secured ownership of the land through foreclosures on Puneño *hacendados* in the 1930s and 1940s.[80]

Among the southern middle sectors, a long-standing political movement reinvigorated the dormant ideal of regional autonomy. Spurred on by recent though limited capitalist developments, regionalist demands erupted as soon as the regional economy experienced increased difficulties due to the decline in international wool prices, and when the state failed to keep its promises in the late 1920s.

THE POLITICS OF REGIONAL FINANCE

During the *civilista* regimes (1899–1912, 1914–19) capitalist integration advanced mainly at the private level. The state was curbed from interfering with the consolidation of autonomously integrated and privately diversified élite groups. Liberalism regulated the affairs between the state and private initiative in a momentary break with the traditional character of the Peruvian state. During Leguía's second term this was overturned as without a degree of state intervention in the economy Leguía's development plans could not be fulfilled. Growing pressure from the working and middle classes was influential in bringing about the change in the role of the state.[81] The ultra-liberal factions of the élite, formed during the *civilista* regimes, criticised Leguía's interventionism and tax projects.[82]

In order of priority, according to Leguía's own statements and those of his followers, in 1919 the political objectives of his government were as follows: (1) democratisation of the national political order; (2) industrialisation; (3) strengthening of the country's defenses; (4) international respectability; and (5) education of the masses.[83] During the initial populist phase of Leguía's eleven-year regime, the *Oncenio*, the first of these objectives was expressed in two actions which were received enthusiastically in the interior regions. One was the organisation in 1919 of regional congresses (legislative bodies at the provincial level) which aroused high expectations among the middle sectors of the interior. The second was the constitutional legalisation and recognition of Indian communities in 1920. Combined with the *Conscripción Vial*, the measures were effective in expanding national integration, furthering capitalist penetration and providing modern regional finance. Leguía was the first modern president to discover the political means to mobilise the countryside.

When Leguía was asked in 1925 what was the acutest problem in Peru he answered 'the Indian'. He argued in favour of integrating the Indians with the nation by providing economic opportunities and education. 'The task is to make [the Indian] an effective part of a larger productive scheme. . . . I say let him rise!'[84] Leguía saw himself as the demiurge of a middle class that would be formed through affordable credit-serviced exploitation of the land, following a strategy of 'least resistance to the financial and social oligarchy'.[85] According to Leguía's acolytes only a strong authority could execute these designs, only Leguía's personality was fit for the task, and therefore – they argued – his second re-election in 1929 was absolutely necessary for the country.[86]

'Leguiísmo' never really became a political ideology beyond the cult of the leader. It was basically a movement of support to a figure who symbolised capitalist progress to aspiring middle class politicians and protected the interests of modernising agro-exporters. Leguía's personalism pervaded his political movement. His mobilising approach to the provincial masses proved positive in terms of capitalist integration, but became dangerous when the expectations of the masses were frustrated following the adoption of a pragmatic, centralist orientation to his regime after 1925.

Leguía concentrated the financial efforts of the state on irrigation projects, urban development and road improvement on the coast. Some of these projects involved scandalous and fraudulent beneficiaries. State-financed public works in the highland provinces were less ambitious but, in the long run, were essential for regional organisation and the integration of rural areas with provincial urban areas.[87] Provincial capitals in the south (Arequipa, Cuzco, Puno) also benefited from the urban development and sanitation works carried out by the Foundation Company – under state contract – in the 1920s. Provincial élite groups by then had already started a private strategy of investment in local urban electric trusts, textile factories and real estate. In Cuzco the group Lomellini-Montes, owners of the factories Huáscar and La Estrella, had formed the Cía. Eléctrica Comercial del Cuzco in 1913, which gained support from Italian capital and the Banco del Perú y Londres in 1917. In Arequipa the Crédito Urbano (1908) was supported by the Banco Italiano. In Huancayo the Sociedad Industrial Huancayo Limitada was formed in 1919.[88] These concerns were supported by Lima banks and their provincial branches, and by foreign capital, clearly taking advantage of the biased state policy which centred on strategic provincial urban centres. The most conspicous representatives of these groups, who formed part of a 'burguesía industrial', dominated provincial politics. Included were Cesare Lomellini, the promoter of Cuzco's electrical trust, who was a senator and later a minister during the Billinghurst administration, and the merchant Emmel who became mayor of Arequipa.[89]

Leguía's political system was based on power being exerted by an executive supported by a legislature, unlike the *civilista* regime which based its power on an élitist congress which limited the functions of the executive. Both of these systems provided the provinces with little effective leverage.[90] Under Leguía, the congressmen who represented the interior provinces were important members of a network which ensured financial and political centralism. These included men like Julio C. Arana, deputy for Loreto; Pedro J. Noriega, senator from Puno; Ing. Eduardo Gonzales Orbegoso, senator of La Libertad; Enrique de la Piedra and Ismael Ganoza Chopitea, representatives of northern provinces; and Francisco Graña, representative for Chincha, among others. Allegiance to Leguía was expected of these political representatives. At the summit of Leguía's political edifice were top executives and businessmen in charge of official financial institutions, such as Pedro Larrañaga y Loyola and Alfredo Alvarez Calderón who had strong connections with foreign capital.[91]

Despite the above, many provincial élite groups continued to be based on old-fashioned landownership, enforced labour recruitment and the local power structure controlled mostly by rural political bosses (*gamonales*). These traditional clientèle networks (*gamonalismo*) thus caused friction in the provinces. By the end of the 1920s the lack of pace in modernisation and an economic crisis in the southern highlands had triggered discontent among the politically and socially displaced sectors.

Decentralism and federalism were espoused in the south, a region which we have seen was poorly integrated with the rest of the country in the 1920s. Cuzco, for example, was strongly influenced by Argentinian culture. In 1927 the trip to Buenos Aires took five days, the same amount of time as a trip to Lima.[92] The economic crisis unleashed in 1929–30 exacerbated dissension and protest against the Leguía regime. In 1927 Leguía's regional spending programmes were abruptly interrupted. Frustrated nativists (*indigenistas*) and regionalists joined the struggle. These movements have been considered as the expression of regional middle class forces opposing *gamonales* and traditional relations of property.[93] However their rejection of the mechanisms of capitalist integration proved to be a political mistake on the part of the decentralists as there was little political support for their cause at the national level. When Leguía fell, the opportunity to lead the country was offered to the decentralists. However only weak and traditional leaders disguised as regionalists came forward. The Partido Federal supported Captain Arístides Pachas, a military leader who misrepresented the regionalist movement in 1931.[94] In a way these political movements, as had the attempts to form regional banks in the south, lacked the necessary resources and infrastructure. National politics, as opposed to regionalist exclusivism, had come to stay in Peru and could not be disregarded by political leaders.

Comandante Luis Sánchez Cerro became popular with the anti-Leguía masses thanks in part to previous political changes which had integrated them into national politics. His movement was semi-fascist and nationalist and was supported by Leguía's enemies among the élite, who saw in Sánchez Cerro a good match for the politically more sophisticated *aprista* party. After Leguía, the vacuum of authority was thus filled temporarily by radical nationalists rather than by regionalists.

Part of the success of Oscar Benavides, Sánchez Cerro's successor, against *aprista* populist ideology and embryonic communism in the 1930s was the shift towards a developmentalist approach. This in effect continued Leguía's policy, amid gradual economic recuperation and the restructuring of the productive sector. The completion of efforts in the 1930s and 1940s to bring about integration made Arequipa and Cuzco poles of growth and gave them control of a slowly changing hinterland. This effectively weakened decentralism and the more belligerent forms of regionalism. From 1932 the decentralist debate was limited to constitutional and congressional matters. Between 1936 and 1939 Benavides advanced further the centralist character of the Peruvian state against the remnants of regional political and fiscal autonomy,[95] which in later years remained more a political tradition than a modern economic alternative.

An adequate central state policy to take care of regional needs was not provided by the state. Consequently regional development in the

1930s and 1940s did not keep the pace with the growth and increase in wealth of Lima and the central coast. The interventionist policies of the state aided rather than diminished the trend toward centralisation. The few projects designed to improve regional development ended in failure. President Manuel Prado's most ambitious design was the formation of national corporations to exploit hitherto untapped national resources: the Corporación del Amazonas (1942) and the Corporación Peruana del Santa (1943).[96]

These undertakings by the state lacked sound planning and did not produce the desired results due to the limited amount of locally available funds, the difficulty in importing machinery during the Second World War, and the lack of foreign financing due to the protracted default of 1931. Of the S/100 million the state was to have provided the Santa Corporation, only eight million had been received by 1944.

Regional banking also did little to help reduce centralisation. Modern regional banking did not become properly established in Peru until the 1960s (the old regional banks of the Guano Age had collapsed after the War of the Pacific). Between 1890 and 1960 commercial banks controlled the basic mechanisms of fund transfers between the provinces through a centralist banking organisation with headquarters in Lima. The contrast between weak regional banking and the thriving involvement of banks in real estate and mortgages in Lima can provide insights into the effects of domestic finance on growing centralisation and income and wealth distribution in Peru.

FINANCING LIMA'S REAL ESTATE

One native institution maintained an advantage over the other native and foreign banks in terms of the quantity of provincial branches it had under its control in the 1895–1930 period. The Banco del Perú y Londres had for many years a virtual monopoly in banking activities in the majority of the commercially important provincial towns and cities. In 1929 it had 19 provincial and four Lima district agencies. No other institution could compete with this network.

It was only from about 1910 onward that the Banco Italiano and the Banco Alemán were able to consolidate a secure hold in two towns (Chincha Alta and Mollendo) and to function in two other growing provincial cities (Arequipa and Trujillo). However by 1929 they only had 10 provincial branches between them. During the First World War the Mercantile Bank of the Americas, which opened its

Lima branch in October 1916, expanded its activities beyond the capital with the opening of agencies in Arequipa and Callao in 1917, Trujillo in 1919 and Chiclayo in 1920.[97] However the business gained by their provincial agencies did not prevent their withdrawal in 1924.

Bank agencies in the provinces concentrated on the principal ports, the northern coastal area, the central coastal Ica–Chincha area, and the southern Arequipa–Mollendo areas. From 1915 onward agencies appeared in the commercial zones of the southern highlands, Cuzco and Puno, thus expanding the Arequipa financial network. It is worthwhile noting that the Banco del Perú y Londres was involved from an early date in Chilean-occupied Tacna and in the Bolivian banking sphere through capital participation in the Banco de Tacna and Banco de la Nación Boliviana. When Tacna was returned to Peru in 1929, the Banco del Perú y Londres opened an agency there.

Irrespective of this spreading of interests in the provinces, the concentration of financial assets in Lima and Callao was overwhelming when compared with the rest of the regions. Between 1926 and 1929 institutions in Lima and Callao held approximately 80 per cent of the small savings accounts in Peru, followed by Arequipa with 9 per cent and Trujillo with 3 per cent.[98] Apart from the establishment of branches of Lima-based institutions, and the unsuccessful Banca Víctor Larco in Trujillo (1922), Banco Departamental de Lambayeque (1922–7) and Banco Gibson in Arequipa (1929–30), investment in regional banking was practically non-existent. In a sense the poor financial structure in the provinces contributed to the early concentration of financial assets in Lima and Callao.

As Table 5.1 shows, financial resources continued to be concentrated in Lima and the coastal region well into the 1960s. Loans by and deposits in commercial banks in areas outside Lima represented only 17–28 per cent of the total after 1926, and the coastal area received more than 90 per cent of commercial loans after 1945. Mortgage loans in the provinces showed an astounding decline from 23 per cent in 1894 to 2 per cent in 1965. Even development banks contributed to this inequity. In 1945 the Banco Agrícola allocated 68 per cent and the Banco Industrial 87 per cent of their loans to the coast. In 1955 the latter bank still only provided 27 per cent of its loans to provinces other than Lima.

Moreover the regions suffered from the paralysis in publicly financed works in 1929, and the provincial élite groups' slow transition to interests beyond commerce and land, especially in the south. The completion under Benavides of the basic public works instigated

Table 5.1 Indicators of Peruvian bank credit's regional concentration, 1894–1965 (in per cent)

Year	All Provinces (Lima excluded)			Commercial Loans			Banco Industrial Loans			
	Commercial Loans	Commercial Deposits	Mortgages	Coast	Sierra	Selva	Provinces	Coast	Sierra	Selva
1894	–	–	23	–	–	–	–	–	–	–
1905	–	–	22	–	–	–	–	–	–	–
1915	–	–	17	–	–	–	–	–	–	–
1926	–	28	–	–	–	–	–	–	–	–
1935	17	19	–	–	–	–	–	–	–	–
1945	28	28	22	90	9	1	27	87	11	2
1955	19	21	6	93	6	1	27	–	–	–
1965	21	23	2	92	7	2	51	70	29	1

Sources: *Memoria*, Dirección de Crédito Público, Inspección Fiscal de Bancos Hipotecarios (1902–7); 'Banco del Perú y Londres, Sección Hipotecaria, Distribución de Préstamos', in *El Comercio* (1894–1901); *Informe*, Inspección Fiscal de Bancos (1926–9); *Memoria*, Superintendencia de Banca (1931–66); *Anuario estadístico del Perú* (1955, 1966).

ten years previously by Leguía at last spurred on capitalism in the interior regions, but this was too late for balanced national development.

Banks in the provinces had provided only commercial services and transfer of funds operations until the appearance of regional banks in the 1960s. The most important reasons why the interior regions were not able to overcome Lima's centralism were the limited provincial markets and production being constrained by traditional landholding and peasant interests which prevented the formation of regional growth poles and financial centres.[99]

As late as 1911 the development of mortgage business in the provinces was still limited.[100] However real estate in or near Lima was a sound investment because of its periodic appreciation during various business cycles and the high speculative profits gained during short inflationary periods. The granting of credit for urban development and speculation in Lima's real estate was one of the most successful financial businesses between 1884 and 1950. Mortgage activities in the Lima region exemplify the growing trend towards concentrated and centralised growth poles. Mortgage transactions brought credit institutions and traditional thrift practises into a new relationship. As early as the 1890s long-term mortgage credit provided capital to real estate proprietors, who in turn opened new deposit accounts in banking institutions.

Immediately after the war with Chile, the Guano Age mortgage banks, which specialised in agrarian mortgages, had serious difficulty in liquidating their assets due to lengthy litigation over debtors' mortgaged properties.[101] For example, in 1888 the real assets of the Banco de Crédito Hipotecario reached only 50 per cent of its liabilities, according to the report of its stockholders' meeting.[102] Agricultural estates had been the main recipients of mortgage loans prior to 1883. In January 1885 the former Banco de Crédito Hipotecario was owed S/1 156 216, that is 31 per cent of its total outstanding mortgages in December 1883, by seven sugar estates. The former Banco Territorial Hipotecario was owed the excessive amount of S/880 000 plus interest by six estates in La Libertad.[103]

Deficiencies in the legal registration of property, the general depression of real estate expressed in a 75 per cent decrease in rents in 1883, and the depreciation of mortgage bonds and paper money posed formidable difficulties to the old style mortgage banks. In the 1880s the general distrust toward the mortgage credit market and its institutions was at its highest. Debtors refused to repay banks in silver currency the amounts which they had been lent in mortgage bonds intended for sale on the Lima stock market. Opposition to attempts by banks to extract loan repayments assumed the form of 'defence of the general interests of agriculture'.[104]

On their part, creditor bankers firmly rejected the demands of mortgage debtors. The president of the former Banco de Crédito Hipotecario, Pedro Gallagher, answered the attacks against his institution, which was undergoing liquidation, as follows: 'Do you think that national or foreign capital will come to the aid of agriculture in a place where the unusual right of the agriculturist to not repay his debts is sanctioned?'[105] The impasse lasted until the enactment of the 1889 Mortgage Law, promoted by banker Payán, and the eradication of paper currency.[106]

After 1889 loans were granted primarily to urban owners rather than to agricultural ones as there was a higher expectation of profit from urban rents and in the past there had been frustrating experiences with indebted estates. In addition mortgage credit was made more available to urban owners because they were more likely to use the credit granted to open a current account with the lending institution.[107] The new law proved to be beneficial to banks.[108] Those who enjoyed the advantages of mortgage credit were large property owners who could mortgage their properties and receive on account, as stipulated by the mortgage law, a minimum of S/1000 on one half of the property's value.[109] Institutional mortgage credit in Peru until the 1920s therefore had little effect on agricultural credit to small and medium sized producers.

Significant consequences of the mortgage credit policy practiced in Peru between 1889 and 1929 were experienced in the urban areas of Lima. The available data on total mortgage distribution by department for the 1894–1907 period shows a marked concentration of outstanding mortgage loans in the department of Lima. At least three-fourths of total banking mortgage loans took place in Lima during this period, and a slight increase in that share was apparent by 1906–7. La Libertad, Arequipa and Callao each had approximately 6 per cent to 7 per cent of the total mortgage loans granted between 1894 and 1898. For the years 1900–6, La Libertad and Ica had between 1 per cent and 3 per cent more of the total than Arequipa, Callao and Ancash. Furthermore, between 1884 and 1913 a sample of clients of the most important institution, the Banco del Perú y Londres, shows that an average 18 per cent of loan recipients were urban residents, especially homeowners in the downtown Lima area.[110]

These facts provide the clue to linking the moderate expansion of mortgage credit between 1890 an 1907 to the renovation observed in the old and traditional areas of Lima after a long period of neglect and decay following the war with Chile. Large urban proprietors were given the means to improve their properties and to augment their urban ownership through privileged 10 to 21 year-term credit.

By 1908 a population increase in Lima of around 40 per cent since 1876, together with a price rise and the concentration of real estate ownership, had produced high rents and overcrowding in populous neighbourhoods. A specialist in sanitation, alarmed at the extremely high 276.1 per 1000 mortality rate among infants up to 12 months of age, and the 62.1 and 11.3 per 10 000 mortality rates due to tuberculosis and typhoid, respectively, wrote: 'We have the highest mortality rates, we do not save in human capital, on the contrary, Lima wastes it in a crazy way'.[111] Only one-fifth of old Lima's population was adequately housed. High rents were blamed for the overcrowding which brought such overwhelming sanitary problems while providing high profits to urban landlords. Likewise mortgage institutions calculated the safety of an individual loan on the basis that the annual rent on the property would return a higher annual yield than would mortgage bonds. Therefore the higher the urban rents the better the mortgage business, in spite of the general housing problems thus created.[112]

The development of mortgage loans went through three distinct phases up to 1930: (1) a moderate increase in mortgage loans between 1889 and 1907; (2) relative stagnation from 1907 to 1921; and (3) extreme expansion between 1921 and 1930. If my previous observation about the strong connection between the increase in mortgage loans and Lima's population and urban expansion is taken into account, it is not surprising to find a strong correlation between each one of these mortgage phases and Lima's growth periods.

The growing importance of mortgage loans vis-à-vis other banking services, especially in the 1920s, was significant. The proportion of total outstanding mortgage loans to total commercial loans and discounts was between a fifth and a sixth in the years 1894, 1915 and 1925, when banks expanded their mortgage business. In 1930 mortgages increased to the previously unseen proportion of almost one-half of total commercial loans and discounts. This clearly shows the critical influence that Lima's physical growth exerted over the highly concentrated Peruvian financial structure during certain periods. Mortgage loans were greater than the portfolio investment of banks, except in 1910 and 1915, years of heavy involvement in securities by the banks, and in 1920 when one important mortgage institution, the Crédit Foncier Peruvien, abandoned the market.

By 1900 the monopoly by the Banco del Callao/Perú y Londres' mortgage section was broken. First the Banco Italiano, and later five other mortgage institutions, attempted to reap profits from the banking opportunities opened by mortgage services. Between 1900 and 1907 overoptimism led to a proliferation of institutions offering not only mortgages but also a variety of other administrative and credit services to urban owners. The list of new institutions of this type included the Crédito Urbano (1900), Cía. Urbana La Victoria (1903), Caja Hipotecaria (1903), Cía. Administradora de Fincas (1906), and a host of others. In addition, since mortgage institutions demanded that fire insurance policies be taken out on the mortgaged properties, native fire insurance companies benefited from the increase in mortgage and urban real estate businesses. By 1906 attempts to improve Lima's and Callao's sewers, and conditions of hygiene in general, were being initiated by the English contractor, E. J. Rumsby.[113]

All the moderate advances in modernisation mentioned above stopped abruptly in 1907. The competition among mortgage and real estate institutions acting in a limited market had extracted its toll. During the years 1907–9 the Crédito Urbano, La Colmena and others went bankrupt. An urban technician noticed that between 1908 and 1916 there was practically no construction in old Lima due to what he called a 'financial crisis'.[114] Another observer pointed out that Lima's housing conditions in 1914 were no better than in 1900 because the increase in housing (18 per cent) had not kept pace with the population increase (31 per cent). He calculated that as a result, urban lots had increased in price by 1000 per cent in those fourteen years.[115]

As old Lima stagnated because of the glutted mortgage market, the organisation of five new realty companies, called *urbanizadoras*, initiated what would become a highly profitable business until well into the 1960s. They used land on the outskirts of Lima to sell lots by instalments at an average 6 per cent interest. The first *urbanizadoras* were La Victoria, El Chirimoyo, La Colmena, Paseo Colón and Avenida de la Unión.[116] Concurrently (in 1908–9) the most important mortgage institutions showed a decrease in their outstanding loans. Investment in suburban real estate and in mortgage bonds to finance old Lima's buildings had a relationship of substitution. Also, expectations of lower yields from mortgage bonds were tied to an observed decline in the general interest rate at the time. Suburban real estate business, on the other hand, depended directly on the increasing price of suburban land, which guaranteed higher profits for investors.

The emergency measures taken by the government and banks with respect to currency during the First World War included mortgage bonds being used as part of the banks' issue of paper money. This prevented mortgage bonds from receiving lower quotations during the early war years. In 1917 the first signs of a recuperation in real estate and mortgage businesses was apparent. The housing shortage and general inflation triggered higher rents and an improvement in mortgage bond yields. Consequently mortgage bond investment increased significantly, overcoming the stagnation of the early war years.[117]

The gap between the population increase and the housing supply in Lima widened from 1908 onwards.[118] By 1922 housing conditions were in a critical situation. A law enacted in 1920 to protect tenants from eviction and rising rents discouraged urban owners in old Lima from renting out their houses. Instead downtown neighbourhoods became increasingly commercial and many buildings deteriorated. In addition the price of land in new neighbourhoods outside old Lima increased at a higher rate between 1917 and 1922 (150 per cent compared with 114 per cent and 109 per cent in the older areas), resulting in windfall profits to realty companies. The boom period for the *urbanizadoras* had began.[119]

The number of real estate companies soared between 1918 and 1927. Fifteen such companies held 35 per cent (759.3 hectares) of Lima's total urban area in 1927. The total number of real estate companies reached 40 in 1925. Estate owners near Lima were lured by high profits to divide their properties into lots for housing. Realty costs were kept low by not complying with sanitary regulations when housing was intended for the lower classes.[120] Banks also engaged in selling suburban lots on instalment plans. The Urbanización La Cerámica was the concern of a special section of the Banco del Perú y Londres. The outward expansion of Lima provided a renewed demand for mortgage loans which, by 1925, were allowed by law on empty lots. From the early 1920s increased mortgage credit to agriculturists, a clear difference from previous mortgage credit policies, also contributed to the expansion of the mortgage market. The number of mortgage loans granted grew remarkably between 1921 and 1929.

In 1920, following the collapse of the foreign mortgage concern Crédit Foncier Peruvien, the Banco del Perú y Londres bought back the Crédit Foncier's assets. However the Banco del Perú y Londres had lost important ground to the Banco Italiano, which pursued an aggressive mortgage policy from 1921 onward. Although other new mortgage institutions had appeared by 1921, in 1925 the Italian bank was far ahead of the Perú y Londres, holding 46 per cent of total mortgage loans compared with 22 per cent for the Perú y Londres.[121]

The post-war golden period of the *urbanizadoras* had receded by 1927, in spite of the persistent housing shortage. Limited demand by the middle class for housing in suburban areas affected adversely the real estate business, which experienced an aggregate loss in 1929. That same year the government abruptly ended the public urban works which had partially sustained the real estate business during the 1920s. Likewise the formation in 1927 of a central public mortgage institution, the Banco Central Hipotecario, which was weakly opposed by the private institutions, monopolised the already declining mortgage market. Under this new state-controlled mortgage system, geared toward providing additional guarantees to foreign creditors to alleviate the serious fiscal situation, mortgage bonds did not grow at the same rate as mortgage loans. The unsound financial situation of the government had eroded the confidence of native investors in mortgage bonds.[122]

In the 1930s and 1940s mortgage credit for urban construction continued under the monopoly of the central mortgage bank. In December 1941 mortgage bonds in circulation amounted to S/ 68 937 000, earning between 6 per cent and 7 per cent[123]. This investment by mostly small investors compared with approximately one-fifth of the amount of deposits in commercial and savings institutions at the time. However the issue of mortgage bonds was highly regulated and did not meet the expectations or needs of urban dwellers. Mortgage loans were primarily granted to credit-worthy capitalists involved in the construction business, which netted approximately 18 per cent to 25 per cent in profits by 1941. There were no building societies in existence, despite interesting projects in that direction.[124] Only in May 1957 was a law promulgated (promoted by Pedro Beltrán), by which *mutual* credit allowed associations of small savers to use credit to build their homes. In the 1950s *barriadas* (urban belt slums) had began to appear as a result of the increasing influx of provincial migrants who were unable to find affordable housing in Lima.[125]

Thus in the 1930s and 1940s the *urbanizadoras* and the companies involved in building and supplying building materials (Fred T. Ley & Company, Fábrica de Cemento Portland, Wiese & Company) benefited from the urban expansion in Lima.[126] The countryside just outside Lima had been radically transformed as a result of the restructuring of agrarian production since the crisis of the 1930s.[127] Most landowners on the outskirts of Lima were able to diversify into the real estate business with relative ease. Credit support was granted especially by the Banco Italiano and the Banco Popular. As in the 1920s, urban developments consisted simply of dividing former sugar and cotton estates into lots. The building of houses had to be financed by the buyer of the individual lot, except for the limited state-sponsored projects such as the 'worker's neighbourhood' of La Victoria during the Benavides regime, and El Porvenir in 1940. In general, by 1950 only a few small savers were able to become homeowners despite the possibilities opened by the urban boom in Lima.

SMALL SAVERS AND INVESTORS

The savings of the lower middle and working classes did not flow directly into the commercial banks in Peru before 1920. Small savers did not have the resources required by commercial banks for the granting of credit or payment of interest on deposits. Among the common people the use of financial instruments was limited to mortgage and public debt bonds, the first because they enjoyed general prestige and the second because they were imposed on the general public by the state. Therefore the facility to obtain credit against collateral was seldom used by the average individual with a low income. Small savings could only be attracted through substantially higher interest on deposits and solid institutional guarantees. Although commercial banks did not try to capture small savings by adopting higher interest rates until the early 1920s, the financial élite did not, however, leave small savings resources untapped.

The only institution allowed to pay interest rates higher than the commercial rate on small savings accounts (below S/1000 until a 1927 legislation) was the Caja de Ahorros. The Caja was under the control of the official munificence institution, Beneficencia Pública de Lima. With its charitable front, the Caja at times offered small savers 30 to 100 per cent more interest than local banks, and the small savings of persons willing to place their trust in this institution were absorbed. The crucial detail is that the Caja was managed by the same élite individuals who led the financial structure. Top financiers or their closest relatives who were members of the Caja's board of inspectors included J. Payán, V. G. Delgado, J. Prado, L. Alzamora, P. Mujica y Carassa, E. Fernandini and D. Olavegoya.[128]

The available statistical information on the composition of the Caja's male depositors by occupation, although insufficient, shows that the principal small savings groups were mainly urban workers, with white collar workers slightly predominating. Among the male depositors who opened accounts in 1900, white collar government workers accounted for 26 per cent, artisans 17 per cent, domestic servants 11 per cent, small merchants 10 per cent, blue collar workers 7 per cent and commercial employees 6 per cent. Women represented 45 per cent (3300 individuals) of the total number of depositors but no information on female composition by occupation is given in the institution's annual reports. However it is known that many working women at the time earned their living at home as seamstresses or as cheap labourers in local textile mills. Two-fifths of the depositors were bachelors (not including minors and widowers) as compared to one-fifth who were married. Nearly 90 per cent were Peruvian and 70 per cent were literate. In 1910 the male white collar share among depositors increased. From a total of 1065 new savings accounts opened by men during that year, the artisans' share declined to 12.3 per cent and that of blue collar workers to 4.6 per cent, while the share of domestic servants increased to 13.8 per cent. Government employees were by far the largest group with 28.7 per cent, which, when added to small merchants and commercial employees, accounted for almost one-half of new depositors. Distribution of depositors by sex, nationality and literacy remained stationary from 1916.[129]

The amounts in the Caja for small savings and current and term deposit accounts were only 7 per cent of the value of total commercial creditor accounts in 1900 and 9 per cent in 1910 and 1917. By official statutory regulation (1884–8), the institution was obliged to grant credit preferentially with securities as collateral. Mortgage bonds were the favourite type of securities used as collateral. Special government permission allowed mortgage loans to be granted by the Caja from 1896, although the Caja's mortgage section was not established until 1904. The Caja also kept part of its assets in low interest-bearing deposits in commercial banks, thus losing the difference it had to pay out on its own higher interest liabilities. In this way working people's savings at the disposition of the Caja's managers were funnelled indirectly into the commercial sphere.

Insignificant amounts were allocated to loans against personally owned gold and silver (*alhajas*) except during the years of the gold hoarding frenzy (1895–1900, 1913–16) when such loans reached 10 to 15 per cent of the amount of loans against securities. The institution was never allowed to compete in the discounting of bills of exchange and other commercial credit instruments. The Caja had very low capital and reserve funds, which accrued annually from only one-half of its meager profits. A firm clientèle that had nowhere else to place its small savings constituted the main source of funds for the Caja.[130]

The general factors affecting the commercial banking system appear to have influenced in great measure the Caja's evolution. The allocation of the Caja's assets was dependent on the business cycle and fluctuations in the securities' market. In addition, rises and falls in income determined the workers' capacity to save during the different periods of export boom and bust and internal inflation. The years 1890–1, which were characterised by improved business activity and increased securities transactions, were years of the institution's recuperation relative to the 1880s. However the sudden decline in the price of silver between 1892 and 1895 posed serious problems which, together with the spreading rumour of a government takeover of private savings, created a panic among the Caja's depositors. In 1908–10 the depression of the securities market prevented the managers of the Caja from investing or lending 24 per cent of its assets, while small depositors kept increasing their savings in spite of declining interest rates.[131]

As can be seen, it was the methods used by the élite, which have been detailed elsewhere, which seriously affected the degree of popular savings, and not the alleged lack of thrift among the masses. An intellectual Peruvian woman once criticised the speculation by the élite on securities, which had served to discourage popular saving: 'Accumulated money means power. It is said the people in our country do not yet have the savings habit. But why are the upper classes, who proclaim themselves educators of the masses, not occupied with forming this custom?'[132] Additional examples of the practice of thrift among Lima's small savers are provided by the activities of hybrid savings institutions which bloomed in the 1900s but soon closed in the critical period of 1907–10 (La Acumulativa, La Colmena and others). For example, La Dotal (1901), a self-proclaimed feminist savings institution, addressed the important savings group of bachelor women and their relatives, urging them to place their small savings in time-maturing 'dowry certificates'.[133]

The period of high inflation (1917–21) showed a marked decline in the amount placed in term deposits by the Caja's medium savers. Standard savings accounts (*libretas de ahorro*) were not affected in the same way, probably due to money illusion (scant awareness of inflation effects) among small savers. The aggregate accounts of the Caja show a clear decline in total assets between 1915 and 1923.

From 1919 the commercial banks began to compete for small savers. It was obvious by then that the future of banking in Peru lay in the expansion of demand factors. In 1919 the Banco del Perú y Londres opened its savings section and by December 1926 it controlled 66 per cent of the Lp2 152 970 total national savings. The Caja ranked second with a share of 26 per cent. In the same year a total of nine institutions offered savings accounts, mainly in Lima (which had 72 per cent the savings), Callao (9 per cent) and Arequipa (8 per cent), with fourteen other provinces having 11 per cent of the share.[134]

In the new institutional setting formed by the participation of commercial banks in the small savings business, total small savings increased 300 per cent between 1921 and 1930. Part of this increase, however, has to be attributed to the change in the legal definition of small savings brought about by the Savings Law of July 1927, which guaranteed and protected savings under S/5000. The previous guarantee covered only up to S/1000. Therefore the accounts of more savers fell into the category of 'small savings' thus raising the total amount, inflation notwithstanding. By 1931 the competition for small savings among banks, and official restrictions on foreign banks, had resulted in only four national institutions conducting the savings business as thus defined. The attempt to establish a central savings bank, whose capital originated from the unpopular reparation agreement Leguía negotiated with the Chilean government over Tacna and Arica in 1929, failed due to the distrust small savers felt toward state management.

Five bankruptcies, including that of the Banco del Perú y Londres and the Caja de Ahorros del Callao, together with the closure of three foreign banks, left the majority of small savings accounts in the hands of the Banco Italiano and the Caja of Lima. At the end of the period small savings continued to expand, but at a slower rate and in a basically commercial financial structure assailed by problems.

Major evidence of a grave flaw in the Peruvian financial structure with respect to small savers is provided by the extensive presence of pawnshops in Lima from 1884–1930. Table 5.2 documents the increasing reliance of the working class on pawnbrokers to meet their urgent financial needs. According to these figures the fastest periods of increase in amounts pawned were 1898–1902 and 1905–7. This old-fashioned form of short-term credit against personal property at extremely high rates of interest funnelled financial resources away from the working class toward the élite, thus exacerbating the unequal distribution of income.[135]

Nevertheless pawnshops were badly needed because of the reluctance of formal financial institutions, including the Caja de Ahorros, to provide credit in small amounts against personal property or future income. Pawnbrokers, to the contrary, were not selective in this respect provided that the interest rate on the loans was high enough to cover defaults and that the pawned object was appraised for loan purposes at no more than 75 per cent of its real value. While the annual interest on commercial credit was approximately 10–12 per cent in the 1890's, the average monthly interest on amounts below S/100 borrowed by pawning items of gold or silver (*alhajas*) was 3–3.5 per cent (36–42 per cent annually). For clothing, furniture or other personal objects it was as high as 7.5 per cent a month. Since, according to some estimates, 80 per cent of all pawned items were

Table 5.2　Pawn loans in Lima, 1888–1913

Year	No. of pawn loans (× 1000)	Total value of pawn loans[a]	Growth index of pawn loans	Auction receipts[a]	Average value of each loan[b]
1888	168	73	1	–	0.43
1889–90[c]	202	89	1.2	–	0.44
1890–91[c]	246	107	1.5	16	0.43
1893	332	118	1.6	–	0.36
1898	485	132	1.8	–	0.27
1901–2[d]	553	198	2.7	34	0.36
1903[e]	568	206	2.8	–	0.36
1904	443	193	2.6	–	0.44
1905	500	213	2.9	–	0.43
1907[f]	555	272	3.7	–	0.49
1908[g]	593	286	3.9	–	0.49
1909–10[h]	618	271	3.7	–	0.44
1911	650	298	4.1	–	0.46
1913	720	320	4.4	–	0.44

Notes: a = nominal Lp × 1000; b = nominal Lp; c = year from Nov. to Oct.; d = year from Dec. to Nov.; e = missing data for June, Nov., Dec.; f = year from Sept. to July, excluding Feb. and Aug.; g = year from Nov. to Oct., excluding Oct.; h = year considered as 12 months between Feb. 1909 and May 1910. Data for missing months replaced by monthly average of the corresponding year.

Sources: 'Parte mensual de la Inspección de Casas de préstamo', *Boletín Municipal* (1889–1913); *El Comercio*, 10 Jan. 1899; Joaquín Capelo, *Sociología*, vol. 2, pp. 74–8.

objects other than *alhajas*, the composite average interest charged by pawnshops reached 6.7 per cent a month.[136]

Popular dissatisfaction with this phenomenon was directed at the usury 'vampires' as pawnbrokers were called at the time. A cheap novel in 1886 profited from the theme and thought it morally correct to

expose . . . the intimate wickedness and ambition consuming the heart of a miser pawnbroker, supporter and accomplice in the past of burglars fondness of others' property. In this way we simply aid justice's vigour in condemning crime and manifesting the sacred splendor of the morale.[137]

Pawnshops were subject to strict regulation and surveillance. Before 1888, when the Lima City Council took charge of taxing and controlling the growing number of pawnshops, the police patrolled these establishments in search of stolen property. In 1889 an ad-hoc system of inspection was created to control 28 pawnshops. The number of pawnshops increased to 47 in 1891, reduced to 43 in 1893 and rose again to the record number of 57 in 1898. In 1911 after some bankruptcies the number became a stable 46.

According to a municipal survey in January 1901 of the 53 pawnshops in Lima, 85 per cent were owned by foreigners (of which 27 were Italian, seven were French, and four were Chinese) and 15 per cent by Peruvians (eight in all).[138] No competition with commercial banks existed in this marginal financial market, so pawnbrokers were able to reap the full benefits from pawn transactions and at the same time become clients of local banks such as the Banco Italiano.

The regulation of pawn interest rates was discussed intensively in financial and theological circles. The old colonial *montes de piedad*, charitable institutions that made loans against personal property at low interest, had curbed 'usury', as high interest on loans was called by the dominant catholic code of the time. Based on these historical precedents the idea of establishing a Banco de Pobres (1901) or similar institutions (La Auxiliar in 1919) with the Church's capital was contemplated during inflationary periods when the working class urgently needed credit.[139]

Despite their supposedly good intentions as members of charitable institutions, important financiers firmly opposed any attempt to limit pawnshop interest rates due to the possibility of similar initiatives being aimed at commercial banking interest charges. According to them, the scientific way to deal with extremely high interest rates was to allow the free play of supply and demand. Also, the high interest rates were justified because of the risk involved in such transactions.[140] No effective limitation on pawn interest rates was achieved until 1918 due to the organised protests of pawnbrokers and the unwillingness of the financiers who controlled financial policy to permit any regulation.[141]

By 1941 savings deposits in Peru still earned only 4 per cent annual interest, and amounted to S/97 539 745, that is, approximately 28 per cent of all deposits in commercial and savings banks.[142] Compared to earlier periods, the contribution by small savers to the financial sector had improved considerably, although the benefits to them did not change much in the 1930s and 1940s. Homeowners had to finance the building of their houses without recourse to housing credit. Small agricultural producers did not receive credit from the Banco Agrícola created in 1931. The same applies to small industrialists in relation to the Industrial Bank (1936). Low interest rates, limited use of their own funds, and inflation (especially in the 1940s) discouraged saving among the general population but provided the élite with additional funds for their oligopolistic businesses.

In conclusion, finance in Peru, through banks acting in close collaboration with regionally-based élite groups (and state intervention in the 1920s and 1930s), developed centralist connections which allowed funds to be transferred to the more dynamic capitalist sectors which represented specialised productive poles of export and urban growth. Even before the massive improvements in urban development and means of communication occurred, complementation of productive and financial activities allowed private groups to overcome structural bottlenecks through the formation of native oligopolies.

The formation of native agrarian and livestock *negociaciones* and *sociedades*, provincial urban trusts and *habilitación* business, which had a relationship of competition combined with instances of collaboration with foreign capital, resulted in unequal capitalist integration between 1884 and 1940. Increasing urbanisation and better means of communication consolidated and encouraged further group and institutional finance in regions of limited integration.

Although the bulk of native financial resources continued to be concentrated in the Lima area and the coastal region, they were not altogether absent from the important provincial urban and productive centres. Neither did the regional surplus flow entirely out of the country. Regional groups with centralist connections retained part of those surpluses to develope modern internal poles of economic growth which contributed to the formation of regional and national markets. However, as in any capitalist process of national integration, certain regions developed at the expense of others, especially the Lima region which benefited most from this competitive process.

Backwardness in the southern regions, reinforced by traditional property ownership, provincial bosses and peasant resistance, produced expectations of change among middle sectors in provincial cities. Frustration with centralist financial and political élite networks resulted in a move towards regionalism, but this received little support at the national level. 1929–32 was an explosive period in which Peruvian society was led almost to the brink of civil war. However, compared to other South American nations (Colombia or Bolivia for example), a liberal export-oriented and modernising leadership dealt with regional inequality without unleashing sustained violent opposition to centralism (at least until the 1970s), extreme regionalism, or territorial loss. After 1932 capitalist integration and developmentalism continued to grow, for better or for worse. Even the southern rural region experienced a revitalisation due to the actions of modernising groups in the 1930s. What did become truncated was the completion of the integrative process as a result of the decline in specialised export activities, which affected the core of the native élite in critical years, the trend toward excessive oligopolisation aided by foreign capital, and, in political terms, authoritarian and misguided state intervention.

From the social perspective, the analysis of the effects of Peruvian finance on income and credit distribution is not favourable. Small savings were neglected by banks and left at the mercy of informal markets until the 1920s. Depression in the 1930s and inflation in the 1940s demoralised small savers and would-be homeowners who were affected by adverse official monetary and credit policies. Likewise, formal credit to small producers, investors and savers was practically non-existant until recent years. In general the popular sectors did not benefit directly from private and public financial evolution. The Peruvian export economy was modernised in part thanks to its native financial structure between 1884 and 1950, but the country was unable to achieve the higher objective of a balanced development.

6 Financial Policies and the State

The state has played a critical role in Latin American socio-economic issues.[1] Assumptions about the supposed weakness of the state in the nineteenth and early twentieth centuries are being thoroughly revised. So are theoretical misconceptions concerning the 'extreme dependency' of Latin American 'liberal' regimes.[2] The search for the roots of authoritarian regimes has contributed to these revisions by stressing the organicist and bureaucratic legacies which survive liberal and democratic governments in modern Latin America.[3] Thus the real character of state interventionism – often seen as an indispensable type of reformism for latecomers to development[4] – is under scrutiny. In addition, the limited results of state-sponsored import substitution industrialisation cast shadows of doubt on the efficiency of the interests behind post-liberal 'autonomous' drives.

One area of research which is proving fruitful in the understanding of the socio-economic role of Latin American states is that of state finances and financial policies. Recent seminal studies have uncovered crucial links between state financial and debt policies with trade, economic and developmental strategies.[5] External loans have received preferential treatment, although the study of internal public debt can perhaps lead to a greater understanding of the interests behind debt and financial strategies. Moreover, relevant information on the social implications of the state's financial role is obtained from the study of the interests behind monetary and exchange manipulation, official regulation and protection, state intervention, and the activities of state financial institutions.

In this chapter I evaluate the changing and often contradictory state measures which I consider have been relevant to Peruvian financial development. I argue that, despite the obvious alternation of predominantly liberal periods and periods of interventionist financial policies, one can detect the continuity of a tradition in state arbitration which had on balance negative effects on the Peruvian financial structure. Even during extreme liberal periods when official regulation and intervention was practically non-existant, the state used patrimonial rights, official monopolies and protectionism to facilitate oligopolisation by domestic and foreign interests. Such

154

measures were not always in the interests of the native agro-exporters and miners who constituted the core of the native élite (and who, according to crude versions of the dependency theory, should have been the major beneficiaries of liberal regimes). However, the most negative effects of the state's participation in domestic financial activities stemmed from unchecked interventionism, excessive external indebtedness, internal debt default and inflationary financial policies which constrained – especially after 1930 – the full potential of the Peruvian private domestic sector.

This chapter will first discuss the situation of weak regulation and the relatively stable monetary conditions which prevailed during the use of the gold standard prior to 1919. It then will proceed to analyse the initial interventionist measures in monetary and banking matters during the debt-ridden regime of President Leguía. Subsequently attention will centre on the 'autonomous' financial policies of the 1930s, and the role of official central and developing banking. Finally the chapter will conclude with an analysis of the decline in the influence of agro-exporters on state financial policies, and the parallel rise of the interests supporting the early attempts at import-substitution industrialisation and the controlist and damaging ('repressive') financial measures of the 1940s.

REGULATION AND POLICY DEBATES BEFORE 1919

The state's finances were in complete disarray after the war with Chile. Private and public funds were exhausted as a result of the forced contributions, amounting to eight million silver soles over a period of ten months, imposed by the occupying Chilean authorities in Lima. After the Chileans left, lack of revenue forced the Peruvian state, controlled by military and civilian *caudillos* until 1899, to rely on local credit, using meagre customs revenues as guarantees, or to obtain funds through levies. Under President Nicolás de Piérola (1895–9) new revenue resources were created, such as taxes on salt consumption, and tax collection was reorganised on the basis of indirect taxation.[6] Due to its financial weakness the state tended to behave complacently toward its foreign and domestic creditors and to respond favourably to liberal business initiatives.

In terms of financial regulation, the state limited itself to legislation that facilitated the use of metal currency, gave monopolistic privileges to certain creditor institutions, favoured the organisation of semi-private tax collection companies, and established minimal control over some financial institutions (mortgage departments, insurance companies and savings institutions). The most outstanding regulatory measures enacted before 1914 were the following:

1. The withdrawal of the devalued fiscal notes (*billetes*) in November 1887 and, subsequently, the consolidation of the internal debt in July 1889 and December 1898 which converted S/97 million in *billetes* at a proportion of 100 to 1, as well as other past liabilities of the state, into debt bonds which earned only 1 per cent interest. In line with the traditional abuse by the state of domestic lenders, the consolidation measures proved disastrous. In 1898 approximately S/11 million in *billetes* were not consolidated because their holders refused to submit to the consolidation terms. In 1901 internal debt bonds were quoted at 7 per cent of their face value, and S/58 million in floating debts were still waiting to be consolidated.[7]

2. The Mortgage Law of 1889, which set the legal conditions for mortgage credit in order to assure loan repayment, and later the establishment of a weak controlling institution, the Inspección Fiscal de Bancos Hipotecarios y Compañías de Seguros.

3. Between 1895 and 1897 a series of minimal capital and asset requirements based on real estate which aided the establishment of native insurance companies.

4. Between 1897 and 1902 decrees favouring the transition to the gold standard.

5. An ineffective Law of Savings Houses in October 1901 which was not enforced until it was modified by another law in 1927.[8]

6. Contracts with privately organised companies authorising tax collection under a system providing for advances to the government against future tax collection (Sociedad Recaudadora de Impuestos in 1898, Compañía Nacional de Recaudación in 1901, Sociedad Recaudadora in 1912, Compañía Salinera in 1907).

7. The formation of the Caja de Depósitos y Consignaciones in 1905 which was given a limited role as a public financial institution in charge of receiving deposits as guarantees for compliance with legal contracts.[9]

Until the first legislation on the issuance of paper money appeared in 1914, commercial banking was almost untouched by state regulation and, like the Lima stock exchange, it ruled its activities according to the liberal and general Commerce Code of 1902. Attempts by Presidents Leguía (1909–12) and Billinghurst (1912–13) to increase state intervention and regulation in finance met with failure. Leguía's efforts to form a national bank on the basis of the Caja de Depósitos y Consignaciones in collaboration with German capital in 1910, and his search for US banks' participation in reorganising tax collection in 1912, did not bear fruit.[10]

Under the liberal conditions allowed by the Peruvian state prior to 1914, the model of banking regulation applied in Peru contained elements copied from the English and French models and, following increased state regulation by 1921, from the US model. The result was a hybrid composite: 'due to the limited conditions offered by the local environment', observed a contemporary in 1917, 'national banks are of a mixed nature: mortgage, discount, issue, agricultural, etc.'[11] French legislation and practice were introduced in 1889 to standardise mortgage transactions and aid individual urban real estate proprietors. Thus some of the conservative banking, reserve and deposit practices in Lima were similar to those applied by private institutions in Paris.[12]

However until 1914 an English-based, liberal model was dominant in Peru. It had as its main characteristic a self-adjusting, inelastic gold currency supply. Interest rate policy was based on discount rate variations which closely followed fluctuations in the exchange rate. In Peru however there was no counterpart to the Bank of England to set the official discount rate. The rigid gold-based monetary policy prevented official intervention in banking and monetary matters as long as private banks were tied to the gold standard and acted by common agreement in setting interest rate policies.[13]

The private financial élite vigorously supported an unregulated financial structure and an inexpensive, non-interventionist state apparatus. Early foreign attempts to obtain state-granted monopolies over the financial structure, as in the case of the Banco Privilegiado, were initially blocked by local financiers.[14] It was in the interests of native bankers and evolving élite groups to take advantage of the space left by the lack of state intervention in areas such as tax collection, public services, public works, transportation, banking and insurance. Exporters also supported the liberal state in order to avoid paying taxes. Miners protested against export taxes in 1884 and 1895 and, with merchant support, obtained liberal tax conditions until 1915 (when Tizón, an author writing on mining taxes, protested against the new imposition of taxes on miners).[15] Sugar producers resisted export taxes in 1914.[16] Likewise official attempts to establish an organised system of direct income tax were consistently rejected by the élite, who favoured instead an increase in indirect taxes.[17]

The intermediary role of semi-public financial institutions was limited to reinforcing élite business. The state granted the management of the Caja de Depósitos y Consignaciones (1905) and the Compañía Nacional de Recaudación (named Sociedad Recaudadora de Impuestos before 1901 and Compañía Recaudadora de Impuestos after 1912) to private investor groups and local banks in order to ensure that local credit would be granted to the government. The assets held by these semi-public institutions comprised judicial deposits, tax collection funds and current accounts.

Total deposits in the Caja de Depósitos reached the respectable sum of Lp18 million (6 per cent in cash, 19 per cent in securities and 21 per cent in current cash accounts) for the period 1905–24, or an average of approximately Lp1 million a year (compared to one-fifteenth of the total amount of commercial banking deposits in 1924). Tax collection by the Cía. Recaudadora amounted to an annual average of Lp1.7 million for the period 1913–21 (Lp13 million in total). The state was provided with advances at a fixed interest of between 3 per cent and 6 per cent from the profit accounts of these semi-public institutions. The remaining profit went to private shareholders. Deposits and funds of these institutions were also invested in stocks and bonds quoted on the Lima Exchange. By these methods an important portion of public funds was transferred into private hands.[18]

The weak position of the state in relation to domestic financial activities was also expressed in exchange and monetary policies. Exchange rate and monetary manipulations by governments in underdeveloped countries have been studied lately as key devices to promote economic growth. Correct handling of exchange and monetary conditions by economic policymakers in alternating periods of export boom and bust might make a difference in the adequate use of trade gains in the first case, or mitigate the negative effects of delayed growth in the second. In simplified terms, an independent floating monetary policy responding to favourable international export conditions (exchange appreciation) can be used to increase necessary imports and ease the conditions of foreign indebtedness. Conversely, during a decline in export trade (exchange depreciation) exchange rate flexibility can be used to stimulate internal diversification, induce import substitution, or delay foreign debt repayment.

Obviously a large variety of constraints condition the effective application of these simplified rules.

Pressure from creditor countries, an immature institutional structure, domestic consumer and saver demands and other political and social concerns act against the smooth adoption of sound exchange and monetary policies. Studies on Brazil and Mexico during the period examined here show fairly pragmatic results from exchange and monetary handling in Brazil (coffee export sheltering), and a less successful outcome in Mexico (worsening of its foreign debt) due to attempts by the Díaz regime to maintain the use of silver currency in spite of the decline in its international price.[19]

In Peruvian financial history there are several episodes that allow revealing evaluations of the official and economic élite's attempts to use exchange policy and monetary measures to their advantage. The first incident involves the abandonment, in 1887, of the drastically depreciated currency notes or *billetes fiscales* of the late Guano Age. From 1875 these notes, which had started as private bank issues (see Chapter 2), depreciated in spite of (some argued because of) the state's financial intervention as guano and nitrate revenues declined. By December 1879 they were quoted at 170 per cent below the scarce silver unit and by 1883, during the Chilean occupation, they had depreciated to the worthless level of 2500 per cent below the value of silver currency.[20]

As a means of payment the *billete* was totally unsatisfactory and it was seldom used in mercantile transactions. However silver currency was scarce due to impositions by Chile following the war with that country, and the extensive flight of capital at the time. The *billete* unavoidably appeared in small, daily transactions due to the shortage of silver currency. In addition it received fragile support from the state, which accepted payment of only 10 per cent of customs rights in *billetes*. Most importantly, lawyers representing heavily indebted agriculturists argued in favour of the need to sustain the legal value of the depreciated notes to allow their clients to pay their debts in *billetes* instead of silver.[21] Years later influential agro-exporters, facing yet another difficult monetary period in 1901, recognised the favourable effects the *billete* depreciation of the 1880s had had in diminishing the pressure of debt on agricultural estates.[22]

The surprising persistence of the *billete* can be explained by the concurrent need of the state and politically influential landowners to finance public and private deficits with devalued currency. It was possible to do away with the *billete* in Peru only when national and foreign creditors, merchants and the reorganised credit institutions articulated their common interests in reconstructing the Peruvian capitalist sector and its foreign credit. For the future advance of capitalism eradication of these fiscal notes was the rational policy to follow if the capital market was to be regenerated (see Chapter 3). Although the survival of the *billete* had had certain advantages for the agro-exporters, they too eventually had to recognise their own need for foreign credit to expand their activities and to recuperate and surpass previous levels of production. An example of the evolution among agro-exporters was the action of Antero Aspíllaga when he was minister of finance in 1887–9. He recognised that the fiscal note could not be enforced as mandatory legal tender, and soon after participated actively in the foreign debt settlement of the claims of British bondholders.[23]

After the abolition of the fiscal notes, merchants and financiers became for some years the recognisable heads of exchange policymaking. Silver currency was preferred because of its initial exchange stability. Foreign capital arrived in 1890, slowly at first, to support the large, predominantly foreign merchant firms and the three existing banks. Therefore the gradual expansion in the use of silver currency, through the active participation of the native Banco del Callao as minting contractor to the Peruvian government, had a temporary rehabilitative effect on internal and external trade mechanisms.

However the international price of silver declined sharply between 1890 and 1902.[24] Peruvian hopes that exchange stability would allow an expansion of international trade were frustrated by this decline. The importation of goods, a crucial activity for merchants, was considerably afflicted, since imports paid for abroad in gold were being bought in devaluating silver in the local market. Banks which had taken the precaution of keeping their capital and reserve accounts in gold, and which also received foreign capital in gold, were forced to lend in silver. This resulted in the shrinking of their profits in spite of rising interest rates. The gains obtained by the banks in buying bills of exchange by discount in London plummeted.[25]

Agricultural exporters on the other hand benefited somewhat from the depreciation of the silver currency, provided that they were not excessively indebted in gold, as their goods were paid for abroad in gold but they paid for local labour and other costs of production in silver.[26] As a consequence, between 1892 and 1897, agro-exporters, those merchants involved primarily in export trade and credit (the most vocal was J. L. Dubois, manager of Graham Rowe & Company), and silver miners afraid of the adverse effects they would suffer from a reduction in the minting of silver currency, consistently opposed the import merchants' and bankers' pleas for the adoption of pro-gold standard measures.

Also affected were the members of the local Banco del Callao's board of directors, who represented the most important economic interests. Opposing strategies of how to deal with the situation began to develop from the first signs, in 1886, of a slump in the price of silver, and later heated debates were held in the national Congress. The bank had established its capital in silver soles in April 1883. In 1887 the silver soles again became the official currency when fiscal notes were taken out of circulation. The bank's conservative merchant-financiers, among whom the most prominent was J. M. Mendoza, thought it convenient to convert the bank's capital to British gold currency in order to follow closely the institution's doctrine that 'the integrity of the real value of the bank's capital should always be preserved'.[27]

However the decision to maintain the bank's capital in gold, while the majority of transactions carried out by the bank had to be in the official silver currency, proved to be a mistake. As profits in silver had to be converted into gold, practically no dividends could be declared from 1891 to 1894, the years of the most radical decline in the price of silver. An intense debate among the directors ensued as to whether or not dividends should be declared, whether capital accounts should be in silver rather than gold in order to at least secure silver dividends and avoid public distrust and, finally, whether the national currency itself should be based on silver or gold.[28]

Two principal factions developed among the directors of the Banco del Callao. The 'gold' group, composed of directors Mendoza, Correa y Santiago and Payán, was at first triumphant. This group favoured the raising of interest rates to cover exchange differences and opposed the distribution of dividends. The 'silver' group was formed by J. L. Dubois and Enrique C. Basadre, who protested against higher interest rates and the non-payment of dividends.[29] This division among the directors mirrored the conflict between importers and exporters in the Lima business élite. Furthermore the men who represented the two opposing views within the confines of the Banco del Callao were the same men who advised members of the Peruvian Congress in 1892 about the best monetary unit to be adopted.[30]

Payán and Mendoza defended the adoption of gold currency by citing the negative effects the depreciation of silver had had on foreign capital participation in the bank and the country by reducing the amount in remittances from abroad. Dubois, who was deeply involved in the export business, argued the need to continue using silver currency whose depreciation was to the advantage of exporters.

The silver group temporarily defeated the gold group, and the bank's capital was reconverted to silver in January 1893. This was done in spite of Payán's plea for the necessity of keeping good contacts abroad, which meant payment of foreign credits in gold, and Mendoza and Piaggio's reluctance to accept conversion to silver because they represented stockholders abroad (shares held abroad amounted to 25 per cent of the bank's total capital stock at the time) who preferred to keep their shares in gold. Dubois, on the other hand, defended his position by expressing the hope that silver currency would experience an increase in value due to a possible change in US monetary policy.[31] Mendoza attacked the interest in exchange profits which lay behind the stance of the silver group, who would be harmed if the gold standard were to be adopted: '. . . sugar producers and other exporters would no longer receive the profit they obtain today from their products sold abroad by paying their labourers and others [in silver for what they receive in gold'].[32] Despite his initial triumph, Dubois became isolated from the rest of the directors in December 1893. As a result, the Board of Directors fell under the control of the gold group. Therefore credit was curtailed, a double interest tariff was applied (lower loan interest for gold and higher for silver), and deposits in gold were eagerly sought.

In response to the profit opportunities offered by exchange depreciation for the establishment of sheltered domestic factories, merchants and banks also participated in the transfer of funds from trade to industrial investments.[33] Protectionist measures were introduced to reinforce the gains from exchange depreciation. In periods when exchange revaluation had an adverse effect on oligopolistic domestic industries, the dominant liberal policymakers provided a degree of official protection for those same industries. This was achieved by raising tariffs on competing imports according to fiscal needs in response to political lobbying by native groups. By 1895 the Piérola regime enacted measures for currency appreciation toward the gold standard and established import taxes with the primary intention of increasing government revenue, which had been drastically reduced in those years. Conveniently, machinery imports were declared to be free of tax. As a result, foreign and local financial interests participated in a costly and shortlived industrial bubble which had started under the shelter of exchange depreciation and was continued by Piérola's protectionism.

During the years of the most intensive protectionist actions (1895–1900), local financiers and merchants worked to obtain a fiscal shelter for their existing investments in domestic industries. Their aim was to establish monopolistic control over the supply of certain manufactured goods. Payán and Piérola worked together to obtain the desired alteration in policy and consensus among the economic élite. Since 1892 financial interests had publicly opposed the 'natural' protection of exchange depreciation because of its negative effects on banking. Opposing protectionist support for depreciation of the silver currency Payán argued in 1892:

> I desire, perhaps more than anyone else, that [our industries] acquire all their possible development and enhancement. I also think they should be granted every type of official protection without causing damage onto others. I aspire they should progress through lawful means which are good and economic management, savings in labour, quality of their products, and the rise of prices in the consumers' market. I condemn the unjust protection of monetary depreciation.[34]

In 1895 a solution which allowed a great advance in tariff protection and the consolidation of oligopolistic groups was agreed upon between financial interests and the revenue-hungry state. Merchants and bankers personally invested in privileged, protected factories with the certainty of a high price for their products, windfall profits and a good opportunity to import machinery and foreign capital. Influential bankers also became principal and honorary directors of industrial concerns in order to deflect any possible competition from the few native lending institutions. Payán was director of the following industrial concerns: Cía. de Fósforos El Sol, Fábrica Nacional de Sombreros de Lana and the Peruvian Cotton Manufacturing Company, among others.

When more than one privileged factory appeared simultaneously, price agreements and production controls were established to guarantee handsome profits for the factories involved. The most prominent protected industries with heavy oligopolistic control and institutional financial support were the manufacturers of textiles (cotton and wool), flour and noodles, matches, beer, cigars, soap, candles and hats. A case in point was the Fábrica de Fósforos El Sol, which was controlled by the directors of the Banco del Perú y Londres. In 1898 the directors of the factory established a joint participation agreement with the American company, Diamond Match, which held 51 per cent of the factory's stock as payment for imported machinery. In 1900 El Sol entered a price agreement with the more efficient local factory La Luciérnaga with the intention of raising the price of matches. In 1902 the El Sol factory was going through a difficult period due to a market glut and so decided to pay La Luciérnaga S/8000 a month to coordinate a reduction in match production for five years. El Sol had serious difficulty in adapting its imported technology (in spite of the paid services of Diamond Match engineers), to produce goods of competitive quality, and in marketing its products regardless of the commercial expertise of the Banco del Perú y Londres and Ayulo & Company. The factory reported an annual loss of Lp7700 in July 1906.[35]

Criticism by liberal agro-exporters of protectionist moves by merchants and financiers climaxed during the sugar export crisis of 1901–2. Since 1896 the liberal commentators Garland and Gubbins had argued that protectionist measures without a central plan had negative effects on the productive structure and fiscal budget. They estimated that approximately S/10 million in revenue and gains from consumer price increases had been diverted from investment in the most economically viable sector (agriculture, cattle raising and mining) to support a handful of industries dependent exclusively on fiscal protection.[36] They considered the defense of the so called 'national industries' to be an act of hypocrisy on the part of opportunistic 'protectionists'. These industries were, according to the liberal position, unfavourable for domestic consumers due to the resultant price increases, but very favourable to foreign-financed imports of industrial machinery and materials. The activities of Peruvian industrialists, according to other anti-protectionist thinkers, were too costly and uneconomical for the country because they lacked industrial knowledge – this had to be imported at a high price, together with foreign technology.[37]

By 1901, however, it was too late to press for the radical eradication of protectionist devices. Agro-exporters had to learn to coexist with protected industries and try also to benefit from them, as some were already doing: 'The interests of industries that were established under the shelter of special laws – even if these laws had little or no public discussion – are as sacred as any other legitimate interest'.[38] Despite the controversy which arose over their actions, the manipulation of protective fiscal measures by the élite did facilitate the transfer of funds from trade, finance and eventually agro-exports to the initially costly manufacturing sector, a sector which survived and, in later years, grew.

The fundamental area of conciliation of interests which acted as a pillar for the Peruvian financial policy between 1902 and 1914 was the final official adoption of the gold standard. The measures dictated by President Piérola toward restricting the amount of silver currency in circulation and the inducement for gold to be imported in 1897, proved surprisingly effective for a majority of interested parties. Foreign capital was enticed with advantageous privileges and arrived in Peru swiftly.[39] The exchange rate stabilised, importation improved, and agro-exporters and industrialists obtained easy foreign credit to implement the modernisation and mechanisation of their production. A rise in prices directly linked to the gold standard measure and exchange rate appreciation was beneficial for producers and suppliers to the domestic market.

Soon, however, there arose some discontent with the gold standard, especially after the end of the sugar export boom in 1901. Agro-export and provincial interests, deprived of currency to fund their transactions, raised their voices in protest. Puno merchants complained about the disappearance of silver currency in the provinces, and contemporary analysts criticised some negative effects arising from the adoption of the gold standard.[40]

Once merchants and bankers had obtained the official adoption of the gold standard in 1902, they sternly and inflexibly promoted its use, regardless of the condition of the export sector and the balance of payment situation. Foreign capital started to contribute to the disproportionate growth of the local capital market and financial speculations ensued with securities floated abroad – these collapsed at the onset of the First World War. During the years of acute reduction in exports (1902, 1907 and 1912) the fixed and inflexible gold parity policy had a negative effect on diversification. Even importers suffered when the internal market contracted, and several merchants went bankrupt. However financial institutions benefited because they were the major holders of gold and they controlled the stability of the exchange rate to support the constant internal appreciation of their gold.

The banks' stubborn determination to retain control of the monetary sphere, and to maintain a stable and high exchange rate to defend their joint portfolio investments with foreign financial capital, continued during the First World War. Their emergency measure of adopting a limited issue of provisional bank notes (*cheques circulares*) damaged the expanding interests of agro-exporters, who had started to enjoy windfall gains in the First World War export boom since 1916. A shortage of currency due to the banks' monetary policies created serious difficulties in the domestic economy. Exporters lost sizeable profits because of the extremely high international value of the Peruvian monetary unit in 1917–19 (about 20 per cent above the British sterling!) and the acute rise in the internal costs of production due to international inflation and the shortage of currency. The banks' control over the issue of *cheques circulares* was severely criticised, as were their foreign financial speculations: 'the Peruvian financiers have become misers with the [gold] metal'.[41]

Criticism of the banks was also levelled by those sectors of the élite who were endangered by the financial crisis which had started with a run on the Banco Alemán Transatlántico on 1 August 1914. Fearful that the run would spread to other institutions, the leading local financiers pressed the government to declare a moratorium lasting several months on banking liabilities. Financial paralysis followed the sudden interruption of international transactions in bills of exchange and gold. A shortage of the means of payment dominated the frantic scramble to prevent financial ruin. A thirst for gold, an instinctive reaction to the uncertainty of the war, was also widespread among Peruvian economic agents during 1914–16. Local banks tried in various ways to hold on to their diminishing gold reserves without consideration for the interests of other sectors.

The influential *civilista* congressman and university professor, José Matías Manzanilla, was among those who blamed the banks for contributing to the public's 'nervous state' due to the vulnerable condition of their liquid reserves just before the crisis developed. According to Manzanilla, a main cause of the banks' weakness was 'the absence of laws to limit their autonomy, and the dangerous liberties taken by stock companies whose stock, sometimes enormously inflated, served as collateral for a considerable number of bank loans . . .'[42] This was an indirect criticism of the local Banco del Perú y Londres.

Although the first legislation on the *cheques circulares* gave the banks the privilege of issue, it nevertheless represented a partial reduction in their previously unrestrained privileges. An official institution, the Junta de Vigilancia, was created to control the private banks' issues and to centralise their gold guarantees. Payán had argued that domestic commercial activities would absorb an issue of no less than two million libras with 25 per cent gold collateral. Deputy Manzanilla and Senator José I. Chopitea (owner of the important sugar estate Laredo), among other congressmen, opposed vigorously Payán's proposal, considering that it provided an excessive advantage to the banks and that it could cause inflation to rise. Other congressmen with strong liberal principles and animosity toward the banks were deputies Francisco Tudela y Varela, Mariano H. Cornejo and Alfredo Solf y Muro, and senator Antonio Miró Quesada.[43] As a result of the protests, the first issue was limited to Lp1 100 000 with 35 per cent gold collateral. All but one of the banks responded in several joint public memoranda warning against the catastrophic consequences of this limited issue which, they argued, would force banks to restrict or refuse credit. Only the Banco Italiano refused to sign the memoranda. It held to the position that the first *cheques circulares* issue was sufficient for the needs of the country. This shrewd move by the Banco Italiano was certainly an attempt to inherit the recently abandoned metal currency tradition and prestige.

The negative effects of the outbreak of the First World War on the gold standard created a serious financial crisis which contributed to the decline of the private banks' authority and to the start of the state's centralising and regulatory powers in monetary and exchange matters. Due to the gold shortage in 1914 the Junta de Vigilancia collected gold deposits from banks to back the private issue of *cheques circulares*. The private banks struggled to maintain their authority over the financial sphere by attempting to influence note issue and gold reserve policies. The US government embargo on gold export in 1917 caused further monetary problems in 1918. With the inauguration of the second Leguía government in 1919, the Junta de Vigilancia increased its regulatory powers and established autonomous control over the issue of notes and over the gold reserves which had accumulated in the United States. Although Peru nominally used the gold standard until 1931, in practice it was a modified gold standard that operated in the 1920s. A floating exchange rate, dependent on export proceeds and the balance of payments, became the principal monetary rule.[44]

LOANS AND INTERVENTION IN THE 1920s

Fiscal and monetary conditions fared satisfactorily in 1919 and the first half of 1920 due to a favourable export situation. In order to implement his economic policy, Leguía counted on revenue from export and import taxation and a series of indirect taxes. Tax collection had been managed by the semi-public Compañía Recaudadora de Impuestos but after 1921 it was brought under sterner government control. In 1927 Leguía created a more centralised fiscal agency for the collection of taxes, as well as setting up several government monopolies whose revenues he pledged to foreign creditors.[45] In addition tariff protection was increased to encourage domestic industry. Road construction, irrigation projects, urban development and a variety of public improvements formed the pillars of Leguía's developmentalist economic policy.[46]

Pressures to reduce the Peruvian exchange rate in 1921 forced the government to assume an unprecedented regulatory interventionist role which affected banking operations and interest rate and credit policies. In May 1921 the Inspección Fiscal de Bancos was created to enforce legal reserve requirements and to standardise the accounting methods of private banks. To avoid a reduction in borrowing, the government decreed a maximum legal interest rate of 10 per cent, and it also took measures to prevent capital from leaving the country. Likewise, radical projects for the creation of an interventionist national bank were prepared by Leguía's officials.

However the 1921 contraction continued its course. Private banks led by the Banco del Perú y Londres strongly opposed state regulation and the national bank project, but Leguía struggled to impose his authority over the Banco del Perú y Londres through political means. The Banco del Perú y Londres' monetary policy directly contradicted Leguía's new financial orientation. A serious conflict between the state and the private institution ensued.

In order to consolidate his government and execute modernising economic measures, Leguía needed a state with enhanced centralising power and increased financial resources.[47] His opposition to the *civilista* political clique stemmed from his previous unsatisfactory attempts to bring about a more efficient economic administration directed by the state and favouring native exporters.[48] Of the private sectors supported by Leguía's measures, perhaps the one that benefited most was the agricultural export sector. The protection given to agriculture by Leguía's government included the waiving of import taxes on insecticides and agricultural machinery, technical support and irrigation projects. The avowed objective of Leguía was 'to make every Peruvian a proprietor'.[49]

Both by background and conviction Leguía favoured strong financial advantages for agro-exporters like himself. Economic development was seen by Leguía as a process starting in the export sector and spreading to the industrial, urban and provincial levels with the help of moderate state intervention. 'President Augusto B. Leguía's work of national reconstruction since 1919 had necessarily to encompass simultaneously a vast and complex public works plan, to defeat the inertia of several centuries and set the base for material advancement'.[50] Public works included motorways, railroads, port facilities, irrigation projects, colonisation in the jungle, urban sanitation, and public parks and monuments. This developmental argument helped to justify financial indebtedness and state intervention.

Old and crude practices to protect the profits and capital of exporters, such as exchange depreciation, were not sufficient for Leguía. A more sophisticated financial structure that would allow credit expansion to exporters was the alternative he argued for in 1902.[51] He decided to confront his stubborn opponents in the traditional financial and commercial spheres who had benefited in the past from concessions obtained from an ultra liberal and financially weak state.

Leguía attempted to control the issue of money, increase tax revenues, limit inflation, impose ceilings on interest rates and regulate the domestic financial structure. All these measures affected the existing privileges of the Banco del Perú y Londres. As early as October 1919, a French diplomat informed Paris that President Leguía was thinking about forming a Peruvian national bank which would have currency issuing privileges. The opinion of the diplomat was that Leguía's plan could only be accomplished with the aid of 'l'argent américain'.[52] Rumours of the proposed Banco de la Nación also reached the ears of the Banco del Perú y Londres' directors, causing unease among them.

In July 1920 minister Fernando Fuchs published his proposals for the national bank. His innovative economic principles were considered radical at the time. Fuchs argued that what he considered a local financial bonanza brought by the export boom had to be consolidated to prevent a crisis when the exceptional international conditions returned to normal. He observed that an excessive amount had already been deposited (Lp17 million) in local banks and considered this money could be more productively allocated. Fuchs thus proposed the creation of a national bank to allow private funds to be used to provide the state with loans for public works and foreign debt servicing, to regulate the money supply and to distribute national capital (through industrial promotion, and so forth) in such a way as to rationalise the contributory system. At the same time the proposed bank would control tax collection. Local bankers reacted with horror to these projects for state intervention in economic activities.[53]

In the tense atmosphere created by conflicting public and private long-term interests, more immediate incidents triggered an overtly aggressive conflict between the government and the Banco del Perú y Londres. Leguía was against any private transfer of funds from the United States by the bank, and in November 1920 he rejected the bank's plan to import Lp100 000 in gold to increase its share of *cheques circulares*. Instead Leguía wanted to maintain complete official control over the funds deposited abroad in joint account with private banks. Furthermore he conceived a very profitable transaction for the state with the funds in the United States, which amounted to $12 million. Between April and June 1921 he pressed for the transfer of the Junta de Vigilancia's dollar funds, held in a deposit account at the National City Bank of New York, to a London sterling account with the expectation of obtaining a handsome profit once the British currency recovered. The English pound actually appreciated in 1922 providing a profit of Lp600 000 for the government.

This action was taken by Leguía in spite of opposition from the local banks who claimed the measure was illegal. The banks had expected to use the gold fund held abroad for their own interests.[54] National City Bank officials had also attempted to dissuade Leguía from transferring the funds. The City Bank's president informed the US Secretary of the Treasury about Leguía's intentions, seeking support from the US government in stopping the transaction. According to the City Bank president, the British government's representative in Lima was cooperating with British financial interests (that is, the Anglo South American Bank) to bring about the gold transfer in order to reduce American financial influence in Peru.[55]

Arguing adverse international conditions, the Banco del Perú y Londres decided at the end of 1920 to raise its interest rates one percentage point in an overt challenge to Leguía's intention to maintain interest rates unchanged. As a response to a government decree in May 1921 regulating investments by banks and restricting the transfer of funds abroad, further interest rate increases were contemplated by the Banco del Perú y Londres.[56] On 11 May 1921 Leguía responded by limiting interest rates to a 10 per cent ceiling. The latter measure by the government was considered by bankers as the ultimate illegal trespass by the state on the banks' sacred liberal right to dictate their own interest rate policy. The outraged directors of the Banco del Perú y Londres decided on 12 May to cancel abruptly all current accounts, arguing that they were no longer profitable because of the interest rate limitation. This measure was intended to exert public pressure on Leguía.

This time Leguía unleashed all of his might against the Banco del Perú y Londres. A decree was enacted on 14 May to allow the gradual cancellation of debtor current accounts as a means of softening the impact on the public of the sudden decision by the Banco del Perú y Londres. At the same time an official attack in the press was orchestrated against the bank and the president of its board of directors, Manuel V. Villarán, a distinguished *civilista* ideologue. He was accused of having political motives which had influenced the bank's recent actions in opposition to the Leguía's government. A public scandal ensued which forced Villarán to resign his post at the bank. Some months later Villarán declared that he had learned from the May 1921 events that it was inconvenient for the bank to have public men among its directors, a practice hitherto ignored.[57] In June 1921 government officials initiated another campaign against the bank, this time in the provinces, by sending alarming information by telegram to erode the bank's prestige. This action caused a run on the bank in Cuzco.[58]

At another level, in August 1921 Leguía's supporters in Congress severely criticised the administration of the Cía. Recaudadora de Impuestos which had been in charge of the Banco del Perú y Londres since 1913. Complaints were made about the excessive expenditure of and profiteering practices by the private tax collecting company. This action formed part of Leguía's attempts to reorganise the tax system and to offer it as a guarantee to foreign lenders.[59]

The Banco del Perú y Londres had a secret weapon to use in its struggle against Leguía, but this would only be used in the event that Leguía radicalised his measures against the private banks. In 1921 the bank's contacts in European financial institutions, through its Committee in Paris, were ready at any moment to start an international diplomatic campaign against Leguía. An urgent telegram sent to Paris by the Banco del Perú y Londres informed supporters there of the alarming local situation. Jacques Kulp, the leading member of the Comité de París, answered immediately:

The situation is known here and has caused a very bad impression on the [French] government and public. Send a telegram if you think diplomatic intervention is opportune. We will then take the necessary actions.[60]

The local directors appreciated the support offered by Paris but decided to postpone any diplomatic action. This did not stop Kulp from informing the French minister of foreign affairs about the trouble the bank had been caused in Peru by Leguía.[61] Obviously any hasty action could be disastrous for the bank due to the wide popularity Leguía enjoyed at the time. However the foreign pressure against Leguía, although subtle and cautious, was quite real and imposed a definite limit on Leguía's 'nationalistic' measures.

The conflict between private banks and the state calmed down somewhat after June 1921. Negotiations concerning financial legislation and the national bank project were carried out in October 1921 between the government, local merchants and the banks. The banks tried to water down the initial Fuchs project for the national bank, as well as the new version of it proposed by the new minister of finance, A. M. Rodríguez Dulanto, because of the dangers 'that the establishment of such bank would entail for circulation, business and the country'.[62] Leguía offered a compromise that would allow a 65 per cent participation by private banks and a 35 per cent government share in the national bank's capital.

Leguía was a complex political personality who constantly played opposing forces against each other for his own advantage. He obtained political benefits by pitting Peruvian public opinion against the Peruvian Corporation,[63] the *civilista* élite against popular movements, and British, French, German and US financial interests against each other. On this occasion he was playing state interests against private interests over the matter of the national bank. Unfortunately for Leguía the swift negative effects of the international recession in 1921 considerably eroded the leverage of the state in its negotiations with the private banks. The government found itself unable to pay its employees' wages and had to ask for emergency loans from the local banks. A military uprising to demand payment of delayed wages to soldiers included among its actions the storming of the Banco del Perú y Londres' agency in Iquitos. The Peruvian exchange rate also dropped as a result of a decline in export prices.

In November 1921 serious accusations passed again between the government and the Banco del Perú y Londres. Once more Leguía's government attempted to spread suspicion against the Banco del Perú y Londres when it implicated the bank in the transfer of funds to political conspirators in Guayaquil. The bank was in effect forced to suspend all fund transfers to Guayaquil.[64] In addition leaflets attacking the private banks were distributed in December 1921 with the intention of forcing the banks to grant emergency loans to the government and to divert the attention of dissatisfied state employees.[65] On behalf of the Banco del Perú y Londres a diplomatic response to the state's aggression was finally being prepared. A telegram was sent to the Paris Committee stating that in due course a communication from Lima would announce that the time had come to exert foreign pressure.[66]

It was at this highly volatile time that a commission of American bankers from the Guaranty Trust Company of New York, led by Nicholas Kelley and further composed of C. W. Van Law and R. S. Rife, arrived in Peru. The commission's aim was to negotiate a financial reorganisation of the Peruvian state in order to guarantee the safety of future American loans to the Leguía government. The recommendation by the commission on the issue of the national bank dispute was accepted by both the private banks and the state. The American commission held that any decision by US banks to grant the badly needed loans to the government was conditional on the establishment of a central bank similar to the US Federal Reserve Bank.[67]

As the government was devoid of funds and in political danger it desperately needed foreign loans to secure financial and political stability. US financial advisors were hired in 1921–2 in the hope of facilitating the granting of credit by US banks. Loan negotiations with the financial firms, the Foundation Company (financed by Morgan & Company, the Chase Manhattan Bank and the Third National Bank), holder of the 1919 sanitation contract, and the Guaranty Trust Company, resulted in the arrival in Peru of William W. Cumberland to occupy the post of customs supervisor. As a result of the condition stipulated by the US financial commission, the Banco de Reserva was established in April 1922 and Cumberland became its first manager.

However in 1922 the loan under discussion with the Guaranty Trust Company fell through and Leguía publicly criticised the American financiers. He briefly redirected his attention toward British financial institutions and was successful in obtaining a loan from Speyer & Company of London. Temporarily out of danger, he continued the state's regulatory drive by establishing in November 1922 minimum capital and domestic investment requirements for banks. These measures, strongly opposed by foreign banks which considered them unconstitutional, were never executed.[68] Cumberland resigned as manager of the Banco de Reserva in 1923. In 1925 another measure, the modification of the 1889 mortgage law to allow mortgage loans on urban building plots, was criticised by the directors of the Banco del Perú y Londres because its policy of granting mortgages exclusively on buildings was affected by the new law.

Leguía's banking regulations contributed decisively to the changed character of the Peruvian financial structure. The establishment of the Banco de Reserva, which was modelled on the US Federal Reserve Bank but lacked some of the latter's powers, allowed the relative centralisation of Peruvian financial activity. Exchange rate stabilisation and controls on inflation were achieved through the new institution to comply with the preconditions for foreign loans. A conciliatory formula for the establishment of the bank was arrived at after negotiation between the government and private banks. Domestic banks, not the state, provided the capital for the bank. Private banks thus had the power to significantly influence official policies.

Agro-exporters and miners held strategic positions in the Banco de Reserva. This situation was criticised in 1931 by E. W. Kemmerer, who recommended its reorganisation. It was, he wrote, 'dominated excessively by a single group of economic interests' and 'its loans and discount transactions were too rigid'.[69] The state, however, obtained the right to appoint three of the bank's directors and used political pressure to enforce the approval of desired policies at times of pressure from foreign creditors. Leguía appointed his relative, Eulogio Romero, as president of the bank in 1922. Romero was replaced in 1925 by a sugar planter and creditor of the state, Augusto Gildemeister, the bank's former vice-president. Eulogio Fernandini, an important miner, was also one of the bank directors appointed by the state.[70] In 1923 Cumberland highlighted the internal situation of the bank in a letter explaining the reasons for his decision to resign: 'As a Manager of the Bank, I am completely subject to the orders of the board of directors, and that board lacks banking knowledge and experience, its integrity not wholly above question, and it is continually threatened with government pressure'.[71]

The Banco de Reserva's activities allowed the expansion of credit and improved monetary flexibility, thereby benefiting local banks during periods of export boom. Its exclusive issuing power, its interest rate authority and its discount, rediscount and clearing house functions were soon praised by private banks. Private banks were able to drop their previously high reserves by 32 per cent between 1922 and 1923 due to the credit expansion made possible by the Banco de Reserva's policies.[72]

Leguía had introduced a fairly effective (at least until 1925) monetary policy based on the flexibility of internal credit monitored by the new reserve bank. In 1920 he arrested the tendency toward rising exchange and interest rates, thus supporting exporters.[73] His regulation of the money supply by paying attention to the state of the balance of payments constituted an attempt toward business expansion.[74] More crucially, the Banco de Reserva had a flexible policy of rediscounting that allowed local banks heavily tied to agricultural loans to expand their credit. All this was good news for agro-exporters, who were also well represented in the Banco de Reserva and in local banks, especially the Banco del Perú y Londres since 1921. But by extending official re-discount credit to the local institutions which had overspecialised in loans to the agro-export sector, the Banco de Reserva contributed to the possibility of a financial disaster should an export crisis occur.[75]

In addition the increasing reliance of the state on foreign loans to finance public works and budget deficits added to a dependence on US banks and curtailed the possibility of taking advantage of cheaper loan offers. Bankers heavily involved in agro-export finance protested against the foreign-induced stabilisation measures applied in 1927.[76] By guaranteeing monetary stability to foreign creditors, Leguía added enticements to foreign lending, although with this he also diminished the possibility that agro-exporters might benefit from currency devaluations. The decline in exports by 1925, and, especially from 1927, emphasised the need by agro-exporters for a declining exchange rate as protection against excessive indebtedness and bankruptcy. Leguía's financial edifice started cracking from the pressure exerted on the one side by his native agro-exporter protégés, and from the other side by US financiers. While export trade and the exchange rate had declined markedly from 1925, the government, urged on by US banks, unwisely augmented its foreign indebtedness.[77] From 1927 the government began to be pressured by its creditors and fiscal agents, Seligman & Company and the National City Bank of New York, to adopt severe exchange stabilisation measures to stop the fall in the Peruvian exchange rate which had resulted from the decline in agro-exports.

The organisation of the Mortgage and Agricultural Bank (1927) and the Savings Bank (1929) was conceived as means to expand the guarantees for foreign creditors of the state and to pacify local interests at the same time. In 1927 an American advisor, George H. Stevenson, was hired as executive head of the Mortgage and Agricultural Bank, and in April that year negotiations were initiated with an American financial firm for a $2 million loan to the bank.[78] Demands for the establishment of a mining bank were also being made at that time. These institutions were the forerunners of the state-sponsored 'development' banking institutions established in the 1930s. However the Mortgage and Agricultural Bank and the Savings Bank of the late 1920s lacked the confidence of the public because of the difficult fiscal situation. They also displaced local institutions from part of the financial market, forcing some of them to follow the tendency to overspecialise in agricultural credit.

Leguía's public works projects and his sponsorship of the native élite called for large budgetary outlays. A large part of his political strategy depended on keeping these two pillars – public works and élite support – from collapsing. The fall in revenue from exports in 1921–2 and 1925–6 threatened to unbalance the state budget, paralyse the programme of public works and depreciate the currency, so Leguía resorted to heavy foreign borrowing. Was this financial decision a mistake? Was the Peruvian government, as it was argued at the time, overambitious and thus had borrowed beyond its means?[79] Or had state intervention, fuelled by foreign funds, in fact contributed to domestic diversification?

The 1920s were years when increased domestic public and private credit financed a spate of road construction which changed the face of Peruvian overland communication.[80] Irrigation works were also made possible by cheap state credit that subsidised the purchase of irrigated land by small cotton growers.[81] Urban development, sanitation and street paving works in Lima and provincial cities made important leaps forward.

The policy of US banks to supply extensive credit to South American governments was part of a movement on the part of US interests to displace British financial and commercial supremacy in countries like Peru. The international financial atmosphere was optimistic, and the future prospects of Peru looked very promising to foreign observers. Leguía was quick to recognise the advantages of providing ample 'facilities for the investment of unemployed capital of industrial countries'.[82]

As compensation for increased state intervention, the export and financial élite demanded a supportive government, increased official credit, and a flexible money supply to bail them out from financial troubles linked to export declines. However foreign creditors also expected gains from state intervention. Local commercial banks lost most of the promising mortgage and small savings markets when the state took control of these in order to increase its financial appeal to foreign creditors. Furthermore, the hiring of foreign contractors, such as the Foundation Company, reduced the returned value of public works financed with borrowed funds. Industrial oligopolies limited the opportunities of industrial finance. Consequently over-specialisation in credit to commercial agriculture continued to increase. This showed in the extensive rediscounting by the Banco de Reserva of commercial banking instruments tied to large estates.[83] In other words, the state was contributing to national infrastructure but hindering local financial diversification.

High hopes were placed on the ability of another bonanza in commercial agriculture to overcome the vulnerable condition of Peruvian finances in 1927. Instead the world crisis of 1929 deeply affected the Peruvian agro-exporter élite and its financial structure. With the fall of Leguía in 1930 the protective net of commercial credit backed by the Banco de Reserva's rediscounts vanished, and several important agrarian concerns were declared bankrupt.[84]

As a consequence of the 1929 depression the pace of Peruvian development declined considerably in the 1930s. The capitalist advance of the 1920s, which had been encouraged by greater and relatively cheaper foreign borrowing, was not experienced with such intensity again in Peru until the 1950s and 1960s. However, despite the proven corruption involved in the process of foreign borrowing, the foreign debt of the 1920s had fewer long-term costs and provided more in terms of infrastructural transformation than the one of the 1870s.

Leguía was ousted by a military coup d'état organised in Arequipa by a group of lieutenant-colonels headed by Luis Sánchez Cerro, who accused Leguía of immoral tyranny, unlawful enrichment and 'false progress'.[85] Leguía's overthrow was accelerated by a much less known conflict among the élite during the final months of his regime. Strained by the world crisis, the agrarian exporters had been demanding the lowering of export taxes, criticising the irrigation projects, and pressing for the abandonment of the strict monetary stabilisation policy imposed by foreign creditors on the Banco de Reserva.[86] Leguía was unable to comply with these demands because of the government's acute financial difficulties at the time.

The last serious political crisis which Leguía confronted just four months before the Sánchez Cerro uprising resulted from the opposition to him by his ex-minister of finance, the senator for Lambayeque Enrique de la Piedra (head of the sugar complex Viuda de Piedra e hijos), and engineer Gerardo Klinge, both directing members of the Sociedad Nacional Agraria (SNA), the influential agriculturists' association.[87] Leguía lashed out against these conspirators, accusing them of planning to overthrow and assassinate him. Thus in May 1930, in the middle of the 'normalisation' financial measures that paralysed public works, Leguía lost an important section of his power base, the agrarian export sector of the Peruvian élite.

However before being ousted Leguía decreed a series of budgetary, regulatory, monetary and fiscal measures which resulted in the de facto devaluation of the Peruvian currency. Nominally use of the gold standard continued,[88] but the monetary unit was changed to the sol de oro instead of the libra. Through a sleight of hand Leguía used funds earmarked for the stabilisation of the Peruvian exchange rate to service the foreign debt. He argued that the Peruvian currency was safely fixed to the gold standard.[89] These measures set the tone for the subsequent monetary and financial decisions that effectively expanded internal monetary circulation and public credit after Leguía's fall.[90]

CENTRAL AND DEVELOPMENT BANKS SINCE 1931

With Leguía's demise in August 1930, political instability, a common feature in South American countries during the years of the depression, intensified the economic crisis in Peru. Little was done between 1930 and 1931 by the military government to halt the plummet in copper, sugar and cotton export prices; thus keeping their promise to proceed in economic and financial matters with 'honest parsimony'.[91]

The Kemmerer Mission was appointed in January 1931 and worked in Peru during a very unstable political period when local opinion was growing in favour of a moratorium on debt repayment, or even default. At the end of its three-month work the mission produced a series of documents concerning private banking regulation, central banking reorganisation, monetary policy based on the gold standard, and budgetary, public credit, customs and tax reforms.[92]

The package of measures recommended by Kemmerer was not implemented as a whole by the Peruvian authorities. Only the individual laws concerning banking regulation (February 1931), and central banking reorganisation and monetary stabilisation (April 1931) were enacted. Even these laws were substantially modified months later in a direction opposite to that which Kemmerer and his assistants had proposed.[93] Rather than limiting credit and monetary manipulation, the newly-created Central Reserve Bank was actually used to guarantee internal loans to the government and expand the monetary and credit systems beyond tight controls.[94]

Kemmerer's banking law made reference to private interests that had in the past dominated the previous reserve bank. He was refering especially to the agrarian export sector,[95] which continued to play an influential role in the country's financial policy in the 1932–50 period despite Kemmerer's reforms. However one of the most important results of his presence in Peru was the liquidation of the Banco del Perú y Londres, which had been closed to the public, with official permission, between October 1930 and February 1931. Kemmerer's assistants dictated that this institution had to be amputated from the Peruvian financial system, and that a regulating institution, the Superintendencia de Bancos, had to be created.[96] This was a heavy blow to the agro-export sector, which was no longer able to rely as heavily on the private commercial banks as it had during Leguía's regime.[97] However the liquidation of the Banco del Perú y Londres was conveniently delayed to allow some agro-exporters to avoid bankruptcy. The agro-exporters then adopted the strategy of directing their complaints and demands for protection and support to the state.

Agrarian export interests proved to be a mixed blessing in the period of economic recovery after 1932. On the one hand cotton production, with its high returned value and improved prices, provided enough foreign currency to uphold the Banco Central's credit manipulations. On the other hand the well organised agrarian élite continued to be influential in the defense of their narrow interests at the political and financial levels.

In the depths of the depression financial backing for the agrarian sector was extremely precarious. The organisation of agro-exporters, Sociedad Nacional Agraria, submitted to the post-Leguía governments long lists of demands, ranging from lower prices for fertilisers to reduced taxation.[98] Informal commercial *habilitadores* (lenders) to agriculturists were seen as oppressive. Foreign interests threatened to take over or foreclose on native agrarian properties which had enjoyed significant financial autonomy in the previous period.

Several proposals were submitted to Congress for it to declare a moratorium on private mortgage loans and enforce the repayment of debts in national currency.[99] Colonel Sánchez Cerro had continued to pay off the foreign debt in the middle of the general business depression of 1930–1. It was only after several destabilising military uprisings that repayment of the debt was questioned. Following advice given by northern sugar planter Rafael Larco Herrera, who was minister of foreign affairs and later minister of finance, the provisional compromise government of David Samanez Ocampo suspended the servicing of the debt on 20 March 1931.[100] This default – which lasted until 1952 – and the abandonment of the gold standard in May 1932 proved to be essential for financial and economic recovery and the survival of agro-exporters.[101]

The Banco Agrícola del Perú, a cherished project of agro-exporters, finally became a reality in 1931. The void left by the Banco del Perú y Londres in the agrarian credit structure was partly filled by the Banco Agrícola – the first official 'development' bank – which provided badly needed credit, unavailable elsewhere, to cotton and sugar planters. The new institution was created in August 1931 as an offshoot of the Banco Central by reducing the latter's capital in favour of the former. In the midst of deep scepticism regarding an agrarian export recovery,[102] the Banco Agrícola represented the Peruvian version of a 'New Deal' to the influential sector of planters led by the SNA. Credit at low interest rates was extended to the most productive estates.

In this way a significant portion of the state's scant financial resources was diverted away from use in exchange stabilisation, as recommended by Kemmerer, and toward the financing of the agrarian export sector. In the 1930s cotton growers were the principal beneficiaries of the Banco Agrícola's 'controlled' loans: in 1932, for example, the bank provided from its total loans (S/10 551 830) approximately 66 per cent to cotton growers, 14.7 per cent to rice growers, 8.3 per cent to sugar producers and 8 per cent to cattle ranchers.[103]

The Banco Agrícola's credit policies succeeded in securing its loans by closely scrutinising the entrepreneurial capacity of the debtor as well as the debtor's accounting methods. Loans were mainly used to finance annual harvests and could only be renewed upon the entire repayment of the previous loan. The commercial agrarian sector was the only one that could benefit from this system of controlled credit because the cost of supervision was too high to be applicable to small loans. Small farmers received only 7.7 per cent of the total loans (S/263 million) between 1931 and 1944. The bank recognised there was a higher risk in lending to small producers not yet organised into cooperatives.[104] Until 1944 not a single loan had been granted to peasant communities because, as the bank managers stated, peasants 'had not requested them'.[105]

In return for sponsoring the Banco Agrícola, the state was able to secure from agriculturists and commercial banks a pool of foreign drafts which were purchased or rediscounted by the Banco Central. This allowed a relative backing of the Peruvian currency, which did not depreciate further and even stabilised between 1933 and 1938.[106] Furthermore, internal credit and expanded circulation were spurred on by a Patriotic Loan in 1932. The first of a series of internal bond issues, it was issued by semi-fascist Sánchez Cerro for the purchase of the defence *matériel* required for the Leticia boundary crisis with Colombia which threatened to become another international conflict similar to the Chaco War.

When General Oscar Benavides assumed power following Sánchez Cerro's assassination in May 1933, he adopted stabilising measures which quickly gained the trust of the holders of the private capital which had not been remitted abroad. This private confidence in the authoritarian Benavides regime facilitated the state's policy of credit expansion and intervention.[107]

Benavides, who remained president from 1933–9, carried out a series of public works which basically completed Leguía's road, port and urban construction projects. These works were intensified after 1936 in combination with social programmes.[108] During the Benavides regime, 3700 miles of roads were built or upgraded (against 10 000 under Leguía), mostly financed by the revenue from the gasoline tax used as security for road building bonds.[109] The Callao dock works, contracted by the New York firm Frederick Snare & Company, were completed in 1935 and provided better facilities for the increased collection of export and import taxes. Additional dry dock construction was executed by Snare through the financial intermediation of the Banco Italiano.[110]

The state's increasing participation in the economy was led by important élite representatives, such as Héctor Boza, minister of public works, with some interruptions between 1933 and 1939.[111] In the long term, the state's promotional role encountered financial and political limitations. The sponsoring by the state of development banks (the Agrícola in 1931, Industrial in 1936 and Minero in 1940) was limited under Benavides but more active during the government of the next president, the civilian Manuel Prado (1939–45).[112] The most successful experience of development banking (*banca de fomento*) was that of the Banco Agrícola described above. The Banco Industrial and the Banco Minero had few resources and consistent operational losses.[113]

The agrarian interests looked with disfavour, however, on intervention by the state beyond direct assistance to agriculture. Agriculturists were opposed to higher taxes on exports, income tax reform or budget expansion, but they favoured monetary devaluation at critical moments.[114] Led by the British-educated ultra-liberal cotton entrepreneur, Pedro Beltrán, the Agrarian National Party was formed in 1936 on the foundations of the SNA to form an electoral alliance with the old *civilista* party in support of the candidacy of Manuel Vicente Villarán. Agrarian export interests envisioned a liberal state similar to the one which had existed prior to 1919. Politically, agro-exporters were conservative and supported repression of the populist *aprista* party. Conversely, the official candidate, Jorge Prado (brother of future president, Manuel Prado), and his moderate 'liberal' movement, represented the continuation of the developmentalist and interventionist trend tied to those sectors of the élite oriented toward industry and the expansion of the internal market. Prado promised toleration of the *aprista* party.[115]

Thus the Peruvian élite showed itself divided in the 1936 elections, which proved a harsh democratic reversal for the wealthy. Before the elections were declared void by Benavides – who continued to rule until 1939 without calling a further election – the candidate supported by the *aprista* party, Luis Eguiguren, was clearly the winner, followed by the fascist candidate Luis Flores, heir to the late Sánchez Cerro.[116]

FINANCIAL CONTROLS AND INDUSTRY IN THE 1940s

In December 1937 President Benavides' daughter, Paquita, married Mariano Peña Prado, a prominent member of the rising Prado group. The marriage helped forge political compromise which favoured industrial interests, state developmentalism and financial intervention. In December 1939, Manuel Prado, Benavides' favourite candidate, was elected president in the midst of a darkening international situation. Prado had been president of the Banco Central between 1934 and 1939[117] and had considerable experience in the use of internal public credit to promote state projects.

Prado conducted a bold expansionist financial policy. Internal bond issues were augmented and the excess liquidity of banks continued. This policy reached its limit when inflation, devaluation and capital being remitted abroad increased. Prado's response was the imposition of exchange and import controls, which caused much concern among exporters. However the large importing houses and dependent industrialists supported the measures of control which were biased in favour of imports consisting of capital goods.[118]

The budding Peruvian industrial sector, as in other Latin American industries during the Second World War, enjoyed import-substitution opportunities despite the high cost of essential imported supplies. However the benefits obtained by importers and industrialists from the interventionist state seriously undermined these opportunities.[119] The establishment of import quotas and exchange controls was doubly advantageous to industrialists. On the one hand costly protection was extended to local manufacturers, on the other hand those imports allowed to enter the country by special import licences were paid for with an artificially cheap foreign currency supplied by the state under presidents Prado and Bustamante.[120] At this time importers and their industrialists dependents became more influential than agro-exporters in financial policy matters.

Domestic industrial production grew, but at the cost of a dramatic increase in the value of imported goods by 1943. Previous gains in foreign trade turned negative. This was due to an import policy too vulnerable to rises in the international price of basic imports (machinery and vehicles, foodstuffs, industrial chemical products, electric appliances). Consumer imports represented 40 per cent of total imports, capital imports 40 per cent and semi-finished products 20 per cent. Inflation loomed, threatening serious problems for the financial sector.[121] This was a case of wasted developmental opportunity which distorted financial development, resource allocation, income distribution and entrepreneurial capacity mainly due to the financial repression encouraged by the state, importers and industrialists.[122]

The export élite's confidence in the state's financial measures declined further with the continuation of controls and salary increases under the regime of José L. Bustamante (1945–8). Inflation increased to a dangerous 45 per cent in 1946 compared with 7.1 per cent in 1945 and 2.9 per cent in 1944. Consequently commercial banks' deposits, savings and assets plummeted between 1945 and 1948.[123]

Bustamante's financial policies and his political openness to the *aprista* party added to the concern felt by the élite – agro-exporters battled fiercely against these policies. The structural economic problems of Peru began to acquire their contemporary character: inadequate food production, increased internal consumption of gasoline and petroleum (which further upset the balance of trade), and oligopolised sectors of the economy. Bustamante became caught in a political mess without having first laid down a coherent industrial alternative to the agrarian export and financial model.

Two of the books written at the time discuss the financial and monetary events of the Bustamante regime. The first is a highly critical treatise on Bustamante's management of state finance by Rómulo Ferrero, who was finance minister during the first year of the Bustamante government. The second is an apologetic and justificatory analysis of the regime's failure by Bustamante himself.[124] Ferrero argued that the basic mistake of the regime's financial policy, which was supported by the *aprista* party, was the excessive expansion of public expenditure and the money supply which had negative inflationary consequences. Prado's regime had already been too expansionist and Bustamante did little to arrest that tendency. Internal debt had risen in its most damaging form, loans by the Central Reserve Bank to the government. Moreover internal debt instruments had depreciated due to decreased public confidence and the state's own moves towards lowering the value of its liabilities through public auctions, the imposition of taxes, and consolidation at lower yields.[125]

Bustamante defended his financial policy by stating that he had inherited the expansionist and inflationary situation from Prado. In part this was true. However Bustamante was either unable or unwilling to do much to turn the situation around. He continued to provide subsidies on food imports – according to him, because there was no alternative.[126] However, domestic production of wheat, rice, meat and dairy products was unable to keep pace with the rising population, and official price controls and taxes on agricultural products had devastating effects on the producers of these products.[127]

Instead of correcting the import, exchange, price and financial controlist strategies which were having such negative effects on national income and the financial structure, Bustamante put the blame on private banks for promoting 'unproductive' ventures such as real estate and construction. According to Bustamante private banks had to discourage inflation by not lending to the public the currency the Banco Central kept on issuing without responsible limits. He was also bitter because private banks did not increase their lending to the Banco Agrícola, and because the bank did not have enough autonomy since many of its directors represented private banking interests. He finally lamented the absence of Peruvian external credit standing which precluded access to much needed foreign loans. Despite his democratic convictions, Bustamante's financial strategies encouraged unsound state financial strategies and interventionism.[128]

General Manuel Odría (1948–56) led the military coup d'état that ousted Bustamante. His authoritarian regime was quick to follow the liberal financial prescriptions of the agro-exporters' leader Pedro Beltrán and American advisor Julius Klein to liberalise exchange and import controls. In 1952 Odría at last settled the defaulted Peruvian foreign debt. Foreign investment flooded in to all sectors, including banking, by December 1953, and inflation was reduced to 12 per cent. Notwithstanding Odría's liberal financial policies, public works that emphasised social promotion were maintained in consonance with the general's demagogic statism.[129] Increased state expenditure and budget deficits were once more financed by foreign credit. In 1953 a loan of $30 million for monetary stabilisation was arranged with the International Monetary Fund, the US Treasury and Chase Manhattan Bank.[130] The foreign trade situation again turned positive. The native mining and agrarian sectors experienced an upturn following the imposition of favourable financial policies, a liberal tax structure and the completion of irrigation works in Piura.[131] Mining and petroleum concessions were arranged with foreign capital as native private and fiscal enterprises had again failed to form a large-scale presence in those sectors. These developments pertain however, to a new cycle of native and foreign finance beyond the scope of the present study.

In conclusion, state intervention had, on balance, negative effects on financial development until 1950. Despite the state's weakness after the war with Chile, elements of state arbitrary intervention and protection were used to encourage rather than to curb oligopoly. The lack of independent public financial institutions reinforced an undemocratic private financial sector. State interventionism between 1884 and 1919 went through a process of convalescence and eventually recovered. After 1919 excessive external indebtedness was caused by ambitious development projects which left limited infrastructural gain. Together with the financial oligopolisation which resulted between 1900 and 1914 under the gold standard, excessive borrowing from abroad between 1925 and 1930 was unquestionably one of the more defective financial policies adopted by the financial élite and the state. The role of foreign borrowing and finance will be discussed more fully in Chapter 7. Finally, monetary and financial manipulation in the 1930s and 1940s led to increased state intervention, officially-induced financial repression and, eventually, to high inflation which constrained the private sector and limited financial development and diversification.

7 Interaction of Foreign and Domestic Finance

Analysis of the role of foreign finance in Peruvian financial evolution has been left for this final chapter. Despite the crucial role played by foreign finance in Peru since before 1884, my argument has hitherto given emphasis to the complex collaboration and competition offered by domestic finance. In previous chapters it has been demonstrated that domestic finance, private and public, accounted for major changes in the Peruvian financial structure. The crucial turning point in the Peruvian agro-export cycle from 1930 on needs, however, a more comprehensive reference to the changing influence of international financial and economic conditions. In this chapter I seek to provide, and evaluate, often overlooked historical evidence on the effects of foreign financial flows on the Peruvian domestic financial sector.

My assessment will centre on the effects of the relationship between foreign and domestic finance in promoting or hindering economic development. I consider primarily the interactive nature of foreign and domestic factors on the financial evolution of Peru rather than condemn outright foreign financial factors as negative – the benefits and the costs of foreign finance in Peru must be weighed against each other.[1]

The role of foreign finance in developing economies is debated continually. Some experts regard foreign portfolio and direct investment as a contributing factor towards development.[2] In contrast, dissenting scholars have considered foreign loans and multinational corporations as distorting elements in what have been termed 'dependent' capital markets.[3] The differing positions in this debate, however, generally rely on incomplete or scant consideration of concrete historical evidence.

In the case of Peru, some argue that foreign interests controlled the major economic sectors, as well as the financial system, until the military coup d'état of 1968 supposedly led to nationalist reforms.[4] According to the critics of the foreign presence in Peru, this experience exemplifies the adverse consequences of foreign penetration. Despite their challenge to what were, until recently, some undisputed assumptions concerning the benefits of foreign investment, the view of these critics is still limited by their disregard of historical data on domestic interests competing and collaborating with foreign concerns, and also by implying praise for state interventionist policies.[5]

In order to critically respond to these historical and conceptual shortcomings, I first establish the pre-1920 background to the flow of foreign finance into Peru that resulted in competition among different foreign interests and, more crucially, blatant cases of the crowding out of domestic financial interests. I then discuss the foreign-supported state intervention in domestic financial matters during the foreign loan cycle of the late 1920s. Next I analyse foreign influence – especially that of foreign corporations and financial monopolies – and the calculated leniency in enforcing repayment of external public loans in the 1930s. Finally I will discuss the determinant role played by the coordinated actions of US public and private interests during and after the Second World War, prior to the regaining of international credit by Peru that started a new cycle of foreign borrowing in the early 1950s.

PRE-1920s FOREIGN FINANCIAL FLOWS

The flow of foreign finance into Peru in the twentieth-century had a modest beginning because of the country's loss of standing in international credit after the War of the Pacific (1879–83) (the nineteenth-century public foreign debt had been in default since 1876). In 1890 the debt to British creditors (approximately £50 million) was dramatically liquidated by the surrender of national assets as a form of repayment.[6] Nevertheless no new foreign credit was granted to the state until 1905–6, and even after that date the contribution of external finance to state projects was kept low until the 1920s loan expansion.

Provision of credit to the native private sector and to semi-private public utility companies between 1895 and 1913 increased earlier and at a much faster rate than to the public sector. Crucial to this private form of foreign portfolio investment was the collaboration between local banks and international financial institutions in forming syndicates to float loans both inside and outside Peru. Likewise the oligopolistic funding of some important local firms had either foreign capital participation, foreign management, or both.

Internationally 1870–1913 was a boom period for capital exportation.[7] Unlike in Argentina and Brazil, where public and municipal loans continued to expand throughout the period, in Peru foreign capital expansion from 1890 took the form of portfolio and direct investments in the private sector linked to exports and urban services. In contrast to the assumption that public foreign debt can be used as a proxy to measure foreign financial cycles, the Peruvian case points to a pattern of alternation between periods of expansion of public loans and periods of increased private portfolio and direct investments, which were not always linked closely to general international trends. In this sense Ady's view that private foreign investment in Latin America was mainly portfolio investment until 1930 (shifting to mainly direct investment thereafter) should be modified.[8]

The major foreign lenders in the pre-1920s were British, French, German and American, in that order of importance. The predominant strategy of foreign lending at that time was that of the British. French and German creditors differed significantly from the British with regard to their approach to Peruvian loans. British merchant-bankers, investors and their leading representatives favoured securing limited loans to the Peruvian state – as had been the practice in the nineteenth century – with pledges of particular state revenues. Likewise the very secure credit conditions imposed by British lenders to the Peruvian private sector consisted of consignment and hedging (purchase of futures) varieties of credit, capital participation, managerial direction, and oligopolistic guarantees. The British also favoured participation in local banking institutions (rather than opening branches of their own banks) to allow managerial influence to be applied where oligopolistic business practices ensured privileged profits.

French financial interests were pressed by their state and diplomatic officials to open wholly French financial institutions in Peru, but they were ultimately unsuccessful in this regard. The French *haute banque* had to conform to the British example of joint ventures with local financial institutions. Confrontation between French, British, German and local interests took a sharp edge at times. The French claims over the nineteenth-century Peruvian debt were not settled until the 1920s. Loans to the Peruvian state were therefore out of the question in the Paris Bourse. The monopolistic crowding out of native financial resources reached its worst with the French venture of the Crédit Foncier Peruvien (discussed in more detail below), which attempted to displace native investors from the mortgage credit market.

German creditors made a successful and competitive appearance in

Lima in 1905–6 with the granting of the first major loans to the Peruvian government for defense purposes. Also, the Lima branch of the Banco Alemán Transatlantico (Deutsche Ueberseeische Bank, a section of the Deutsche Bank, Berlin), which had been established there in 1905, was the only fully foreign banking institution until 1916. This German bank introduced modern banking practices, such as the provision of individual safety-deposit boxes, and provided institutional consignment credit to agro-exporters. Local interests tied to British creditors struggled to avert the penetration and possible dominance of German financial interests.[9] During the First World War German banking interests were blacklisted and then temporarily liquidated.

A fourth noticeable form of financial inflow from approximately 1900 was the placing of financial assets by North American firms in local banks and among native owners. Among these firms the most important were the Cerro de Pasco Copper Corporation (a Guggenheim interest), the International Petroleum Company, a subsidiary of Standard Oil (Rockefeller interests), W.R. Grace & Company and the Vanadium Company. Executives of these foreign companies were represented on the boards of directors of local financial institutions, trade associations, and the stock market. By striking business agreements and combining interests with local financial personalities, US interests were able to buy out native properties and legal rights over rich but under-capitalised mining sites in the Peruvian highlands. This not only helped displace native miners but also led to the importation of input material for copper mining and other oligopolies.[10]

A crucial form of interaction between foreign finance and local private capital was the dependence of native agro-exporters on foreign commercial credit until the First World War, as discussed in Chapter 3. Credit for financing the trading and production of agricultural exports was provided for the most part by foreign merchant houses with branches in Peru, but also by merchant bankers in London and Liverpool. This relationship constituted a source of conflict as well as of collaboration. Agro-export was a sensitive area where native investors still retained substantial property rights.

However in an economy like Peru's, exposed as it was to volatile international fluctuations, foreign investors strove increasingly to control the most profitable activities, including the financial sector. Native financial resources were thus removed from several of the most profitable businesses and had to focus on areas of relatively higher risk or areas of no interest to foreigners. The initial blatant displacement of native financial interests, as in the cases of the Peruvian Corporation, Cerro de Pasco, International Petroleum and Crédit Foncier, gave way to a subtler strategy of joint ventures, especially in the financial market and the highly concentrated industrial sector.

The first significant example of the effects of this crowding out was the settlement of the nineteenth century foreign debt. The Peruvian Corporation obtained from the state railway concessions that placed this British association of bondholders in almost total control of the railway system in Peru. The fact that the Peruvian Corporation provided only modest profits, or even incurred losses, to its shareholders does not exclude the fact that it actually prevented access by local or other foreign resources to many economic opportunities linked to railway transportation.[11]

On its part the Cerro de Pasco Corporation started its activities in Peru by secretly buying mines and land in the Morococha–Cerro de Pasco area of the central sierra in the early 1900s. Guggengheim interests guaranteed substantial financial support, and a significant number of the Peruvian miners who sold their properties seemed to have made a lucrative decision because they received considerable payments that were later reinvested in other sectors.[12] The Empresa Socavonera Cerro de Pasco, a native concern which had held exclusive rights to drainage works since 1902 and which had financial connections in Lima, managed to strike a favourable deal by obtaining stock shares in the Cerro Corporation in exchange for its drainage rights in Cerro de Pasco.

The Banco del Perú y Londres owned a substantial amount of the Socavonera's shares that were accepted as first class collateral from its clients. Powerful officials of the Banco del Perú y Londres were among the Socavonera's directors, managers and shareholders. Financial and technical problems assailed the Socavonera, although it triumphed in its legal disputes with the Cerro Corporation. Foreign pressure resulting from a settlement between British and US investors in matters of railway use, and the willingness of the Banco del Perú y Londres to cash in its participation in the Socavonera, resulted in the selling out of the native Socavonera to US interests. The final arrangement took approximately ten years (1904–14) to negotiate.[13]

French attempts to establish a dominant financial presence in Peru constituted another clear example of crowding out. The participation of the Société Générale and the Banque de Paris in the capital stock of the Banco del Perú y Londres, and the partnership of these three institutions in a joint mortgage venture in 1912, the Crédit Foncier Peruvien, were sought by French financial investors in order to gain local representation and a better position from which to press French financial claims. The high profits of the Banco del Perú y Londres were an additional reason for the French institutions' participation in the local bank's activities. When a stronger defence of their interests in Peru was needed, the Paris banks attempted to gain control over the Banco del Perú y Londres. The French attempts conflicted with the existing British and local management of the institution. The conflict became clear to the local directors in 1913 when news from Paris alerted them to measures taken by the Société Générale and the Banque de Paris to monopolise the European transactions of the Banco del Perú y Londres (thus conflicting with the finance commissions of banking partners in London), and to dominate the Crédit Foncier Peruvien. In a meeting of the Banco del Perú y Londres' board of directors it was stated that the real purpose of these French actions was to force

> . . . us to exert our influence over the public and government in Peru to acquire the Muelle y Dársena [del Callao] which the Société Générale has been seeking to sell for some time now. It was recalled that the [Perú y Londres] bank had assisted the Société Générale in every way it could and that it was willing to do the same again, but present circumstances make it impossible from every point of view to bring about the successful conclusion of the matter.[14]

At first the Société Generale and the Banque de Paris found that the Banco del Perú y Londres offered the advantage of a foreign managerial presence, which made it more reliable and trustworthy. In an accurate observation on the Banco del Perú y Londres' directive body, but with an obvious underestimation of the importance of the local savings that comprised the bulk of the local bank's undertakings, a French diplomat informed Paris: 'The Council of that institution is almost entirely composed of foreigners, and the funds for its establishment and development have been provided by foreign savings'.[15] The Paris banks' decision to participate in the Banco del Perú y Londres finally swept away any hope for the establishment of an entirely French bank in Peru:

We will never have a completely French bank in Lima . . . because the Bank Perú y Londres is supported by the French banks of the rue Boudreau, by the Société Générale, the Banque de Paris et des Pays Bas and the Comptoir Nationale. These groups will not compete with each other by creating a rival bank. Neither is it probable that other French groups will choose the option of trying to replace them.[16]

As soon as the Banco del Perú y Londres shares were quoted in Paris in 1907, French representation in its board of directors increased from one to two, including the head of the French merchant house Harth & Company in Lima. The line of action followed by the Paris banks, supported by French diplomats, consisted thereafter of efforts to increase French representation and influence on the board. In a 1909 letter to the French minister of finance, the French minister of foreign affairs recommended that he personally alert the manager of the Banco del Perú y Londres to the French government's desire to see French interests better represented in the bank.[17] A French diplomatic representive in Lima had informed Pichon, the minister of foreign affairs in Paris, about the unacceptability of having a German employee of Harth & Company replace the former French director in the bank because of the dangerous German business competition in Peru. Instead another Frenchman was suggested and the bank's manager agreed to nominate him in light of such strong pressure.

French pressure was also exerted to form a committee of the Banco del Perú y Londres in Paris which would have general counselling powers. Moreover French diplomats argued that the number of French representatives on the bank's board of directors should be raised to three if major financial transactions with French participation were to be successful in Paris and London, 'to provide the French presence in this country an instrument of action in exact proportion to the resources that we supply to Peruvian finance'.[18]

Eventually, due to French urging and to an increase in French capital participation in the Banco del Perú y Londres, a committee composed of three to five members was formed in December 1909 in Paris. The Paris Committee was similar to that which the Banco Nacional de Mexico had in Paris, that is, it had the power to propose financial business of importance in Europe and to organise representation of French stockholders. The Paris Committee of the Banco del Perú y Londres had, however, a majority of the British–Peruvian bloc. Initially this committee helped to carry out important international transactions (the Lima Municipal Loan, the loan guaranteed by salt consumption taxes), but a new modification of the bank's statutes in February 1913 enhanced the administrative power of the committee. Thereafter the reformed committee proved to be ill-fated because it divided the bank's power of decision and became a cause of conflict within the board of directors.

As a result of the 1913 statutes, the directors in Lima had to comply with the veto power of the Paris Committee in every transaction above Lp100 000 and had to submit the bank's annual balances and accounts for approval in Paris. The Société Générale's and the Banque de Paris' interest in controlling the Banco del Perú y Londres was behind the granting of these new powers to the Paris Committee.[19]

The mortgage affair of the Crédit Foncier Peruvien was a major reason for the subsequent decline of the Banco del Perú y Londres. In the period 1907–12, the mortgage section of the local bank was remarkably stable compared with its other banking activities, although the 1907 depression had caused a temporary slowdown in mortgage business in Peru. The bank's local management was convinced, however, that real estate financing would provide exceptional investment opportunities in the near future. With this in mind the bank provided prompt credit and the benefit of its international connections to the city council for urban improvements and services. In 1911 manager José Payán obtained the quotation in London of an Lp600 000 municipal loan bond issue. The issue received a poor initial response so the local bank had to advance additional credit of Lp70 000 to secure the success of the foreign loan to the municipality of Lima by purchasing the privately owned water supply company (Empresa del Agua). All of this financing prepared the foundations for the later real estate boom in Lima.[20]

After contributing to the preparations for a profitable real estate business, the next step taken by the Banco del Perú y Londres' administration toward the sharing and eventual surrender of its mortgage business to a French capitalised corporation was a mistake. The objective of the mortgage combination was to attract cheap foreign capital in order to control the mortgage business in Lima by reducing mortgage interest from its annual rate of 8 per cent, 'with the objective of monopolising and increasing the loans, and avoiding competition, we think that the interest should not be more than 6 per cent'.[21]

The result of Payán's deals in Paris was the formation in March 1912 of the Crédit Foncier Peruvien, which had a minority participation by the Banco del Perú y Londres and the Anglo South American Bank, who held collectively 337 000 out of 1 250 000 francs in capital shares. The majority of the institution's capital was held by the Société Générale–Banque de Paris group. The Crédit Foncier had its headquarters in Paris and an agency in Lima, managed by five directors of the Banco del Perú y Londres. The most important decisions concerning the institution's financial policy were made in Paris. Immediately after the establishment of the Crédit Foncier, the Paris Banque Priveé advanced 12 500 000 francs at 89 per cent discount, after finance charges, in 5 per cent mortgage bonds to be repaid within 37 years of the establishment of the Crédit Foncier. In its turn the Crédit Foncier had acquired all the Banco del Perú y Londres' mortgage credits in Peru, which were then sold to the Banque Priveé. Later the Banco del Perú y Londres acquired 500 000 francs in bonds of the crédit Foncier from the Banque Priveé, at the value of 90.5 per cent (1.5 per cent above the initial loan granted by the Banque Priveé for the purchase of bonds in Peru) 'as a means of inspiring confidence considering the political movements in Lima'.[22]

An important clause in the statutes of the Crédit Foncier stated that new mortgage loans would be offered in Lima at 6.5 per cent annual interest and that the old mortgage loans would have their interest rates lowered from 8 to 6.5 per cent. Soon difficulties arose because of contradictions between the Crédit Foncier's administration in Paris and the Lima agency controlled by the local directors of the Banco del Perú y Londres. In April 1912 the Lima representatives communicated to Paris that the Banco del Perú y Londres would suffer serious difficulties and conflicts with local mortgage bond investors because of the extremely short period of time scheduled for cancelling the old mortgage bonds.

The Lima mortgage bond investors were deeply disturbed by the fact that their Lp408 000, previously placed in reliable mortgage bonds, would have no secure alternative allocation. As a consequence, there was a danger that investors would look abroad for profit opportunities. Another consequence would be an increase in the amount deposited in local banks. The Banco del Perú y Londres did not have the capacity to absorb more deposits because of the already excessive amounts it held in relation to the limited possibilities for investment in Peru at the time.[23] The proposal by the local directors for a slower amortisation of the displaced mortgage bonds was rejected, however, in Paris. Payán responded from Paris that cancellation of the bonds should be completed by July of that same year because otherwise the Crédit Foncier in Paris would have to defray interest costs at 6 per cent during the entire period of cancellation. The shorter the time of cancellation the better for the French intermediaries. Peruvian investors had to be sacrificed.

The local board of directors was forced to comply with this order from Paris. Damage to the bank's prestige in Lima resulted, as well as negative economic effects brought about by the displacement of native capital by foreign financing.[24] Even though the cancellation was completed rapidly, the Crédit Foncier complained in March 1913 that it had suffered a net loss of £2130 due to the cost of gold transfers to Lima and lost interest. Payán had recommended not selling too many bills of exchange in Lima in consideration of the depreciatory effects such a move would have had on the local currency and exchange market.[25]

The most acute conflict, which almost broke all the relations between Lima and Paris, arose from the decision in March 1913 by the Paris administration to raise the interest rate on mortgage loans to 8 per cent. Until then the financial results of the first year of the Crédit's activity in Lima had been considered quite good, despite the difficulties it had caused in terms of capital supply. On this occasion the local directors reacted in absolute opposition to the Paris administration's determination to raise interest rates. The granting of mortgage credit was frozen, thereby causing further difficulties among customary credit recipients who expected loans at low interest rates. Also, because the Crédit Foncier operated in Lima from the Banco del Perú y Londres' main headquarters, the bank's prestige was profoundly affected and a vast advantage was given to competitor institutions that were lending at a low 6.5 per cent interest. The answer by the French to the local directors' opposition to raising the rate was an attempt in June 1913 to gain absolute control over the Crédit Foncier by the Banque de Paris–Société Générale group. The local directors reacted to this attempt by proposing to sell their participation in the Crédit Foncier and to reopen the Banco del Perú y Londres' old mortgage section. It was too late, however, to attempt to disengage from the Crédit Foncier.[26]

Preoccupation over losing its precious Paris financial connections finally became the main argument that forced the local directors in January 1914 to comply with the Parisian request for an increase in the mortgage loan interest rate 'with the intention of avoiding any reasons for friction with the gentlemen in Paris'.[27] Thereafter the Credit Foncier's mortgage business in Lima collapsed absolutely and, contrary to its designs, the Banco del Perú y Londres lost its supremacy over the mortgage market to other institutions (Banco de Crédito Hipotecario, Banco Italiano).

Why did local financiers so keenly desire foreign participation and thus allow extensive foreign control and management, a policy that eventually brought many difficulties? The local administrators of the Banco del Perú y Londres, for example, saw in their partnership with British and French financial capital a guarantee for maintaining the bank's supremacy over the Peruvian market and for successfully overwhelming the competition. Since 1879 the London and Paris financial markets had been closed to new Peruvian ventures and foreign concerns had been careful to avoid Peruvian partners. Thus no large investments with mixed participation, except the Banco del Perú y Londres' 1897 merger, occurred in Peru between 1880 and 1907.

Suddenly, around 1907, as a consequence of an international recession, foreign capital began to pour into the reduced Lima market in search of untapped opportunities. British, French, German and Italian interests competed with each other and with local interests to secure exclusivity in the allocation of loans and in financial oligopolies. Local enthusiasm for this liberally available foreign capital was excessive and produced an adverse crowding out of local financial assets. The accepted economic supposition at the time was that foreign capital in any quantity was good *per se* in countries like Peru.

International financial interests, however, observed the added competition from foreign interests with increasing concern. Monopolistic and oligopolistic control of business in Peru had become a common practice. The swift and competitive arrival of German financial interests in Peru (as well as in Chile, Colombia and Brazil) was soon considered a threat by other financial actors. German penetration was especially strong in the financial sector and from there it developed a solid network with the trading, oceanic transportation and export sectors.

From its initial loan arrangements with the Peruvian government in 1905, and relying on German diplomatic assistance, the Lima section of the Banco Alemán Transatlántico also entered the interconnected mortgage and insurance businesses in 1906.[28] From 1905–13 the Berlin headquarters of the Banco Alemán Transatlántico reported high annual dividends of 9 per cent, but this decreased to 6 per cent in 1914–15 due to the effects of the First World War.[29]

German interests, however, were effectively prevented from

granting public loans because of the monopoly enjoyed by the Banco del Perú y Londres and its British and French partners, much to the chagrin of German diplomats who criticised this exclusive arrangement between the Peruvian government and its non-German creditors.[30] But the most dangerous challenge to German financial interests in Peru arose as a consequence of open hostility from businesses owned by the allies, especially from US concerns, during the First World War. This business warfare resulted in the loosening of the foothold gained by German agro-export concerns. The most important firms targeted and blacklisted were the Banco Alemán Transatlántico, the Gildemeister sugar planting and refining concerns, the merchant company Hilbck & Company and Weiss & Company among several other trade, mining and cotton-producing firms.[31]

Active US opposition to German interests resulted in internal conflicts among the German business community in Peru. Before the war the Guaranty Trust Company of New York had close financial relations with the Banco Alemán Transatlántico. In 1917 the US bank began blocking cheques from German companies in Peru. Likewise W. R. Grace & Company, under British pressure, initiated in 1916 a legal procedure against the delivery of coal to Gildemeister & Company by local intermediaries who had bought the coal from Grace.[32] Grace's competitor in provincial trade at the time was the German Hilbck & Company. Grace & Company, the Guaranty Trust and other US banks broke their previous contracts with the Banco Alemán Transatlántico in 1917, and refused to accept German bills of exchange.[33]

A German firm, Weiss & Company, continued to trade – in products formerly shipped to Britain – with the USA despite the American actions against German companies. This caused a reaction among the German business community against Weiss. Likewise Gildemeister & Company had a serious conflict over a large credit contract with the Banco Alemán Transatlántico and the Guaranty Trust Company. The quarrel almost resulted in a duel between the owner and manager, respectively, of the German firms. Conveniently, the Gildemeister concerns cancelled all their financial relations with the German bank and started working with US banks.[34] In a coded telegram, the beleaguered manager of the German bank suggested transforming the bank into a private local concern to avoid persecution and confiscation.[35]

As a result of these events German and other European financial interests dwindled in Peru and were increasingly replaced by US interests that swiftly consolidated in Peru during the First World War. As a British journal commented in 1916 'Europe cannot supply a loan to Peru for many a day. So that Peru is forced to turn to the Americans, and thus to the Standard Oil interests, themselves closely concerned with oil concessions in the country'.[36]

LOAN EXPANSION UNDER LEGUÍA

A dramatic change in the credit conditions in Peru occurred between 1916 and 1920. After experiencing initial trade and financial disruptions caused by the onset of the First World War, a significant increase in cotton and sugar prices resulted in windfall profits for native agriculturists.[37] Many agro-exporters were able to repay their debts to foreign merchants, acquire agricultural properties or pay off existing mortgages on them, and even have enough financial assets remaining to buy stock in banks and other financial institutions.

Concurrently British, French and German capital began to be removed from Peru due to a shortage of capital in war-torn Europe and fears of a post-war international recession. Apart from native élite groups, two other players entered the competition to fill the financial vacuum left by the withdrawal of European capital. They were US investors and the Peruvian state under reformist President Augusto B. Leguía. The Peruvian branch of the Mercantile Bank of the Americas (organised in New York by the Guaranty Trust Company) opened its business in Lima in 1916 to compete in the financing of crops for exportation and to promote trade with the US. The Mercantile Bank also competed with domestic banks for control over the local market of bills of exchange.

Confronted with the high price of Peruvian currency during the First World War, the Mercantile Bank – on behalf of US overseas trade interests – pressed for a depreciation of the libra exchange rate against the dollar. Such a depreciation would increase US access to local currency. As the main buyer of Latin American products during the war, US trade was suffering from the high exchange rates of some Latin American currencies. In the autumn of 1917 the US Department of State and the Federal Reserve Board initiated negotiations for currency 'stabilisation' with the governments of Argentina, Uruguay, Chile, Bolivia and Peru. In March 1918 the Department of State discouraged the manager of the Mercantile Bank in Lima from pursuing any action regarding the Peruvian exchange rate that might interfere with the negotiations between the Federal Reserve Board and the Peruvian government. This was part of the growing pressure being applied by the US to expand the supply of paper money. Local banks were on the whole against this move.[38]

Despite an initial success by the Mercantile Bank, the Banco del Perú y Londres was able to displace the US bank from agricultural finance by increasing its supply of credit to agriculture, especially to sugar producers who were vulnerable to fluctuating sugar prices in the 1920s.

US financial interests were nevertheless able to displace European financial influence in Peru in the financing of Peruvian state loans by the late 1920s. The approval of US loans to the Peruvian state did not, however, have an easy start. Initially, American bankers and financial syndicates contacted and received advice from the US Department of State which demanded from borrowing Latin American states certain financial reforms before loans could be granted to them.[39] As discussed in Chapter 6 these reforms included the establishment of central banks to be modelled after the US Federal Reserve Bank, fiscal reorganisation, balanced budgets, and the implementation of sound monetary policies. They also demanded the presence of US advisors in certain key posts of institutions such as customs houses and central banks.[40]

Between 1918 and the first half of 1920 the financial situation of the Peruvian state was satisfactory thanks to an increase in export duty revenues linked to the high prices resulting from the First World War export boom. In 1920 the foreign public debt amounted to Lp2 895 000 ($13.3 million), including a loan for Lp980 587 guaranteed by revenue from salt, and Lp600 000 lent to Lima's city council. By June 1920, however, signs of an international recession brought down abruptly Peruvian export prices.[41] As a result, foreign importers had to allow considerable extensions or reductions of between 20 per cent and 50 per cent on credits previously granted to native agriculturists.[42]

Leguía was in power at the time thanks to a coup d'état staged to remove the opposition to his inauguration – apparently the coup was financed by Royal Dutch Shell in exchange for the promise of a petroleum concession.[43] By June 1920 Leguía's regime was beginning to suffer dire financial straits. Worsening the situation, import and export duties fell from Lp2.2 million and Lp1.4 million respectively, in June 1921 to Lp1.1 million and Lp0.4 million in June 1922.[44]

Leguía was placed in the difficult position of not being able to pay the salaries of the armed forces and state bureaucracy and he was in desperate need of foreign credit to avert his overthrow.[45]

Consequently Leguía took seriously US demands for reforms. For example, the introduction of income tax was discussed, although this failed to materialise. In 1922 he appointed William W. Cumberland, a State Department economist who had graduated from Princeton (where he had studied under Edwin W. Kemmerer, the money doctor), as financial advisor to the Peruvian government. Later Cumberland was also appointed president of the newly created Banco de Reserva, an appointment which was strongly opposed by local banks.[46] Despite these measures, US credit was not contracted in 1921 because of the severe terms offered by US bankers (Guaranty Trust and National City Bank).

However Leguía was able to temporarily weather the storm because of the profit that resulted from the exchange and transfer of the Junta de Vigilancia's gold funds from New York to London.[47] The first US loan was finally contracted in July 1922 – floated in New York by Blyth, Witter & Company and White, Weld & Company with the Guaranty Trust Company acting as loan commissioner – for $2.5 million at 8 per cent interest. The future revenue from export and import taxes on petroleum products was offered as guarantee for the loan.[48] A loan was raised in London in December 1922 by Baring Brothers and J. Henry Schroeder & Company (represented in Lima by the Anglo–South American Bank) for £1.25 million to cover arrears in governmental salaries and pensions. For this loan the revenue from internal guano sales, administered by the reorganised Cía. Administradora del Guano which at the time was under British control, was offered as guarantee.[49] In October 1923 another loan of £10 million to consolidate previous debts was under discussion in London by the Westminster Bank and Schroeder & Company.[50] In effect Leguía was playing US and British financial interests against each other – he was following the same strategy with regard to US and British petroleum interests.[51]

Subsequent US loans included a sanitation loan signed in October 1924 for $7 million to contract for the works of the US Foundation Company, a syndicate composed of Morgan & Company, Chase Manhattan Bank and the Third National Bank; the petroleum loan of 1925 for $7.5 million; a second sanitation loan in June 1926; and a loan for $30 million (gold bonds) in August 1926 which was guaranteed by several fiscal rents. For each of these loans the Guaranty

Trust Company acted as commissioner, and Blyth, Witter & Company and White Weld & Company brokered the loans in New York. An additional loan for the purchase of submarines for the Peruvian navy was contracted with the US Electric Boat Company in 1926, and the tobacco loan of 1927 for $15 million was arranged with a US syndicate composed of J. & W. Seligman & Company, the National City Bank, W. H. Rollins & Company and others. Seligman also participated in the 1927 loan for the port of Callao.

By now Leguía, through his diplomatic approach, had drawn closer to the United States, as evidenced by the president of the US having consented to arbitrate in the territorial dispute between Chile and Peru.[52] Leguía's financial difficulties continued, however, owing to a pattern of recklessness in debt management. A British diplomat observed:

> As it happens with many other countries, the last course the Peruvian government are willing to adopt is retrenchment; on the contrary they continue to pass measures involving additional expenditure whether the necessary funds are available or not, so that with insufficient revenues coming in, it resolves itself into a scramble as to who shall get possession of the small sums trickling into the Treasury. Notwithstanding these happy-go-lucky methods, it seems that sooner or later debts are liquidated, and when the turn of the tide in trade produces temporary prosperity enabling the republic to secure credit abroad, she continues her onward march and marks a further stage in development.[53]

The dangers of the Peruvian loan practice were seriously increased as a result of a major breakthrough in the US policy towards Peruvian public debt in December 1927 when a loan for $100 million, at a discounted value of 86 per cent and at 6 per cent interest, was granted by a group of New York bankers headed by J. & W. Seligman and the National City Bank without the backing of pledges of specific revenues (as had been the practice in British and US loan granting in the past), but rather against the general credit of the country. The loan, the first series of the Empréstito Nacional Peruano, was to be applied to the conversion (refinancing) of all the previous and outstanding foreign issues (excluding the 1922 guano loan), the stabilisation of exchange, the establishment of an agricultural bank, and public works.[54] As in the case of the 1927 tobacco loan, the Peruvian institution of judicial deposits (Caja de Depósitos y Consignaciones) was in charge of providing the payments for the Empréstito loan. A second series of the Empréstito was floated in 1928 for $25 million and £2 million. A Lima municipal loan was also contracted in 1928 for $3 million with the US firms E. H. Rollins & Sons and the Grace National Bank.

Leguía mainly used the increased supply of foreign credit for infrastructural works, which presented many opportunities for graft, a serious but 'invisible' problem in Latin American debt issues. Foreign observers doubted the moral integrity of Leguía's officers and family members, as well as the soundness of Leguía's financial judgement.[55] The results of Leguía's private involvement in cotton financing and trading attested to his flawed estimations of the forward value of cotton and sugar in the early 1920s.[56] Moreover it is doubtful that his public works programme was carried out with utmost efficiency because of the hasty nature of many projects. Nevertheless the huge increase in the number of roads, improved sanitation, urban development, and irrigation works during his presidency attested to at least partial success in making proper use of foreign credit.[57]

The most negative effects of foreign credit in Peru in the 1920s were, however, those that resulted from the expansion of foreign loans to bolster state interventionism. Monopolies of ridiculous proportions were established. Crowding out continued in modified forms. In February 1926 the government sanctioned a monopoly which would provide it with £200 000 annually. This was in exchange for a twenty year concession to the Swedish Match Company (Svenska Tandische Aktiebolaget, Stockholm) to import matches from Europe. The monopoly agreement implied the closing down of the two local match factories,[58] and the importation of matches from elsewhere was prohibited. The use of cigarette lighters by individuals was allowed only by special license, and the importation of cars with fixtures for lighters was forbidden.[59]

Industrial monopolies granted by the state to foreign and native concerns multiplied in the late 1920s. Exclusive rights for the manufacture of specific products, granted for periods of up to ten years, resulted in higher tariffs and state revenues and limited industrial promotion. For example a British subject, Arthur B. Wells, was given an official monopoly for the production of sewing thread in October 1926.[60] A total of 64 industrial monopolies and concessions were granted as follows: 2 in 1920, 6 in 1924, 6 in 1926, 22 in 1927, 14 in 1928, 8 in 1929, and 6 in 1930.[61] There is a noticeable correlation between the rise in the number of monopolies granted by the state and the increase in public borrowing from abroad from around 1926–7 (some of these monopolies, however, did not materialise).

Instances of crowding out multiplied as a result of the concessions granted in the 1920s. Among the most notable examples of foreign businesses displacing local ones were the British interests of the Marconi Telegraph Company, the Italian and Swiss interests in the electrical conglomerate Empresas Eléctricas Asociadas, the Swedish Match Company, the Peruvian Glass & Bottle Company, the Foundation Company, Cía. Peruana de Cemento Portland, and Frederick Snare and Company. The state's agreements with foreign interests also included one in 1926 with the Cerro de Pasco Corporation for the advanced payment of Lp120 000 for export duties on minerals and metals. However a concession with British subject H. V. Holden, former negotiator (together with Gildemeister & Company) of a loan from Rothschild to the government for a monopoly on the sale of gasoline in Peru, did not materialise.[62]

During the same period, despite the fairly stable monetary policy imposed by US creditors, overspecialisation on the part of local banks on short-term agricultural credit proved disastrous. The Banco de Reserva had a policy of rediscounting the financial instruments of banks heavily involved in commercial credit to planters. Leguía could not easily correct this because of his commitment to agricultural interests. Ultimately, in 1929–30, the Banco del Perú y Londres and the Leguía government had a bitter disagreement about financial policy and monetary matters. American advisors suggested that the Banco de Reserva raise its interest rate and restrict credit in order to stabilise the declining exchange rate and control inflation. The Banco del Perú y Londres opposed any increase in interest rates and the restriction of credit since these measures would put a strain on the liquidity of the already troubled institution.[63] With the hope of obtaining government protection against bankruptcy, the Banco del Perú y Londres had become a heavy creditor of the state. This caused concern among American creditors who were alarmed by the increase in the local floating debt incurred by the Peruvian government.

According to a diplomatic report, however, by September 1928 local banks had placed restrictions on granting credit to the state because of its adverse financial policies and the conditions pressed for by the Banco de Reserva.[64] Agricultural creditors who hoped for a loosening of local credit conditions were behind the complaints voiced by the Banco del Perú y Londres. In November 1929 interest rates jumped from 8 per cent to 10 per cent. Time was running out for the Banco del Perú y Londres, and the fall of Leguía in 1930 finally removed the bank's last weak defence against bankruptcy. Embittered and witnessing the loss of internal support, Leguía criticised Seligman & Company in December 1929 because ' . . . the fiscal agents [Seligman & Company] had been prepared to see the whole country go to smash . . . and showed a complete lack of desire to be helpful'.[65]

After the fall of Leguía foreign capital continued to exert an important influence. After 1930 mineral and petroleum concessions were to prove crucial in the relationship between foreign capital and the state, and local financial and monetary policies were to be affected by that relationship. The native private sector was also to suffer further as a result of foreign financial power in Peru.

FOREIGN FINANCE DURING THE 1930s

Despite the financial crash of 1929–32, a politically powerful lobby of agro-exporters, who had turned against Leguía in the crucial year 1930, was able to retain certain influence over the state in terms of financial policy. The financial programme established by the emergency government in the early 1930s allowed many agro-exporters to survive.

It has been argued that a factor of primary importance in Peru's economic recovery in the 1930s might have been the avoidance of the complete collapse of the Peruvian agro-industry through a swift adaptation to cotton rather than sugar production with the financial support of the state. The departure from the gold standard (without introducing exchange controls) and the supply of 'controlled' credit to cotton producers aided the trend toward crop substitution. Significantly, several finance ministers and high officials of the Banco Central de Reserva during this period faithfully represented agro-exporting interests. However the financial recovery of the 1930s, supported by foreign finance, was to result in a reduction in the importance of agro-exports in the Peruvian economic and financial structure.

The second important factor of Peruvian recovery was the suspension of the servicing of foreign loans in 1931, and the replacement of foreign credit by domestic credit. This restructuring of public borrowing was aided by the local banks and especially by the most important among them, the Banco Italiano, which had excess deposits to allocate and was oriented in its business toward the internal market. The purchase of internal debt bonds by local banks proved helpful to the state in meeting its military, road building and current expenses. Foreign creditors observed these developments with remarkable patience out of concern for internal stability.

The tactful strategy followed by foreign financial interests in Peru during the years of the depression was threefold. In the first place, foreign creditors assumed a cautious approach to the delicate issue of the repayment of foreign loans until the Peruvian economy recovered. Secondly, there was the consolidation and expansion of already existing, as well as new, monopolies and oligopolies. Thirdly, encouragement was given to import machinery to supply the budding though costly import-substitution industrialisation.

During the most difficult moments of the depression in Peru, foreign creditors considered political stability to be paramount in safeguarding their Peruvian concerns, and as a consequence loan repayments were not urgently demanded. Instead they opted for special arrangements with the Peruvian state. In 1930 the Canada-based petroleum concern tied to Standard Oil, the International Petroleum Company (IPC), was anxious to secure from the government a monopoly on the sale of petroleum in Peru, but political turmoil prevented the deal from being closed. However President Luis Sánchez Cerro was in desperate need of funds to pay the army, the navy and the police. IPC lent the government $1.5 million in December 1930, and monopoly concessions were soon after granted to IPC.[66]

Another example of foreign influence on domestic affairs was the US Cerro de Pasco Corporation, which was encountering considerable business and labour difficulties. The Pasco Corporation called on the armed forces, under the orders of Sánchez Cerro, to suppress what was termed at the time a communist insurrection in Morococha. Thus the insistence by foreign interests for political stability contributed to the consolidation of the authoritarian regimes of Sánchez Cerro and his successor General Oscar R. Benavides.

Some foreign oligopolistic interests, like the Pasco Corporation, experienced difficult financial times in Peru during the depression. The Liverpool-based merchant house Graham Rowe had lent considerable sums, provided by the Martins Bank, to agricultural concerns. Like the Banco del Perú y Londres, which had overextended its agricultural credit, Graham Rowe was not able to repay its creditor bank and was therefore forced into liquidation in October 1931.[67]

Table 7.1   Peruvian public debt, 1876–1966* (millions of US dollars)

		Foreign Debt						Internal Debt		
					Types of Creditors**					
Year	Pledges on Re- venues	General Credit	Total	Interest (%)	% govt	% private	% int.	Funded	Floating	Total
1876	180	–	180	5.5		100		–	–	–
1889	250	–	250	6.0		100		–	–	38
1990	15	–	15	6.0		100		–	–	38
1920	13	–	13	6.0		100		–	–	26
1925	25	–	25	8.0		100		–	–	30
1929	–	88	88	6.0		100		–	–	36
1933	–	105	105	6.0		100		15	29	44
1937	–	119	119	6.0		100		18	40	58
1945–48	–	167	167	6.0		100		38	99	137
1950	–	113	113	6.5				84	11	95
1954	–	95	95	6.5	31	48	21	68	41	109
1960	–	162	162	6.5						
1966	–	579	579	6.5						

* Includes interest in arrears.
** Govt = government agencies; int. = international banks and organisations

Sources: Corporation of Foreign Bondholders, *Annual Reports* (1873–86); UK Department of Overseas Trade, *Reports* (1922–55); Rómulo Ferrero, *La política fiscal*; German Suárez and Mario Tovar, *Deuda pública externa*; Gianfranco Bardella, *Un siglo en la vida económica*.

In another example, the National City Bank advanced $600 000 in May 1932 to help keep alive the Gildemeister sugar estate Casa Grande, a sugar complex that had the largest sugar cane crushing mill in the world and in which German interests had been involved.[68]

Considering the rather bleak prospects for foreign business in Peru some sober foreign observers argued that the resumption of payment of both the principal and the interest on foreign loans was not possible until the international market price of Peruvian commodities improved, and until political stability allowed a reduction in government expenditure.[69] As can be seen from Table 7.1, from a total foreign debt of $105 million at 6 per cent interest, Peru owed approximately $18 per person in 1933 among an estimated population of six million people. In addition the internal debt (funded and floating) amounted to $44 million, and kept on increasing thereafter.

A 1934 article in *The Times* of London argued that payments to service the debt were dependent upon the demand for Peruvian primary products abroad. The article considered that although Peru had made steps towards economic recovery by 1933, and confidence in the government of President Benavides was on the rise, foreign debt payments would continue in abeyance until the more developed countries organised their economies to bring the demand for Peruvian products back to normal.[70]

However in December 1933 J. Henry Schroeder & Company, representing the creditors of the 1922 guano loan, complained that the Peruvian government had used the proceeds of the guano sales under the administration of the Guano Company to purchase arms and aircraft from the US and Japan.[71] British creditors remained sternly opposed to the guano loan being treated by the Peruvian government in the same manner as the US loans. These creditors proposed that His Majesty's Government should condemn any move in that direction and should also disallow any trade agreement which did not give due consideration to the rights of British bondholders.[72] Likewise, in 1935 the British holders of the 1924 centenary loan of S/5 million protested against the unilateral reduction, from 8 per cent to 6 per cent, of the interest rate paid to them.[73]

US creditors took a different stand from that of the British. Following the US congressional investigations into foreign loans in the early 1930s, the mood of US creditors was one of resigned patience. J. Rafael Oreamuno, a Costa Rican by birth and a representative of the US holders of Peruvian bonds, believed after visiting Peru in January 1935 that the time for serious discussions on debt repayment had not yet arrived.[74] In the meantime the Peruvian government had managed to allocate S/2 million for debt servicing and two million more for redemption of its public debt. Oreamuno was of the opinion that if Peru was left alone for the next two years its economic situation would improve sufficiently for a better debt arrangement to be offered.

In 1937 Oreamuno considered that time had come, and that Peru should pay in full what it owed.[75] The Peruvian government, however, continued to allocate only the S/4 million mentioned above, following the example of Chile. This amount was unsatisfactory to US creditors but constituted, according to Oreamuno, at least an official recognition of the debt. Consequently the June 1937 report of the US Securities and Exchange Commission did not favour the application of sanctions on Peru to enforce repayment.[76]

Unwilling to accept the unilateral action by the Peruvian government, in November 1935 the chairman of the British Council of Foreign Bondholders proposed to the Peruvian minister of finance a negotiated settlement of the debt to Britain. According to British diplomats in Peru, the two most important obstacles to the formation of a surplus in Peruvian fiscal finances that could be assigned to the servicing of foreign debts were, first, the extensive development programme launched by the Benavides government to revitalise the economy and, second, the demands by Peruvian congressmen to divert funds to their constituencies for banal and decorative purposes. However, as agro-export interests continued to compete with foreign interests in the arena of financial and monetary policies, in 1937 both Oreamuno and the British Ambassador in Lima had doubts about the sincerity of the Peruvian government's willingness to pay.[77]

Difficulties in resuming repayment of the foreign debt continued until 1952 with approximately the same characteristics as described previously. The major change from the viewpoint of foreign financial interests was the encouragement given to the importation of foreign machinery for protected local industries. In 1938 machinery, tools and metal goods accounted for 40 per cent of the value of all Peruvian imports.[78] The other major import items eroding the Peruvian balance of trade were food products such as wheat, rice and dairy products, which had accounted for approximately 40 to 50 per cent of domestic local consumption since the mid-1920s when urban centres expanded considerably.[79]

Selective protectionist legislation, import quotas, and foreign exchange controls went hand in hand. These measures, gradually imposed during the regimes of President Manuel Prado and José Luis Bustamante, benefited the interests of industrialists and their allies among the foreign importers.

The link between credit and foreign imports had been established since the beginning of the century. In 1933 the British Ambassador noted that on the sugar estates of Anglophil agro-exporter Antero Aspíllaga, the British machinery that had been in use in previous decades was not being replaced by new British imports owing to the lack of trade credit. Instead new German technical devices that were procured with credit provided by German importers were being introduced.[80] According to official statistics, the Peruvian balance of trade had suffered a considerable decline due to a rapid rise in imports (machinery, chemical products and foodstuffs) between 1938 and 1945.[81]

A local banking institution that benefited from this change in the direction of foreign trade was the Banco Italiano, which relied on US, Swiss and Italian capital support. Foreign banking institutions preferred to support this leading local institution of an already oligopolised financial sector. The liquidation of the Banco del Perú y Londres left several US creditors of this bank with considerable financial claims. Among the major creditors were the National City Bank, W. R. Grace & Company and M. Samuel.

In contrast support of the Italian bank offered considerable advantages.[82] The Banco Italiano, unlike the Banco del Perú y Londres, had oriented its loans toward Lima's expanding urban and service markets that were in need of credit in the 1920s, and the Italian owners of factories and commercial establishments were the bank's main clients. The Banco Italiano became the most solid institution in the Peruvian banking system and local savings and deposits flooded into it. It also pursued a conservative loan policy, and had acted as the agent for the Guaranty Trust Company of New York in the 1920s.[83]

The fascist political sympathies of some managers of the Banco Italiano, especially its head Gino Salocchi, a close friend of President Benavides, were instrumental in providing commercial credit to the government for the purchase of Italian military equipment in the 1930s.[84] Despite these fascist connections, Swiss, French and US investors continued to favour the Banco Italiano rather than branches of foreign banks that were not able to compete in the Peruvian banking structure. The Banco Italiano changed its name to Banco de Crédito in 1941 to avoid political persecution during the war, and thus was able to continue its successful business.

The Banco Italiano's support to foreign oligopolies and monopolies was substantial. The huge electrical concern, the EE.EE.AA, which had been restructured in 1910 and again in the 1920s with the participation of British, French and Swiss capital, was closely tied to the Banco Italiano in the 1920s and 1930s. Other major corporations, like the Cerro de Pasco Corporation, were good clients of the bank. Most importantly, the process of concentration of the local industry depended on the financial and credit backing of the Banco Italiano. Under these circumstances the following multinationals invested in Peru: the ITT-dominated Compañía Peruana de Teléfonos (1930), Goodyear (1943), and thanks to the liberal mining and petroleum laws (1950, 1952), the Southern Peru Copper Corporation (American Smelting and Refining Company, 1952), the Marcona Mining Company (1952), Anderson Clayton & Company, Constructora Emkay, Morrison-Knudsen Company, General Motors (1952) and Sears (1955).[85] Only in the 1950s, with the establishment of new banks with modern banking methods (Banco Continental, with the substantial participation of the Rockefeller's Chase Manhattan Bank), and with the increase in influence of US financial interests, was there to be a degree of challenge to the Banco Italiano's dominance over the local banking business.

FINANCIAL CONSEQUENCES OF THE SECOND WORLD WAR

During the Second World War US financial interests reinforced the change in the Peruvian economic and financial structure which had occurred following a drastic shift in the international market for Latin American exports. By 1940 Europe had effectively disappeared as a market for Peruvian cotton, Chilean copper and Brazilian coffee. Formerly Europe had accounted for approximately 35–40 per cent of the Latin American import–export trade, and nearly 75 per cent of Peruvian cotton exports. Economic collapse, political vulnerability and increased defence costs against Axis designs in Latin America were feared by the US authorities. Consequently US agencies soon geared to provide loans and reorient Latin American foreign trade towards the US economic sphere.[86]

When the US entered the war in 1941 the trade situation in Latin America was altered due to the lend-lease of military equipment and the US defence programmes. This also meant major restructuring of Latin American infrastructures and basic economies within the framework of Roosevelt's Good Neighbour policy that offered economic and financial rewards to aligned Latin American states.

A man who proved to be central as an ideologist and policymaker in consolidating the new US strategy towards Latin America was Nelson A. Rockefeller. In an economic environment influenced by the work of economist John Maynard Keynes, Rockefeller represented influential US private interests that aimed to reconcile state goals with those of private corporations, aiding rather than opposing the rising economic and financial role of the state in the 1930s and 1940s.[87]

According to the ultimate goals of this novel coordination between US public and private efforts, Latin American countries were to be transformed into semi-peripheral economies that would increasingly absorb US products, especially used and new industrial equipment.[88] Thus, under the Axis threat, the Latin American tendency toward state intervention – as opposed to previous liberal policies – was encouraged and supported by US private and public interests. At the end of the war, a renewed liberal reversal of US trade and foreign policy further undermined traditional private interests in Latin America and contributed to the post-war rise in inflation in Peru. The aim to transform the Latin American élite into US-modelled 'middle classes' was reinforced after the war, supported by Rockefeller's own non-profit private organisations that worked actively in the area.

Axis influence in Latin America prior to and during the Second World War was especially strong in Argentina and Bolivia. German networks of communications and airlines throughout Latin America constituted strategic threats. Before the German invasion of Russia in June 1941, American strategists feared a possible Axis thrust to the south beyond Northern Africa and thence across the Atlantic to South America. Brazil therefore became a cornerstone of US military and logistical strategic planning. Likewise the Japanese threat in the Pacific made US military leaders aware of the strategic importance of Ecuador.[89]

Economically, German interests had strong banking and trading relations with South America, including the handling of a proportion of US goods exported to Latin America. In the case of Peru, the Banco Alemán Transatlántico facilitated the importation of German and US products. Also, among the economically influential Italian concerns in Peru, the Banco Italiano was the backbone of fascist symphathies that expressed themselves in the local press. In addition, by June 1941 Japan was the major purchaser of Peruvian cotton.[90]

Fascist economic and financial ideology encouraged self-sufficient economic activities which coincided with some practices of several Latin American populist and authoritarian leaders in the 1930s, including Benavides in Peru. Monopolistic ventures in Italy were supported by a corporate policy of privileges through tariff protection and official subsidies. This policy was not unlike the Peruvian state's increasing support to local monopolies and oligopolies, including of course the Banco Italiano and its clients among the import-substitution industrialists. Added to this, nazi and fascist aversion to the gold standard was probably influential in Latin American monetary policies in the 1930s.[91]

After a trip to Latin America in 1930, Nelson Rockefeller was appointed head of a newly created institution, the Office of the Coordinator of Inter-American Affairs (CIAA). He was assigned the task of deflecting Axis influence and implementing the Good Neighbour policy in close coordination with the Advisory Committee of the

Council of National Defense, the Departments of State and Commerce, and the Export–Import (EXIM) Bank.

The energetic Rockefeller introduced crucial measures to US–Latin American relations during the war, some of which were projected beyond the short and medium term. These measures were of three types. First, the CIAA recommended the planning of strategic defence actions, to be coordinated by ad hoc committees in Latin American countries. These defence actions involved the elimination of Axis ownership or control of the telecommunications facilities in Latin America, and the acquisition of such networks by private US negotiations with prior consultation and coordination with the Department of State; and the construction of telegraph, telephone and medical facilities for the US army and navy in Brazil, Ecuador and the Caribbean.[92]

The second type of measure coordinated by Rockefeller involved a so-called economic warfare policy aimed at the elimination of Axis and pro-Axis economic influence, and in particular the influence of pharmaceutical, chemical and other industrial cartels.[93]

The third measure related to the delicate question of Latin American domestic economic and financial matters, the stability of which were considered essential in avoiding internal turmoil that could lead to Axis influence. These matters included the burning issue of price controls on Latin American imports and exports, exchange stability, cooperation projects, agricultural and other development projects, and loans and credits.

During the war Latin American countries depended on US imports. Thus the prices of Latin American exports were tied to US prices. Under the war controls and regulations imposed by the US Office of Price Administration, strategic Latin American products such as rubber, cotton and copper were to be kept under a certain level agreed with Latin American governments. The Good Neighbour policy emphasised cooperation in the supply of these products. In the case of Peru, however, native cotton growing interests protested against such agreements.[94]

Because the US could not fulfil the high demand for imports by Latin America due to war controls, gold funds for up to $3 billion belonging to South American countries alone had accumulated in US banks by the end of 1943. As a consequence exchange stability was not a problem at that time, except for Chile and Bolivia. In addition, as a preemptive measure, from the start of the war the EXIM Bank had extended credit to Latin American countries for stabilisation purposes. Peru was granted $25 million, but this was not used owing to the Peruvian position with respect to its defaulted foreign debt.[95]

Except for Peru, the consequence of the accumulation of the Latin American gold funds in the US was that part of those funds were used to repay outstanding or defaulted Latin American bonded debts. The total outstanding debt was reduced from $1.67 billion to $1.20 billion between 1939 and 1944.[96]

Rockefeller's office was also instrumental in the signing of cooperation agreements, of which the most strategic and important were those with Mexico and Brazil that expressly aimed to provide political support to, respectively, the Camacho and Vargas regimes.[97] A multitude of specific agreements were targeted at long-term agricultural improvements to alleviate war-caused food shortages, improvements in sanitation and other infrastructural developments for which US Federal funds were allocated. These outlays were criticised by Senator Hugh Butler who believed that goodwill could not be purchased. Rockefeller answered these criticisms by pointing out the strategic importance of Latin America to the US and detailing the specific outlays by the office under his administration.[98] Towards the end of the war the CIAA recommended the continuation of developmental projects in Latin America and the need for the provision of 'sufficiently liberal' financial and credit facilities.[99] The provision of low interest loans tied to specific US trade and economic goals would continue after the war through the activities of the EXIM Bank, the World Bank and other governmental and intergovernmental agencies that had substantial US presence.

However, when the war was finally over the long-term plans of the CIAA were not implemented as Rockefeller had envisioned due to US foreign and economic policies being concentrated on European and global affairs. He nevertheless continued his objective for the transformation of Latin American economies towards what he considered higher levels of development, which implied the formation of industrial and financial 'middle classes'. This time he deployed his own private interests in the 1940s and 1950s to encourage the activities of such non-profitmaking organisations as the Inter-American Development Commission (IADC), with none other than J. Rafael Oreamuno as vice chairman, the American International Association, and the International Basic Economy Corporation.[100]

IADC staff pointed out several shortcomings in the post-war foreign financing of economic activities in Latin America. For example the loans by the World Bank for government and government-sponsored projects fostered nationalisation and state intervention. The EXIM Bank's credit policy was directed at US exporters and not at Latin American importers. And, most crucially, financial facilities for the development of private enterprise were lacking. However, as the example of an important IADC project in Peru proved, Rockefeller's agency ultimately aimed at the takeover by the Peruvian government of the projects it had initiated. The case in question was the Manual Industry Mission in Peru, headed by a Mr. Bailey who dealt with the influential (and pro-interventionist) politician Haya de la Torre to obtain government support for the highly publicised factory in 1945.[101]

The supposedly crucial 'middle classes' envisioned by Rockefeller and supported by US public and private interests, consisted of a small group of import-substitution industrialists who received state and financial support through subsidies, controls and tariff protection, as discussed in the previous chapter. Rising inflation in Peru after the Second World War resulted in additional benefits to these industrialists, but rising costs to the saving public and the financial structure.

REGAINED INTERNATIONAL CREDIT

Not until 1952 did the Peruvian government negotiate a definitive solution to its old (pre-1930) debt. In 1947 there had been a new attempt to settle the issue unilaterally by the regime of Bustamante y Rivero. These attempts failed despite Bustamante's eagerness to regain access to foreign credit.[102] Odría was successful in deposing Bustamante because of fears of the *aprista* party's rise to power, and through his opposition to the economic and financial management that had introduced foreign exchange controls. Odría reintroduced orthodox financial policies in an attempt to stabilise the currency and lower inflation.[103] US financial advisor Julius Klein contributed to these changes. These measures were relatively effective. Furthermore, the export boom which took place during the Korean War allowed correction of the Peruvian negative balance of trade.

In addition to these internal rearrangements, in 1952 Odría renegotiated the foreign debt. By 1955 repayment schedules were agreed on the condition of a debt reduction by which foreign creditors would forgo the interest accrued on the Peruvian defaulted debt between 1930 and 1946.[104] With the availability of new foreign loans as a result of this arrangement, Odría was finally able to carry out his programme of public works and social security.

New loans from foreign creditors were contracted for a total amount of $980 million between 1950 and 1965. Approximately 48 per cent of this amount was granted by private suppliers of goods, 31 per cent by US and other government agencies, and 21 per cent by international banks and organisations (Table 7.1).[105] A substantial portion of these loans were, however, tied to specific purchases of imports.

Unlike the funds from the previous cycle of public loan expansion, the new loans were not necessarily linked to developmental purposes. In fact, many loans in the 1950s and 1960s were used for military and defence purposes.[106] This pattern was to be continued in the 1970s, when large foreign commercial loans were made available to a military government keen on bureaucratic expansion.

In conclusion, crowding out effects, state interventionism fuelled by foreign public loans and, in general, internationally-led flows of foreign capital and foreign policy pressures, limited the developmental effects of foreign finance in Peru. By inhibiting the growth of the local private sector, foreign capital and the state removed the possibility of financially viable capitalism in Peru, and fostered instead a bureaucratically-led economic environment where graft and unsound economic decisions proliferated.

8 Conclusion

The evidence discussed in this study has provided interesting insights into Peruvian financial development and its long-term interaction with the export economy. It can be concluded that, at least until 1950, overall modern financial evolution was relevant to the country's particular economic growth and diversification. Export growth and modernisation developed hand in hand with domestic financial resources. Compared to the financial performance of other Latin American countries, Peru's was not altogether disfavourable and even showed dynamism by the 1960s.

However, a deeper analysis of key financial factors, subperiods, acute fluctuation relating to international cycles, and the continuation of the dangerous trend towards oligopolisation and state intervention, shows an undermining of the earlier more positive results of financial intermediation.

Private domestic finance demonstrated an initially dynamic response to economic incentives and made important contributions to the export economy's modernisation, diversification and integration. Between 1884 and 1930 native financial institutions and élite groups combined competition and collaboration with foreign capital, and struggled for native financial autonomy. By 1930–50, however, increased financial concentration and oligopolisation – reinforced by state intervention and foreign capital – had detrimental effects on the regional and social distribution of credit, wealth and income.

Public finance demonstrated, on balance, a negative effect on the domestic financial structure. Since the disastrous Guano Age, and with renewed intensity by the late 1920s, the legacies of state arbitrary intervention, deficit finance, abused domestic debts, and excessive reliance on foreign loans, have resulted in the gradual weakening of the relatively small but crucial private sector, and the strengthening of authoritarian trends linked to state control and financial repression.

Foreign finance endeavoured to displace native capital from crucial financial sectors, with variable emphasis according to the ebbs and flows of international financial and trade cycles. By granting loans to the state and investing in the domestic financial system, foreign interests reinforced the lack of collaboration between the private and public sectors.

The wider implications of this study stress the need to combine the analysis of private and public domestic finance with that of foreign financial factors to form an integrated and comprehensive historical model for use in the study of Latin American export-led financial processes. Financial dependence can not be taken for granted during a period of export-led modernisation. As shown by the Peruvian case, financial dependence was paradoxically enhanced by state intervention and foreign public credit aimed at encouraging and protecting costly import-substitution industrialisation.

The export-led financial model was replaced in part by an even more oligopolistic and state-controlled financial model. The consequences of this include the rise of new economic and financial élites, as well as the eruption of authoritarian regimes, some even with populist appeal, which did little to improve the distribution of income and wealth.

The recent expansion of state financial interests and the 'nationalisation' of financial systems in Latin America are a consequence of financial repression and foreign indebtedness. The private sector in several countries has been thoroughly weakened and has lost its ability to make sound financial decisions in response to economic incentives. The financial interests of Latin American states and foreign banks predominate over viable local economic projects, and have paved the way for bureaucratic and unsound financial decisions.

Appendix A: Comparing Peruvian Financial Performance

According to the indices that measure the quantitative evolution of banking assets and the amount of total financial assets relative to domestic output and wealth,[1] one can establish that there was fluctuating but, in the main, positive financial development in Peru between 1885 and 1965. If my limited estimates for the pre-1965 ratio of financial instruments to gross national product (GNP) are interpolated with the more precise contemporary measurements of economists,[2] as has been done in Table A.1, one observes considerable progress in the Peruvian financial structure from 1960 to 1965, progress which was more pronounced than between 1935 and 1945.

However long-term financial development was obviously not sustained, according to the ratio of financial assets to GNP. This index might not be adequate in expressing financial development if, for example, there is a sudden decline of the GNP denominator (due to an export bust), or if the financial assets are inflated due to excessive speculation or lack of productive credit allocation opportunities. It is thus necessary to consider the more precise financial interrelations ratio (FIR, ratio of financial assets to tangible assets), and analyse in detail the fluctuations and phases of development of a particular financial structure.

More precise approximations of the Peruvian FIR are difficult as there is a lack of statistical information on national wealth. It is possible however to identify five distinct cycles in Peruvian modern financial development: 1884–1901, 1902–15, 1916–30, 1931–9 and 1940–50. These cycles determined long-term performance. The evolution of commercial and savings banks' total assets, deposits and loans shown in Figure 3.1 shows an overall tendency towards a rise.

Compared to Mexico, Peru's financial development seems to have been somewhat smaller – approximately half that of Mexico if measured by the ratio of financial assets over GNP for 1929–60 – as well as less marked in its fluctuations. However, estimates of the Peruvian ratio for 1905 and 1910 are slightly higher than Mexico's despite this country's lead in the proportion of banking assets to exports for the same years. Even this advantage of Mexico disappeared and Peru apparently took the lead between 1925 and 1950. According to specialists Mexico underwent a true financial revolution from 1939, following a steep decline and poor financial performance between 1910 and 1938.

Peruvian financial development was nearer to and even marginally more than that of Colombia if we observe the evolution in the number of banking institutions and the ratio of banking assets to exports between 1914 and 1950. For the years 1965–9 Colombian and Brazilian ratios of financial assets to GNP were, on average, respectively only four-fifths and two-thirds that of Peru.[3]

219

Table A.1   Indices of financial development: various countries, 1850–1965

Year	Total Financial Assets/GNP				Financial Interrelations Ratio (FIR)		
	Peru	Mexico	US	Gt Britain	Mexico	India	US
1850	–	–	1.33	4.95	–	0.64	0.47
1875	0.59	–	2.29	3.44	–	0.47	0.64
1885	–	–	–	–	–	–	–
1895	–	0.27	4.61	6.41	–	0.40	0.71
1905	0.44	0.38	–	–	–	–	–
1910	0.65	0.52	–	–	–	–	–
1914	0.74	–	3.47	5.70	–	0.34	0.83
1925	0.68	–	–	–	–	–	–
1929	0.56	1.03	5.61	6.96	0.36	0.30	1.29
1939	0.74	1.55	5.17	7.54	0.64	0.38	1.32
1950	0.59	1.33	3.90	5.71	0.74	0.45	1.17
1960	0.78	–	–	–	–	–	–
1965	1.72	1.48	4.42	4.77	0.68	0.57	1.28

Year	Banking Assets/Exports			Number of Banking Institutions						
	Peru	Colombia	Mexico	Peru A	Peru B	Colombia A	Colombia B	Mexico A	Mexico B	US A
1850	–	–	–	–	–	–	–	–	–	–
1875	–	–	–	16	–	–	–	–	–	–
1885	0.23	–	–	3	–	–	–	10	–	–
1895	1.14	–	0.99	4	5	–	–	–	–	–
1905	0.93	–	1.42	6	12	–	–	35	63	–
1910	1.15	–	3.56	6	14	–	–	–	–	24 514
1914	1.55	–	–	7	21	14	–	–	–	–
1925	1.87	1.09	0.85	12	28	35	–	76	66	–
1929	1.43	1.97	–	15	36	16	–	–	–	23 719
1939	2.52	1.80	1.42	13	87	–	–	124	61	14 534
1950	2.15	–	1.83	16	184	14	171	414	846	14 146
1960	2.17	–	3.60	30	658	18	522	462	2346	13 472
1965	–	–	–	30	688	–	–	461	3108	13 600

Note: A = number of banks' headquarters; B = number of branches and agencies

Sources: For Peru, author's estimates based on Carlos Camprubí, *Historia de bancos*, pp. 119, 217; *Extracto Estadístico del Perú* (1918–1966); Carlos Boloña, 'Tariff Policies in Peru'; *Cuentas Nacionales del Perú* and *Memoria*, Banco Central de Reserva; *Memoria y estadística bancaria*, Superintendencia de Bancos; Alfonso Quiroz, 'Financial Institutions', pp. 432–39; Clark Reynolds, 'Flow of Funds', pp. 68–70. On the number of banking institutions in Peru and Colombia in 1914, US Department of Commerce, *Banking*

Opportunities in South America, by William Lough, Special Agents Series no. 106, p. 66. Ratios of financial assets to GNP and FIR for Mexico, US, Great Britain and India from Raymond Goldsmith, *Comparative National Balance Sheets*, Table 19. On US banking institutions, Peter Rose, *The Changing Structure* Table 1.3. For Mexico, Raymond Goldsmith, *Financial Development of Mexico* Tables 14, 15; Leopoldo Solís, *La realidad económica mexicana* Table iii.2; María E. Cordero, 'Evolución financiera de México' Table 1; Elia Ramírez Bautista, *Estadísticas bancarias* Tables 1, 35, 39; José A. Bátiz, 'Trayectoria de la banca'; John K. Thompson, *Inflation, Financial Markets* Table ii.1; O. Ernest Moore, *Evolución de las instituciones financieras* Table 2; Nacional Financiera S. A., *Statistics on Mexico* Tables 7.3, 6.1; Dwight S. Brothers and Leopoldo Solís, *Mexican Financial Development* Tables i.a, ii.b. For Colombia, William McGreevey and Jorge Rodríguez, 'Colombia: Comercio exterior' Table ii.b; Antonín Basch, *El mercado de capitales en Colombia*; Jorge Franco Holguín, *Evolución de las instituciones*; Paul Drake, *Money Doctor*, pp. 46–8.

In a comparison with developed economies Peru's financial assets/GNP ratio clearly lagged behind: one-fifth and one-eighth of that of the US and Great Britain, respectively, in 1875 and 1914, one-tenth and one-twelfth in 1929, and one-seventh and one-tenth from 1939 onwards.

In general Peru, Mexico and India lacked the swift and sustained increase in their financial assets/GNP and FIR ratios exhibited by the US between 1850 and 1913. Nor did the ratios of the poorer countries remain consistently high after 1914 the way they did in the US. Also, the increase in number of main banking offices in Peru, Colombia and Mexico was inverse to the decreasing number of main offices in the restructured US banking system from the 1930s. This was probably due to the increasing number of regional and development banks and the state's financial intervention in Latin America. However an increase in the number of branches of banks was common to the four countries after 1940, especially in Mexico and the US.

According to this brief comparative overview one can not consider the financial evolution in Peru was as substantial as Goldsmith found it to be in Mexico.[4] Peru's position in Latin American financial development by 1965 can be considered intermediate, but above that of other countries which are similar in size, such as Colombia. Compared to developed financial structures the Peruvian one was quite limited in its evolution.

Despite Peru's relatively moderate results in financial development one can not dismiss its historical achievements, which regretably have been blurred by the pessimist view that the costs of the export financial model outweighed its benefits.[5] The Peruvian financial structure did have positive effects, but these are often overlooked. Likewise the Peruvian financial institutions and élite can not be thought of simply as pro-foreign. Evidence points to their having had a complex relationship with foreign financial interests, as well as to their relative autonomous financial manipulations in certain historical episodes. Timing in this regard is crucial and should be taken into account in an overall evaluation of historical evidence.

Appendix B: Domestic Banking Data, 1872–1952

Table B.1   Basic statistics of Peruvian banking assets, deposits and loans, 1872–1952, millions of (1913) soles

Year	Price Index 1913	Price Index 1935	Assets 1913	Deposits 1913	Loans 1913
1872	1.16	0.61	30.4	11.4	24.4
1873	1.19	0.63	27.1	8.2	23.7
1874	1.20	0.63	23.5	8.1	19.9
1875	1.20	0.63	19.3	6.5	16.8
1876	–	–	–	–	–
1877	–	–	–	–	–
1878	–	–	–	–	–
1879	–	–	–	–	–
1880	–	–	–	–	–
1881	–	–	–	–	–
1882	–	–	–	–	–
1883	0.48	0.25	4.2	3.3	4.2
1884	0.49	0.26	6.1	4.5	4.9
1885	0.51	0.27	5.5	3.9	3.9
1886	0.54	0.29	6.7	5.2	5.9
1887	0.53	0.28	9.1	6.4	5.7
1888	0.54	0.29	13.0	10.0	8.1
1889	0.57	0.30	16.1	13.3	10.5
1890	0.51	0.27	–	–	–
1891	0.53	0.28	–	–	–
1892	0.61	0.32	–	–	–
1893	0.72	0.38	–	–	–
1894	0.80	0.42	19.1	14.5	13.3
1895	0.79	0.42	18.6	15.2	10.3
1896	0.81	0.43	20.5	16.7	12.6
1897	0.84	0.44	18.3	16.3	13.1
1898	0.72	0.38	27.1	20.6	17.8
1899	0.79	0.42	26.1	19.7	18.6
1900	0.78	0.41	32.1	22.7	22.3
1901	0.92	0.49	24.2	21.0	20.9
1902	0.92	0.49	34.1	24.5	24.8
1903	0.91	0.48	40.5	29.0	28.4
1904	0.92	0.49	45.2	29.7	28.2
1905	0.92	0.49	54.3	35.5	31.4
1906	0.92	0.49	57.7	40.9	37.9
1907	0.92	0.49	69.3	43.8	44.8

1908	0.93	0.49	103.7	47.0	46.9
1909	0.94	0.50	83.8	45.4	43.1
1910	0.94	0.50	80.2	59.9	50.7
1911	0.94	0.50	120.2	67.9	57.2
1912	0.95	0.50	135.8	80.6	67.3
1913	1.00	0.53	103.0	81.1	66.1
1914	1.03	0.54	103.9	52.1	59.7
1915	1.09	0.58	104.6	40.2	48.3
1916	1.20	0.63	105.0	48.1	41.9
1917	1.42	0.75	105.6	55.6	38.7
1918	1.67	0.88	112.6	60.5	37.5
1919	1.90	1.01	136.8	60.0	40.8
1920	2.09	1.11	152.2	74.6	54.5
1921	2.05	1.08	137.1	66.3	51.7
1922	1.90	1.01	108.9	70.5	56.8
1923	1.89	1.00	116.4	74.6	55.6
1924	1.92	1.02	131.3	87.5	70.8
1925	2.02	1.07	138.6	84.7	81.7
1926	2.03	1.07	132.0	83.7	80.3
1927	2.03	1.07	137.4	82.3	84.2
1928	1.92	1.02	140.6	92.7	87.5
1929	1.86	0.98	167.7	94.6	96.8
1930	1.78	0.94	124.7	69.7	73.6
1931	1.75	0.93	109.1	58.3	66.3
1932	1.70	0.90	122.4	60.0	78.8
1933	1.80	0.95	119.4	70.6	52.2
1934	1.88	0.99	153.2	86.7	62.8
1935	1.89	1.00	165.6	100.0	72.5
1936	1.92	1.02	209.4	116.1	89.6
1937	2.05	1.08	212.7	124.9	90.7
1938	2.05	1.08	232.2	141.5	101.5
1939	2.15	1.14	219.5	150.7	105.6
1940	2.48	1.31	219.4	166.5	104.4
1941	2.90	1.53	214.1	156.6	101.4
1942	3.67	1.94	216.1	167.0	85.3
1943	4.14	2.19	252.4	197.3	107.0
1944	4.30	2.28	292.1	234.0	129.8
1945	4.49	2.38	317.8	247.0	140.8
1946	4.83	2.56	340.2	265.2	181.0
1947	6.50	3.44	281.7	223.1	158.9
1948	8.16	4.32	245.2	181.1	145.5
1949	11.40	6.03	224.2	159.1	124.5
1950	13.28	7.03	256.6	175.2	132.2
1951	15.40	8.15	255.6	183.8	149.1
1952	15.83	8.38	313.7	221.0	185.5

Sources: Perú, Ministerio de Hacienda, Dirección General de Estadística, *Estadística de precios*; Alfonso Quiroz 'Financial Institutions', Appendix A: *Extracto Estadístico del Perú*, 1933; *Anuario Estadístico del Perú*, 1945, 1954, 1966; Paul Gootenberg's Price Index 1800–1873, in *Carneros y Chuño*; Carlos Boloña, 'Tariff Policies', p. 351.

Appendix C: Commercial Banks' Credit Allocation by Economic Sector

Table C.1   Commercial banks' percentage credit allocation by economic sector, 1884–1969; Banco del Perú y Londres (1884–1930), aggregate data (1947–69)

Year	Agric.	Livest.	Mining	Fishing	Industry	Trade	Constr.	Govnt	Public Cos.	Other	Total
1884	3.5	–	1.5	–	13.4	30.0	22.5	16.0	7.0	6.1	100
1899	8.0	–	–	–	11.0	29.0	20.0	13.5	5.0	13.5	100
1907	3.0	–	–	–	4.0	8.7	13.0	37.0	22.0	12.3	100
1915	27.0	–	5.0	–	6.0	28.0	2.1	21.0	1.0	9.9	100
1920	34.0	–	1.0	–	5.0	32.0	1.0	12.0	2.5	12.5	100
1925	35.0	–	–	–	–	18.0	–	31.0	5.0	11.0	100
1947	12.8	1.7	1.3	–	22.7	36.6	5.1	5.0	4.5	10.3	100
1949	12.7	2.0	1.3	–	26.1	36.6	4.2	4.3	2.0	10.8	100
1951	11.2	1.7	1.4	–	27.7	42.2	4.1	1.6	1.0	9.1	100
1953	13.1	1.7	1.3	–	24.8	43.2	5.2	2.2	0.6	7.9	100
1955	14.0	2.3	1.3	–	25.3	41.7	3.9	0.8	0.8	9.9	100
1957	13.9	1.9	1.6	–	25.8	41.3	4.6	0.4	0.8	9.7	100
1959	12.6	2.1	1.4	–	25.8	40.9	5.0	0.8	1.0	10.4	100
1961	10.9	2.3	1.5	–	28.9	40.8	4.5	0.4	1.6	9.1	100
1963	9.7	2.2	1.5	–	31.3	39.5	4.2	0.5	2.3	8.8	100
1965	8.8	2.2	1.3	5.3	25.3	39.6	4.4	0.4	2.8	9.9	100
1967	8.6	1.8	1.0	4.9	24.8	39.1	5.8	0.2	1.1	12.7	100
1969	8.0	1.3	0.5	3.7	29.2	30.7	8.8	0.1	0.8	16.9	100

Sources: BPLS; *Memoria*, Superintendencia de Bancos, 1947–1969; *Anuario Estadístico del Perú*, 1954, 1966; *Memoria*, Banco Central de Reserva del Perú, 1972, 1973.

Appendix D: Clients of the Banco del Callao and the Banco del Perú y Londres, 1884–1930

Primary information was obtained from records of the meetings of the boards of directors, as well as from those of shareholders meetings, on 6970 individual banking transactions from 1884–1930. This is a significant sample of the banking operations of the Banco del Callao and its successor the Banco del Perú y Londres. Complementary sources such as official tax records, national and urban guides for professions, and scattered biographical information from sundry literature, were used to complete information on these banks' clients. All amounts in different currencies (soles, Peruvian libras, dollars, francs) were converted to sterling using official exchange rates. Information has been arranged by sub-periods in Table D.1.

Table D.1   Types of transactions and occupation of clients, Banco del Callao and Banco del Perú y Londres, 1884–1930 (in per cent)

	1884–98	*1899–1906*	*1907–14*	*1915–19*	*1920–5*	*1926–30*
Occupation:						
Merchants	30.0	29.0	8.7	28.0	32.0	18.0
Proprietors	22.5	20.0	13.0	2.1	1.0	–
Government	16.0	13.5	37.0	21.0	12.0	31.0
Agriculturists	3.5	8.0	3.0	27.0	34.0	35.0
Miners	1.5	–	–	5.0	1.0	–
Industrialists	13.4	11.0	4.0	6.0	5.0	–
Semi-public Cos.	7.0	5.0	22.0	1.0	2.5	5.0
Professionals	4.0	7.0	5.0	3.0	4.0	–
Financiers	1.0	3.0	3.0	2.6	5.0	–
Other	1.1	3.5	4.3	4.3	3.5	11.0
Total	100.0	100.0	100.0	100.0	100.0	100.0
Transactions:						
Current accounts	26.5	18.5	22.0	32.0	29.0	22.5
Discounts	17.6	19.5	15.0	49.0	32.0	27.0
Short-term loans	35.3	24.3	42.0	16.0	36.0	46.0
Long-term loans	20.6	37.5	21.0	3.0	2.6	4.0
Total	100.0	100.0	100.0	100.0	100.0	100.0

Sources: Banco del Callao and Banco Perú y Londres, 'Directorio', 'Accionistas', BPLS; Alfonso Quiroz, 'Financial Institutions', pp. 441–4.

Notes and References

Note on Abbreviations

AMEF	Archives du Ministère de l'Economie et des Finances, Paris
ANF	Archives Nationales de la France, Paris
AAL	Archivo Arzobispal de Lima, Lima
AGI	Archivo General de Indias, Seville
AGN	Archivo General de la Nación, Lima
AHN	Archivo Histórico Nacional, Madrid
BNL	Biblioteca Nacional de Lima, Lima
BAP	Bundesarchiv, Potsdam
BPLS	Superintendencia de Banca y Seguros, Archivo Sección Liquida-ciones, Banco del Perú y Londres en Liquidación, Lima
MAE	Archives du Ministère des Affaires Etrangères, Paris
WRGP	W. R. Grace & Co. Papers, New York
GLL	Guildhall Library, London
PRO	Public Record Office, Kew Gardens, London
RAC	Rockefeller Archive Center, Pocantico Hills, North Tarrytown, New York
USNA	US National Archives, Washington, D.C.
Lp	Peruvian libra
S/	Peruvian sol
£	Pound sterling
d.	Penny sterling
$	US dollar

1 Introduction

1. Roberto Cortés Conde and Shane Hunt (eds), *The Latin American Economies*; John Coatsworth, *Growth Against Development*; Colin Lewis, 'The Financing of Railway Development'; Frederick Weaver, *Class, State, and Industrial Structure*; Stephen Haber, *Industry and Underdevelopment*; Steven Topik, *The Political Economy*.
2. Peter Klarén and Thomas Bossert, *Promise of Development*; James Rippy, *British Investment in Latin America*; Irving Stone, 'British Direct and Portfolio Investment'; D. C. M. Platt, *Business Imperialism*; H. S. Ferns, *Britain and Argentina*.
3. Alec Ford, *The Gold Standard*; idem, 'Notes on the Working of the Gold Standard'; Charles Kindleberger, *Keynesianism vs. Monetarism*.
4. Heraclio Bonilla, *Guano y burguesía*, pp. 165–6; Ernesto Yepes del Castillo, *Perú 1820–1920*, pp. 158–9.
5. Recent important exceptions are Carlos Marichal, *A Century of Debt*; Paul Drake, *The Money Doctor*; Bill Albert, *South America*; Winston Fritsch, *External Constraints*.
6. Rondo Cameron (ed.), *Banking and Economic Development*; idem,

Banking in the Early Stages of Industrialization; Raymond Goldsmith, *The Determinants of Financial Structure*; Alexander Gerschenkron, *Economic Backwardness*; Charles Kindleberger, *The Formation of Financial Centers*.

7. Raymond Goldsmith, *Financial Structure and Development*; Edward Shaw, *Financial Deepening*; Ronald McKinnon, *Money and Capital*; Nathaniel Leff, 'Capital Markets'; Albert Fishlow, 'Lessons from the Past'.

8. Carlos Marichal, *A Century of Debt*, pp. 6–11; J. A. Hobson, *Imperialism*; Barbara Stallings, *Banker to the Third World*, pp. 164–5.

9. See for example André G. Frank, *Capitalism and Underdevelopment*; and, for the supposedly 'enclave' economies such as the Peruvian, Fernando H. Cardoso and Enzo Faletto, *Dependency and Development*, p. 102.

10. Barbara Stallings, *Banker to the Third World*, pp. 49, 178; Keith Griffin, 'Monopoly Power', p. 8; Antonín Basch and Milic Kybal, *Recursos nacionales*, pp. 3–16, 41.

11. John H. Clapham, *The Bank of England*; Raymond de Roover, *Rise and Decline*; R. Ehrenberg, *Capital and Finance*; E. C. Corti, *The Rise of the House of Rothschild*; Lewis Corey, *The House of Morgan*; Harold Cleveland and Thomas Huertas, *Citibank*.

12. Raymond Goldsmith, *Financial Intermediaries*; Simon Kuznets, *Capital in the American Economy*.

13. 'Trato de Martín Antolínez con los judíos' in Ramón Menéndez Pidal (ed.), *Cantar de Mío Cid*, vol. 3, p. 1029.

14. Gobierno, Lima, leg. 817, Archivo General de Indias, Seville (hereafter AGI); Audiencia de Lima, Juzgado General de Censos, leg. 39, Archivo General de la Nación, Lima (hereafter AGN); 'Libro manual de los caudales correspondientes a la Dirección General de Censos y Obras Pías', 1822, Libros de Cuentas, serie C-15, libro 1553, AGN.

15. *The Bullionist*, 13 Dec. 1879, in Corporation of Foreign Bondholder Council, *The Newspaper Cuttings of the Council of Foreign Bondholders in the Guildhall Library, London*, microfilm publication (hereafter CFB) vol. 9, p. 48.

16. US Senate, Finance Committee Hearings, *Sale of Foreign Bonds*, vol. 1, p. 1587.

17. P. G. M. Dickson, *The Financial Revolution*; James C. Riley, *International Government Finance*.

18. James D. Tracy, *A Financial Revolution*; Violet Barbour, *Capitalism in Amsterdam*; Jelle C. Riemersma, *Religious Factors*.

19. James Riley, *International Government Finance*, pp. 2–3; P. G. M. Dickson, *The Financial Revolution*, pp. 11–12.

20. Ramón Carande, *Carlos V y sus banqueros*; James Boyajian, *Portuguese Bankers*.

21. James Riley, *International Government Finance*, pp. 165–74.

22. Geoffrey Parker, 'War and Economic Change', pp. 49–71; Violet Barbour, *Capitalism in Amsterdam*, p. 81.

23. P. G. M. Dickson, *The Financial Revolution*, pp. 54–6.

24. Gonzalo Anes et al., *El Banco de España*; Richard Herr, *The Eighteenth Century*.

25. John Lynch, *The Spanish–American Revolutions*; Peggy Liss, *Atlantic Empires*; Carlos Camprubí, *El Banco de la Emancipación*; Leonor Ludlow and Carlos Marichal (eds), *Banca y poder en México*.
26. Karl Polanyi, *The Great Transformation*, pp. 14–17; David Bushnell and Neill Macaulay, *The Emergence of Latin America*, pp. 180–5.
27. Paul Gootenberg, *Between Silver and Guano*; Alfonso Quiroz, *La deuda defraudada*; Barbara Tenembaum, *The Politics of Penury*; Samuel Amaral, 'El descubrimiento de la financiación inflacionaria'.
28. D. C. M. Platt (ed.), *Latin America and British Trade*; Carlos Camprubí, *Historia de bancos*; William Glade, *The Latin American Economies*; Christopher Abel and Colin Lewis (eds), *Latin America*.
29. Stanley Chapman, *The Rise of Merchant Banking*; Michael Edelstein, *Overseas Investment*.
30. Charles Jones, 'Commercial Banks and Mortgage Companies'; Charles Joslin, *A Century of Banking in Latin America*.
31. Jaime Zabludowski, 'Money, Foreign Indebtedness and Export Performance'.
32. Alec Ford, *The Gold Standard*, pp. 12–15.
33. Benjamin Keen and Mark Wasserman, *A History of Latin America*, Ch. 10; André G. Frank, *Capitalism and Underdevelopment*.
34. Thomas Skidmore and Peter Smith, *Modern Latin America*, p. 45.
35. Fernando H. Cardoso and Enzo Faletto, *Dependency and Development*, pp. 74–5; Celso Furtado, *Economic Development*, pp. 50–3.
36. David Collier, *Squatters and Oligarchs*; Manuel Burga and Alberto Flores Galindo, *Apogeo y crisis*.
37. Rosemary Thorp and Geoffrey Bertram, *Peru*; Florencia Mallon, *The Defense of Community*; Peter Klarén, *Modernization and Aprismo*.
38. Carlos Díaz Alejandro, *Essays*; Carlos Waisman, *Reversal of Development in Argentina*; Clark Reynolds, *The Mexican Economy*. My argument is *not* a version of neoliberal revisionism. I do not dispute the need for a degree of state intervention in economic emergencies as occurred in the 1930s. However even Keynes believed that long-term and persistent state intervention beyond certain limits – as verified in Latin America after 1930 – was counterproductive.
39. 'Persistence of inward-looking development strategies in the 1960s and 1970s made the [Latin American] region vulnerable to a debt crisis and not well situated to respond dynamically once the crisis broke out', Robert Devlin, *Debt and Crisis*, p. 237.
40. Carlos Boloña, 'Tariff Policies', pp. 29–36.
41. Rosemary Thorp and Geoffrey Bertram, *Peru*, Ch. 4.
42. Returned value is defined as the share of export receipts accounted for by local inputs and labour: Rosemary Thorp and Geoffrey Bertram, *Peru*, pp. 40, 153.
43. Rory Miller, 'British Business in Peru', pp. 22, 40, 152; Geoffrey Bertram, 'Development Problems', p. 29.
44. Héctor Maletta and Alejandro Bardales, *Perú*, vol. 1, pp. 35, 41; *Extracto Estadístico del Perú* (1919).
45. José Barbagelata and Juan Bromley, *Evolución urbana*, pp. 104–9. Rory Miller has raised several questions on the reliability of the 1876 census for Lima due to undercounting (based on physical evidence of urban

growth in the 1860s and 1870s and the 1891 and 1896 Lima censuses) in an unpublished paper presented at the International Congress of Americanists, Amsterdam, 1988.

46. Barbara Stallings, *Banker to the Third World*; Michael Edelstein, *Overseas Investment*, pp. 301–3.

47. Antony Gibbs & Sons Ltd, Merchants and Foreign Bankers, 'Private Information Book (Foreign Customers), 1865–98', '1859–1902', and '1884–1908', mss. 11 038A, B, C, and 11 069, Guildhall Library, London (hereafter GLL).

48. Alejandro Garland, 'La nueva política internacional sudamericana' (1906?), cited in Alberto Salomón 'El desarrollo económico del Perú' p. 350.

49. Rosemary Thorp and Geoffrey Bertram, *Peru*; Peter Klarén, *Modernization and Aprismo*; Florencia Mallon, *The Defense of Community*; Rory Miller (ed), *Region and Class*.

2 The Colonial and Post-Independence Heritage

1. John Noonan, *The Scholastic Analysis of Usury*; Marjorie Grice-Hutchinson, *Early Economic Thought*.

2. Julio Cotler, *Clases, Estado y Nación*; Ernesto Yepes del Castillo, *Peru*, p. 184; Heraclio Bonilla, *Guano y burguesía*, p. 63.

3. Shane Hunt, 'Growth and Guano', pp. 255–319; Paul Gootenberg, *Between Silver and Guano*; W. M. Mathew, *Gibbs and Peruvian Guano*.

4. Linda Greenow, *Credit and Socioeconomic Change*; David Brading, *Miners and Merchants*, p. 100.

5. *Censo* defined both mortgages (*censo al quitar*) and liens (*censo perpétuo* and *censo enfitéutico*) in Spain and its colonies at the time. When I use the word *censo*, I refer to the first of these definitions.

6. *Mercurio Peruano*, no. 27 (1791) p. 250; similar monetary aspects in 1686 and 1786 discussed in Manuel Moreyra Paz Soldán, *La moneda colonial en el Perú*, pp. 153–5, 257–9.

7. Manuel Vaquerizo Gil, 'Los censos al quitar'; Ubaldo Gómez Alvarez, *Estudio histórico*, pp. 235, 297–8; Arnold Bauer, 'The Church in the Economy of Spanish America'.

8. 'Espediente sobre competencia entre censuatarios y censualistas, de si deben pagar los censos de las fincas arruinadas por el terremoto del año 1746. Años 1747 a 1754', Sección Gobierno, Audiencia de Lima, leg. 509, AGI; Susan Ramirez, *Provincial Patriarchs*.

9. Sección Censos, 1700–1829, leg. 17, Archivo Arzobispal de Lima; Brian Hamnett, 'Church Wealth in Peru'.

10. Manuel de Silva to Consejo, 12 Aug. 1748, Gobierno, Lima, leg. 509, ff. 435–6, AGI.

11. Gonzalo Anes et al., *Banco de España*; James Riley, *International Government Finance*, pp. 165–74.

12. José Muñoz Pérez, 'Los proyectos sobre España e Indias'; Marcelo Bitar Letayf, *Los economistas españoles*; Peggy Liss, *Atlantic Empires*; Gaspar Melchor de Jovellanos, 'Informe de la Sociedad Económica de Madrid'; Pablo de Olavide, 'Informe de Olavide sobre la Ley Agraria'.

13. 'Expediente sobre la venta de los bienes de obras pías en los reinos de Indias', Gobierno, Lima, leg. 769; letter from Diego Miguel Bravo de Lagunas, 12 Oct. 1811, 'Amortización y consolidación 1780–1830', Indiferente, leg. 1702; Abascal to President of Castilla, 8 April 1809, Gobierno, Lima, leg. 738, AGI.

14. Tribunal del Consulado, 'Toda Imposición, 1819', leg. 349, libro 1237A, serie H-3, AGN; 'Informe que presenta la comisión de la deuda española y secuestros', 20 Feb. 1865, Manuscritos 1865-D2845, Biblioteca Nacional, Lima (hereafter BNL); 'Sobre el préstamo del millón y medio', Consulados, leg. 794, AGI.

15. *Mercurio Peruano*, no. 1 (1791) pp. 1–7; no. 23 (1791) pp. 209–16; John Fisher, *Silver Mines and Silver Mining*; idem, *Commercial Relations*; on the disputed effectiveness of Bourbon economic and financial reforms, Carlos Malamud and Pedro Pérez Herrero, 'Le reglamente du commerce libre'.

16. Gobierno, Lima, legs. 860, 874, 913, AGI; Consejos, leg. 20.319, AHN.

17. Rose Marie Buechler, *The Mining Society of Potosí*; Miguel Molina Martínez, *El Tribunal de Minería*.

18. 'El Consulado y comercio del Perú . . .', año 1774, Gobierno, Lima, leg. 874, AGI.

19. Alberto Flores Galindo, *Aristocracia y plebe*; Timothy Anna, *Fall of the Royal Government*, p. 120.

20. Vicente Rodríguez Casado and J. A. Calderón Quijano (eds), *Memorias*; Manuel de Mendiburu, *Diccionario histórico-biográfico*; Timothy Anna, *Fall of Royal Government*, pp. 114–19. Anna's argument that the extreme poverty of the Peruvian colony was a factor in favour of Peruvian independence 'by default' explains better the period 1815–21 than the fiscal and public debt reforms between 1777 and 1815.

21. Taxes created as part of Abascal's fiscal reforms in 1815 and which charged one peso for each 'fanega' of wheat imported, and 5 per cent on rents of Lima's *propiedades rústicas*.

22. Armando Nieto, *Contribución a la historia del fidelismo*, pp. 115–35.

23. Bernardo de Monteagudo, *Memoria*.

24. 'Deuda española liquidada hasta 1821', 1865-D12853, BNL.

25. *El Peruano* (3 July 1851).

26. Peru, *Cuestión entre el Perú y España*, pp. 4, 18.

27. 'Deuda española liquidada hasta 1821', BNL. Post-1821 Spanish government debts and *secuestro* amounts not included.

28. Timothy Anna, *Fall of Royal Government*, p. 114.

29. Bernardo Monteagudo, *Memoria*; 'Informe que presenta la Comisión de la deuda española y secuestros', 20 Feb. 1865, 1865-D2845, BNL; and 'Expediente relativo al acopio y organización de datos de la deuda española antigua y secuestros', (based on documents of the Tribunal de Cuentas, Dirección del Crédito Nacional and Tesorería Departamental, as well as 268 cases of *secuestros*), Feb. 1865, 1865-D2811, BNL; Alberto Flores Galindo, *Aristocracia y plebe*, p. 220.

30. Juan Rolf Engelsen, 'Agricultural Expansion', p. 10; Manuel Burga, *De la encomienda a la hacienda capitalista*, p. 148; Alfonso Quiroz, *Deuda*

defraudada, pp. 29–30. Some of these properties were later given back to the former owners or compensated for through internal debt bonds.

31. Carlos Palacios Moreyra, *La deuda anglo–peruana*, pp. 29–31; W. M. Mathew, 'The First Anglo–Peruvian Debt'; a similar case for Mexico in Reinhard Liehr, 'La deuda exterior'.

32. Paul Gootenberg, *Between Silver and Guano*, Ch. 5; Tribunal del Consulado, 'Expediente relativo a la relación de comerciantes de abono para el pago de derechos de aduana', 1866-D2810, BNL.

33. Tribunal del Consulado, 'Razón rectificada de las personas acotadas para el empréstito de cien mil pesos', Lima 23 Nov. 1837, 1837-D10367, BNL.

34. Alfonso Quiroz, *Deuda defraudada*, pp. 44–5.

35. Paul Gootenberg, *Between Silver and Guano*, pp. 155–6; Alfonso Quiroz, *Deuda defraudada*, Ch. 7.

36. W. M. Mathew, *Gibbs and Peruvian Guano*, pp. 58–60.

37. Shane Hunt, 'Growth and Guano', p. 275; W. M. Mathew, *Gibbs and Peruvian Guano*, p. 71.

38. Shane Hunt, 'Growth and Guano', pp. 262–4; Alfonso Quiroz, *Deuda defraudada*, pp. 23–5; José Deustua, *La minería peruana*; Fernando Casós, *La minería y la agricultura*, pp. 92–103, 113; *South Pacific Times*, 30 Sept. 1875, in CFB, vol. 3, p. 76; *Star & Herald*, 8 March 1878, in CFB, vol. 7, p. 176.

39. Alfonso Quiroz, *Deuda defraudada*, pp. 95–108; Heinrich Witt, *Diario y observaciones*, pp. 237–40.

40. Comisión Especial del Crédito Público, *Informe*; Junta de Examen Fiscal, *Informes*; *El Peruano* (31 Oct. and 4 Nov. 1857).

41. Juan Engelsen, 'Agricultural Expansion', pp. 57–8; Alfonso Quiroz, *Deuda defraudada*, pp. 159–65.

42. Emilio Dancuart, *Anales de la Hacienda Pública*, vol. 5, pp. 46–8; Manuel de Mendiburu, 'Noticias biográficas', p. 167; *El Peruano* (31 March 1857). If the conversion of the debt to the Tacna–Arica railway contractor Joseph Hegan (2 million pesos, not included in the consolidation) is added, the amount of debt conversion in 1853–4 totals 11 million pesos (see Table 2.6).

43. 'Objections of Thornton, Richmond and others that it is not advisable to admit domestic debt of any nation and particularly of Peru', 28 Aug. 1954, Hambros Bank Ltd, ms. 19 156, GLL.

44. Alfonso Quiroz, *Deuda defraudada*, pp. 62–3; *El Peruano* (19 Feb. 1857).

45. Correspondence, prospectus, application, allotment lists, receipts relating to 1853 substitution, Hambros Bank Ltd, ms. 19 156, GLL.

46. Heraclio Bonilla, *Guano y burguesía*; Julio Cotler, *Clases, Estado y Nación*; Javier Tantaleán, *Política económico-financiera*; Alfonso Quiroz, *Deuda defraudada*.

47. José Clavero, *El coronel de milicias*. Zaracondegui & Company went bankrupt in 1874; Carlos Camprubí, *Historia de bancos*, pp. 52–3.

48. Manuel Argumaniz Muñoz, 'Memorias inéditas', vol. 3, pp. 5, 14.

49. Carlos Camprubí, *Historia de bancos*, pp. 3–4; José A. Rodulfo, *Representación*.

50. Alberto Regal, *Castilla constructor*; Jorge Dulanto Pinillos, *Ramón Castilla*, p. 128; José Clavero, *El coronel de milicias*, p. 38; Protocolos Notariales, Felipe Orellana, 1865, no. 500, f. 224v, AGN.

51. Men like Felipe Barreda, José Canevaro, Carlos Delgado, Felipe Gordillo, Manuel Pardo and Clemente Villate; W. M. Mathew, *Gibbs and Peruvian Guano*, pp. 186–9, 194.

52. Robert Greenhill and Rory Miller, 'The Peruvian Government'; Heraclio Bonilla (ed.), *Las crisis económicas*.

53. Federico Blume, *Observaciones*, p. 12.

54. Cecilia Méndez, 'La otra historia del guano' and subsequent discussion; Juan Engelsen, 'Agricultural Expansion', pp. 52–7.

55. E. M., *La moneda en el Perú*; Alfonso Quiroz, *Deuda defraudada*, pp. 117–19; Manuel Moreyra Paz Sodán, 'El oro de California'.

56. José A. Rodulfo, *Representación*, pp. 8–10.

57. Manuel Moreyra Paz Soldán, 'El Oro de California'; *Documentos sobre el contrato de conversión*.

58. Carlos Camprubí, *Historia de bancos*, pp. 119–20.

59. Banco de la Providencia, *Exposición*; Una víctima de la Providencia, *Consideraciones*.

60. Manuel Argumaniz Muñoz, 'Memorias inéditas', vol. 4, p. 5.

61. Luis B. Cisneros, 'El negociado Dreyfus' (Havre, 1870), reprinted in idem, *Obras completas*, pp. 227–8.

62. Banco del Perú, *Reflexiones*.

63. José María Pando, *Reclamación de los vulnerados derechos*; Paul Gootenberg, *Between Silver and Guano*, pp. 34–6; Juan Engelsen, 'Agricultural Expansion', pp. 31–3; Alberto Flores Galindo, *Aristocracia y plebe*, pp. 48–53.

64. Juan Engelsen, 'Agricultural Expansion', pp. 10, 21, 18–9.

65. Alfonso Quiroz, *Deuda defraudada*, pp. 155–7; Manuel Argumaniz Muñoz, 'Memorias inéditas', vol. 3, p. 16.

66. Juan Engelsen, 'Agricultural Expansion', pp. 144–5.

67. Alfonso Quiroz, *Deuda defraudada*, pp. 159–65; Juan Engelsen, 'Agricultural Expansion', pp. 58–9.

68. Watt Stewart, *Chinese Bondage in Peru*, p. 25; Luis Cisneros, *Obras completas*, pp. 23–4.

69. Juan Engelsen, 'Agricultural Expansion', pp. 167–79; Manuel Argumaniz Muñoz, 'Memorias inéditas', vol. 3, p. 6.

70. Alfonso Quiroz, *Deuda defraudada*, pp. 88–90.

71. Cabildo Metropolitano, 'Representación elevada al Arzobispo de Lima Dn. José Sebastián Goyeneche y Barreda', Lima, 5 Jan. 1865, 1865-D8449, BNL; *El Peruano* (17 Dec. 1864); Pilar García Jordán, 'Estado moderno'.

72. Carlos Camprubí, *Historia de bancos*, pp. 61–4; Tribunal del Consulado, 'Expediente relativo a la suscripción de accionistas del Banco de Crédito Hipotecario', Lima, 27 Aug. 1866, 1866-D2809, BNL.

73. José Santos Morales, *Proyecto de un Banco Hipotecario*.

74. 'Obligación de la Sra. Da. María de Arauzo al Banco de Crédito Hipotecario', 17 March 1870, 1870-D12763, BNL.

75. Federico Blume, *Observaciones*, p. 11.

76. 'Documentos de las operaciones financieras realizadas entre el Gobierno peruano y la Casa Gibbs', Lima, Aug. 1858, 1858-D2214, BNL.
77. Daniel Ruzo, *Contestación a la carta*, citing earlier criticisms against Pardo by Bogardus. Also 'Sobre el juicio seguido por la Inspección Fiscal del Perú en Europa contra los Sres. Thomson Bonar y Cia. relativo al cobro indebido de comisiones por empréstitos correspondientes a los años 1862–65. París 26 enero 1874', 1874-D3254, BNL.
78. Luis Cisneros, *Obras completas*, pp. 213–21, 365.
79. Shane Hunt, 'Growth and Guano', pp. 275–6.
80. Jorge Basadre, 'Prologue', in Juan Copello and Luis Petriconi, *Estudio*, p. iii.
81. Jacinto López, *Manuel Pardo*, pp. 3, 13–18; Evaristo San Cristóbal, *Manuel Pardo y Lavalle*, pp. 14, 19–24; Manuel Pardo, 'Memoria que el ex-Secretario de Estado en el despacho de Hacienda y Comercio presenta al Jefe Supremo Provisorio de la República' (1867) in ibid., pp. 327–99.
82. Jorge Dulanto Pinillos, *Nicolás de Piérola*, p. 104.
83. 'Sobre las medidas a adoptarse para cubrir el déficit del Presupuesto de la República', Lima, 7 Sept. 1869, 1869-D2655, BNL.
84. On the origins and creditworthiness of Auguste Dreyfus' business in Peru one can read the following report from the Lima branch of Antony Gibbs & Sons to their London office on 12 Aug. 1863: the Dreyfus' house 'have hitherto done [import] business through Templeman & Bergman . . . it is now their intention to set up store separate from T & B. We don't know what means they may have, not in fact much about them but we should recommend caution in case they should enter into business relation with you', in 'Private information book on merchant firms, chiefly foreign 1859–1902', Antony Gibbs & Sons, ms. 11038B, GLL.
85. Heraclio Bonilla, *Guano y burguesía*, pp. 69–116.
86. Jorge Dulanto Pinillos, *Nicolás de Piérola*; Alberto Ulloa, *Don Nicolás de Piérola*; Heraclio Bonilla, *Guano y burguesía*, pp. 74–6.
87. Jorge Dulanto Pinillos, *Nicolás de Piérola*, pp. 57–61.
88. Later on Piérola had interests in the Banco Nacional, financed by Dreyfus and competitor of the Banco del Perú y Londres which was co-owned by Manuel Pardo, Piérola's political enemy; Alberto Ulloa, *Don Nicolás de Piérola*, pp. 84–90; Carlos Camprubí, *Historia de bancos*, pp. 90–6.
89. *Stock Exchange Review*, June 1874, in CFB, vol. 1, p. 242.
90. Consejo de Ministros, 13 July 1871 session, 1871-D4674, BNL.
91. Carlos Palacios Moreyra, *Deuda anglo-peruana*, pp. 128–32.
92. 'Peruvian Government 5 per cent consolidated loan 1872', prospect signed by J. Henry Schröder & Company, in CFB, vol. 1.
93. 'Memorandum de la operación financiera de 1872 de £36,000,000', 1872-D4655, BNL.
94. *The Pacific Mail*, 1 Dec. 1873, in CFB, vol. 1, p. 54.
95. Juan Maiguashca, 'A Reinterpretation of the Guano Age'; Carlos Marichal, *A Century of Debt Crises*, pp. 108–11.
96. Carlos Camprubí, *Historia de bancos*, p. 125.

97. Federico Blume, *Observaciones*, p. 3.
98. Carlos Camprubí, *Historia de bancos*, pp. 119, 129, 217.
99. *The Financier*, 22 Sept. 1874, in CFB, vol. 1.
100. *Star & Herald*, 21 Aug. 1875, in CFB, vol. 2, p. 342.
101. Profit earnings of Huth Grunning partnership, 1868–73, Frederick Huth & Company, ms. 10 702/4, GLL.
102. Graham Rowe to F. Huth & Company (London), Lima 27 March 1876, Frederick Huth & Company, ms. 10 703/1, GLL.
103. *The Bullionist*, 15 April 1876, in CFB, vol. 4.
104. *South Pacific Times*, 10 Sept. 1875, in CFB, vol. 5.
105. Federico Blume, *Observaciones*, p. 8; *South Pacific Times*, 28 Oct. 1876, in CFB, vol. 5, p. 204.
106. Carlos Camprubí, *Historia de bancos*, pp. 321–9.
107. Article in the *South Pacific Mail* reprinted in the *Brazil & River Plate Mail*, 6 July 1878, in CFB, vol. 7, p. 304.
108. Bancos del Perú, Nacional del Perú y La Providencia, 'Bases que proponen para el establecimiento de una sociedad que administre el Estanco del Salitre y del contrato que debe regir con el Supremo Gobierno', Lima, July 1873, 1873-D3504, BNL.
109. Gibbs & Sons to President of Associated Banks Delegates, Lima 2 Dec. 1876, in Antony Gibbs & Sons Papers, ms. 11 121, GLL.
110. 'Que no hay remedio? . . .' [1874] in Luis Cisneros, *Obras completas*, vol. 3, pp. 361–78; *Star & Herald*, 21 Aug. 1876, in CFB, vol. 5.
111. Jorge Basadre, *Sultanismo, corrupción y dependencia*, pp. 85–8.
112. Daniel Ruzo, *Important statement with reference to the Peruvian loans of 1870 and 1872 by a Peruvian bondholder* (London: Green & Son, 1876) in CFB, vol. 3.
113. *South Pacific Times*, 6 June 1876, in CFB, vol. 5; and 29 March 1877, in CFB, vol. 6; *Star & Herald*, 5 Sept. and 21 Sept. 1876, in CFB, vol. 6. Meiggs died in 1877.
114. *Brazil & River Plate Mail*, 6 July 1878, in CFB, vol. 7, p. 304; and 23 Jan. 1877, in CFB, vol. 5, p. 345.
115. *The Bullionist*, 13 Dec. 1879, in CFB, vol. 9, p. 48.
116. Lucas León, *Exposición*.

3 The Domestic Financial Structure, 1884–1950

1. Ernesto Yepes del Castillo, *Perú 1820–1920*, pp. 158, 194–6; Julio Cotler, *Clase, Estado y Nación*, p. 39; José Luis Rénique, 'La burguesía peruana'.
2. Carlos Malpica, *Los dueños del Perú*, pp. 20–21, hardly an academic book but extremely popular, as well as a populariser of dependency authors such as Jorge Bravo Bresani.
3. Mario B. Ordóñez, *La técnica y la práctica*, pp. 11–12; José Vargas Patrón, 'La estructura'.
4. José Payán, 'Breve reseña histórica del Banco del Callao' in 'Correspondencia de J. Payán', Superintendencia de Banca, Banco del Perú y Londres en Liquidación, Lima (hereafter BPLS); Luis N. Bryce,

Memoria de hacienda in *Memoria*, Ministerio de Hacienda, 1886; Joaquín Capelo, *Sociología de Lima*, vol. 3, p. 129; Carlos Camprubí, *José Payán*.

5. Banco del Callao, 'Accionistas', 24 Jan. 1888, pp. 143–4, BPLS.
6. The Banco del Callao consistently denied credit to estate owners because 'The bank did not undertake operations to finance rural properties', Banco del Callao, 'Directorio', 2 Nov. 1887, p. 130, BPLS.
7. Joaquin Capelo, *Sociología de Lima*, vol. 2, p. 74.
8. Héctor Harvey, 'El Banco Agrícola'; Bill Albert, 'External Forces'.
9. Michael Grace to A. Leslie, 17 April 1884, Box 58, no. 155, p. 292, W. R. Grace & Company Papers, Columbia University Library, New York (hereafter WRGP).
10. Peter Klarén, *Modernization and Aprismo*, pp. 5–12; *Mútuo e hipoteca* entries, Escribano Carlos Sotomayor, nos 777–83, years 1881–9, AGN.
11. Michael Gonzales, *Plantation Agriculture*, pp. 27, 33–35; Gerardo Klinge, 'La agricultura en el Perú', pp. 73–5.
12. Antero Aspíllaga, Alejandro Garland and Augusto Leguía, *La crisis del azúcar*; José Ramírez Gastón, *Sociedades de crédito agrícola mutual*; ibid., *Medio Siglo*, pp. 4–5; 'El Banco Agrícola del Perú', *El Economista Peruano*, vol. 3, no. 36 (Feb. 1912) p. 420.
13. Ashbourne to Edie, 21 Dec. 1928, Gibbs, ms. 11 115, vol. 3, p. 727, GLL.
14. The houses of Frederick Huth, Antony Gibbs, Dreyfus, Lachambre, Canevaro, among others, had stopped doing significant business in Peru by 1884.
15. Gibbs and Huth partnership, 'Balance Sheet, Lima 10th April 1873', Gibbs, ms. 10 702/4, p. 19, GLL; Box 1, WRGP; Heinrich Witt, *Diario y observaciones*, pp. 58–74.
16. Grace to Eyre, 18 April 1884, 'Michael P. Grace, Private', WRGP; Alfonso Quiroz, 'Las actividades comerciales y financieras'.
17. F. Clement Simon, 'Renseignements generaux,' Lima 1 Oct. 1909, F¹²7270, p. 97, Archives Nationales de la France, Paris (hereafter ANF); Carlos Camprubí, *José Payán*, p. 63.
18. Stanley Chapman, *The Rise of Merchant Banking*; Bill Warren, *Imperialism*.
19. For references to corruption and pay-off methods during the years 1884–99: Box 81, 1890, 'E. E[yre].', p. 25; Box 67, no. 24, pp. 234–7; and Box 72, no. 13, pp. 391–2, WRGP. At higher levels bribery was more subtle: 'The advance of a thousand pounds to Monocle [Nicolás de Piérola] which we authorized, half of your account, we did in view of the many services which we have received heretofore at his hands, and we did not consider at all policy to refuse him this amount, he being the leader of a large political party, and may at any future time come to the front again', M. P. Grace to E. Eyre, 27 Aug. 1884, Box 58, no. 155, p. 292, WRGP.
20. Rory Miller, 'The Making of the Grace Contract'.
21. Eyre to Lima house, 11 April 1898, Box 72, no. 13, pp. 66–7, WRGP.
22. Banco Alemán Transatlántico, *Juicios criminales*.
23. Ashbourne to Edie, 21 Dec. 1928, op. cit.

24. Iris Freyre, 'Exportaciones e Industria', p. 12; Bill Albert, 'Peruvian Sugar', pp. 53a, 222a.
25. Leguía to British Minister, Lima, 16 Jan. 1895, FO61, no. 409, Public Record Office, Kew Gardens, London (hereafter PRO).
26. Hilbck, Kuntz & Company financial role in Cajamarca, O.L. 649.114, leg. 1223, year 1899, AGN; Rodrigo Montoya, *Capitalismo y no capitalismo*.
27. US Department of Commerce, *Peruvian Markets*, p. 27.
28. Eyre to London house, 28 Feb. 1905, Box 74, no. 20, and Box 72, no. 11, p. 243, WRGP.
29. *El Comercio* (21 Feb. 1885).
30. José Payán's letterbook, 'Correspondencia de J. Payán', p. 19, BPLS.
31. Banco del Callao, 'Directorio', vol. 2, 11 June 1891, BPLS; ibid., p. 151; Banco del Callao, 'Accionistas', vol. 4, 4 Aug. 1893, p. 93, BPLS.
32. Payán to J. H. Reid, 15 Sept. 1902, quoted in Carlos Camprubí, *José Payán*, p. 39.
33. Bancos Hipotecarios, *Observaciones*, pp. 17–24; Banco de Crédito Hipotecario, *Memoria*, pp. 8–9; Manuel Olaechea, *Causa seguida*.
34. César A. Ugarte, *Bosquejo*, p. 93.
35. *La Gaceta Comercial*, vol. 3, no. 87 (30 June 1902) p. 549; ibid., vol. 5, no. 103 (30 Nov. 1904) pp. 788–9; Pont to Freyeinet, 22 March 1882, B31.345, Archives du Ministère de l'Economie et des Finances, Paris (hereafter AMEF).
36. F. Abril to Director General de Gobierno, Trujillo 3 Jan. 1888, and 'Comunicado del Ministerio de Relaciones Exteriores a Ministro de Gobierno', 16 Jan. 1888, Manuscritos, 1888-D5505, BNL.
37. Alejandro Garland, *Sistema monetario del Perú*.
38. *Memoria*, Ministro de Hacienda, (1890).
39. *El Financista*, vol. 4, no. 219 (30 April 1918) p. 674.
40. M. P. Grace to J. T. North, 27 Nov. 1882, Box 58, no. 153, p. 101, WRGP; Harold Blakemore, *British Nitrates and Chilean Politics*, p. 53; Alfonso Quiroz, 'Actividades comerciales', p. 236.
41. *El Comercio* (8 Jan. 1887); Beneficencia Pública de Lima, *Donación Sevilla*; Jorge Basadre, *Historia*, 6th ed., vol. 9, pp. 179–80.
42. *Revista de Cambios y Valores*, no. 19 (30 Nov. 1891).
43. Banco del Callao, 'Accionistas', vol. 1, 24 Jan. 1888, pp. 142–3; 'Directorio', 23 Aug. 1887, p. 124, BPLS; Banco del Callao, '24a. Memoria semestral', 31 Dec. 1888.
44. James Dorion, *Banco privilegiado del Perú*, pp. 11–12.
45. Dorion, agent of a French syndicate, was in search of an official bank monopoly against the liberal banking of the time, L. N. Bryce et al., *Exposición*.
46. Banco del Callao, '22a. Memoria Semestral' in Callao, 'Accionistas', 24 Jan. 1888, vol. 4, pp. 142–3, BPLS.
47. 'Memoria del balance a 31 de diciembre de 1887', in Banco Callao, 'Directorio', 24 Jan. 1888, vol. 1, pp. 142–3; and 'Memoria del balance a 31 diciembre de 1888', in idem. 'Accionistas', 28 Feb. 1889, vol. 1, p. 12, BPLS.

48. José Payán, 'Memorandum referente al comercio de Lima' (1911?) in Carlos Camprubí, *José Payán*, pp. 62–4; José Payán, 'Correspondencia de J. Payán', BPLS; Banco Callao, '26a. Memoria semestral', 31 Dec. 1894.

49. *Revista de Cambios y Valores* (of Joaquin Godoy), 1890–7; *El Comercio*, 1890–1900; *Tipos de Cambio y Valores* (of Paul Ascher), 1887–90; *Letras y Valores* (of A. S. Finnie), 1895–6; Cámara Sindical de la Bolsa Comercial, 'Memoria anual' in *Boletín de la Bolsa Comercial de Lima*, 1900–30.

50. Box 76, no. 76, p. 172, WRGP.

51. M. P. Grace to J. W. Grace, 22 Nov. 1898, Box 69, no. 32, p. 28, WRGP.

52. *El Comercio* (12 Oct. 1899); *El Economista*, vol. 2, no. 88, (22 May 1897).

53. Banco del Perú y Londres, 'Directorio', vol. 1, nos 66, 76, 97, 118, 119, 123, Sept. 1898–Oct. 1899, BPLS.

54. *El Comercio* (7 Feb. 1888), (6 July 1888), and (12 July 1888).

55. José Ramírez Gastón, *Crédito agrícola mutual*, p. 12; *El Financista*, vol. 4, no. 177; 'El banco agrícola del Perú', *Economista Peruano*, vol. 3, no. 36 (29 Feb. 1912); Joaquín Capelo, *Sociología de Lima*, vol. 3, p. 130.

56. Banco del Callao, 'Accionistas', 20 June 1892, p. 55, BPLS.

57. *El Comercio* (9 Feb. 1895), (3 March 1895), (3 Jan. 1889), and (30 Dec. 1888).

58. *Revista de Cambios y Valores*, no. 15 (31 July 1895).

59. Beneficencia Pública de Lima, *Donación Sevilla*, p. 100.

60. Banco del Callao, 'Directorio', 8 Feb. 1895, vol. 1, p. 115, BPLS.

61. José Payán, 'Les hipothèques au Pérou. Leur Development', Paris, 8 July 1911, Crédit Foncier Peruvien, BPLS.

62. First Law of Insurance Companies, *El Economista*, vol. 1, no. 16 (28 Dec. 1895); *Memoria*, Dirección del Crédito Público Inspección Fiscal de Compañías de Seguros (1902) pp. 116–19. Native insurance companies continued, however, to reinsure with companies abroad.

63. *El Comercio* (13 Oct. 1899).

64. 'El apoderado fiscal y las cías. de seguros', *El Comercio* (23 Aug. 1888), in representation of 17 British, one US, one Swiss, and one German insurance companies.

65. 4th and 5th articles of Insurance Companies' Law signed by Nicolás de Piérola, *El Economista*, vol. 1, no. 16 (28 Dec. 1895).

66. 'Las compañías peruanas de seguros', *La Gaceta Comercial*, vol. 7, no. 132 (1 Feb. 1907) p. 2046.

67. *El Comercio* (16 April 1898).

68. Banco del Perú y Londres, 'Directorio', no. 128, 6 Nov. 1899, pp. 272, 284; vol. 2, no. 170, 27 Aug. 1900, p. 59; vol. 3, no. 291, 22 Dec. 1902, p. 29; no. 310, 4 May 1903, p. 67; no. 370, 27 June 1904; and no. 446, 11 Dec. 1905, p. 339, BPLS.

69. *Revista de Cambios y Valores*, no. 83 (31 March 1897). See also *El Economista*, vol. 2, no. 68 (2 Jan. 1897).

70. Ignacio Meller, *Patrón oro o bimetalismo*.

71. Banco Callao, 'Accionistas', 28 Feb. 1889, p. 12; and 30 June 1892, p. 54, BPLS; Ignacio Meller, *Patrón oro o bimetalismo*, p. 25.
72. *Revista de Cambios y Valores*, no. 1 (30 June 1890); ibid. nos 39–50 (July 1893–April 1894).
73. Banco del Callao, 'Accionistas', 30 June 1892, vol. 4, pp. 49–51; ibid., 3 Jan. 1893, pp. 77–9, BPLS.
74. Antero Aspíllaga, Luis Dubois and Juan Gildemeister, *Informe en mayoría*; Pedro Correa y Santiago and José Payán, *Informe en minoría*; Banco del Callao, 'Directorio', 30 Sept. 1892, vol. 2, no. 610, p. 251, BPLS.
75. José Payán, *La cuestión monetaria*, pp. iv, 7–8; Carlo Camprubí, *José Payán*, pp. 32–8.
76. *Revista de Cambios y Valores*, no. 67 (Nov. 1895).
77. Jorge Basadre, *Historia*, 5th ed., vol. 6, pp. 3003–23.
78. *Revista de Cambios y Valores*, vols. 69–79 (Jan.–Nov. 1896).
79. *Revista de Cambios y Valores*, nos. 85–92 (May–Dec. 1897); 'Cuestión monetaria: carta protesta de comerciantes e industriales', *El Comercio* (2 Oct. 1897).
80. Article by Nicanor Tejerina, *El Comercio* (19 Aug. 1897); speech by Olivio Chiarella at the general meeting of the Sociedad Nacional de Agricultura, ibid. (6 Sept. 1897); M. G. del R[iego], 'Revista económica del mes de abril', ibid. (3 May 1898).
81. 'Revista económica del mes de junio', *El Comercio* (1 July 1898); Joaquín Godoy, '102a. Revista', ibid. (5 Oct. 1898); 'Crisis monetaria en Cajamarca', ibid. (6 Feb. 1900).
82. *La Gaceta Comercial*, vol. 2, no. 53 (10 Oct. 1901) p. 85; ibid. vol. 1, no. 33 (13 March 1901); Stinson to Munro, 'Brief History of Peruvian Currency and Banking', 24 Oct. 1929, Department of State, Division of Latin American Affairs, 823.515/123, microcopy 746, roll no. 22, p. 9, US National Archives, Washington, DC (hereafter USNA).
83. *Extracto Estadístico del Perú* (1929–33).
84. See appendix D.
85. Alejandro Garland, *Sistema monetario*, pp. 29–30.
86. Manuel Yrigoyen, *Bosquejo*, p. 14; Jorge Basadre, *Historia*, 5th ed., vol. 7, p. 3422.
87. *La Gaceta Comercial*, vol. 7, no. 139 (15 May 1907).
88. Ministre to Pichon, Lima 19 Aug. 1908, B31.345, AMEF.
89. *La Gaceta Comercial*, vol. 7, no. 130 (1 Jan. 1907).
90. 'La política bancaria moderna y nuestros bancos nacionales', *El Financista*, vol. 4, no. 219 (30 Nov. 1918), defends banks' role in 'financing' industry.
91. *El Comercio* (23 Jan. 1907).
92. *Economista Peruano*, vol. 1, no. 3 (May 1909); ibid., vol. 3, no. 36 (29 Feb. 1912); 'Pérou, rapport commercial, année 1911', F¹²7270, ANF; *El Comercio* (1 Jan. 1910).
93. *Revista de Cambios y Valores* (30 Nov. 1891).
94. Klobukowski to Delcasse, 12 Oct. 1904, B31.345, no. 1, AMEF.
95. These distinctions are also discussed in Geoffrey Bertram, 'Development Problems', and Bill Albert, 'Peruvian Sugar'.

96. Banco Italiano, *Estatutos*.
97. A comparison between the Banco del Perú y Londres and the Banco Nacional de México, respectively the leading institutions in their countries in the 1884–1910 period, reveals they have common characteristics: a high concentration of banking activities, foreign participation, and state connections. The Mexican bank had more regional linkages and enjoyed issue privileges which the Peruvian institution lacked, Leonor Ludlow and Carlos Marichal (eds), *Banca y poder en México*, p. 258.
98. Banco del Perú y Londres, 'Accionistas', 26 Dec. 1906 and 18 March 1907, vol. 2, pp. 58–62, BPLS.
99. *El Financista*, vol. 3, no. 143 (30 April 1915).
100. *El Financista*, vol. 3, no. 157 (16 Oct. 1915) p. 255.
101. Banco Popular del Perú, *Estatutos*, 2nd article.
102. Felipe Portocarrero Suárez, 'El Imperio Prado', pp. 147–52.
103. Peru, Ministerio de Hacienda, Dirección General del Crédito Público, *Memoria*, p. 133.
104. Bolsa Comercial de Lima, 'Memoria', 1900, anexo 1; ibid., 1905.
105. Peru, Ministerio de Hacienda, Dirección Crédito Público, *Memoria*, pp. 116–19, 128–9.
106. *Peru To-Day*, vol. 3, no. 4, (June 1911) p. 23; *Extracto Estadístico del Perú* (1931–3), p. 65; *Economista Peruano*, vol. 6, no. 3 (Jan. 1915).
107. *El Financista*, vol. 2, no. 104 (30 Jan. 1914) p. 26; Klobukowski to Delcasse, Lima 12 Oct. 1904, B31.345, AMEF.
108. Bolsa Comercial de Lima, 'Memoria', in *Boletín de la Bolsa Comercial*, 1900–30.
109. *La Gaceta Comercial*, vol. 7, no. 138, suplemento (1 May 1907) p. 2126; ibid., no. 139; *El Financista*, vol. 3, no. 156 (23 Sept. 1915).
110. *El Financista*, vol. 2, no. 102 (9 Jan. 1914); ibid., vol. 3, no. 149 (23 June 1915) p. 177.
111. *El Financista*, vol. 1, no. 82 (19 July 1913).
112. Joaquín Capelo, *Sociología de Lima*, vol. 3, p. 143, and vol. 1, pp. 49–94; Empresa del Gas, *La Empresa del Gas de Lima*.
113. 'Nuevas urbanizaciones', *Boletín Municipal*, vol. 18, no. 897 (2 Feb. 1918) p. 6985; Bolsa Comercial, 'Memoria'.
114. B. M. Anderson, *Effects of the War*, pp. 5–8.
115. Banco del Perú y Londres, 'Directorio', vol. 7, no. 991, 31 July 1914, pp. 250–2; 'Comité', vol. 1, no. 2, 5 Sept. 1914, p. 3, BPLS.
116. Banco del Perú y Londres, 'Directorio', vol. 7, no. 997, 12 Aug. 1914, pp. 267–72, BPLS.
117. Banco del Perú y Londres, 'Comité', vol. 1, no. 46, 28 Oct. 1914, p. 63, BPLS; Jorge Basadre and Rómulo Ferrero, *Historia*, pp. 90–1.
118. Banco del Perú y Londres, 'Directorio', vol. 8, no. 1028, 13 Feb. 1915, p. 100, BPLS.
119. Banco del Perú y Londres, 'Comité', vol. 1, no. 67, 21 Nov. 1914, p. 91, BPLS.
120. Banco del Perú y Londres, 'Directorio', vol. 8, no. 1015, 19 Nov. 1914, p. 55, BPLS; L. S. Rowe, *Early Effects of the War*, pp. 26–7.
121. French and British shareholders of the Banco del Perú y Londres

declined from 73 per cent of total shares in 1913 to 34 per cent in 1921, 'Accionistas', 1913–21, BPLS. The agro-industrial complexes of Santa Bárbara, Puente Piedra, Paramonga and San Nicolás were either taken over or substantially capitalised by natives during 1917–21; Informaciones Mercantiles e Industriales, *El Perú en su centenario*; Bill Albert, 'Peruvian Sugar', p. 140a.

122. Jorge Basadre, *Historia*, 6th ed., vol. 9, p. 300.
123. Heraclio Bonilla and Alejandro Rabanal, 'La Hacienda San Nicolás', pp. 3–47.
124. Banco del Perú y Londres, 'Directorio', vol. 11, no. 1255, 26 June 1919, pp. 20–1; 'Comité', vol. 5, no. 1017, 25 June 1919, p. 60, BPLS.
125. Banco del Perú y Londres, 'Comité', vol. 3, no. 764, March 1918, p. 314, BPLS.
126. Banco del Perú y Londres, 'Directorio', vol. 11, no. 1257, July 1919, p. 34, BPLS.
127. Ibid., no. 1293, March 1920, p. 185, BPLS.
128. Banco del Perú y Londres, 'Accionistas', vol. 3, pp. 25–7, 42–5, BPLS.
129. Rosemary Thorp and Geoffrey Bertram, *Peru*, Ch. 5; Elizabeth Dore, *The Peruvian Mining Industry*, Ch. 4.
130. *Informe*, Inspección Fiscal de Bancos (1922 and 1925); *El Financista*, vol. 9, no. 274 (Dec. 1921); Ribot to Pichon, 8 July 1919, B32.896, AMEF.
131. Gianfranco Bardella, *Un siglo en la vida económica*, pp. 213–14.
132. William Bollinger, 'The Rise of the U.S. Influence'; Bill Albert, 'Peruvian Sugar', p. 140a.
133. Dejean la Batie to G. Leygues, 23 Nov. 1920, B32.896, pp. 2–4, AMEF.
134. Banco del Perú y Londres, 'Directorio', vol. 13, no. 1390, Feb. 1922, p. 274, BPLS.
135. Batie to Leygues, 23 Nov. 1920, AMEF; *El Financista*, vol. 7, no. 269 (May 1921) p. 1531; *Informe*, Inspección Fiscal de Bancos (1921), pp. 4–5.
136. *Memoria*, Banco de Reserva del Perú (1923) p. 2; Adolfo Berger, 'Los depósitos bancarios'.
137. *Memoria*, Banco de Reserva del Perú (1925), pp. 3–4.
138. *Memoria*, Banco de Reserva del Perú (1926).
139. *Memoria*, Banco de Reserva del Perú (1928); Banco del Perú y Londres, 'Comité', vol. 11, no. 1825, 21 Nov. 1929, p. 70, BPLS.
140. *Informe*, Inspección Fiscal de Bancos, 1921–9.
141. Iris Freyre, 'Exportaciones e industria', p. 4.
142. Administrators of A. B. Leguía deceased, 'Account of Receipts and Payments', 28 Feb. 1935, Frederick Huth & Company Papers, ms. 10 706/2, GLL.
143. Boal to Secretary of State, 28 Oct. 1927, Department of State 823.52/ 10, microcopy 746, roll no. 23., USNA.
144. Rosemary Thorp and Carlos Londoño, 'The Effects of the Great Depression'.
145. US Department of Commerce, Bureau of Foreign and Domestic Commerce, 'Manufacturing in Peru', p. 1.

146. 'Annual General Meeting of Shareholders of Banco Italiano', *The West Coast Leader* (hereafter *WCL*) vol. 20, no. 1046 (1 May 1932) p. 4; '45th Annual Report of the Banco Italiano', *WCL*, vol. 21, no. 1098 (7 March 1933) p. 21.

147. On Italian political and financial connections in Peru see Orazio Cicarelli, 'Fascist Propaganda' and 'Fascism in Peru'; Gianfranco Bardella, *Un siglo en la vida económica*, pp. 266, 314–17.

148. Banco Italiano, *Lima, 1889–1939*, p. 11.

149. *Memoria y Estadística Bancaria*, Superintendencia de Banca (1934–40); *Situación de las Empresas Bancarias del Perú*, Superintendencia de Banca, (1931–45); Maisch Gonzalo Portocarrero, *De Bustamante*, p. 21.

150. Gianfranco Bardella, *Un siglo en la vida económica*, p. 351.

151. Ibid., pp. 371–3; Felipe Portocarrero Suárez, 'Imperio Prado', pp. 152, 164.

4 Elite Groups and Private Financial Management

1. Nathaniel Leff, 'Capital Markets in Less Developed Countries'; Robert Maushammer, 'Investor Groups', pp. 14–16.

2. Francois Bourricaud, 'Notas sobre la oligarquía peruana' in Bourricaud et al., *La oligarquía en el Perú*, p. 30; Manuel Burga and Alberto Flores Galindo, *República Aristocrática*, pp. 95–6.

3. Ernesto Yepes del Castillo, *Perú 1820–1920*, pp. 158–9; Jorge Bravo Bresani, 'Mito y realidad de la oligarquía peruana' in Bourricaud et al., *La oligarquía*, p. 86; Julio Cotler, *Clase, Estado y Nación*, pp. 132, 146; Daniel Carbonetto, 'El modelo de acumulación descentrado y dependiente', p. 71.

4. Dennis Gilbert, *La oligarquía peruana*, pp. 49–52; Geoffrey Bertram, 'Development Problems', pp. 258–9, 279; Rosemary Thorp, 'Endeudamiento o inversión directa', p. 33.

5. A 1925 article by J. M. Rodríguez in *Economista Peruano*; Manuel Capuñay, *Leguía*, p. 92.

6. César Ugarte, *Bosquejo historia económica*, p. 78.

7. W. E. Dunn, *Peru*, pp. 21–2.

8. Francois Bourricaud, *Power and Society in Peru*; Bourricaud et al., *La oligarquía en el Perú*; Carlos Malpica, *Dueños del Perú*; Mariano Valderrama and Patricia Ludman, *La oligarquía terrateniente*, pp. 3–14.

9. See the works of Low, Maushammer, Miller, Albert, Gilbert, Thorp and Bertram cited below.

10. Nathaniel Leff, *Underdevelopment and Development*, Ch. 3; Winston Fritsch, *External Constraints in Brazil*.

11. Abraham Rodríguez Dulanto, 'La agricultura nacional', *Revista Universitaria*, vol. 2, no. 9 (1907) p. 5; Alberto Salomón, 'El desarrollo económico del Perú'. Both were influential University of San Marcos professors in the faculty of Political and Economic Sciences and later finance ministers in different administrations.

12. *Economista Peruano*, vol. 2, no. 36 (1912).

13. José Payán, 'Les hypothèques au Pérou: leur developpement', type-

script: Paris, 8 July 1911, Crédit Foncier, BPLS.

14. Francisco García Calderón, *Le Pérou Contemporain*, pp. 272–89, 324–9.
15. Manuel Vicente Villarán, 'Condición legal de las comunidades indígenas', *Revista Universitaria*, vol. 2, no. 14 (1907) p. 3.
16. Carlos Lisson, *Breves apuntes sobre la sociología del Perú*, a publication financed by Manuel Candamo and Ignacio de Osma.
17. Hildebrando Fuentes, 'Política financiera del Perú', *Anales Universitarios*, vol. 26 (1899) p. 5; Manuel Capuñay, *Leguía*, p. 71.
18. *Economista Peruano*, vol. 4, no. 35 (1912).
19. Cited in René Hooper López, *Leguía*, p. 54.
20. Manuel V. Villarán, *Las profesiones liberales en el Perú* (Lima, 1900), cited in Salomón 'El desarrollo económico del Perú', p. 356. On tasks for economic autonomy: Francisco García Calderón, *Latin America*, pp. 383–5.
21. See Chapter 3; Bill Albert, 'Peruvian Sugar', p. 140a.
22. Robert Maushammer, 'Investor Groups', pp. 166, 199.
23. Diana Balmori, Stuart Voss and Miles Wortman, *Notable Family Networks*.
24. Nathaniel Leff, 'Industrial Organization'; Stanley Chapman, 'British-Based Investment Groups'.
25. Herbert Klein, 'The Creation of the Patiño Tin Empire'.
26. Alberto Flores Galindo et al., 'Oligarquía y capital comercial en el sur peruano'; Rory Miller, 'The Coastal Elite'.
27. Robert Maushammer, 'Investor Groups', p. 299. Family groups such as Ayulo, Pardo, Nicolini, Gildemeister, Cillóniz, Aspíllaga, Beltrán and others.
28. Jesús Chavarría, 'La desaparición del Perú colonial'. On modern changes dating from the 1850s see works by Gootenberg and Quiroz cited previously.
29. Carlos Camprubí, *Historia de Bancos*, p. 252; Robert Greenhill and Rory Miller, 'Peruvian Government and Nitrate Trade'.
30. Rory Miller, 'The Making of the Grace Contract'; Alfonso Quiroz, 'Actividades comerciales y financieras'.
31. Carlos Camprubí, *José Payán*, pp. 62–4; Rory Miller, 'The Grace Contract'.
32. David Chaplin, *The Peruvian Industrial Labor Force*, pp. 99–100.
33. Enrique Ramírez Gastón, *Muelle y Dársena del Callao*; Dora Mayer, *La conducta de la compañía minera Cerro de Pasco*; J. A. Hobson, *Imperialism*.
34. Alfred Chandler, *The Visible Hand*.
35. Correspondence between directors of W. R. Grace & Company and Peruvian businessmen (Payán, Prado, Derteano, Llaguno), WRGP.
36. Perú, Cámara de Senadores, *Diario de los debates del Congreso Ordinario de 1889*, 5 Sept. 1889 session, pp. 237–8.
37. Banco del Perú y Londres, 'Accionistas' (1900–14), BPLS.
38. José Pardo, *Perú*; Carlos Capuñay, *Leguía*, pp. 33–4; A. Ulloa Cisneros, *Leguía*.
39. 'Solicitudes para guía de remisión de barras de plata al tesorero del gremio de mineros (12 miners)', Hacienda, year 1890, O.L. 591–607,

AGN; Federico Moreno, *El Petróleo bajo el punto de vista industrial*; Alaine Low, 'Effects of Foreign Capital'.

40. 'Memoria del Presidente [Isaac Alzamora] de la Empresa Socabonera del Cerro de Pasco' (including stockholders list of 71 members), *La Gaceta Comercial*, vol. 6, no. 127 (1906) p. 1213.
41. Alaine Low, 'Effects of Foreign Capital', p. 4; Dirk Kruijt and Menno Vellinga, *Labor Relations and Multinational Corporations*, pp. 44–5.
42. 'Cuadro de las empresas organizadas dentro y fuera del Perú y establecidas en el país durante el decenio 1886–1896', *El Economista*, vol. 2, no. 69 (1897) pp. 263–4; Compañía Minera Sayapullo, *Memoria y balance anual*, 1908–11.
43. The following treatment of the Riva Agüero-Osma family is based on manuscript data from the uncatalogued section (Papeles Varios) of the Archivo Histórico Riva Agüero, Lima.
44. Mariano de Osma, *Causas de mi encarcelamiento*; *Cuestión célebre de la Hacienda Naranjal*.
45. Banco del Perú y Londres, 'Directorio', vol. 11, 17 July 1919, BPLS.
46. Confidential information on important Peruvians, FO371, 20644, PRO.
47. Forbes to Eden, 22 July 1936, FO371, 19801, PRO.
48. Appendix to article by Alfonso Quiroz, 'Financial Leadership'.
49. Dennis Gilbert, *Oligarquía peruana*, p. 121.
50. Banco del Perú y Londres, 'Directorio', vol. 1, 24 April 1899; vol. 2, 15 Oct. 1900 and 4 March 1901; vol. 14, 14 Feb. 1924, BPLS; on the background of the Carrillo de Albornoz family see Alfonso Quiroz, *Deuda defraudada*, pp. 149–59.
51. René Hooper López, *Leguía*, pp. 24–5.
52. Ibid., p. 25.
53. 'Claim of Messrs. Kearsley and Cunningham against Mr. A. B. Leguía', 8 Aug. 1928, FO371, 13508, PRO.
54. Ibid.
55. Tribunal de Sanción Nacional, legs. 517, 519, AGN. On proven bribe taking by Juan Leguía, from American representatives of the Seligman loans, see US Senate, Finance Committee Hearings, *Sale of Foreign Bonds*; Jorge Basadre, *Historia*, 5th ed., vol. 9, p. 4119.
56. Administrators of A. B. Leguía, deceased, 'Accounts of Receipts and Payments', 28 Feb. 1935, Frederick Huth & Company Papers, GLL.
57. Bancos del Callao/Perú y Londres, 'Directorio'; 'Accionistas' (1884–1930), BPLS.
58. Florencia Mallon, *The Defense of Community*, pp. 174–5.
59. Felipe Portocarrero Suárez, 'El Imperio Prado'; Florencia Mallon, *The Defense of Community*, p. 273.
60. Loan of £36 000 to the Molineros de Bellavista: Callao, 'Directorio', vol. 1, 10 Jan. 1888, BPLS; Gianfranco Bardella, *Setenta y cinco años*, p. 90; Banco Italiano, *Memoria* (1926–31).
61. James Gilbart, 'Condiciones para ser banquero', *La Gaceta Comercial*, vol. 4, no. 127 (1906) p. 1189.
62. Rodrigo Montoya, *Capitalismo y no-capitalismo*, pp. 95–7.
63. Geoffrey Bertram, 'Modernización y cambio', which shows the tension between modernising landowners, the foreign railway firm, local mer-

chants and traditional Indian alpaca herdsmen in Puno.

64. Banco del Perú y Londres, 'Accionistas', 31 Jan. 1929.
65. Beneficencia Italiana, Club Italiano, Circolo Sportivo Italiano.
66. Janet Worral, 'Italian Immigration to Peru', p. 216; Emilio Sequi and Enrico Calcagnoli, *La Vita Italiana*; Comitato de Lima per la Esposizione de Milano, *L'Italia al Peru*; Banco Italiano, Lima: *1889–1930*.
67. Carl Herbold, 'Developments in the Peruvian Administrative System', pp. 81–2, 88; Carlos Capuñay, 'El Perú financiero de 1919 a 1924'.
68. Geoffrey Bertram, 'Development Problems', pp. 6, 258–9, 279, 365.
69. US Department of State 823.154/10, microcopy 746, roll no. 10, USNA.
70. Superintendencia de Banca y Seguros, *Banco del Perú y Londres en liquidación: memoria anual* (Lima: Imprenta Gil, 1931) p. 17.
71. US Department of State 823.154/20, microcopy 746, roll no. 10, USNA.
72. US Department of State 823.5611, microcopy 746, roll no. 27, USNA.
73. On charges of corruption in Leguía's administration, see Geoffrey Bertram, 'Development Problems', pp. 51–2 and R. Thorp and C. Londoño, 'The Effects of the Great Depression'; Jorge Basadre, 'Leguía y el leguiísmo', p. 135.
74. Germán Reaño and Enrique Vásquez, *El Grupo Romero*, pp. 47, 56.
75. Felipe Portocarrero Suárez, 'El Imperio Prado'.
76. Robert Maushammer, 'Investor Groups'.
77. Felipe Portocarrero Suárez, 'Economic elites in Peru, 1900–68', Ph.D. diss. in progress, Oxford University, 1991.
78. Enrique Vásquez Huamán, 'Entrepreneurial dynamics and economic groups in Peru: case studies', Paper presented at the 47th International Congress of Americanists, New Orleans, 1991.
79. Frits Wils, *Industrialization*, p. 24.

5 Financial Aspects of Regional and Income Inequalities

1. Charles Kindleberger, *The Formation of Financial Centers*, pp. 2, 6, citing the works of Hoselitz, Gershenkron, and Cameron who centre on the role of banking as agent of industrialisation, and Goldsmith, Shaw and MacKinnon who focus on the efficiency of financial transfers.
2. Cynthia Taft Morris, 'The Measurement of Economic Development', pp. 145–81.
3. Frank Tipton, *Regional Variations*.
4. Efraín Gonzales de Olarte, *Economías regionales del Perú*, pp. 201–3; Rodrigo Montoya, *Capitalismo y no-capitalismo*, pp. 60–70.
5. Manuel Burga and Alberto Flores Galindo, *República Aristocrática*, p. 11; Alberto Flores Galindo, *Arequipa y el sur andino*, pp. 7, 143–4.
6. Florencia Mallon, *The Defense of Community in Peru*, pp. 137, 181; David Slater, *Territory and State Power*.
7. José C. Mariátegui, *Siete ensayos*, pp. 18–19.
8. Guido Pennano, 'Desarrollo regional y ferrocarriles'; Nils Jacobsen, 'Desarrollo económico y relaciones de clase'; Dirk Kruijt and Menno Vellinga, *Labor Relations*, pp. 25–6.
9. Efraín Gonzales de Olarte, *Economías regionales*, p. 83; Carol Smith, *Regional Analysis*.

10. Frank Tipton, *Regional Variations in Germany*, p. 5.
11. R. E. Caves, 'Vent for Surplus Models'. External market opportunities served as a base for further and complementary economic growth in advanced regions in 18th century England and 19th century Germany. This, by the way, was understood as follows by Peruvians of the time: '[El Perú es un] país cuya vida depende del movimiento comercial internacional porque el pequeño desenvolvimiento de la industria no permite atender a las demandas del propio mercado y porque otros países reclaman las materias primas que para su elaboración en ellas dan nuestra agricultura y nuestra minería', Informaciones Mercantiles e Industriales, *El Perú en su centenario*, p. 110.
12. Kindleberger makes a good case for the need for financial centres to maximise the efficiency of financial transfers and inter-regional payments in his *The Formation of Financial Centers*. Some authors prefer to define the process as one of 'internal colonialism' when the less developed regions lag continually behind the growth poles, José Tamayo Herrera, *Historia social e indigenismo*, p. 25.
13. Robert Brown, *Transport and Economic Integration*.
14. Compare with German regional development in 1861–90 and Colombian and Bolivian acute regional problems: Frank Tipton, *Regional Variations*, pp. 14–15, 150; James Park, *Rafael Núñez*, p. 23; Charles Bergquist, *Coffee and Conflict*, pp. 49–50; José Roca, *Fisonomía del regionalismo boliviano*, p. 12.
15. Peter Klarén, *Modernization and Aprismo*, p. 3; Lewis Taylor, 'Earning a Living in Hualgayoc, 1870–1900', in Rory Miller (ed.) *Region and Class*, p. 120; Clifford Smith, 'Patterns of Urban and Regional Development in Peru on the Eve of the Pacific War', ibid., pp. 77–101, particularly on the subject of Lima's primacy and the relative importance of its secondary and tertiary sectors; Florencia Mallon, *The Defense of Community*, p. 57.
16. Peter Klarén, *Modernization and Aprismo*, p. xvii; Florencia Mallon, *The Defense of Community*, p. 186; both emphasise the role of foreign capital, although Klarén considers it the 'motor force' while Mallon emphasises 'collaboration and competition' between foreign and native interests.
17. Alberto Flores Galindo, *Areguipa y el sur*, pp. 100–14; Manuel Burga and Reátegui Wilson, *Lanas y capital mercantil en el sur*, p. 181. Nelson Manrique contrasts the north and central highlands regions (oriented toward the internal market) with the southern region (organised for export), *Colonialismo y pobreza campesina*, p. 199.
18. Héctor Maletta, 'Perú, país campesino?', pp. 10–12; Héctor Maletta and Alejandro Bardales, *Peru*, vol. 2; Clifford Smith, op. cit.; David Werlich, *Peru*, p. 227.
19. Peter Klarén, *Modernization and Aprismo*, pp. 26, 30. Yellow fever was eradicated from the coast only in 1922, bubonic plague in the 1930s, and malaria not until 1946–55: Marcos Cueto, *Excelencia en la periferia*.
20. José Barbagelata and Juan Bromley, *Evolución urbana de Lima*, pp. 104–9; José Tamayo Herrera, *Historia del Cuzco*, p. 128.
21. 'Eastern Peru: Iquitos and North Eastern Peru' by V. H. S., *WCL*, vol.

12, no. 627 (19 Feb. 1924) pp. 1, 23: 'Keen commercial competition caused ridiculous credits to be given with nothing as security and huge losses had to be borne'. Immigration projects (Tomenotti concession) also failed. See also Guido Pennano, *La economía del caucho*, pp. 57–8.

22. The main steamer companies in 1920 were the Cía. Peruana de Vapores (financed by stock subscription among Lima investors), the Chilean Cía. Sudamericana de Vapores, both of which stopped at each port on a more or less regular basis, and the Pacific Steam Navigation Co. (English), Grace Line (North American), and Toyo Kisen Kaisha (Japanese) which served the major ports only. In the smaller ports 'the coastwise steamer is the only means of traffic and communication with the outer world, and the going and coming of the weekly or biweekly steamer is an important event. A motley crowd and curiously mixed cargo is discharged and received at each stop: live cattle, sheep, hogs and horses . . .', in 'Southern Peru' by reporter Nelson Rounsevell, *WCL*, vol. 12, no. 624 (29 Jan. 1924) p. 2.

23. Guido Pennano, 'Desarrollo regional', p. 143; Félix Alvarez-Brun, *Ancash*, p. 190; José Tamayo Herrera, *Historia del Cuzco*, pp. 95–9, and *Indigenismo en el Altiplano*, pp. 81–2.

24. Rory Miller, 'Railways and Economic Development', pp. 27–52.

25. José Tamayo Herrera, *Historia del Cuzco*, p. 130; Fiona Wilson, 'Indigenous and Immigrant Commercial Systems', p. 127.

26. *WCL*, vol. 11, no. 595, 4 July 1923.

27. Lima-Chosica motorway, *WCL*, vol. 11, no. 600 (14 Aug. 1923) p. 20; Ayacucho-Huancayo, *WCL*, vol. 12, no. 636 (22 April 1924) p. 1; Manuel Capuñay, *Leguía*, pp. 197–207.

28. W. E. Dunn (acting US Commercial Attaché in Lima), *Road Construction in Peru*, also printed in *WCL*, vol. 12, no. 638 (6 May 1924).

29. *WCL*, vol. 11, no. 597 (24 July 1923) p. 9.

30. Félix Alvarez-Brun, *Ancash*, p. 238; José Tamayo Herrera, *Historia del Cuzco*, p. 131; Fiona Wilson, 'Indigenous and Immigrant Commercial Systems', p. 141.

31. 'Years ago an attempt was made to acclimatize the camel to the deserts of northern Peru. The attempt failed, though the feasibility of such an enterprise had until recently many converts. The motor car and the motor truck have, we believe, given the final *coup de grace* to the mirage of the Peruvian camel', *WCL*, vol. 12, no. 620 (1 Jan. 1924) p. 1.

32. David Werlich, *Peru*, pp. 158, 213.

33. Bryan Roberts, 'The Social History of a Provincial Town' p. 153; Fiona Wilson, 'Indigenous and Immigrant Commercial Systems', p. 135.

34. *WCL*, vol. 11, no. 596 (17 July 1923) p. 1.

35. Banco del Perú y Londres, 'Directorio'; 'Informes de sucursales', BPLS.

36. Informaciones Mercantiles e Industriales, *Perú en su centenario*; William Parker (ed.), *Peruvians of To-Day*; Juan P. Paz Soldán, *Diccionario biográfico*.

37. 'The Port of Pisco and the Beverage', by Nelson Rounsevell, *WCL*, vol. 12, no. 621 (8 Jan. 1924) p. 3.

38. *WCL*, vol. 12, no. 622 (15 Jan. 1924) pp. 1, 11.

39. *WCL*, vol. 11, no. 582 (4 April 1923), and no. 601 (21 Aug. 1923); the total official cost of the Imperial project was Lp.436 000 (Labarthe and Thorp/Londoño cite 922 000 instead). By July 1923 the project had rendered 8000 hectares (20 000 acres) of fertile land; R. Thorp and C. Londoño, 'The Effects of the Great Depression', p. 86.

40. Informaciones Mercantiles e Industriales, *Perú en su centenario*, pp. 32–4: '. . . como la producción [de algodón] se encuentra en gran parte en manos de pequeños agricultores cuya capacidad económica es deficiente y que carecen de capitales para una explotación progresiva, las grandes firmas habilitadoras son una rueda matriz en el engranaje de la industria'.

41. Ibid., p. 23.

42. Pablo Macera (comp.), 'Palto', pp. 46–7, 58, 68. This is a collection of primary sources from the Achivo del Fuero Agrario, Lima.

43. Luis Ponce Vega, 'La crisis mundial de 1929 y la agricultura de la costa nor central', in Heraclio Bonilla (ed.), *Crisis económicas*, p. 226.

44. 'The Department of La Libertad', by Nelson Rounsevell, *WCL*, Trujillo Number (Nov. 1923) p. 5.

45. Pablo Carbone, 'El problema agrario'.

46. José Reaño García, *Historia del leguiísmo*, p. 209.

47. 'El negocio de habilitación está inteligentemente relacionado con el giro que explota de preferencia y así los préstamos que en esa forma realiza en favor de pequeños productores, lo son conscientemente para los que los invierten en sembríos de arroz y cereales', Informaciones Mercantiles e Industriales, *Perú en su centenario*, p. 12.

48. 'The Ford agency in Trujillo claims the largest sales of any agency outside Lima, which is another evidence of the influence of highway improvement on automobile sales', *WCL*, Trujillo Number (Nov. 1923) p. 1.

49. Ibid., p. 10.

50. *WCL* (Nov. 1923) p. 15; vol. 14, no. 703 (4 Aug. 1925) supplement 1. Leases were signed on average for a period of 20 years.

51. *WCL* (Nov. 1923) p. 17.

52. *WCL*, vol. 14, no. 731 (16 Feb. 1926) supplement, p. 1.

53. *WCL*, Trujillo Number (Nov. 1923) p. 9.

54. 'Million Dollar Transaction', *WCL*, vol. 12, no. 630 (11 March 1924) p. 1.

55. Forbes to Eden, 22 Feb. 1937, 'Leading personalities in Peru', FO371, 20644, FO371, A1361/1361/35, PRO.

56. Lewis Taylor, 'Cambios capitalistas'.

57. Jesús Silva Santisteban, *Cajamarca*, pp. 69–70.

58. Alaine Low, 'Effects of Foreign Capital', Ch. 4.

59. Michael Gonzales, 'Capitalist Agriculture'.

60. Alaine Low, 'Effects of Foreign Capital', p. 5a; Florencia Mallon, *The Defense of Community*, pp. 181–2.

61. Fiona Wilson, 'Indigenous and Immigrant Commercial Systems', p. 137.

62. Florencia Mallon, *The Defense of Community*, p. 175; Bolsa de Lima, *Boletín*.

63. Alaine Low, 'Effects of Foreign Capital'; Informaciones Mercantiles e

Industriales, *Perú en su centenario*, pp. 106–8; William Parker (ed.), *Peruvians*, pp. 327–8.

64. Informaciones Mercantiles e Industriales, *Perú en su centenario*, pp. 126–9.
65. Florencia Mallon, *The Defense of Community*, pp. 176, 182.
66. Bryan Roberts, 'The Social History of a Provincial Town' p. 146.
67. Informacions Mercantiles e Industriales, *Perú en su centenario*, pp. 82–3.
68. Florencia Mallon, *Defense of Community*, p. 273; Bryan Roberts, 'The Social History of a Provincial Town', p. 155.
69. Nelson Manrique, *Mercado interno y región*, pp. 265–8.
70. Bryan Roberts, 'The Social History of a Provincial Town', p. 147.
71. Nelson Rounsevell, 'Southern Peru', *WCL*, vol. 12, no. 624 (29 Jan. 1924) p. 1.
72. Alberto Flores Galindo, *Areguipa y el sur*, pp. 105–6; Baltazar Caravedo, 'Poder central y descentralización'.
73. 'Cuzco the Ancient Capital of the Incas' by Hiram Bingham, article in *WCL* based on his book *Inca Land* published in 1911.
74. José Tamayo Herrera, *Historia en el Altiplano*, pp. 84–6; Janine Brisseau Loaiza, *Le Cuzco dans sa region*, p. 162.
75. Manuel Burga and Wilson Reátegui, *Lanas y capital mercantil*, p. 118; Nelson Manrique, *Colonialismo y pobreza*, pp. 200, 210.
76. Manuel Burga and Wilson Reátegui, *Lanas y capital mercantil*, pp. 24, 181–182.
77. José Tamayo Herrera, *Historia en el Altiplano*, p. 91.
78. Banco del Perú y Londres, 'Accionistas', 31 Jan. 1929, BPLS.
79. Geoffrey Bertram, 'Modernización y cambio', pp. 3–22, which shows the tension between a minority of modernising landowners, the foreign railway firm, local merchants and traditional Indian alpaca herdsmen in Puno; Nelson Manrique, *Colonialismo y pobreza*, p. 197; Rodrigo Montoya, *Capitalismo y no capitalismo*, p. 50; for a discussion on the timing of hacienda growth after the War of the Pacific see Rory Miller, 'The Wool Trade'.
80. José Tamayo Herrera, *Historia en el Altiplano*, pp. 104–5.
81. Julian Laite, 'Miners and National Politics'.
82. Informaciones Mercantiles e Industriales, *Perú en su centenario*, pp. i–iii: '. . . la atención gubernativa no se interesa en el auge industrial sino en clavar sobre el productor los tentáculos succionadores del impuesto'.
83. José Reaño García, *Leguiísmo*, p. 37.
84. 'Leguía, the South American Roosevelt', interview by Isaac F. Marcosson, *WCL*, vol. 14, no. 702 (July 1925) pp. 4–5.
85. Ibid. p. 5.
86. José Reaño García, *Leguiísmo*, Prologue.
87. Janine Brisseau Loaiza, *Le Cuzco dans sa region*, p. 170.
88. Informaciones Mercantiles e Industriales, *Perú en su centenario*, p. 82.
89. Luis Valcárcel, *Memorias*, p. 37; José Tamayo Herrera, *Historia del Cuzco*, p. 108.
90. Rory Miller, 'Coastal Elite'.

91. José Reaño García, *Leguiísmo*, pp. 328–31.
92. José Tamayo Herrera, *Historia del Cuzco*, p. 102.
93. José Luis Rénique, 'De la fe en el progreso al mito andino', Baltazar Caravedo, 'Poder central y descentralización'. On a progressive alternative proposed by a distinguished decentralist in 1932 see Emilio Romero, *El descentralismo*.
94. José Tamayo Herrera, *Historia en el Altiplano*, p. 99; José Luis Rénique 'Los descentralistas arequipeños y la crisis política de 1930', in José Deustua and José Luis Renique, *Intelectuales, indigenismo y descentralismo*, pp. 97–115.
95. Baltazar Caravedo, *Descentralismo y democracia*; Emilio Romero, *Descentralismo*.
96. Darío Saint Marie, *Perú en cifras*, pp. 112–20, 258–9. The Amazonas Corporation exploited rubber during the Second World War. The Santa Corporation was an hydroelectric and iron industrial complex in the province of Ancash, 'Memoria de la Corporación Peruana del Santa', *Revista de Hacienda*, vol. 26 (1946) p. 451.
97. On the Mercantile Bank of the Americas branch activities and its 'German' methods used in Peru to aid importers and exporters see *Economista Peruano*, vol. 5, no. 140 (28 Feb. 1921) p. 6; *El Financista*, vol. 5, no. 183 (Oct. 1916); Pates de la Fosse to Briand, 26 Aug. 1916, B32.896; and Ribot to Pichon, 31 Oct. 1919, B32.896, AMEF.
98. *Informe*, Inspección Fiscal de Bancos, years 1926–9.
99. Geoffrey Bertram, 'Modernización y cambio'.
100. José Payán, 'Les hypothèques au Pérou. Leur Development', Paris, 8 July 1911, Crédit Foncier Peruvien, BPLS.
101. Banco de Crédito Hipotecario, *Memoria correspondiente al año 1883*; Bancos Hipotecarios, *Observaciones para el pago en metálico*; *El Comercio* (2–3 Jan. 1885).
102. *El Comercio* (6 July 1888).
103. *El Comercio* (5 Jan. 1885 and 2 Jan. 1888); Banco de Crédito, *Memoria*, appendix 2.
104. *El Comercio* (2 Jan. 1885); Bancos Hipotecarios, *Observaciones para el pago en metálico*, p. 24.
105. *El Comercio* (3 Jan. 1885).
106. *El Comercio* (7 Feb. 1888), 6 July 1888 and 12 July 1888.
107. *El Financista*, vol. 4, p. 177 (30 July 1916), p. 147.
108. *Memoria*, Dirección del Crédito Público, Inspección Fiscal de Bancos Hipotecarios, 1907, p. 5.
109. José Ramírez Gastón, *Sociedades de crédito agrícola*, p. 12; *El Financista*, vol. 4, p. 177; 'El banco agrícola del Perú', *Economista Peruano*, vol. 3 (29 Feb. 1912) p. 36; Joaquín Capelo, *Sociología*, vol. 3, p. 130.
110. Alfonso Quiroz, 'Financial Institutions', p. 444.
111. Rómulo Eyzaguirre, *Enfermedades evitables*, p. 13.
112. Banco del Callao, *Estatutos*, p. 4; Alejandro Garland, *Peru in 1906*, p. 262.
113. *Memoria*, Dirección del Crédito Público, Inspección Fiscal de Bancos Hipotecarios, 1906, pp. 4–5; *El Comercio* (13 Feb. 1900), (19 April 1903); *Economista Peruano*, vol. 4, no. 283 (16 Feb. 1901); *Gaceta*

Comercial, vol. 4, no. 127 (15 Nov. 1906); and no. 123 (Aug. 1906); Banco del Callao, *Estatutos*; 'Sanitary Progress in Peru', *Peru To-Day*, vol. 3, no. 9 (Nov. 1910) pp. 24–7, and no. 10 (Dec. 1910) pp. 25–9.

114. Alberto Alexander, *Estudio*, pp. 25–8.

115. Ricardo Tizón y Bueno, *El plano de Lima*, pp. 53–5.

116. Ibid., p. 51; *Boletín Municipal*, vol. 15, no. 757 (3 July 1915).

117. Alberto Alexander, *Estudio*, pp. 4, 28.

118. José Barbagelata and Juan Bromley, *Evolución urbana de Lima*, p. 108.

119. Alberto Alexander, *Los problemas urbanos de Lima*, p. 12; Jorge Basadre, *Historia de la República*, 5th ed., vol. 9, 4184; Alberto Alexander, *Estudio*, pp. 34–5; Peru, Ministerio de Fomento, Dirección de Salubridad, Inspección Técnica de Urbanizaciones y Construcciones, *Segundo informe sobre el registro sanitario*, p. 5.

120. 'Nuevas urbanizaciones', *Boletín Municipal*, vol. 18, no. 897 (2 Feb. 1918) p. 6985; Compañía Urbanizadora San Isidro, *1a. memoria*; Alberto Alexander, *Los problemas urbanos*.

121. *Boletín de la Bolsa Comercial*, 'Memoria', 1925, anexo no. 1; Banco Popular del Perú, *Sección hipotecaria*.

122. *Informe*, Inspección Fiscal de Bancos, years 1926, 1928 and 1929.

123. *Memoria*, Superintendencia de Banca, year 1941.

124. Walter E. Norris, 'Banco del Hogar y Ahorros'.

125. David Collier, *Squatters and Oligarchs*, Ch. 2.

126. Antonio Zapata, 'Chalet y material noble'.

127. 'El fin de una industria cuatro veces centenaria', *La Vida Agrícola*, vol. 15, no. 175 (June 1938) pp. 441–4.

128. *Memoria de la Caja de Ahorros* (1908, 1910, 1916, 1929); José Payán, 'Correspondencia de J. Payán', BPLS.

129. Carlos Camprubí, *Sociedad de Beneficencia Pública*, pp. 86–8; *Memoria de la Caja de Ahorros* (1901, 1910, 1916).

130. Carlos Camprubí, *Sociedad de Beneficencia Pública*, p. 89; Beneficencia Pública de Lima, Caja de Ahorros, *Datos concernientes al movimiento de la oficina principal*; *Memoria de la Caja de Ahorros* (1917), p. 20; *Extracto Estadístico del Perú* (1926–8).

131. Carlos Camprubí, *Sociedad de Beneficencia Pública*, pp. 94–5; *Peru To-Day*, vol. 2, no. 8 (Oct. 1910) p. 29; *Memoria de la Caja de Ahorros* (1910) p. 6.

132. Dora Mayer, 'Moralidad en los negocios', *La Gaceta Comercial*, vol. 6, no. 123 (Aug. 1906) p. 1155.

133. *El Comercio* (21 Feb. 1902); *La Gaceta Comercial*, vol. 1, no. 31 (Feb. 1901) vol. 6, no. 123 (Aug. 1906).

134. Carlos Camprubí, *Sociedad Beneficencia Pública*, p. 111.

135. 'El préstamo sobre prenda', *Economista Peruano*, vol. 3, no. 73 (June 1915).

136. José Payán, 'Correspondencia de J. Payán', p. 78, BPLS; Federico Eyzaguirre and César Panizo, *Memorandum*, p. 4. Capelo estimated in 1895 an average pawn interest of 5 per cent a month in his *Sociología*, vol. 2, p. 75.

137. Antenor Vascones, *Estudios morales*, p. 4. On popular distrust of usury pawnbrokers see also Joaquín Capelo, *Sociología*, vol. 2, p. 77.
138. Inspección de Casas de Préstamo, 'Relación de las casas de préstamo que actualmente existen en la capital', *Boletín Municipal* (1st semester 1901) p. 37.
139. Federico Eyzaguirre and César Panizo, *Memorandum*; 'Banco de Pobres', *El Comercio* (23 Jan. 1903); Rubén L. Olivares, *El negocio del dinero y la usura*.
140. Payán to Director de la Beneficencia, undated (probably 1895), José Payan, 'Correspondencia de J. Payán', pp. 72–8, BPLS, in which the author criticises a project by Sr. Habich proposing limits on pawnshop interest rates and the Caja's intervention in the pawn business; E. de la Riva Agüero, 'Infome sobre un proyecto de reglamentación para las casas de préstamo', *Boletín Municipal*, vol. 4, no. 83 (3 April 1886) p. 687, also warns on the 'very grave innovation' of controlling interest rates, as argued in a project by Sr. Félix A. Deglane.
141. Letter from Albino Crocco, president of Sociedad de Casas Prestamistas, *Boletín Municipal* (1st semester 1901) p. 69; 'Reclamo de los dueños de casas de préstamos', *El Comercio* (24 Feb. 1888), 'Casas de préstamo', *El Comercio* (1 Feb. 1901). Regulation rules of 1903 and 1904 did not limit interest rates. Ceilings on pawn interest were established by decree on 26 June 1918.
142. Walter E. Norris, 'Banco del Hogar y Ahorros', p. 4.

6 Financial Policies and the State

1. Alfred Stepan, *The State and Society*, ch. 1, pp. 39–40; James Malloy (ed.), *Authoritarianism and Corporatism*.
2. Steven Topik, *The Political Economy*; Paul Gootenberg, *Between Silver and Guano*; Nils Jacobsen, 'Free Trade, Regional Elites and Internal Market'.
3. Guillermo O'Donnell, *Modernization and Bureaucratic-Authoritarianism*; Fernando Uricoechea, *Patrimonial Foundations*.
4. Abraham Lowenthal (ed.), *The Peruvian Experiment*; E. V. K. Fitzgerald, 'State Capitalism in Peru: A Model of Economic Development and Its Limitations', in Abraham Lowenthal and Cynthia McClintock (eds), *The Peruvian Experiment Reconsidered*, pp. 65–93, xiii, xv.
5. Carlos Marichal, *A Century of Debt*; Bill Albert, *South America*; Winston Fritsch, *Economic Policy in Brazil*; Paul Gootenberg, *Between Silver and Guano*; Steven Topik, *The Political Economy*.
6. *El Financista*, vol. 1, no. 80 (28 June 1913).
7. Wenceslao Valera, *Deuda interna*; Rafael Quiroz, *Estudio sobre la deuda interna*, p. 16; Ricardo Tizón y Bueno, *La deuda interna*, p. 3.
8. Carlos Camprubí, *Sociedad de Beneficencia Pública*, p. 89.
9. The Caja de Depósitos assumed central tax collecting functions in 1921. Caja de Depósitos y Consignaciones, Departamento de Recaudación, *Informe, año 1927*; *Memoria*, 1924.
10. US Department of State 823.51, microcopy 746, roll no. 1, USNA.

11. *El Financista*, vol. 5, no. 195 (20 April 1917) p. 360.
12. B. M. Anderson, *Effects of the War on Money*, pp. iii, 7. On French mortgage and deposit practices, ibid., p. 27.
13. Alec Ford, *The Gold Standard*, pp. 16–17.
14. James Dorion, *Banco Privilegiado*; Banco del Callao, 'Directorio', year 1889, BPLS.
15. Ministre au Pérou to Ministre des Affaires Etrangères, 20 Feb. 1884, F¹²6578, ANF; 'La Cámara de Comercio de Lima', Archivo de Hacienda, year 1895, 621–1181, AGN; Ricardo Tizón y Bueno, *Sobre Tributación Minera*, p. 22.
16. Rory Miller, 'Coastal Elite', p. 109.
17. Fernando Tola, *Los impuestos en el Perú*.
18. Caja de Depósitos y Consignaciones, *Memoria*, pp. 6–11. Peru, Cámara de Diputados, Documentos Parlamentarios, *Dictamen*, p. 13.
19. Carlos Díaz Alejandro, *Essays*; Winston Fritsch, *Economic Policy in Brazil*; Jaime E. Zabludowski, 'Money, Foreign Indebtedness and Export Performance'.
20. J. M. Rodríguez, *El billete fiscal*, pp. 7–8; César Ugarte, *Bosquejo de historia económica del Perú*, pp. 92–3.
21. Alberto Ureta, *La moneda de plata y el billete fiscal*.
22. A. Aspíllaga, A. Garland and A. Leguía, *Crisis del azúcar*, p. 16.
23. Alfonso Quiroz, 'Actividades comerciales y financieras', p. 243.
24. Ignacio Meller, *Patrón de oro*, p. 25.
25. José Payán, *Cuestión monetaria*, pp. 7–8. On comments about the interest of the Banco del Callao in raising the exchange rate, Paul Faure to Ministre des Affaires Etrangères, 10 Feb. 1892, Lima 20, Archives du Ministère des Affaires Etrangères, Paris (hereafter MAE).
26. José Payán, op. cit.; Emilio Romero, 'La vida financiera en el Perú'.
27. Banco del Callao, 'Directorio', vol. 1, shareholders meeting, 27 July 1886, BPLS.
28. Banco del Callao, 'Accionistas', 30 June 1892, p. 49; 2 Sept. 1892, p. 68; 3 Jan. 1893, p. 77; 'Directorio', vol. 2, no. 610, 30 Sept. 1892, pp. 250–1, BPLS.
29. Ibid., no. 595, 3 June 1892, p. 221; no. 597, 17 June 1892, pp. 227–8; no. 598, 24 June 1892, pp. 229–30, BPLS.
30. P. Correa y Santiago and J. Payán, *Informe en minoría*; A. Aspíllaga, L. Dubois and J. Gildemeister (important agro-exporters), *Informe en mayoría*.
31. Banco del Callao, 'Accionistas', extraordinary session, 30 June 1892, pp. 60–3; 3 Jan. 1893, pp. 77–8, BPLS. Another defender of the gold position, Stromsdorfer, stated that 'en el seno de la Junta no cabía discusión entre la conveniencia de conservar el capital en oro o plata, porque este punto estaba de tal manera resuelto, que en Lima las casas de comercio hasta de tercer orden tenían constituído su capital en libras esterlinas, y que si esas casas hacían esto para prevenir toda fluctuación perjudicial, con cuanta mayor razón debía hacerlo el banco, por la importancia de sus recursos y su influencia moral', ibid., 30 June 1892, p. 62.

32. Banco del Callao, 'Directorio', vol. 2, no. 610, 30 Sept. 1892, p. 251, BPLS.
33. Rosemary Thorp and Geoffrey Bertram, *Peru*, p. 29.
34. José Payán, *Cuestión monetaria*, p. 8. Felipe Barreda y Osma (linked to the manufacturing and financial interests of the Pardo group) defended himself publicly by writing a protectionist appeal against liberal siege in his pamphlet *Los derechos de aduanas y las industrias nacionales*.
35. Fábrica de Fósforos El Sol, 'Actas de Accionistas y Directorio', 1898–1906, BPLS. Import tariff on matches was established in 1896, J. R. Gubbins, *Lo que se ve*, p. 6.
36. Alejandro Garland, *Las industrias en el Perú*; *El Fisco y las industrias nacionales*; *Reseña industrial del Perú*; J. R. Gubbins, *Lo que se ve*. On the discussion between Gubbins and Garland defending liberal positions and the 'protectionists' Barreda and Ricardo García Rosell see Julio Revilla, 'Industrialización temprana', p. 20.
37. Manuel Capuñay, *Leguía*, p. 46.
38. Alejandro Garland, *Artículos económicos*, p. 2.
39. Ignacio Meller, *Patrón de oro*, p. 44.
40. 'Cuestión monetaria en Puno', *El Comercio*, 20 Aug. 1897; Alejandro Garland, *Sistema monetario*, p. 29; Aníbal Maúrtua, *El Banco de la República Peruana*, p. 5.
41. Benjamín Roca, *Opiniones*.
42. José Manzanilla, *Finanzas y economía*, p. 27.
43. Jorge Basadre, *Historia*, 5th ed., vol. 8, p. 3785.
44. Geoffrey Bertram, 'Development Problems', p. 35; Stinson to Munro, 'Brief History', 24 Oct. 1929, microcopy 746, roll no. 22, p. 16, USNA.
45. Monopolies included those on guano, salt, alcohol, matches and tobacco, Albert Giesecke, 'Recent Financial Reforms in Peru', *WCL*, vol. 18, no. 936 (21 Jan. 1930) p. 7; *Revista Universitaria* (April 1928) pp. 582–675.
46. Augusto Leguía, *El Oncenio y la Lima actual*; René Hooper López, *Leguía*; biased criticisms of Leguía's policies in Pedro Ugarteche, *La política internacional peruana* and Jose Ramírez Gastón, *Medio siglo*, p. 39; Paul Drake, *Money Doctor*, pp. 216–17.
47. Augusto Leguía, *El oncenio y la Lima actual*.
48. Jorge Basadre, *Historia*, 5th ed., vol. 8, p. 3747.
49. Peru, Ministerio de Fomento, *La labor constructiva del Perú*.
50. Ibid.
51. A. Aspíllaga, A. Garland and A. Leguía, *La crisis del azúcar*.
52. Ribot to Pichon, 31 Oct. 1919, B32.896, AMEF.
53. Fernando Fuchs, *Memoria*, pp. 32–5; idem., *Prospecto*. On Leguía's ministers' 'progressive' and developmental economic policies see Carl Herbold, 'Developments in the Peruvian Administrative System', pp. 81–2.
54. Banco del Perú y Londres, 'Directorio', vol. 12, nos. 1350 and 1351, 27 April and 4 May 1921, pp. 147–50, BPLS.
55. President of National City Bank to Andrew W. Mellon, 1 June 1921, US Department of the Treasury, Box 162, File No. 1, USNA. Also US

Department of State, *Papers Relating to the Foreign Relations of the United States*, pp. 663–6.

56. Banco del Perú y Londres, 'Directorio', vol. 12, no. 1352, 12 May 1921, pp. 155–17, BPLS.
57. Ibid., no. 1354, 21 May 1921, p. 162; vol. 13, no. 1401, 12 April 1922, p. 30, BPLS.
58. Ibid., vol. 12, no. 1357, 9 June 1921, p. 170, BPLS.
59. Perú, Cámara de Diputados, *Dictamen*. An imprecise interpretation of Leguía's motives for removing the control of the tax collection company from the Banco del Perú y Londres in Howard L. Karno, 'Augusto B. Leguía', p. 156.
60. Banco del Perú y Londres, 'Directorio', vol. 12, no. 1354, 21 May 1921, p. 165, BPLS.
61. Comité Banque Pérou et Londres to Ministre des Affaires Etrangères, 21 May 1921, Perou 46, MAE.
62. Banco del Perú y Londres, 'Directorio', vol. 12, no. 1374, 13 Oct. 1921, p. 209, BPLS.
63. Interview with President Leguía by A. S. C. (representative of the Peruvian Corporation), 20 June 1925, Peruvian Corporation Archive, B3/6, University College, London.
64. Banco del Perú y Londres, 'Directorio', vol. 12, no. 1380, 24 Nov. 1921, p. 238, BPLS.
65. Ibid., no. 1387, 5 Jan. 1922, pp. 260–2, BPLS. Leaflet: 'Cruel burla o refinada maldad de los banqueros?'
66. Ibid., no. 1389, 24 Nov. 1921, p. 242, BPLS.
67. Ibid., no. 1384, 16 Dec. 1921, p. 253, BPLS; US Department of the Treasury, Box 162, File No. 1, USNA. See also French minister in Peru to Ministre des Affaires Etrangères, 4 Feb. 1922, B32.896, AMEF.
68. Telegram to Secretary of State, 24 Nov. 1922, US Department of State 823.516/34–36, microcopy 746, roll no. 22, USNA.
69. Banco de Reserva del Perú, *Legislación*, vol. I, p. 7.
70. Dejean de la Batie to Ministres des Affaires Etrangères, 6 April 1922, B32.896, AMEF; Poindexter to Secretary of State, 29 June 1925, US Department of State, 823.516/46, microcopy 746, roll no. 22, USNA.
71. Cumberland to Secretary of State, 30 Oct. 1923, US Department of State, 823.516/41, microcopy 746, roll no. 22, USNA.
72. Stinson to Munro, 'Brief History', microcopy 746, roll no. 22 p. 19, USNA.
73. *Informe*, Inspección Fiscal de Bancos, 1921, anexo no. 7, pp. 33–7.
74. For a laudatory comment on Leguía's early monetary measures (Ley 4500, June 1922) see Lizardo Alzamora, *El billete de banco*, p. 149.
75. Caja de Depósitos y Consignaciones, *Memoria*; *Memoria*, Banco de Reserva del Perú, 1922–30; Banco del Perú y Londres, 'Directorio', 1921–8, BPLS.
76. Oscar Arrús, *La estabilización de nuestra moneda*.
77. Manuel Yrigoyen, *Bosquejo*, p. 98.
78. US Department of State, 823.5032, microcopy 746, roll no. 1, USNA.
79. Testimony by Lawrence Dennis: US Senate, Finance Committee Hearings, *Sale of Foreign Bonds*, vol. I, p. 1587; José Ramírez Gastón,

Medio siglo, pp. 29–41.
80. Fiona Wilson, 'Indigenous and Immigrant Commercial Systems', p. 127.
81. Gerardo Klinge, 'Política de Irrigación', *La Vida Agrícola*, vol. 13, no. 137 (April 1935) p. 262.
82. 'Interview with President Leguía', by John Clayton, *WCL*, vol. 16, no. 842 (3 April 1927) p. 22; Barbara Stallings, *Banker to the Third World*.
83. *Memoria*, Banco de Reserva, 1922–30.
84. 'Peruvian Business Depression' (based on cable from US Commercial Attaché, L. W. James), *WCL*, vol. 15, no. 777 (4 Jan. 1927) p. 24; Rosemary Thorp and Carlos Londoño, 'The Effects of the Great Depression'.
85. 'Manifesto to the Nation', *WCL*, vol. 18, no. 967 (26 Aug. 1930) pp. 1, 16–17; 'Sentence of the Tribunal of National Sanction (Second Court) Against Ex-President Augusto B. Leguía and His Son', *WCL*, vol. 19, no. 987 (13 Jan. 1931) p. 6.
86. 'Tribute to President Leguía', *WCL*, vol. 17, no. 896 (16 April 1929) p. 1; *Banquete presidencial al Presidente de la República* (Lima: Imp. Torres Aguirre, 1929).
87. 'Political Conspiracies', *WCL*, vol. 18, no. 950 (29 April 1930) p. 1; 'New Directorate of the National Agrarian Society', ibid., vol. 27, no. 954 (May 1930); Rosemary Thorp and Geoffrey Bertram, *Peru*, p. 401, note 2. Years later Klinge explained that the conflict was unleashed by the 1924 Olmos irrigation project that had limited the water supply of large sugar planters in Lambayeque, among them Piedra, so as to irrigate lands newly colonised by small landholders, 'Política de irrigación', *La Vida Agrícola*, vol. 12, no. 137 (1935) pp. 245–69; 'Importante problema de colonización en Lambayeque', ibid., vol. 12, no. 140 (1935) pp. 521–4.
88. 'Project of Currency Stabilization', *WCL*, vol. 18, no. 939 (11 Feb. 1930) p. 11; 'Sun Life [Assurance Co.] May Suspend New Business', ibid., vol. 18, no. 946 (1 April 1930) p. 1. Nominally 1 US dollar = 3.57 *soles*. However the dollar was often quoted at over 4 *soles*.
89. Reginald Gubbins, 'Steps Toward Normalization of Peruvian Finances', *WCL*, vol. 18, no. 939 (4 Feb. 1930) p. xix.
90. 'Peru's Credit Position defined by Institute of International Finance – Peru Will Adopt Gold Standard When Free Convertibility of Notes Can Be Maintained', *WCL*, vol. 18, no. 954 (27 May 1930) p. 3.
91. *WCL*, vol. 18, no. 967 (26 Aug. 1930) p. 16.
92. 'Arrival of Kemmerer Mission', *WCL*, vol. 19, no. 987 (13 Jan. 1931) p. 1; 'Kemmerer Mission Completes Work', ibid., vol. 19, no. 1001 (21 April 1931) p. 1; Oscar Arrús, *La estabilización de nuestra moneda*; Paul Drake, *Money Doctor*, p. 34.
93. *WCL*, vol. 19, no. 1002 (28 April 1931) p. ii. The gold value of the Peruvian *sole* was lowered: instead of an equivalence to $0.40 it was nominally fixed at $0.28 (0.421254 fine gold grams). However, the *sole* was quoted freely below this limit until it stabilised at 6.50 *soles* = $1.
94. 'Extension of credit accompanied by a prudent increase in existing circulation would be an effective means of solving the present economic

crisis of Peru', statement in Arequipa by A. Martinelli, Minister of Finance under President David Samanez in *WCL*, vol. 20, no. 1045 (16 Feb. 1932) p. 7. Internal loans started in May 1931, when sugar planter Rafael Larco Herrera was minister of finance and Manuel Olaechea president of the Banco Central de Reserva: *WCL*, vol. 19, no. 1006 (26 May 1931) p. 1; 'Customs vales', ibid., vol. 19, no. 1053 (9 April 1932) p. 1.

95. Banco de Reserva del Perú, *Legislación*, vol. I, p. 7. Drake finds this a common trait in Kemmerer's advisory services to Andean governments, *The Money Doctor*, pp. 28, 42–3.

96. 'Law Creating Superintendence of Banks', *WCL*, vol. 19, no. 993 (24 Feb. 1931) p. 1; 'Liquidation of the Banco del Perú y Londres', ibid., p. 19. In May 1931 the Caja Nacional de Ahorros, created by Leguía in 1929, was also liquidated. See also Superintendencia de Banca, *Memoria* and *Banco del Perú y Londres en liquidación*.

97. Complaints about the lost opportunities for 'economic progress' after the liquidation of the Banco del Perú y Londres in Carlos Urquiaga, *Algunas notas*, p. 4.

98. 'Sociedad Nacional Agraria', *WCL*, vol. 18, no. 974 (14 Oct. 1930) p. 19; 'El problema azucarero', *La Vida Agrícola*, vol. 14, no. 158 (1937) pp. 35–8.

99. 'Proposed Moratorium on Mortgage Loans', *WCL*, vol. 20, no. 1051 (5 April 1932) p. 2; 'Obligations Contracted in Foreign Money. Lima Chamber of Commerce Voices its Protest Against Recent Legislation', *WCL*, vol. 20, no. 1071 (23 Aug. 1932) p. 4.

100. 'Peruvian National Loans: Service Suspended by Supreme Decree', *WCL*, vol. 19, no. 997 (24 March 1931) p. 1.

101. 'El cambio', *La Vida Agrícola*, vol. 13, no. 146 (Jan. 1936) pp. 21–4.

102. *WCL*, vol. 19, no. 1018 (18 Aug. 1931) p. 1; ibid., vol. 19, no. 1027 (20 Oct. 1931) p. 1. An important agro-exporter was the Vice President of the Banco Central, Pedro G. Beltrán; *Boletín mensual*, Banco Central de Reserva, vol. 1, no. 1 (Sept. 1931).

103. 'Farmer's Bank of Peru', *WCL*, vol. 21, no. 1092 (17 Jan. 1933) p. 25; 'El Banco Agrícola y la Superintendencia de Bancos', *La Vida Agrícola*, vol. 12, no. 139 (1935) pp. 439–41 and vol. 12, no. 144 (1935) pp. 915–18.

104. Small farmers received as much as 12.8 per cent in 1944. No credit was granted to them between 1931 and 1933; Darío Saint-Marie, *Perú en cifras*, pp. 104–11; 'Crédito agrícola: crédito para el pequeño agricultor', *La Vida Agrícola*, vol. 12, no. 138 (1935) pp. 343–6; 'Memoria del Banco Agrícola del Perú', ibid., vol. 14, no. 170 (1938) pp. 95–100.

105. Darío Saint Marie, *Perú en cifras*, p. 111; 'La labor del Banco de Fomento Agropecuario del Perú', *La Crónica*, 31 May 1959, pp. 10–11.

106. 'Policy of Central Reserve Bank of Peru', *WCL*, vol. 22, no. 1172 (31 July 1934) pp. 20–1, and 'Monetary Policy of the Central Bank', vol. 22, no. 1191 (11 Dec. 1934) p. 7; Gonzalo Portocarrero Maisch, *De Bustamante a Odría*, pp. 37–8.

107. Emilio Romero, 'La evolución económica del Perú', *WCL*, vol. 21, no. 1121 (8 Aug. 1933) p. 1.

108. Comedores Populares, Workers' Social Insurance and housing projects.
109. David Werlich, *Peru*, pp. 158, 213; Antonello Gerbi, *El Perú en marcha*.
110. *WCL*, vol. 22, no. 1144 (16 Jan. 1934) pp. xii; ibid., vol. 24, no. 1265 (12 May 1936) p. 7.
111. Manuel Beltroy, *Peruanos notables de hoy*.
112. 'Memoria del Banco Industrial del Perú correspondiente el año 1944' in *Memoria*, Ministerio de Hacienda (1945) vol. II.
113. Banco Industrial del Perú, *Veinte años de vida*; Peru, Ministerio de Hacienda, 'Memoria del Banco Minero del Perú correspondiente al año 1943', *Revista de Hacienda*, no. 18 (1944). This bank had repeated annual losses which were covered by tax revenues.
114. 'Los agricultores y la política', *La Vida Agrícola*, vol. 13, no. 150 (1936) pp. 385–6; Gonzalo Portocarrero Maisch, *De Bustamante a Odria*, pp. 28, 85–7.
115. Ibid., pp. 22, 40; *WCL*, vol. 23, no. 1245 (24 Dec. 1935) p. 1.
116. Gonzalo Portocarrero Maisch, 'La oligarquía frente a la reivindicación democrática'.
117. *Boletín mensual*, Banco Central de Reserva, 1934–9.
118. Rómulo Ferrero, *La política fiscal*, p. iv; Gonzalo Portocarrero Maisch, *De Bustamante a Odria*, p. 33; Felipe Duffaut, *Un plan técnico*.
119. Gianfranco Bardella, *Un siglo en la vida económica*, pp. 327, 338–44.
120. Rómulo Ferrero, *La política fiscal*, p. 51.
121. Alberto Arca Parró, 'Perú en cifras', in Darío Saint Marie, *Perú en cifras*, pp. 49, 53–4; Rómulo Ferrero, 'El comercio en el Perú', ibid., pp. 342–3; 'Memoria del Banco Industrial del Perú' in *Memoria*, Ministerio de Hacienda (1940) p. 755; 'La inflación puede considerarse como un ahorro forzado . . .' according to Rómulo Ferrero, first Minister of Finance under José L. Bustamente, *Memoria*, Ministerio de Hacienda (1945), p. 245; Rómulo Ferrero, *Política fiscal*, p. 6.
122. 'El Banco Industrial y la agricultura', *La Vida Agrícola*, vol. 13, no. 157 (Dec. 1936) pp. 935–8; Gonzalo Portocarrero Maisch, *De Bustamante a Odria*, pp. 43–5; criticism of the industrialisation strategy of high profits, self-finance and financial repression in Guillermo Garrido-Lecca and Gerald T. O'Mara, *The Urban Informal Credit Market*, pp. 48–9.
123. Jorge Jelicic, 'La Memoria del Banco de Reserva y la situación económica del Perú', *Mercurio Peruano*, vol. 242 (1947) pp. 254–68.
124. Rómulo Ferrero, *Política fiscal*; José Bustamante y Rivero, *Tres años de lucha*.
125. Rómulo Ferrero, *Política fiscal*, pp. 25–33, 65.
126. José Bustamante y Rivero, *Tres años de lucha*, pp. 194–5.
127. Gerardo Klinge, *Política agrícola-alimentaria*, pp. 13–14, 82, 95; B. Diez Canseco, *De espaldas al desarrollo agrario peruano*, p. 12.
128. José Bustamante y Rivero, *Tres años de lucha*, pp. 215–18, 240.
129. Felipe Portocarrero Suárez, Arlette Beltrán and Alex Zimmerman, *Inversiones públicas en el Perú*, pp. 32–3.
130. 'Peruvian Economy. Quarterly Report on the Economic Situation of Peru as of March 31, 1954', (issued by the Banco Continental) *Peruvian Times* (Lima) 7 May 1954, p. 6; David Collier, *Squatters and Oligarchs*.

131. 'Almuerzo a Odría', *Boletín de la Sociedad Nacional Agraria*, vol. 5, no. 202 (1953) pp. 3–8; Manuel A. Odría, *La política económica del Perú*; Cámara Algodonera del Perú, *Memoria correspondiente al año 1951*.

7 Interaction of Foreign and Domestic Finance

1. In a methodological sense I basically agree with Ady: 'neither in the effects of POI [Private Overseas Investment] upon the balance of payments nor in its effects upon domestic resources is a zero sum game played between capital exporting and recipient countries: i.e., it is not the case that what one side gains represents a parallel loss to the other', 'Private Overseas Investments and the Developing Countries', in Peter Ady (ed.), *Private Foreign Investment*, pp. 3–34.
2. Raymond Vernon, *Sovereignty at Bay*; ibid., *Storm Over Multinationals*; for a helpful discussion see Paul Sigmund, *Multinationals in Latin America*.
3. R. Barnet and R. Müller, *Global Reach*; Peter Evans, *Dependent Development*, p. 10; Carlos Marichal, *A Century of Debt Crises*, p. 5.
4. Anthony Ferner, *La burguesía industrial*, p. 56; Carlos Malpica, *El mito de la ayuda exterior*, p. 23; J. Michael Deal, *El Estado e inversión extranjera*, pp. 13–15; Fernando Sánchez Albavera, *Minería*, p. 19.
5. Relevant empirical studies of the foreign presence in Peru include Charles Goodsell, *American Corporations*; Adalberto Pinelo, *The Multinational Corporation*; Geoffrey Bertram, 'Development Problems'.
6. Rory Miller, 'The Making of the Grace Contract'.
7. Michael Edelstein, *Overseas Investment*; Carlos Marichal, *A Century of Debt Crises*, chs 5–6.
8. Peter Ady (ed.), *Private Foreign Investment*, p. 5.
9. Auswärtiges Amt, Peru, 4742, p. 129, Bundesarchiv, Potsdam (hereafter BAP); Dirección General del Banco Alemán Transatlántico (Deutsche Ueberseeische Bank, Berlin), *Memoria y balance* (Barcelona: López Robert, 1911); Frederic Clement-Simon to Ministre des Affaires Etrangères, Lima 18 Jan. 1909, AMEF; *Peru Today*, vol. 4, no. 2 (May 1912) pp. 89–92; *El Financista*, vol. 2, no. 111 (9 April 1914) p. 111.
10. Alaine Low, 'Effects of Foreign Capital'.
11. Rory Miller, 'Railways and Economic Development', pp. 27–52.
12. Alaine Low, 'Effects of Foreign Capital', p. 4.
13. Banco del Perú y Londres, 'Directorio', vol. 3, no. 385, 10 Oct. 1904, pp. 220–1, BPLS; *Gaceta Commercial*, vol. 6, no. 127 (1906) p. 1213; Ernesto Yepes del Castillo, *Perú 1820–1920*, pp. 150–1, 178. The Cerro de Pasco Corporation became the owner in 1926 of a sizeable native cattle breeding concern, the Sociedad Ganadera Junín, whose shares were among the most profitable on the Lima Exchange. Litigation with the local owners of the Sociedad Ganadera for damage claims, due to pollution in the mining area adjacent to the cattle lands, concluded in the sale of the property for Lp342 000 to the US company; J. P. Trant, *Report*, p. 21.
14. Banco del Perú y Londres, 'Directorio', vol. 7, no. 929, 9 June 1913,

p. 27, BPLS. The Société Générale was pressing to sell its interests in the Callao wharf to the Peruvian government at a high price but President Billinghurst was strongly opposed to the purchase.

15. Simon to Pichon, 5 July 1909, B31.345, AMEF.
16. Ibid.
17. Pichon to Ministre des Finances, 12 Nov. 1909, B31.345, AMEF.
18. Simon to Pichon, 15 Aug. 1909, and 8 Oct. 1909, B31.345, AMEF.
19. Banco del Perú y Londres, 'Directorio', vol. 5, no. 638, July 1909, p. 122; 'Accionistas', vol. 2, 13 Aug. 1910, p. 92; ibid., Extraordinaria, 20 Feb. 1913, pp. 114–15, BPLS.
20. Banco del Perú y Londres, *Ley sobre venta de inmuebles por mensualidades*. The law enacted in 14 Nov. 1900 limited interest rates on sales of houses to 10 per cent; Banco del Perú y Londres, 'Directorio', vol. 5, no. 706, 2 June 1910, pp. 247–8; vol. 6, no. 811, 23 May 1911, pp. 9–13; and no. 849, 14 Dec. 1911, p. 112, BPLS; *Boletín Municipal*, vol. 14, no. 686 (21 Feb. 1914); and 15, no. 732 (9 Jan. 1915).
21. Payán to Board of Directors about the formation of the Crédit Foncier Peruvien: Banco del Perú y Londres, 'Directorio', vol. 6, no. 863, 14 March 1912, pp. 172–4, BPLS.
22. Ibid., no. 874, 30 May 1912, p. 214.
23. Ibid., no. 867, April 1912, pp. 190–191; also *Informe*, Inspección Fiscal de Bancos Hipotecarios (1912).
24. Banco del Perú y Londres, 'Directorio', vol. 6, no. 868, 18 April 1912, p. 198, BPLS.
25. Crédit Foncier Peruvien, 'Note sur les frais de transfert de fonds á Lima', 6 March 1913, loose typescript, BPLS.
26. Banco del Perú y Londres, 'Directorio', vol. 6, no. 914, March 1913, p. 340; ibid., vol. 7, no. 929, 9 June 1913, pp. 23–6; no. 930, 12 June 1913, p. 34; no. 931, 19 June 1913, p. 37, BPLS.
27. Ibid., no. 961, 8 Jan. 1914, pp. 154–5.
28. Trade report for 1906 by Otto Lahrius, Auswärtiges Amt, Peru, 4804, BAP; ibid., p. 10.
29. Deutsche Ueberseeisches Bank, Berlin, Annual Balance Sheets, Auswärtiges Amt, 4804–6, BAP.
30. Kaiserlich Deutsche Gesandtschaft, Lima 22 Feb. 1913, Reichsamt des Innern, 4741, p. 32, BAP; Report on the monopoly concession to the British-controlled Borax Consolidated in southern Peru, Lima 8 June 1913, ibid., 4736, pp. 10–11.
31. Report by Perl, 23 April 1919, Auswärtiges Amt, Peru, 4745, p. 220, BAP.
32. Report by Perl, Buenos Aires 20 Feb. 1917, Auswärtiges Amt, Peru, 4745, pp. 207–8, BAP; Report by Vietinghoff, Lima 7 Aug. 1916, Reichsamt des Innern, 4736, p. 54, BAP.
33. Report by Perl, Lima 24 Aug. 1917, Auswärtiges Amt, Peru, 4745, p. 284, BAP.
34. Report by Perl, Lima 18 May 1917, Auswärtiges Amt, Peru, 4745, pp. 275–7, BAP.
35. Telegram, Madrid 3 July 1919, Auswärtiges Amt, Peru, 4806, p. 169, BAP.

36. *The Observer* (6 Feb. 1916).
37. A British economic survey stated in 1921: 'Up to and including the first year of the war [the First World War], Peru was a comparatively poor country, but improved communications consequent on the opening of the Panama Canal, and the demand that then arose for her principal products – copper, sugar, and cotton – inaugurated an era of prosperity unknown since before the war with Chile', F. W. Manners (Commercial Secretary to H.M. Legation, Lima), *Report on the Finance, Industry and Trade of Peru to October 31, 1921* (London: HMSO, 1922), p. 5, reproduced in *Economic Surveys 1920–1961*, United Kingdom, Board of Trade.
38. Banco del Perú y Londres, 'Directorio', vol. 3, no. 751, Jan. 1918, p. 293, BPLS; Secretary of State to Fred I. Kent (Federal Reserve Board), 28 March 1918; and M. G. McAdoo to Secretary of State, 25 Sept. 1918, US Department of the Treasury, Box 162, file no. 1, USNA.
39. Frank H. Mackaman, 'United States Loan Policy', p. 569.
40. Ibid., p. 574; Paul Drake, *The Money Doctor*, p. 215.
41. F. W. Manners, 'Peru, Economic Report: January 1920–February 1921', Lima 26 Feb. 1921, FO371, 5610, A2123/2123, PRO; Manners, *Report on the Finance of Peru* (1922), op. cit., pp. 5–6.
42. Ibid., p. 8; A. J. Hill, *Report*, p. 6.
43. According to Adalberto Pinelo, *The Multinational Corporation*, p. xii, based on a confidential enclosure with the report of the US Trade Commissioner in Lima, Carlton Jackson, to the Bureau of Foreign and Domestic Commerce, 5 Aug. 1920, US Department of State, 823.6363/32, USNA.
44. A. J. Hill, *Report*, p. 5.
45. 'The dissatisfaction caused by the failure of the Government to pay the civil service and the army during many months was widespread, and the latter especially was ready to give ear to the persuasions of the enemies of President Leguía, as many officers with their families were practically starving'. Grant Duff to Foreign Office, Lima, 4 Jan. 1923, FO371, 8478, A558/558/35, PRO.
46. 'The Reminiscences of William Wilson Cumberland', interviews by Wendell H. Link, April–May 1951, typescript, pp. 124–53, Oral History Research Office, Columbia University, New York.
47. 'Peruvian Account in the Bank of England', FO371, 5610, 2408, PRO; Manners, *Report on the Finance of Peru* (1922), op. cit., p. 8; Confidential reports of US Ambassador to Lima, William Gonzales, 7 April 1921 and 22 May 1921, US Department of State, 823.51, microcopy 746, roll no. 1, USNA.
48. Germán Suárez and Mario Tovar, *Deuda pública externa*, Appendix X.
49. Grant Duff to FO, Lima 4 Jan. 1923, FO371, 8478, A617/558/35, PRO; Suárez and Tovar, *Deuda public externa*, Appendix X.
50. 'New Loan for Peruvian Government', London 22 Oct. 1923, FO371, 8478, A6287/956, PRO.
51. Adalberto Pinelo, *The Multinational Corporation*, pp. 24–5.
52. J. P. Trant to Foreign Office, Lima 26 Aug. 1923, FO371, 8478, A5807/558/35, PRO.

53. Herbert Harvey, 'Peru: Annual Report, 1924', Lima July 1925, FO371, 10632, A2304/2304/35, PRO.
54. Lord H. Hervey to Foreign Office, Lima 21 Dec. 1927, FO371, 12787, A470/127/35, PRO; Frank Mackaman, 'United States Loan Policy', pp. 520–1.
55. 'The whole presidential family and the Cabinet are feathering their own nests at the expense of the country . . . there is not an honest man among them', Bentick to Foreign Office, Lima 30 April 1929, FO371, 13507, A3600/2406/35, PRO. On Leguía's favourite son, Juan, it was reported that he was 'notorious for violence, drunkness, brawling, etc. . . . [obtained] commission of recent loans . . . [and] holds many contracts and concessions from Government', Darrell Wilson, 'Leading Personalities in Peru', Lima 24 Feb. 1934, FO371, 17555, A2627/2627/35, PRO. With reference to customs administration: 'Graft was rampant', Cumberland, 'Reminiscences', op. cit., p. 125; [Leguía] 'was one of the biggest simpletons in finance whom I have ever known', ibid., p. 129.
56. 'This is a very bad case. President Leguía gambled in cotton futures with the firm's money', British diplomatic comments in 'Claim of Messrs. Kearsley & Cunningham against Mr. A. B. Leguía', 8 Aug. 1928, FO371, 13508, A5418/4687/35, PRO.
57. Albert Fishlow, 'Lessons from the Past'.
58. Lord Harvey, 'Peru: Annual Report, 1925', FO371, 11160, A2480/2480/35, PRO. An agreement between the US International Match Corporation, which had interests in the two local match factories closing down, and the Swedish Match Company, also made the monopoly possible.
59. J. P. Trant, *Report*, p. 34.
60. Harvey to Foreign Office, Lima 2 Nov. 1926, FO371, 11160, A6417/6417/35, PRO.
61. Darrell Wilson, *Economic Conditions in Peru*, pp. 46–8.
62. Lord Harvey, 'Annual Report, 1926', FO371, 12019, A2497/2497/35, PRO.
63. Banco del Perú y Londres, 'Board of Directors', vol. 16, no. 1734, Feb. 1929, p. 112; no. 1825, 21 Nov. 1929, p. 70, BPLS.
64. 'A large part of the floating debt is in the form of short term notes held by banks, construction companies etc., and . . . its substantial increase apparently restrained only by the reluctance of the local banks themselves, continues to be a source of concern to the Fiscal Agents handling the Peruvian National loans (J. W. Seligman & Co. and the National/City Bank of New York)', US vice consul to Secretary of State, 8 Nov. 1928, US Department of the Treasury, Box 162, file no. 2, USNA.
65. Mayer to Secretary of State, 26 Dec. 1929, US Department of State, 823.516/23, microcopy 746, roll no. 22, USNA.
66. FO371, 1482, A8407/532/35, PRO; Adalberto Pinelo, *Multinational Corporations*.
67. Dalton to Foreign Office, Lima 16 Oct. 1931, FO371, 15112/A6182/6110/35, PRO.

68. Hobson to Foreign Office, Lima 9 May 1932, FO371, 15852, A3713/5/35, PRO.
69. Sir R. Lindsay to Foreign Office, Washington, DC, 16 Dec. 1931, quoting the *Special Bulletin on Securities in Default of the Institute of International Finance*, no. 48 (1931), in FO371, 15110, A5959/210/35, PRO.
70. Extract from *The Times*, 6 Feb. 1934 in 'Peru: Foreign Debt Prospects', FO371, 17552, A1250/282/35, PRO.
71. Letter by J. Henry Schröder & Co., 15 March 1934, FO317, 17552, A2227/169/35; Wilson to Foreign Office, Lima 3 March 1934, A2628/169/35; A4673/169/35, PRO.
72. G. W. Dawes & Co. to Foreign Office, 7 Feb. 1935, FO371, 18721, A1214/192/35, PRO.
73. Forbes to Foreign Office, Lima 10 Sept. 1935, FO371, 18722, A8700/192/35, PRO.
74. Forbes to Foreign Office, Lima 25 Jan. 1935, FO371, 18721, A1703/192/35, PRO.
75. FO371, 20644, A1598/908/35, PRO.
76. Sir R. Lindsay to Foreign Office, Washington 11 June 1937, FO371, 20644, A4468/908/35, PRO.
77. Forbes to Foreign Office, Lima 12 Jan. 1937, FO371, 20644, A908/908/35, PRO.
78. *Peru: Review of Commercial Conditions* (London, 1944), p. 6, in *Economic Surveys 1920–1961*, United Kingdom, Board of Trade.
79. J. P. Trant, *Report* (1926) p. 8.
80. FO371, 16597, A8605/66741/35, PRO.
81. Alberto Arca Parró, 'Perú en cifras', in Darío Saint Marie, *El Perú encifras*, pp. 49, 53–4; Rómulo A. Ferrero, *La Política fiscal*, p. 6.
82. Bentick to Foreign Office, Lima 14 May 1931, FO371, 15110, A3645/210/35, PRO.
83. *Report on the Finance, Industry and Trade of Peru* (1922), p. 6, in *Economic Surveys 1920–1961*, United Kingdom, Board of Trade.
84. Orazio Cicarelli, 'Fascism in Peru'.
85. Charles Goodsell, *American Corporations*.
86. 'Development of Economic Warfare', Rockefeller Family Archives, Record Group 4 (Nelson A. Rockefeller, personal), Series 0 (Washington, DC files), subseries CIAA, box 8, folder 61, Rockefeller Archive Center, Pocantico Hills, North Tarrytown, NY (hereafter RAC); 'Trade of the American Republics in the Early Period of the War', R.G. 4, S. 0, CIAA, box 12, folder 9, RAC.
87. Elizabeth Cobbs, '"Good Works at a Profit"', pp. 70, 284.
88. CIAA, 'Economic Report', no. 12, 7 Dec. 1944, 'Post-war development plans and projects in Latin America' by R. H. Rowntree, R.G. 4, S. 0, CIAA, box 3, folder 19; 'Latin America as a market for Government stocks of Machinery and Equipment', Washington, DC, 1944, mimeo., ibid., folder 19, RAC; Elizabeth Cobbs, "Good Works at a Profit", p. 293.
89. CIAA, Content Directive, 'Japan vis à vis Latin America', R.G. 4, S. 0, CIAA, box 3, folder 20; Memorandum on Bolivian Junta, Robert Miller to Nelson Rockefeller, 11 Jan. 1944, ibid. box 3, folder 21;

Memorandum for the Secretary of State: relations with Argentina, 18 July 1945, ibid., box 4, folder 28, RAC.

90. Antonello Gerbi to Nelson Rockefeller, 'Letters from Peru', R.G. 4, S. 0, CIAA, box 37, folder 23, pp. 9–10, RAC.

91. 'Bankruptcy of Fascist Economy Through the Eyes of Italian Economists', by George A. Tesoro, Feb. 1943, Bureau of Latin American Research, Washington, DC, R.G. 4, S. 0, box 3, folder 19, RAC.

92. 'Recommendation of Policy and Program Action', 30 Jan. 1942, R.G. 4, S. 0, box 4, folder 31 and 34, RAC. The coordinating committee in Peru included representatives of the following private US firms: National City Bank, Anderson, Clayton & Company, W. R. Grace & Company and the Cerro de Pasco Corporation.

93. 'Report of Special Committee on Private Monopolies and Cartels', 30 Jan. 1942, R.G. 4, S. 0, CIAA, box 5, folder 39; 'Development of Economic Warfare', op. cit., RAC.

94. Memorandum on Peru, R.G. 4, S. 0, CIAA, box 3, folder 23; 'Price controls and the Americas' by Seymour E. Harris, Chief of Export Price Control, ibid., box 3, folder 18; 'A Brief account of the activities of the procurement agencies of the U.S. Government in acquiring natural rubber in foreign countries with particular reference to Latin America', ibid., box 12, folder 100, RAC; A. Gerbi and N. Rockefeller, 'Letters from Peru', op. cit., p. 12.

95. 'Latin American Gold and Foreign Exchange Holdings', May 1944, R.G. 4, S. 0, CIAA, box 12, folder 100; 'Activities of Export-Import Bank', ibid., folder 99, RAC.

96. 'Dollar debt of the Latin American republics', R.G. 4, S. 0, CIAA, box 12, folder 99; Memorandum from Raymond Fisher to Nelson Rockefeller, 16 Oct. 1947, 'Status of Latin American external bond holdings', ibid., folder 100, RAC.

97. 'Recommendation for the creation of the Brazilian–American Commission for Economic Cooperation similar to the Mexican–American Commission for Economic Cooperation created by Presidents Roosevelt and Camacho in 1943', R.G. 4, S. 0, CIAA, box 4, folder 30, RAC.

98. Hugh Butler, US Senator for Nebraska, 'Our Deep Dark Secrets in Latin America', *The Readers Digest*, vol. 43, no. 260 (Dec. 1943) pp. 21–5; 'Statement of the Office of the Coordinator of Inter-American Affairs in connection with report of US Senator Hugh A. Butler', R.G. 4, S. 0, CIAA, box 10, folder 79, RAC.

99. CIAA, 'Economic Report', op. cit.

100. IADC, 'Information for the members of the Commission', Washington, DC, 6 May 1946, R.G. 4, S. 0, IADC, box 24, folder 164; Elizabeth Cobbs, 'Entrepreneurship as Diplomacy'.

101. Memorandum by Charles C. Pineo, 26 Feb. 1948, R.G. 4, S. 0, IADC, box 23, folder 157; J. Rafael Oreamuno to Nelson Rockefeller, 31 July 1945, ibid., box 24, folder 167, RAC.

102. José Bustamante y Rivero, *Tres años de lucha*, pp. 238–45.

103. Germán Suárez and Mario Tovar, *Deuda pública externa*, p. 17.

104. Ibid., p. 18.

105. Ibid., p. 14, Table 1.

106. Felipe Portocarrero Suárez, Arlette Beltrán, and Alex Zimmerman, *Inversiones públicas*.

Appendix A

1. Raymond Goldsmith, *Comparative National Balance Sheets*, pp. 2, 44; idem., *Premodern Financial Systems*, pp. 1–9.
2. Clark Reynolds, 'Flow of Funds'; based on 1965 figures elaborated by M. Cobo del Prado Collado and Guillermo Garrido Lecca, *Estudio piloto de activos y pasivos financieros en el Perú y sus interrelaciones sectoriales en el periodo 1965–1970*, Simposio sobre el Mercado de Capitales en el Perú, Comisión Nacional de Valores (Lima, 1972). Reynolds asks for the reasons of 'the failure of Peru's high degree of financial intermediation [in the 1960s] to foster a more dynamic growth process', p. 69. For an answer to this question see Rosemary Thorp, 'La función desempeñada'.
3. Clark Reynolds, 'Flow of Funds', p. 70.
4. Raymond Goldsmith, *Financial Development*, p. 15.
5. Carlos Malpica, *El mito de la ayuda exterior*, p. 23; Octavio Diez Canseco, *De espaldas al desarrollo agrario peruano*, pp. 12–15; Ernesto Yepes del Castillo, *Perú 1820–1920*, pp. 158–64.

Bibliography

ABEL, CHRISTOPHER and LEWIS, COLIN (eds), *Latin America, Economic Imperialism, and the State: The Political Economy of the External Connection from Independence to the Present* (London: Athlone Press, 1985).

ADY, PETER (ed.), *Private Foreign Investment and the Developing World* (New York: Praeger, 1971).

ALBERT, BILL, 'An Essay on the Peruvian Sugar Industry 1880–1920', mimeo (Norwich: University of East Anglia, 1976).

—— 'External Forces and the Transformation of Peruvian Coastal Agriculture, 1880–1930', in *Latin America, Economic Imperialism and the State*, edited by C. Abel and C. Lewis (London: Athlone Press, 1985) pp. 231–41.

—— *South America and the First World War: the Impact of War on Brazil, Argentina, Peru and Chile* (Cambridge University Press, 1988).

ALEXANDER, ALBERTO, *Estudio sobre la crisis de la habitación en Lima* (Lima: Imp. Torres Aguirre, 1922).

—— *Los problemas urbanos de Lima y su futuro* (Lima: La Prensa, 1927).

ALVAREZ-BRUN, FÉLIX, *Ancash: una historia regional peruana* (Lima: P. L. Villanueva, 1970).

ALZAMORA, LIZARDO, *El billete de banco en el Peru* (Lima: Imp. Gil, 1932).

AMARAL, SAMUEL, 'El descubrimiento de la financiación inflacionaria. Buenos Aires, 1790–1830', *Investigaciones y Ensayos*, vol. 37 (1988) pp. 379–418.

ANDERSON, B. M., *Effects of the War on Money, Credit and Banking in France and the United States*, Carnegie Endowment for International Peace, Preliminary Economic Studies of the War, no. 15 (New York: Oxford University Press, 1919).

ANES, GONZALO, et al., *El Banco de España: una historia económica* (Madrid: Banco de España, 1970).

ANNA, TIMOTHY, *The Fall of the Royal Government in Peru* (Lincoln: University of Nebraska Press).

ANONYMOUS, *Cuestión célebre de la Hacienda Naranjal* (Lima, 1876?).

ARGUMANIZ MUNOZ, MANUEL, 'Memorias inéditas', typescript (1858–68), 4 vols. Private library of Félix Denegri Luna, Lima.

ARRÚS, OSCAR, *La estabilización de nuestra moneda* (Lima: El Comercio, 1931).

ASPÍLLAGA, ANTERO, DUBOIS, LUIS and GILDEMEISTER, JUAN, *Informe en mayoría de la comisión para el estudio de la depreciación en el valor de la moneda nacional de plata* (Lima, 1892).

—— GARLAND, ALEJANDRO and LEGUÍA, AUGUSTO, *La crisis del azúcar: informe de la comisión oficial*, Peru, Ministerio de Fomento (Lima: Imp. Torres Aguirre, 1902).

BALMORI, DIANA, VOSS, STUART and WORTMAN, MILES, *Notable*

Family Networks in Latin America (University of Chicago Press, 1984).

BANCO ALEMÁN TRANSATLÁNTICO (Deutsche Ueberseeische Bank, Berlin), *Memoria y balance* (Barcelona: López Robert, 1911).

—— *Juicios criminales por extorsión y chantaje contra Reynaldo Gubbins socio y representante de Gubbins & Co. Lima* (Lima: Imp. Rávago, 1928).

BANCO DE CRÉDITO HIPOTECARIO, *Memoria del Banco de Crédito Hipotecario correspondiente al año 1883* (Lima: Imp. del Teatro, 1884).

BANCO DEL CALLAO, *Estatutos de la sección hipotecaria* (Lima: Gil, 1889).

BANCO DE LA PROVIDENCIA, *Exposición que hacen al público el directorio y accionistas* (Lima: Imp. El Comercio, 1868).

BANCO DE RESERVA DEL PERÚ, *Legislación* (Lima: Imp. Torres Aguirre, 1944).

BANCO DEL PERÚ, *Reflexiones contra el proyecto de convertir al Banco del Perú en dueño y empresario del ferrocarril de Eten* (Lima: Imp. Masías, 1876).

BANCO DEL PERÚ Y LONDRES, *Ley sobre venta de inmuebles por mensualidades; formulario para contratos y transferencias* (Lima: Imp. Gil, 1908).

BANCOS HIPOTECARIOS, *Observaciones sobre el procedimiento de los banco hipotecarios al ejecutar sus deudas para el pago en metálico* (Lima, 1883).

BANCO INDUSTRIAL DEL PERÚ, *Veinte años de vida del Banco Industrial del Perú 1936–1956* (Lima, 1956).

BANCO ITALIANO, *Estatutos del Banco Italiano* (Lima: Imp. Fabbri, 1899).

—— *Banco Italiano, Lima, 1889–1939* (Lima: Tipografía Varese, 1939).

—— *Memoria* (Lima, 1926–31).

BANCO POPULAR DEL PERÚ, *Estatutos del Banco Popular del Perú, Sociedad Cooperativa de Crédito Limitada* (Lima: 1899).

—— *Sección hipotecaria* (Lima: Imp. Gil, 1921).

BARBAGELATA, JOSÉ and BROMLEY, JUAN, *Evolución urbana de la provincia de Lima* (Lima: Lumen, 1945).

BARBOUR, VIOLET, *Capitalism in Amsterdam in the 17th Century* (Ann Arbor: University of Michigan Press, 1963).

BARDELLA, GIANFRANCO, *Setenta y cinco años de vida económica del Perú, 1889–1964* (Milan: Banco de Crédito, 1964).

—— *Un siglo en la vida económica del Perú. Banco de Crédito del Perú, 1889–1989* (Lima: Banco de Crédito, 1989).

BARNET, R. and MÜLLER, R., *Global Reach: The Power of the Multinational Corporation* (New York: Simon & Schuster, 1974).

BARREDA Y OSMA, FELIPE, *Los derechos de aduanas y las industrias nacionales* (Lima: Imp. F. Moreno, 1900).

BASADRE, JORGE, 'Leguía y el leguiísmo', in *Primer panorama de ensayistas peruanos* (Lima: Editora Latinoamericana, 1958).

—— *Historia de la República del Perú*, 5th ed., 11 vols (Lima: Editorial Historia, 1964).

—— *Historia de la República del Perú*, 6th ed., 17 vols (Lima: Editorial Universitaria, 1968).

—— *Sultanismo, corrupción y dependencia en el Perú republicano* (Lima: Ed. Milla Batres, 1979).

—— and FERRERO, RÓMULO, *Historia de la Cámara de Comercio de Lima* (Lima: Santiago Valverde, 1963).

BASCH, ANTONÍN, *El mercado de capitales de Colombia* (Mexico: CEMLA, 1968).

—— and KYBAL, MILIC, *Recursos nacionales de inversión en América Latina* (Mexico: CEMLA, 1971).

BÁTIZ, JOSÉ A., 'Trayectoria de la banca en México hasta 1910', in *Banca y poder en México*, edited by Leonor Ludlow and Carlos Marichal (Mexico: Grijalbo, 1986) pp. 267–97.

BAUER, ARNOLD, 'The Church in the Economy of Spanish America: Censos and Depósitos in the Eighteenth and Nineteenth Centuries', *Hispanic American Historical Review*, vol. 63 (1983) pp. 707–33.

BELTROY, MANUEL, *Peruanos notables de hoy* (Lima, 1957).

BENEFICENCIA PÚBLICA DE LIMA, *Donación Sevilla* (Lima: Imprenta Gil, 1890).

—— Caja de Ahorros, *Datos concernientes al movimiento de la oficina principal y su sección hipotecaria* (Lima: Imprenta Gil, 1921).

BERGER, ADOLFO, 'Los depósitos bancarios desde el punto de vista de su cuantía y con relación al estado general del orden económico, financiero y político del país', *Revista Universitaria*, vol. 21 (1927) pp. 793–807.

BERGQUIST, CHARLES, *Coffee and Conflict in Colombia, 1886–1910* (Durham, NC: Duke University Press, 1978).

BERTRAM, GEOFFREY, 'Development Problems in an Export Economy: A Study of Domestic Capitalists, Foreign Firms and Government in Peru, 1919–1930', Ph.D. dissertation, Oxford University, 1974.

—— 'Modernización y cambio en la industria lanera del Peru 1919/1930: un caso frustrado de desarrollo', *Apuntes*, vol. 6 (1977) pp. 3–22.

BITAR LETAYF, MARCELO, *Los economistas españoles y sus ideas sobre el comercio con las Indias* (Mexico: Instituto Mexicano de Comercio Exterior, 1975).

BLAKEMORE, HAROLD, *British Nitrates and Chilean Politics, 1886–1896: Balmaceda and North* (London: Athlone Press, 1974).

BLUME, FEDERICO, *Observaciones sobre el proyecto del Banco Central* (Lima: Imp. Masías, 1876).

BOLLINGER, WILLIAM, 'The Rise of the U.S. Influence in the Peruvian Economy, 1860–1921', M.A. thesis, UCLA, 1972.

BOLOÑA, CARLOS, 'Tariff Policies in Peru, 1880–1980', Ph.D. dissertation, Oxford University, 1981.

BONILLA, HERACLIO, *Guano y burguesía en el Perú* (Lima: IEP, 1974).

—— (ed.), *Las crisis económicas en la historia del Perú* (Lima: CLHES-Ebert, 1986).

—— and RABANAL, ALEJANDRO, 'La Hacienda San Nicolás (Supe) y la Primera Guerra Mundial', *Economía*, no. 2 (1979) pp. 3–47.

BOURRICAUD, FRANCOIS, *Power and Society in Contemporary Peru* (New York: Praeger, 1970).

—— et al., *La oligarquía en el Perú* (Lima: IEP, 1971).

BOYAJIAN, JAMES, *Portuguese Bankers at the Court of Spain, 1626–1650*

(New Brunswick: Rutgers University Press, 1983).

BRADING, DAVID, *Miners and Merchants in Bourbon Mexico 1763–1810* (Cambridge University Press, 1971).

BRISSEAU LOAIZA, JANINE, *Le Cuzco dans sa region. Etude de l'aire d'influence de une ville andine* (Talence: CEGT/Institut Français d'Etudes Andines, 1981).

BROTHERS, DWIGHT S. and SOLÍS, LEOPOLDO, *Mexican Financial Development* (Austin: University of Texas Press, 1966).

BROWN, ROBERT, *Transport and Economic Integration of South America* (Washington, DC: The Brookings Institution, 1966).

BRYCE, L. N. et al., *Exposición que hace al Sr. Ministro de Hacienda la comisión nombrada para emitir opinión sobre el proyecto de 'El Banco Privilegiado del Perú* (Lima: Imp. Gil, 1889).

BUECHLER, ROSE MARIE, *The Mining Society of Potosí, 1776–1810* (Syracuse University Press, 1981).

BURGA, MANUEL, *De la encomienda a la hacienda capitalista: el valle del Jequetepeque del siglo XVI al XX* (Lima: IEP, 1976).

—— and FLORES GALINDO, ALBERTO, *Apogeo y crisis de la República Aristocrática* (Lima: Ediciones Rikchay, 1979).

—— and REÁTEGUI, WILSON, *Lanas y capital mercantil en el sur: la casa Ricketts, 1895–1935* (Lima: IEP, 1981).

BUSHNELL, DAVID and MACAULAY, NEILL, *The Emergence of Latin America in the Nineteenth Century* (New York: Oxford University Press, 1988).

BUSTAMANTE Y RIVERO, JOSÉ L., *Tres años de lucha por la democracia en el Perú* (Buenos Aires: Artes Gráficas Chiesino, 1949).

CAJA DE DEPÓSITOS Y CONSIGNACIONES, *Memoria*, no. 39, 2nd semester, 1924 (Lima: Imp. Gil, 1925).

—— Departamento de Recaudación, *Informe, año 1927* (Lima: Imp. Ed. Cervantes, 1928).

CÁMARA ALGODONERA DEL PERU, *Memoria correspondiente al año 1951* (Lima: 1952).

CAMERON, RONDO (ed.), *Banking in the Early Stages of Industrialization* (New York: Oxford University Press, 1967).

—— (ed.), *Banking and Economic Development: Some Lessons of History* (New York: Oxford University Press, 1972).

CAMPRUBÍ, CARLOS, *Historia de los bancos en el Perú (1860–1879)* (Lima: Lumen, 1957).

—— *El Banco de la Emancipación* (Lima: P. L. Villanueva, 1960).

—— *José Payán y de Reina (1844–1919): su trayectoria peruana* (Lima: P. L. Villanueva, 1967).

—— *Sociedad de Beneficencia Pública de Lima, Caja de Ahorros de Lima: un siglo al servicio del ahorro, 1868–1968* (Lima: P. L. Villanueva, 1968).

CAPELO, JOAQUÍN, *Sociología de Lima*, 4 vols (Lima: Imp. Masías/La Industria, 1896–1902).

CAPUÑAY, MANUEL, *Leguía: vida y obra del constructor del gran Perú* (Lima: E. Bustamante, 1951).

CAPUÑAY, CARLOS, 'El Perú financiero de 1919 a 1924', *La Nueva Economía*, vol. 10, no. 109 (1944) pp. 15–16.

CARANDE, RAMÓN, *Carlos V y sus banqueros*, 3 vols (Madrid: Revista de Occidente, 1943–67).
CARAVEDO, BALTAZAR, 'Poder central y descentralización: Perú, 1931', *Apuntes*, vol. 9 (1979) pp. 111–29.
—— *Descentralismo y democracia* (Lima: GREDES, 1988).
CARBONE, PABLO, 'El problema agrario en el Departamento de La Libertad', BA thesis: UNMSM, 1932. Reprinted by Seminario de Historia Rural Andina, Lima, mimeo. 1976.
CARBONETTO, DANIEL, 'El modelo de acumulación descentrado y dependiente', in *El Perú de Velasco*, Carlos Franco et al., vol. 1 (Lima: CEDEP, 1986) pp. 29–98.
CARDOSO, FERNANDO H. and FALETTO, ENZO, *Dependency and Development in Latin America* (Berkeley: University of California Press, 1979).
CASÓS, FERNANDO, *La minería y la agricultura al punto de vista del progreso* (Lima: Imp. El Comercio, 1876).
CAVES, RICHARD E., 'Vent for Surplus Models of Trade and Growth', in *Trade, Growth and the Balance of Payments*, R. E. Baldwin et al. (Amsterdam: North Holland, 1965) pp. 95–115.
CHANDLER, ALFRED D., *The Visible Hand: the Managerial Revolution in American Business* (Cambridge, Mass: Harvard University Press, 1977).
CHAPLIN, DAVID, 'The Peruvian Industrial Labor Force (Princeton University Press, 1967).
CHAPMAN, STANLEY, 'British-Based Investment Groups Before 1914', *Economic History Review*, vol. 38 (1985) pp. 230–51.
—— *The Rise of Merchant Banking* (London: Unwin Hyman, 1988).
CHAVARRÍA, JESÚS, 'La desaparición del Perú colonial (1870–1919)', *Aportes*, vol. 23 (1972) pp. 120–53.
CICARELLI, ORAZIO, 'Fascist Propaganda and the Italian Community in Peru during the Benavides Regime, 1933–1939', *Journal of Latin American Studies*, vol. 20 (1988) pp. 361–88.
—— 'Fascism in Peru during the Benavides Regime, 1933–39: the Italian Perspective', *Hispanic American Historical Review*, vol. 70 (1990) pp. 403–32.
CISNEROS, CARLOS B., *Sinópsis estadística del Perú 1908–1912* (Lima: Imp. Unión, 1912).
CISNEROS, LUIS B., *Obras completas* (Lima: Ed. Gil, 1939).
CLAPHAM, JOHN H., *The Bank of England: A History, 1797–1914*, 2 vols (Cambridge University Press, 1944).
CLAVERO, JOSÉ, *El coronel de milicias Pedro Gonzales Candamo* (Lima: Imp. El Lucero, 1904).
CLEVELAND, HAROLD and HUERTAS, THOMAS, *Citibank, 1812–1970* (Cambridge, Mass: Harvard University Press, 1985).
COATSWORTH, JOHN, *Growth Against Development: the Economic Impact of Railroads in Porfirian Mexico* (DeKalb: Northern Illinois University Press, 1981).
COBBS, ELIZABETH A., '"Good Works at a Profit": Private Development and United States–Brazil Relations, 1945–1966', Ph.D. diss. Stanford University, 1988.

—— 'Entrepreneurship as Diplomacy: Nelson Rockefeller and the Development of the Brazilian Capital Market', *Business History Review*, vol. 63 (1989) pp. 88–121.

COLLIER, DAVID, *Squatters and Oligarchs: Authoritarian Rule and Policy Change in Peru* (Baltimore: Johns Hopkins University Press, 1976).

COMISIÓN ESPECIAL DEL CRÉDITO PÚBLICO, *Informe de la . . . sobre los vales consolidados y tachados* (Lima: Imp. F. Moreno, 1856).

COMITATO DE LIMA PER LA ESPOSIZIONE DE MILANO, *L'Italia al Peru: Ressegna della Vita e dell'Opera Italiana nel Peru* (Lima: Litografía Fabbri, 1905–6).

COMPAÑÍA URBANIZADORA SAN ISIDRO, *1a memoria* (Lima: International Publishing Co., 1921).

COPELLO, JUAN and PETRICONI, LUIS, *Estudio sobre la independencia económica del Perú* (Lima: UNMSM, 1971).

CORDERO, MARÍA E., 'Evolucion financiera de México: Porfiriato y revolución', *Revista Mexicana de Sociología*, vol. 38, no. 2 (1976) pp. 359–87.

COREY, L., *The House of Morgan* (New York: Grosset & Dunlap, 1930).

CORREA Y SANTIAGO, PEDRO and PAYÁN, JOSÉ, *Informe en minoría de la comisión para el estudio de la depreciación de la plata* (Lima, 1892).

CORTÉS CONDE, ROBERTO and HUNT, SHANE, (eds.), *The Latin American Economies: Growth and the Export Sector, 1880–1930* (New York: Holmes & Meier, 1985).

CORTI, EGON C., *The Rise of the House of Rothschild* (New York: Cosmopolitan Books, 1928).

COTLER, JULIO, *Clase, Estado y Nación en el Perú* (Lima: IEP, 1978).

CUETO, MARCOS, *Excelencia científica en la periferia: actividades científicas e investigación biomédica en el Perú, 1890–1950* (Lima: GRADE-CONCYTEC, 1989).

DANCUART, EMILIO, *Anales de la Hacienda Pública del Perú: historia y legislación fiscal de la República*, 6 vols (Lima: Stolte/La Revista, 1902–1903).

DEAL, J. MICHAEL, *El Estado e inversión extranjera en el proceso de industrialización peruano* (Lima: CISE, 1976).

DEUSTUA, JOSÉ, *La minería peruana y la iniciación de la República, 1820–1840* (Lima: IEP, 1986).

—— and RÉNIQUE, JOSÉ LUIS, *Intelectuales, indigenismo y descentralismo en el Perú* (Cusco: Centro B. Las Casas, 1984).

DEVLIN, ROBERT, *Debt and Crisis in Latin America: The Supply Side of the Story* (Princeton University Press, 1989).

DÍAZ ALEJANDRO, CARLOS, *Essays on the Economic History of the Argentine Republic* (New Haven: Yale University Press, 1970).

DICKSON, P. G. M., *The Financial Revolution in England: A Study in the Development of Public Credit 1688–1756* (London: Macmillan and St. Martin's Press, 1967).

DIEZ CANSECO B., OCTAVIO, *De espaldas al desarrollo agrario peruano* (Lima: Imp. Americana, 1960).

Documentos sobre el contrato de conversión de moneda feble publicados en

'*El Peruano*' *y otros periódicos* (Lima: Imp. El Comercio, 1864).

DORE, ELIZABETH, *The Peruvian Mining Industry: Growth, Stagnation, and Crisis* (Boulder: Westview Press, 1988).

DORION, JAMES, *Banco privilegiado del Perú: refutación del informe presentado por la comisión compuesta por los ss. Bryce, Dubois, Correa, Villarán y Payán* (Lima: Imp. R. Masías, 1889).

DRAKE, PAUL, *The Money Doctor in the Andes: The Kemmerer Missions, 1923–1933* (Durham: Duke University Press, 1989).

—— 'Debt and Democracy in Latin America, 1920s–1980s', in *Debt and Democracy in Latin America*, edited by B. Stallings and R. Kaufman, pp. 39–58. (Boulder, Colorado: Westview Press, 1989).

DUFFAUT, FELIPE, *Un plan técnico para la industrialización integral y coordinada del País* (Lima: Gráfica Stylo, 1945).

DULANTO PINILLOS, JORGE, *Ramón Castilla* (Lima: Impresiones y Publicidad, 1945).

—— *Nicolás de Piérola* (Lima: Impresiones y Publicidad, 1947).

DUNN, W. E., *Peru: A Commercial and Industrial Handbook*, US Department of Commerce, Bureau of Foreign and Domestic Commerce, Trade Promotion Series, no. 25 (Washington, DC: GPO, 1925).

—— *Road Construction in Peru* (Washington, DC: GPO, 1924).

EDELSTEIN, MICHAEL, *Overseas Investment in the Age of High Imperialism: the United Kingdom 1850–1914* (New York: Columbia University Press, 1982).

EHRENBERG, R., *Capital and Finance in the Age of the Renaissance: A Study of the Fuggers and Their Connections* (New York: A. M. Kelley, 1928).

E. M., *La moneda en el Perú* (Lima: Tip. Alfaro, 1859).

EMPRESA DEL GAS, *La Empresa del Gas de Lima y el H. Concejo Provincial* (Lima: Imp. El Comercio, 1891).

ENGELSEN, JUAN ROLF, 'Social Aspects of Agricultural Expansion in Coastal Peru', Ph.D. diss., UCLA, 1977.

EVANS, PETER, *Dependent Development: The Alliance of Multinational, State, and Local Capital in Brazil* (Princeton University Press, 1979).

EYZAGUIRRE, FEDERICO and PANIZO, CÉSAR, *Memorandum sobre el Banco de Pobres* (Lima: Imp. Torres Aguirre, 1901).

EYZAGUIRRE, RÓMULO, *Enfermedades evitables: mortalidad infantil* (Lima: Imp. Opinión Nacional, 1906).

FERNER, ANTHONY, *La burguesía industrial en el desarrollo peruano* (Lima: ESAN, 1982).

FERNS, H. S., *Britain and Argentina in the Nineteenth Century* (Oxford: Clarendon Press, 1960).

FERRERO, RÓMULO A., *La política fiscal y la economía nacional* (Lima: Lumen, 1946).

FISHER, JOHN, *Silver Mines and Silver Mining in Colonial Peru, 1776–1824* (Liverpool: Centre for Latin American Studies, 1977).

—— *Commercial Relations Between Spain and Spanish America in the Era of Free Trade, 1778–1796* (Liverpool: Centre for Latin American Studies, 1985).

FISHLOW, ALBERT, 'Lessons from the Past: Capital Markets During the

19th Century and the Interwar Period', *International Organization*, vol. 39 (1985) pp. 383–439.

FLORES GALINDO, ALBERTO, *Arequipa y el sur andino: ensayo de historia regional (siglos xviii–xx)* (Lima: Editorial Horizonte, 1977).

—— *Aristocracia y plebe: Lima 1760–1930* (Lima: Mosca Azul, 1984).

—— PLAZA, ORLANDO and ORÉ, TERESA, 'Oligarquía y capital comercial en el sur peruano (1870–1930)', *Debates en sociología*, vol. 3 (1978) pp. 53–75.

FORD, ALEC, *The Gold Standard, 1880–1914: Britain and Argentina* (Oxford: Clarendon Press, 1962).

—— 'Notes on the Working of the Gold Standard Before 1914', in *The Gold Standard in Theory and Practice*, edited by Barry Eichengreen (London and New York: Methuen, 1985) pp. 141–65.

FRANCO HOLGUÍN, JORGE, *Evolución de las instituciones financieras en Colombia* (Mexico: CEMLA, 1966).

FRANK, ANDRÉ GUNDER, *Capitalism and Underdevelopment in Latin America: Historical Studies of Chile and Brazil* (New York: Monthly Review Press, 1967).

FREYRE, IRIS, 'Exportaciones e Industria en el Perú: el caso de Grace y Paramonga', mimeo (Lima: U. Católica-CISEPA, 1976).

FRITSCH, WINSTON, *External Constraints on Economic Policy in Brazil, 1889–1930* (London: Macmillan, 1988).

FUCHS, FERNANDO C., *Prospecto para el establecimiento del Banco de la Nación* (Lima: Imp. Torres Aguirre, 1920).

—— *Memoria de Hacienda correspondiente al año 1920* (Lima: Imprenta Opinión Nacional, 1920).

FURTADO, CELSO, *Economic Development of Latin America: Historical Background and Contemporary Problems*, 2nd. ed. (Cambridge University Press, 1976).

GARCÍA CALDERÓN REY, FRANCISCO, *Le Pérou Contemporain* (Paris: Dujarrig, 1907).

—— *Latin America: its Rise and Progress* (London: F. Unwin, 1913).

GARCÍA JORDÁN, PILAR, 'Estado moderno, Iglesia y secularización en el Perú contemporáneo (1821–1919)', *Revista Andina*, vol. 6 (1988) pp. 351–401.

GARLAND, ALEJANDRO, *Las industrias en el Perú* (Lima: Imp. del Estado, 1896).

—— *El Fisco y las industrias nacionales* (Lima: Imprenta del Estado, 1900).

—— *Artículos económicos publicados en El Comercio* (Lima: Imprenta La Industria, 1901).

—— *Reseña industrial del Perú* (Lima: Imp. La Industria, 1905).

—— *Peru in 1906* (Lima: Imprenta La Industria, 1908).

—— *Sistema monetario del Perú* (Lima: Imp. Opinión Nacional, 1908).

GARRIDO-LECCA, GUILLERMO and O'MARA, GERALD T., *The Urban Informal Credit Market in a Developing Country Under Financial Repression: the Peruvian Case* (Austin: University of Texas, 1974).

GERBI, ANTONELLO, *El Perú en marcha: ensayo de geografía económica* (Lima: Banco Italiano/Editorial Torres Aguirre, 1941).

GERSCHENKRON, ALEXANDER, *Economic Backwardness in Historical Perspective* (Cambridge, Mass: Harvard University Press, 1962).

GLADE, WILLIAM, *The Latin American Economies: A Study of Their Institutional Evolution* (New York: Van Nostrand, 1969).

GOLDSMITH, RAYMOND, *Financial Intermediaries in the American Economy since 1900* (Princeton University Press, 1958).

—— *The Determinants of Financial Structure* (Paris: OECD, 1966).

—— *The Financial Development of Mexico* (Paris: OECD, 1966).

—— *Financial Structure and Development* (New Haven: Yale University Press, 1969).

—— *Comparative National Balance Sheets: A Study of Twenty Countries, 1688–1978* (University of Chicago Press, 1985).

—— *Premodern Financial Systems: A Historical Comparative Study* (Cambridge University Press, 1987).

GÓMEZ ALVAREZ, UBALDO, *Estudio histórico de los préstamos censales del Principado de Asturias (1680–1715)* (Luarca: Bibliófilos Asturianos, 1979).

GONZALES, MICHAEL, 'Capitalist Agriculture and Labour Contracting in Peru, 1880–1905', *Journal of Latin American Studies*, vol. 12 (1980) pp. 219–315.

—— *Plantation Agriculture and Social Control in Northern Peru, 1875–1932* (Austin: Texas University Press, 1985).

GONZALES DE OLARTE, EFRAÍN, *Economías regionales del Perú* (Lima: IEP, 1982).

GOODSELL, CHARLES, *American Corporations and Peruvian Politics* (Cambridge, Mass: Harvard University Press, 1974).

GOOTENBERG, PAUL, *Between Silver and Guano: Commercial Policy and the State in Postindependence Peru* (Princeton University Press, 1989).

—— '*Carneros y Chuño*: Price Levels in Nineteenth-Century Peru', *Hispanic American Historical Review*, vol. 70 (1990) pp. 1–56.

GREENHILL, ROBERT and MILLER, RORY, 'The Peruvian Government and the Nitrate Trade, 1873–1879', *Journal of Latin American Studies*, vol. 5 (1973) pp. 107–131.

GREENOW, LINDA, *Credit and Socioeconomic Change in Colonial Mexico: Loans and Mortgages in Guadalajara, 1720–1820* (Boulder, Colorado: Westview Press, 1983).

GRICE-HUTCHINSON, MARJORIE, *Early Economic Thought in Spain 1177–1740* (London: Allen & Unwin, 1978).

GRIFFIN, KEITH, 'Monopoly Power, Material Progress and the Economic Surplus', in *Financing Development in Latin America*, edited by Keith Griffin (London: Macmillan, 1971) pp. 2–19.

GUBBINS, J. R., *Lo que se ve y lo que no se ve* (Lima, 1899).

HABER, STEPHEN, *Industry and Underdevelopment: Industrialization of Mexico, 1890–1940* (Stanford University Press, 1989).

HAMNETT, BRIAN, 'Church Wealth in Peru: Estates and Loans in the Archdiocese of Lima in the Seventeenth Century', *Jahrbuch für Geschichte . . . Lateinamerikas*, vol. 10 (1973) pp. 113–32.

HARVEY, HÉCTOR, 'El Banco Agrícola del Perú', *La Vida Agrícola*, vol. 13, no. 152 (July 1936) p. 570.

HERBOLD, CARL F., 'Developments in the Peruvian Administrative System, 1919–1939', Ph.D., Yale University, 1973.

HERR, RICHARD, *The Eighteenth Century Revolution in Spain* (Princeton University Press, 1958).

HILL, A. J., *Report on the Finance, Industry and Trade of Peru* (London: HMSO, 1923).

HOBSON, J. A., *Imperialism: A Study* (London: Nisbet, 1902).

HOOPER LÓPEZ, RENÉ, *Leguía: ensayo biográfico* (Lima: Ediciones Peruanas, 1964).

HUNT, SHANE, 'Growth and Guano in Nineteenth-Century Peru', in *The Latin American Economies: Growth and the Export Sector, 1880–1930*, edited by R. Cortés Conde and Shane Hunt (New York: Holmes & Meier, 1985) pp. 255–319.

INFORMACIONES MERCANTILES E INDUSTRIALES, *El Perú en su centenario* (Lima: Sanmarti, 1921).

JACOBSEN, NILS, 'Desarrollo económico y relaciones de clase en el sur andino (1780–1920): una réplica a Karen Spalding', *Análisis*, vol. 5 (1979) pp. 67–81.

—— 'Free Trade Regional Elites, and the Internal Market in Southern Peru, 1895–1932' in *Guiding the Invisible Hand: Economic Liberalism and the State in Latin American History*, edited by Joseph Love and Nils Jacobsen (New York: Praeger, 1988) pp. 145–175.

JONES, CHARLES, 'Commercial Banks and Mortgage Companies', in *Business Imperialism, 1840–1930: An Inquiry Based on British Experience in Latin America*, edited by D. C. M. Platt (Oxford: Clarendon Press, 1977) pp. 18–52.

JOSLIN, CHARLES, *A Century of Banking in Latin America* (London: Oxford University Press, 1963).

JOVELLANOS, GASPAR MELCHOR DE, 'Informe de la Sociedad Económica de Madrid al Real y Supremo Consejo de Castilla en el expediente de Ley Agraria', in *Biblioteca de autores españoles*, vol. 50, no. 2 (Madrid: Rivadeneyra, 1859) pp. 79–138.

JUNTA DE EXAMEN FISCAL, *Informes de la . . . creada por resolución suprema en febrero de 1855 para revisar los expedientes relativos al reconocimiento de la deuda interna consolidada* (Lima: Imp. del Estado, 1857).

KARNO, HOWARD L., 'Augusto B. Leguía: The Oligarchy and the Modernization of Peru, 1870–1930', Ph.D. diss., UCLA, 1970.

KEEN, BENJAMIN and WASSERMAN, MARK, *A History of Latin America*, 3rd ed. (Boston: Houghton Mifflin, 1988).

KINDLEBERGER, CHARLES, *The Formation of Financial Centers: A Study in Comparative Economic History* (Princeton: Studies in International Finance, 1974).

—— *Keynesianism vs. Monetarism and Other Essays in Financial History* (London: Allen & Unwin, 1985).

KLARÉN, PETER, *Modernization, Dislocation, and Aprismo* (Austin: University of Texas Press, 1973).

—— and BOSSERT, THOMAS, *Promise of Development: Theories of Change in Latin America* (Boulder: Westview Press, 1986).

KLEIN, HERBERT, 'The Creation of the Patiño Tin Empire', *Inter-American Economic Affairs*, vol. 9 (1965) pp. 3–23.

KLINGE, GERARDO, 'La agricultura en el Perú', in *Perú en cifras: 1944–*

1945, edited by Darío Saint Marie (Lima: Editorial Internacional, 1945) pp. 73–5.

—— *Política agrícola-alimentaria* (Lima: Imprenta Torres Aguirre, 1946).

KRUIJT, DIRK and VELLINGA, MENNO, *Labor Relations and Multinational Corporations: the Cerro de Pasco Corporation in Peru (1902–1974)* (Assen: Van Gorcum, 1979).

KUZNETS, SIMON, *Capital in the American Economy: Its Formation and Financing* (Princeton University Press, 1961).

LAITE, JULIAN, 'Miners and National Politics in Peru, 1900–1974', *Journal of Latin American Studies*, vol. 12 (1980) pp. 317–40.

LEFF, NATHANIEL, 'Capital Markets in the Less Developed Countries: the Group Principle', in *Money and Finance in Economic Growth and Development*, edited by Ronald McKinnon (New York: M. Dekker, 1976) pp. 97–122.

—— 'Industrial Organization and Entrepreneurship in the Developing Countries: the Economic Groups', *Economic Development and Cultural Change*, vol. 26 (1978) pp. 661–77.

—— *Underdevelopment and Development in Brazil. Reassessing the Obstacles to Economic Development*, vol. 2. (London: Allen & Unwin, 1982).

LEGUÍA, AUGUSTO B., *El Oncenio y la Lima actual: memorias completas del Presidente Leguía "Yo tirano, yo ladrón"* (Lima: Imprenta J.C.L., 1936).

LEÓN, LUCAS, *Exposición de las causas determinantes de la aflictiva situación del Banco Garantizador* (Lima: Imp. Solís, 1882).

LEWIS, COLIN, 'The Financing of Railway Development in Latin America, 1850–1914', *Ibero-Amerikanisches Archiv*, vol. 9 (1983) pp. 255–78.

LIEHR, REINHARD, 'La deuda exterior de México y los "merchant bankers" británicos 1821–1860', *Ibero-Amerikanisches Archiv*, vol. 9 (1983) pp. 415–39.

LISS, PEGGY, *Atlantic Empires: The Network of Trade and Revolution, 1713–1826* (Baltimore: Johns Hopkins University Press, 1983).

LISSON, CARLOS, *Breves apuntes sobre la sociología del Perú en 1886* (Lima: Imprenta Gil, 1887).

LÓPEZ, JACINTO, *Manuel Pardo* (Lima: Imp. Gil, 1947).

LOW, ALAINE, 'The Effects of Foreign Capital on Peruvian entrepreneurship, 1890–1975', B. Phil. thesis, Oxford University, 1976.

LOWENTHAL, ABRAHAM (ed)., *The Peruvian Experiment: Continuity and Change Under Military Rule* (Princeton University Press, 1975).

—— and MCCLINTOCK, CYNTHIA (eds), *The Peruvian Experiment Reconsidered* (Princeton University Press, 1983).

LUDLOW, LEONOR and MARICHAL, CARLOS (eds), *Banca y poder en México 1800–1925* (Mexico: Grijalbo, 1986).

LYNCH, JOHN, *The Spanish-American Revolutions, 1808–1826* (New York: Norton, 1973).

MACERA, PABLO (comp.) 'Palto: hacendados y yanaconas del algodonal peruano (documentos 1877–1943)', mimeo (Lima: Seminario de Historia, 1976).

MACKAMAN, FRANK H., 'United States Loan Policy, 1920–1930: Diplomatic Assumptions, Governmental Politics, and Conditions in Peru and Mexico', Ph.D. diss., University of Missouri, 1977.

MAIGUASHCA, JUAN, 'A Reinterpretation of the Guano Age, 1840–1880', Ph.D. dissertation, Oxford University, 1967.

MALAMUD, CARLOS and PÉREZ, HERRERO, PEDRO, 'Le reglamente du commerce libre en Espagne et en Amerique: principaux problemes d'interpretation', in Groupe Interdisciplinaire de Recherche, *L'Amerique espagnole á l'epoque des lumières. Tradition, innovation, representations* (Paris: CNRS, 1987).

MALETTA, HÉCTOR, 'Perú, país campesino? Aspectos cuantitativos de su mundo rural', *Análisis*, vol. 6 (1978) pp. 3–51.

—— and BARDALES, ALEJANDRO, *Perú: las provincias en cifras 1876–1981*, 3 vols (Lima: AMIDEP, 1987).

MALLON, FLORENCIA, *The Defense of Community in Peru's Central Highlands: Peasant Struggle and Capitalist Transition, 1860–1940* (Princeton University Press, 1983).

MALLOY, JAMES (ed.), *Authoritarianism and Corporatism in Latin America* (Pittsburgh University Press, 1977).

MALPICA, CARLOS, *Los dueños del Perú*, 12th ed. (Lima: Peisa, 1981). (1st ed., 1964).

—— *El mito de la ayuda exterior* (Lima: Ensayos Sociales, 1977).

MANRIQUE, NELSON, *Colonialismo y pobreza campesina: Caylloma y el valle del Colca, siglos xvi–xx* (Lima: DESCO, 1986).

—— *Mercado interno y región: la sierra central 1820–1930* (Lima: DESCO, 1987).

MANZANILLA, JOSÉ M., *Finanzas y economía: discursos parlamentarios*, 3rd ed. (Lima: Imp. Gil, 1941).

MARIÁTEGUI, JOSÉ CARLOS, *Siete ensayos de interpretación de la realidad peruana*, 2nd ed. (Lima: Ed. Librería Peruana, 1934). (1st ed., 1928).

MARICHAL, CARLOS, *A Century of Debt in Latin America: From Independence to the Great Depression, 1820–1930* (Princeton University Press, 1989).

MATHEW, W. M., *The House of Gibbs and the Peruvian Guano Monopoly* (London: Royal Historical Society, 1981).

—— 'The First Anglo-Peruvian Debt and Its Settlement, 1822–49', *Journal of Latin American Studies*, vol. 2 (1970) pp. 81–98.

MAÚRTUA, ANÍBAL, *El Banco de la República Peruana: plan económico-financiero* (Lima: Emp. Tip. Unión, 1915).

MAUSHAMMER, ROBERT J., 'Investor Groups, Informal Finance and the Economic Development of Peru', Ph.D. diss., University of Wisconsin, 1970.

MAYER, DORA, *La conducta de la compañía minera Cerro de Pasco* (Callao: Imprenta del Concejo Provincial, 1914).

McGREEVEY, WILLIAM and RODRÍGUEZ, JORGE, 'Colombia: comercio exterior, 1835–1962', in *Compendio de estadísticas históricas* edited by Miguel Urrutia and Mario Arrubla (Bogota: Universidad Nacional de Colombia, 1970) pp. 106–208.

McKINNON, RONALD, *Money and Capital in Economic Development* (Washington, DC: Brookings Institution, 1973).

MELLER, IGNACIO, *Patrón de oro o bimetalismo: ensayo sobre aspectos nuevos de un problema antiguo* (Lima: Imp. Gil, 1932)

MÉNDEZ, CECILIA, 'La otra historia del guano: Perú 1840–1879', *Revista Andina*, vol. 5 (1987) pp. 7–46.

MENDIBURU, MANUEL DE, *Diccionario histórico-biográfico del Perú* (Lima: Imp. Enrique Palacios, 1931).

—— 'Noticias biográficas de los generales que ha tenido la República peruana', *Revista Histórica*, vol. 15 (1960).

MENÉNDEZ PIDAL, RAMÓN (ed.), *Cantar de Mío Cid* (Madrid: Bailly, 1911).

MILLER, RORY, 'The Making of the Grace Contract', *Journal of Latin American Studies*, vol. 8 (1976) pp. 73–100.

—— 'Railways and Economic Development in Central Peru, 1890–1930', in *Social and Economic Change in Modern Peru, 1890–1930*, Rory Miller et al. (University of Liverpool, Centre for Latin American Studies, 1976) pp. 27–52.

—— 'The Coastal Elite and Peruvian Politics, 1895–1919', *Journal of Latin American Studies*, vol. 8 (1976) pp. 97–120.

—— 'British Business in Peru, 1883–1930', Ph.D. diss., Cambridge University, 1978.

—— 'The Wool Trade of Southern Peru, 1850–1915', *Ibero-Amerikanisches Archiv*, vol. 8 (1982) pp. 297–311.

—— 'The Grace Contract, the Peruvian Corporation, and Peruvian History', *Ibero-Amerikanisches Archiv*, vol. 9 (1983) pp. 319–48.

—— (ed.), *Region and Class in Modern Peruvian History* (University of Liverpool, Institute of Latin American Studies, 1987).

MOLINA MARTÍNEZ, MIGUEL, *El Tribunal de Minería de Lima (1875–1821)* (Sevilla: Diputación Provincial, 1986).

MONTEAGUDO, BERNARDO DE, *Memoria sobre los principios políticos que seguí en la administración del Perú y acontecimientos posteriores a mi separación* (Quito, 1823).

MONTOYA, RODRIGO, *Capitalismo y no capitalismo en el Perú* (Lima: Mosca Azul, 1980).

MOORE, O. ERNEST, *Evolución de las instituciones financieras en México* (Mexico: CEMLA, 1963).

MORENO, FEDERICO, *El Petróleo bajo el punto de vista industrial* (Lima: Imprenta Masías, 1891).

MOREYRA PAZ SOLDÁN, MANUEL, 'El oro de California y Australia y su repercusión monetaria en el Perú', *Revista Histórica*, vol. 26 (1962–3) pp. 236–58.

—— *La moneda colonial en el Perú: capítulos de su historia* (Lima: Banco Central de Reserva, 1980).

MORRIS, CYNTHIA TAFT, 'The Measurement of Economic Development: Quo Vadis?' in *Comparative Development Perspectives*, edited by Gustave Ranis et al. (Boulder: Westview Press, 1984) pp. 145–81.

MUÑOZ PÉREZ, JOSÉ, 'Los proyectos sobre España e Indias en el siglo XVIII: el proyectismo como género', *Revista de Estudios Políticos*, vol. 81 (1955) pp. 169–95.

NACIONAL FINANCIERA, J. A., *Statistics on Mexico* (Mexico: Nacional Financiera, 1963).

NIETO, ARMANDO, *Contribución a la historia del fidelismo en el Perú*

(1808–1810) (Lima: Instituto Riva Agüero, 1960).

NOONAN, JOHN, *The Scholastic Analysis of Usury* (Cambridge, Mass: Harvard University Press, 1967).

NORRIS, WALTER E., 'Banco del Hogar y Ahorros', project submitted to the Superintendencia de Bancos, typescript (Lima, 1942).

ODRÍA, MANUEL A., *La política económica del Perú* (Lima: Dirección General de Informaciones, 1953).

OLAECHEA, MANUEL P., *Causa seguida por Arrieta Hermanos contra el Banco Territorial Hipotecario* (Lima: Imp. Camaná, 1885).

OLAVIDE, PABLO DE, 'Informe de Olavide sobre la Ley Agraria', *Boletín de la Real Academia de Historia*, vol. 139 (1956) pp. 357–462.

OLIVARES, RUBÉN L., *El negocio del dinero y la usura* (Lima: Sanmartí y Cía., 1923).

ORDÓÑEZ, MARIO B., *La técnica y la práctica en la banca peruana* (Lima: Imprenta UNMSM, 1963).

OSMA, MARIANO DE, *Causas de mi encarcelamiento: mis cuestiones ante los tribunales* . . . (Lima, 1868).

PALACIOS MOREYRA, CARLOS, *La deuda anglo-peruana 1822–1890* (Lima: Studium, 1983).

PANDO, JOSÉ MARÍA, *Reclamación de los vulnerados derechos de los hacendados de las provincias litorales del Departamento de Lima* (Lima: Imp. Concha, 1833).

PARDO, JOSÉ, *Perú: cuatro años de gobierno constitucional* (New York, 1919).

PARK, JAMES, *Rafael Núñez and the Politics of Colombian Regionalism, 1863–1886* (Baton Rouge: Louisiana State University Press, 1985).

PARKER, GEOFFREY, 'War and Economic Change: The Economic Costs of the Dutch Revolt', in *War and Economic Development. Essays in Memory of David Joslin*, edited by J. M. Winter (London: Cambridge University Press, 1975) pp. 49–71.

PARKER, WILLIAM B. (ed.), *Peruvians of To-Day* (New York: Kraus Reprint Corporation, 1967) (Original edition, New York: Hispanic Society, 1919).

PAYÁN, JOSÉ, *La cuestión monetaria en el Perú* (Lima: Imp. Torres Aguirre, 1892).

PAZ SOLDÁN, JUAN P., *Diccionario biográfico de peruanos contemporáneos* (Lima: Gil, 1917).

PENNANO, GUIDO, 'Desarrollo regional y ferrocarriles en el Perú: 1850–1879', *Apuntes*, vol. 9 (1979) pp. 135–42.

—— *La economía del caucho* (Iquitos: CETA, 1988).

PERÚ, *Cuestión entre el Perú y España* (Lima: Imprenta del Estado, 1864).

—— Cámara de Senadores, *Diario de los debates del Congreso Ordinario de 1889* (Lima: Imprenta del País, 1897).

—— Ministerio de Hacienda, Dirección General del Crédito Público, *Memoria del Director en 1902* (Lima: Imp. Torres Aguirre, 1903).

—— Ministerio de Hacienda, *Leyes, decretos y resoluciones gubernativas expedidas por este ramo en los años 1913–1914* (Lima: Imprenta Americana, 1922).

—— Ministerio de Hacienda, Dirección General de Estadística, *Estadística*

de precios y mimeros indicadores (Lime: Imp. Americana, 1920).
—— Cámara de Diputados, Documentos Parlamentarios, *Dictamen de la Comisión Parlamentaria Investigadora de la Cía. Recaudadora de Impuestos* (Lima: Imp. T. Scheuch, 1921).
—— Ministerio de Fomento, Dirección de Salubridad, Inspección Técnica de Urbanizaciones y Construcciones, *Segundo informe sobre el registro sanitario y catastro de la propiedad urbana de Lima* (Lima: La Prensa, 1928).
—— Ministerio de Fomento, *La labor constructiva del Perú en el gobierno del Presidente don Augusto B. Leguía* (Lima: Imprenta Torres Aguirre, 1930).
PINELO, ADALBERTO, *The Multinational Corporation as a Force in Latin American Politics: A Case Study of the International Petroleum Company in Peru* (New York: Praeger, 1973).
PLATT, D. C. M. (ed.), *Latin America and British Trade, 1806–1914* (Edinburgh: T. & A. Constable, 1972).
—— (ed.), *Business Imperialism, 1840–1930: An Inquiry Based on British Experience in Latin America* (Oxford: Clarendon Press, 1977).
POLANYI, KARL, *The Great Transformation: the Political and Economic Origins of Our Time* (Boston: Beacon Press, 1957).
PORTOCARRERO MAISCH, GONZALO, 'La oligarquía frente a la reivindicación democrática (las opciones de la derecha en las elecciones de 1936)', *Apuntes*, vol. 12 (1982) pp. 61–73.
—— *De Bustamante a Odría: el fracaso del Frente Democrático Nacional 1945–1950* (Lima: Mosca Azul, 1986).
PORTOCARRERO SUÁREZ, FELIPE, 'El Imperio Prado (1890–1970): orígenes, auge y decadencia de un grupo económico familiar', Magister thesis, Universidad Católica 1986.
—— 'Economic Elites in Peru, 1900–68', Ph.D. diss. in progress, Oxford University, 1991.
—— BELTRÁN, ARLETTE AND ZIMMERMAN, ALEX, *Inversiones públicas en el Perú (1900–1968): una aproximación cuantitativa* (Lima: Universidad del Pacífico, 1988).
QUIROZ, ALFONSO, 'Las actividades comerciales y financieras de la Casa Grace y la Guerra del Pacífico, 1879–1890', *Histórica*, vol. 8 (1983) pp. 214–54.
—— 'Financial Institutions in Peruvian Export Economy and Society, 1884–1930', Ph.D. diss., Columbia University, 1986.
—— *La deuda defraudada: consolidación de 1850 y dominio económico en el Perú* (Lima: Instituto Nacional de Cultura, 1987).
—— 'Financial Leadership and the Formation of Peruvian Elite Groups, 1884–1930', *Journal of Latin American Studies*, vol. 20 (1988) pp. 49–81.
QUIROZ, RAFAEL, *Estudio sobre la deuda interna* (Lima, 1901).
RAMÍREZ BUSTAMANTE, ELIA, *Estadísticas bancarias: promedios anuales de los balances mensuales de los bancos mexicanos* (Mexico: Instituto Nac. de Antropología, 1985).
RAMIREZ, SUSAN, *Provincial Patriarchs: Land Tenure and the Economics of Power in Colonial Peru* (Albuquerque: University of Mexico Press, 1986).
RAMÍREZ GASTÓN, ENRIQUE, *Muelle y Dársena del Callao: refutación del contrato de privilegio por 50 años* (Lima: Imprenta Masías, 1886).

RAMÍREZ GASTÓN, JOSÉ M., *Sociedades de crédito agrícola mutual* (Callao: Soc. Tip. Chalaca, 1904).
—— *Medio siglo de la política económica y financiera del Perú 1915–64* (Lima: La Confianza, 1964).
REAÑO, GERMÁN and VÁSQUEZ, ENRIQUE, *El Grupo Romero: del algodón a la banca* (Lima: Universidad del Pacífico, 1988).
REAÑO GARCÍA, JOSÉ, *Historia del leguiísmo, sus hombres y sus obras* (Lima: T. Scheuch, 1928).
REGAL, ALBERTO, *Castilla constructor: las obras de ingeniería de Castilla* (Lima: Inst. Ramón Castilla, 1967).
RÉNIQUE, JOSÉ LUIS, 'La burguesía peruana y la penetración imperialista, 1910–1930', *Socialismo y Participación*, vol. 33 (1986) pp. 47–64.
—— 'De la fe en el progreso al mito andino: los intelectuales cusqueños', *Márgenes*, vol. 1 (1987) pp. 9–33.
REVILLA, JULIO, 'Industrialización temprana y lucha ideólogica en el Peru: 1890–1910', *Estudios Andinos* (1984) p. 20.
REYNOLDS, CLARK, *The Mexican Economy: Twentieth-Century Structure and Growth* (New Haven: Yale University Press, 1970).
—— 'Flow of Funds: The Use of the Flow of Funds Analysis in the Study of Latin American Capital Market Development', in Organization of American States, Capital Markets Development Program, III Annual Meeting (1973), Mexico, DF.
RIEMERSMA, JELLE C., *Religious Factors in Early Dutch Capitalism, 1550–1650* (The Hague: Mouton, 1967).
RILEY, JAMES C., *International Government Finance and the Amsterdam Capital Market 1740–1815* (Cambridge University Press, 1980).
RIPPY, JAMES, *British Investments in Latin America, 1822–1949* (Minneapolis: University of Minnesota Press, 1959).
ROBERTS, BRYAN, 'The Social History of a Provincial Town: Huancayo, 1890–1972', in *Social and Economic Change in Modern News*, Rory Miller et al. (University of Liverpool, Centre for Latin American Studies, 1976) pp. 136–93.
ROCA, BENJAMÍN, *Opiniones sobre el problema del cambio* (Lima: Imp. Gil, 1918).
ROCA, JOSÉ, *Fisonomía del regionalismo boliviano* (La Paz: Ed. Amigos del Libro, 1979).
RODRÍGUEZ, J. M., *El billete fiscal* (Lima: Imp. Torres Aguirre, 1887).
RODRÍGUEZ CASADO, VICENTE and CALDERÓN QUIJANO, J. A. (eds), *Memorias del gobierno del virrey Abascal, 1806–1816*, 2 vols (Sevilla: Escuela de Estudios Hispanoamericanos, 1944).
RODULFO, JOSÉ A., *Representación de . . . al Congreso Nacional solicitando se le autorice a fundar un banco conforme al proyecto que presenta* (Lima: Imp. El Comercio, 1861).
ROMERO, EMILIO, 'La vida financiera en el Perú desde el año 1884', *Revista de la Facultad de Ciencias Económicas UNMSM*, vol. 14 (1939) p. 12.
—— *El descentralismo*, 2nd ed. (Lima: Tarea, 1987).
ROOVER, RAYMOND DE, *The Rise and Decline of the Medici Bank,*

1397–1494 (Cambridge, Mass: Harvard University Press, 1963).

ROSE, PETER, *The Changing Structure of American Banking* (New York: Columbia University Press, 1987).

ROWE, L. S., *Early Effects of the War Upon the Finance, Commerce and Industry of Peru*, Carnegie Endowment for International Peace (New York: Oxford University Press, 1920).

RUZO, DANIEL, *Contestación a la carta dirigida por el señor don Manuel Pardo a los editores de 'El Comercio', de Lima, el 7 de abril de 1872* (London: Loma, 1872).

SAINT MARIE, DARÍO (ed.), *Perú en cifras* (Lima: Editorial Internacional, 1945).

SALOMÓN, ALBERTO, 'El desarrollo económico del Perú: discurso pronunciado en la ceremonia de apertura del año académico', *Revista Universitaria*, vol. 13 (1918) pp. 348–428.

SÁNCHEZ ALBAVERA, FERNANDO, *Minería, capital transnacional y poder en el Perú* (Lima: DESCO, 1981).

SAN CRISTÓBAL, EVARISTO, *Manuel Pardo y Lavalle: su vida y su obra* (Lima: Imp. Gil, 1945).

SANTOS MORALES, JOSÉ, *Proyecto de un Banco Hipotecario destinado exclusivamente a la agricultura* (Lima: Imp. Larriega, 1868).

SEQUI, EMILIO and CALCAGNOLI, ENRICO, *La Vita Italiana nella Repubblica del Perú* (Lima: La Voce d'Italia, 1912).

SHAW, EDWARD, *Financial Deepening in Economic Development* (New York: Oxford University Press, 1973).

SIGMUND, PAUL E., *Multinationals in Latin America: The Politics of Nationalization* (Madison: University of Wisconsin Press, 1980).

SILVA SANTISTEBAN, JESÚS, *Cajamarca: divulgación de temas agropecuarios de la provincia, año 1944* (Lima: Ministerio de Agricultura, 1945).

SKIDMORE, THOMAS and SMITH, PETER, *Modern Latin America*, 2nd ed. (New York: Oxford University Press, 1989).

SLATER, DAVID, *Territory and State Power in Latin America* (London: Macmillan, 1989).

SMITH, CAROL A., *Regional Analysis* (New York: Academic Press, 1976).

SOLIS, LEOPOLDO, *La realidad económica mexicana: retrovisión y perspectivas* (Mexico: Siglo Veintiuno, 1970).

STALLINGS, BARBARA, *Banker to the Third World: U.S. Portfolio Investments in Latin America, 1900–1986* (Berkeley: University of California Press, 1987).

STEPAN, ALFRED, *The State and Society: Peru in Comparative Perspective* (Princeton University Press, 1978).

STEWART, WATT, *Chinese Bondage in Peru: A History of the Chinese Coolies in Peru, 1849–1874* (Westport, Conn: Greenwood Press, 1970).

STONE, IRVING, 'British Direct and Portfolio Investment in Latin America Before 1914', *Journal of Economic History*, vol. 37 (1977) pp. 690–722).

SUÁREZ, GERMÁN, and TOVAR, MARIO, *Deuda pública externa, 1920–1966* (Lima: Banco Central de Reserva, 1967).

SUPERINTENDENCIA DE BANCA Y SEGUROS, *Banco del Perú y Londres en Liquidación: memoria anual* (Lima: Imprenta Gil, 1931–3).

TAMAYO HERRERA, JOSÉ, *Historia social del Cuzco republicano* (Lima: Ed. Universo, 1981).

―――― *Historia social e indigenismo en el Altiplano* (Lima: Ed. Treinta y Tres, 1982).

TANTALEÁN, JAVIER, *Política económico-financiera y la formación del Estado: siglo XIX* (Lima: CEDEP, 1983).

TAYLOR, LEWIS, 'Cambios capitalistas en las haciendas de Cajamarca', *Apuntes*, vol. 14 (1984) pp. 79–110.

TENEMBAUM, BARBARA, *The Politics of Penury: Debts and Taxes in Mexico, 1821–1856* (Albuquerque: University of New Mexico Press, 1986).

THOMPSON, JOHN K., *Inflation, Financial Markets, and Economic Development: The Experience of Mexico* (Greenwich, Conn: JAI Press, 1979).

THORP, ROSEMARY, 'La función desempeñada por las instituciones financieras en el proceso de ahorro peruano, 1960–1969', in *Simposio sobre el Mercado de Capitales en el Perú* (Lima: Comisión Nacional de Valores, 1972).

―――― 'Endeudamiento o inversión directa: consideraciones a partir del caso peruano', in *El Perú frente al capital extranjero: deuda e inversión*, edited by Eduardo Ferrero (Lima: CEPEI, 1985) pp. 25–38.

―――― *Economic Management and Economic Development in Peru and Colombia* (London and Pittsburgh: Macmillan Press and Pittsburgh University Press, 1991).

―――― and BERTRAM, GEOFFREY, *Peru 1890–1977: Growth and Policy in an Open Economy* (New York: Columbia University Press, 1978).

―――― and LONDOÑO, CARLOS, 'The Effects of the Great Depression on the Economies of Peru and Colombia', in *Latin America in the 1930s: the Role of the Periphery in World Crisis*, edited by Rosemary Thorp (London: Macmillan, 1984) pp. 81–113.

TIPTON, FRANK, *Regional Variations in the Economic Development of Germany During the Nineteenth Century* (Middletown, Conn: Wesleyan University Press, 1976).

TIZÓN Y BUENO, RICARDO, *Sobre Tributación Minera* (Lima: Imp. Centro Editorial, 1915).

―――― *El plano de Lima* (Lima: Imprenta Centro Editorial, 1916).

―――― *La deuda interna* (Lima: Tip. Estanco del Tabaco, 1931).

TOLA, FERNANDO, *Los impuestos en el Perú* (Lima: Imp. Gil, 1914).

TOPIK, STEVEN, *The Political Economy of the Brazilian State, 1889–1930* (Austin: University of Texas Press, 1987).

TRACY, JAMES D., *A Financial Revolution in the Habsburg Netherlands: Renten and Renteniers in the County of Holland, 1515–1565* (Berkeley: University of California Press, 1985).

TRANT, J. P., *Report on the Commercial, Economic and Financial Conditions in Peru* (dated October 1926), UK Department of Overseas Trade (London: HMSO, 1927).

UGARTE, CÉSAR A., *Bosquejo de la historia económica del Perú* (Lima: Imp. Cabieses, 1926).

UGARTECHE, PEDRO, *La política internacional peruana durante la dictadura de Leguía* (Lima: Imprenta Castrillón, 1930).

ULLOA, ALBERTO, *Don Nicolás de Piérola: una época de la historia del Perú* (Lima: Imp. Santa María, 1950).

ULLOA CISNEROS, A., *Leguía: apuntes de cartera 1919–24* (Lima: CIP, 1933).

UNA VÍCTIMA DE LA PROVIDENCIA, *Consideraciones dedicadas al Supremo Gobierno sobre el peligro de la emisión de billetes de banco sin garantía* (Lima: Tip. Alfaro, 1866).

URETA, ALBERTO L., *La moneda de plata y el billete fiscal* (Lima: Imp. El Nacional, 1884).

URICOECHEA, FERNANDO, *The Patrimonial Foundations of the Brazilian Bureaucratic State* (Berkeley: University of California Press, 1980).

URQUIAGA, CARLOS, *Algunas notas sobre las concentraciones bancarias y el proyecto para la formación del Banco del Estado* (Lima: F. M. Villacorta, 1933).

US DEPARTMENT OF COMMERCE, *Banking Opportunities in South America* by William Lough, Special Agents Series no. 106 (Washington, DC: GPO, 1915).

—— *Peruvian Markets for American Hardware*, miscellaneous series no. 39 (Washington, DC: GPO, 1916).

—— Bureau of Foreign and Domestic Commerce, Latin American Section, 'Manufacturing in Peru', special circular no. 324 (Washington, DC: GPO, 1934).

US DEPARTMENT OF STATE, *Papers Relating to the Foreign Relations of the United States*, 1921, vol. 2 (Washington, DC: GPO, 1936).

US SENATE, Finance Committee Hearings, 72nd Congress, 1st Session, *Sale of Foreign Bonds or Securities in the United States* (Washington, DC: GPO, 1932).

VALCÁRCEL, LUIS E., *Memorias* (Lima: IEP, 1981).

VALDERRAMA, MARIANO and LUDMAN, PATRICIA, *La oligarquía terrateniente: ayer y hoy* (Lima: Universidad Católica, 1979).

VALERA, WENCESLAO, *Deuda interna* (Lima: El Tiempo, 1898).

VAQUERIZO GIL, MANUEL, 'Los censos al quitar, nueva fuente para el estudio de la financiación. Un ejemplo: la Junta de Voto, 1591–1605', *Altamira*, vol. 1 (1975) pp. 275–94.

VARGAS PATRÓN, JOSÉ A., 'La estructura del mercado bancario comercial en el Perú: un análisis histórico, 1850–1978', *Ciencia Económica*, vol. 4 (1982) pp. 209–33.

VASCONES, ANTENOR, J., *Estudios morales. Don Jaime el prestamista o los vampiros de la humanidad* (Lima: Imp. Prince, 1886).

VÁSQUEZ HUAMÁN, ENRIQUE, 'Entrepreneurial Dynamics and Economic Groups in Peru: Case Studies', paper presented at the 47th International Congress of Americanists, New Orleans, 1991.

VERNON, RAYMOND, *Sovereignty at Bay* (New York: Basic Books, 1971).

—— *Storm Over Multinationals* (Cambridge, Mass: Harvard University Press, 1977).

WAISMAN, CARLOS, *Reversal of Development in Argentina: Postwar Counterrevolutionary Policies and Their Structural Consequences* (Princeton University Press, 1987).

WARREN, BILL, *Imperialism: Pioneer of Capitalism* (London: Verso, 1980).

WEAVER, FREDERICK, *Class, State, and Industrial Structure: The Historical Process of South American Industrial Growth* (Westport: Greenwood Press, 1980).

WERLICH, DAVID, *Peru: A Short History* (Carbondale: Southern Illinois University Press, 1978).

WILS, FRITS, *Industrialization, Industrialists and the Nation-State in Peru* (Berkeley: University of California Press, 1979).

WILSON, DARRELL, *Economic Conditions in Peru (August, 1924)*, UK Department of Overseas Trade (London: HMSO, 1934).

WILSON, FIONA, 'The Conflict Between Indigenous and Immigrant Commercial Systems in the Peruvian Centrel Sierra, 1900–1940', in *Region and Class in Modern Peruvian History*, edited by Rory Miller (University of Liverpool: Institute of Latin American Studies, 1987) pp. 125–161.

WITT, HEINRICH, *Diario y observaciones sobre el Perú (1824–1890)* (Lima: COFIDE, 1987).

WORRAL, JANET, 'Italian Immigration to Peru: 1860–1914', Ph.D. diss., Indiana University, 1972.

YEPES DEL CASTILLO, ERNESTO, *Perú 1820–1920: un siglo de desarrollo capitalista* (Lima: IEP, 1972).

YRIGOYEN, MANUEL, *Bosquejo sobre los empréstitos contemporáneos del Perú* (Lima: Sanmarti, 1928).

ZABLUDOWSKI, JAIME, 'Money, Foreign Indebtedness and Export Performance in Porfirist Mexico', Ph.D. dissertation, Yale University, 1984.

ZAPATA, ANTONIO, 'Chalet y material noble: las mentalidades sobre la vivienda en la Lima del siglo XX,' in *Tiempos de ira y amor*, Carlos Degregori et al. (Lima: DESCO, 1991) pp. 139–82.

Statistical Series, Periodicals and Microfilm Collections

Anales Universitarios (Lima, 1862–1905).

Anuario Estadístico del Perú, Dirección Nacional de Estadístico (Lima, 1944–66).

Boletín de la Bolsa Comercial de Lima, 'Memoria Anual' (Lima, 1900–1930).

Boletín Mensual, Banco Central de Reserva (Lima, 1931–).

Boletín Municipal (Lima, 1895–1915).

Cuentas Nacionales del Perú, Banco Central de Reserva (Lima, 1960–74).

Economista Peruano (Lima, 1908–21).

Economic Surveys, 1920–1961 United Kingdom, Board of Trade, microfiche publication (Cambridge: Chadwyck Healey, 1977).

El Comercio (Lima, 1850–1950).

El Economista (Lima, 1895–1901).

El Financista (Lima, 1912–30).

El Peruano (Lima, 1850–1950).

Extracto Estadístico del Perú, Ministerio de Hacienda, Dirección General de Estadística (Lima, 1918–33).
Informe, Inspección Fiscal de Bancos (Lima, 1921–30).
La Gaceta Comercial (Lima, 1900–7).
La Vida Agrícola (Lima, 1924–1952).
Letras y Valores (of A. S. Finnie) (Lima, 1895–6).
Memoria, Banco Central de Reserva del Perú (Lima, 1931–73).
Memoria, Banco de Reserva del Perú (Lima, 1922–30).
Memoria de la Caja de Ahorros, Beneficencia Pública de Lima (Lima, 1901–29).
Memoria, Dirección del Credito Público, Inspección Fiscal de Bancos Hipotecarios, and Inspección Fiscal de Compañías de Seguros (Lima, 1902–7).
Memoria, Ministerio de Hacienda (Lima, 1886–).
Memoria y Estadística Bancaria, Superintendencia de Banca y Seguros (Lima, 1931–69).
Mercurio Peruano (Lima, 1791–5).
The Newspaper Cuttings of the Council of Foreign Bondholders in the Guildhall Library, London, Corporation of Foreign Bondholder Council, microfilm publication (East Ardsley: EP Microform, 1975).
Peru Today (Lima, 1909–14).
Revista de Cambios y Valores (of Joaquín Godoy) (Lima, 1890–7).
Revista de Hacienda (Lima, 1944–).
Revista Universitaria (Lima, 1906–38).
Situación de las Empresas Bancarias del Perú, Superintendencia de Banca y Seguros (Lima, 1931–50).
The West Coast Leader (Lima, 1913–40).
Tipos de Cambio y Valores (of Paul Ascher) (Lima, 1887–90).

Archival and Manuscript Sources

Archives du Ministère de l'Economie et des Finances, Paris (AMEF), pays étrangers, Pérou.
Archives du Ministère des Affaires Etrangères, Paris (MAE), correspondence consulaire, politique et commerciale, Pérou.
Archives Nationales de la France, Paris (ANF), documents du Ministère des Finances sur Pérou.
Archivo Arzobispal de Lima, Lima (AAL), sección Censos.
Archivo General de Indias, Seville (AGI), secciones: Gobierno, Audiencia de Lima; Indiferente General; Consulados.
Archivo General de la Nación, Lima (AGN), secciones: Real Audiencia de Lima, Juzgado de la Caja General de Censos; Libros de Cuentas, Hacienda, series C-15, H-3; Protocolos Notariales, testamentos y tasaciones; Libros Manuscritos Republicanos, serie H-4; Ministerio de Hacienda, correspondencia.
Archivo Histórico Nacional, Madrid (AHN), secciones: Consejos Supresos, Indias, Escribanía de Cámara; Inquisición; Jesuitas, Lima.
Biblioteca Nacional de Lima, Lima (BNL), sección Manuscritos.

Bundesarchiv, Potsdam (BAP), Auswärtiges Amt, Deutsche Reichbank, Reichministerium des Innern.

Columbia University, Butler Library, Manuscript Collections, W. R. Grace & Co. Papers, New York, New York (WRGP); Oral History Research Office.

Guildhall Library, London (GLL), Papers of Antony Gibbs and Sons Ltd, Merchants and Foreign Bankers; Papers of Hambros Bank Ltd; Papers of Frederick Huth & Co.

Peruvian Corporation Archive, University College, London.

Public Record Office, Kew Gardens, London (PRO), Foreign Office, Correspondence on Peru.

Rockefeller Archive Center, Pocantico Hills, North Tarrytown, New York (RAC), Rockefeller Family Archive.

Superintendencia de Banca y Seguros, Archivo Sección Liquidaciones, Banco del Perú y Londres en Liquidación, Lima (BPLS); Banco del Callao, 'Actas del Directorio', 3 vols, 'Actas de Juntas de Accionistas', 1 vol.; Banco del Perú y Londres, 'Actas del Directorio', 17 vols, 'Actas de Accionistas', 3 vols, 'Actas del Comité de Directorio', 12 vols, 'Correspondencia de José Payán', 'Préstamos Agrícolas', 1929–30; Fábrica de Fósforos El Sol, 'Actas de Directorio y Accionistas', 1898–1906, 1 vol.; Crédit Foncier Peruvien.

US National Archives, Washington, DC (USNA), Department of the Treasury; Department of State, Microfilm Publications, Microcopy 746.

Index

287